HOW TO USE & CARE FOR

WOODWORKING TOOLS

HOW TO USE & CARE FOR

WOODWORKING TOOLS

Alan and Gill Bridgewater

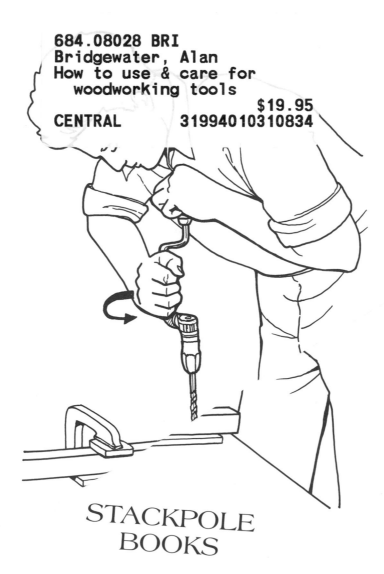

STACKPOLE
BOOKS

To Alec Williamson
For his inspirational stories

Published by
STACKPOLE BOOKS
5067 Ritter Road
Mechanicsburg, PA 17055
www.stackpolebooks.com

Printed in the United States of America

10 9 8 7 6 5 4 3 2 1

FIRST EDITION

Cover Design by Wendy Reynolds
Cover photograph by Ian Parsons
Interior line drawings by the authors

Library of Congress Cataloging-in-Publication Data

Bridgewater, Alan.
    How to use and care for woodworking tools / Alan and Gill Bridgewater. — 1st ed.
        p.   cm.
    Includes index.
    ISBN 0-8117-2794-7
    1. Woodworking tools. I. Bridgewater, Gill. II. Title.
TT186.B75   1998
684'.08'0284—dc21   98-9266
                                                        CIP

Contents

Acknowledgments vii

Introduction ix

1 THE WORKSHOP 1

2 SAWS 7

3 PLANES 45

4 JOINERY AND
   CABINET CHISELS 83

5 WOODCARVING CHISELS
   AND GOUGES 105

6 WOODTURNING CHISELS, GOUGES,
   AND SCRAPERS 133

7 WOODWORKING MACHINES 156

8 PRIMARY MARKING AND
   TESTING TOOLS 176

9 DRILLING TOOLS 187

10 KNIVES AND SCRAPERS 198

11 HAMMERS AND MALLETS 209

12 CLAMPS, CRAMPS,
    AND HOLDFASTS 215

Metric Conversions 225

Index 226

Acknowledgments

We would like to thank all the manufacturers who have over the years supplied us with the best of the best, and given us their time: Tim Effrem, President, Wood Carvers Supply (woodcarving tools); Jim Brewer, Research and Marketing Manager, Freud (Forstner drill bits); John P. Jodkin, Vice President, Delta International Machinery (band saws); Dawn Fretz, Marketing Assistant, De-Sta-Co. (clamps); Paragon Communications, Evo-Stick (PVA adhesive); Frank Cootz, Public Relations, Ryobi America Corp (thickness planer); Glen Tizzard, Draper Tools UK; Legno Ltd (veneers). A special thanks must go to Friedrich Wilhelm Emmerich, of E. C. E. Planes in Germany, for providing us with a selection of his world famous wooden planes—wonderful!

Introduction

There is something uniquely ravishing and enchanting about traditional woodworking tools. It's not only that the glorious coming together of hardwood, forged steel, threaded gunmetal, and knurled brass makes for a stunningly beautiful visual object, but more than that, a good honest traditional woodworking tool has about it an aura that speaks of strength, mystery, and alchemy.

In times past, the use of woodworking tools and related skills were considered to be so singular that woodworkers developed closed societies and guilds to defend the mystery. An old guy once told me that his great grandfather who had been an apprentice cabinetmaker in London—this must have been about 1830 or thereabouts—told him that an unwritten rule in the woodshop was that the tools had to be treated with respect and knowledge of their function had to be kept a closely guarded secret. In fact, when an outsider entered the workshop and started asking questions, cloths were surreptitiously thrown over the tools, and the men would shy away from giving straight answers. Their thinking was, of course, that the best way of keeping the craft strong was to show nothing and say little. And if that wasn't enough, if and when a "gentleman" stranger did start poking around and asking questions; then there was much bowing and scraping and obsequious doffing of caps—"yes sir, no sir, three bags full sir"—and he was given a load of hooey to throw him off the track. The end result of this behavior was that when these selfsame gentlemen wrote accounts of how such and such a woodworking tool was used and who used it, they more often than not came up with the most extraordinary rubbish, or at least a very "thin" account of the real facts.

And so it was that up until modern times the whole subject of woodworking was more or less divided into two camps. In one camp there were all the professional woodworkers who were actually using the tools, making the items, and saying nothing, and in the other camp there were the know-nothing, do-nothing "gentlemen" amateurs who wrote a great deal about "honest sweat" and other nonsense. This state of affairs was, and still is, encouraged by the tool manufacturers, who grade their planes, chisels, and the like, as being "professional" or "amateur." The joke is that whereas "professional" tools are generally pretty sensible good quality full-size strong tools (good grade steel, solid brass fixtures and fittings, and hardwood handles) the "amateur," "gentleman," or "hobby" tools tend to be a bit smaller, a great deal shinier, and a lot more expensive—altogether less for more! Its almost as if the manufacturers are of the opinion that amateurs have such delicate and fragile sensibilities that they can't contend with a tool unless it is small, lightweight, and pretty. And, would you believe, some tool manufacturers still grade their tools as being only suitable for "ladies"!

What this all adds up to is a sad state of affairs, where beginners who are using these inferior tools are confused because they can't achieve good quality work. The pity is that more often than not these beginners are so discouraged by their poor achievements that they think they are never going to make the grade. What they can't know, of course, is that it is their pretty "hobby" tools that are at fault, rather than their efforts. And if this isn't bad enough, we now have a situation where not only have most of the professionals moved over to using machines but, worse yet, more and more beginners are also being beguiled into using handheld power tools. So where we once had professionals doing their very best to protect the mysteries of the craft, we now have the professionals so busy revving up their machines and working against the clock trying to bully chipboard, plywood, and plastics into shape that they themselves have to a great extent forgotten how to use the traditional tools. Where once the mysteries were hidden and protected, now they are fast becoming lost!

The good news is that out of this mess and mayhem a new breed of artist-amateur woodworker is evolving. He or she is concerned not only with making furniture and such for money—although this is great when it happens—but, much more exciting, with experiencing the pure therapeutic pleasure of working with wood hand tools. These artist-woodworkers are amateurs in the true sense of the word: a person who engages in a pastime for love rather than for professional gain. They don't need to beat the clock by working with machines, nor do they need to use a heap of chipboard and plastics, but rather, they are becoming involved with woodworking simply because they enjoy the sensory pleasure of touching and handling the tools and the wood. And the wonderful thing is that these new woodworkers have by chance hit upon the simple truth that the way into the craft—the way to understand the mystery—is to get close to the tools and the materials.

Our aim in writing this book is to cut through all the baloney and to tell it how it really is. We have spent the last twenty years collecting tools, we have handled the wood, we have struggled and strived to build several workshops, we have spent time working alongside the old woodworkers who know all the wrinkles, and we have generally done our level best over the years to understand how the tools and the wood come together.

To our way of thinking, the best way of learning about woodwork is to get hold of good quality tools and to disassemble them and see how they work. You don't need a lot of money, or a big workshop, or lots of machines. All you need is enthusiasm and a desire to become involved. The best way forward is to take a good tool like a block plane, and a nice piece of hardwood like, say, maple, and then to see what you can do with them. So, for example, you might set the wood securely in a vise so that the end grain is uppermost and try using the plane. If the wood cuts up rough, then disassemble the plane and hone the bevel. Make sure that the sole of the plane is smooth and clean, then reset the blade so that it takes the finest cut and try again. Study the way a skewed stroke makes for a cleaner cut. See how the grain splits out if it is unsupported, and so on. And so you continue, touching and handling the tools and the wood until, little by little, you begin to understand how they work together.

If you look through the book, you will see that we have set the various chapters out in such a way that we start with the tools, progress through to step-by-step activities, and finish with working drawings for projects. The idea is that you should first discover all there is to know about the anatomy of the tool—its weight, the way it is constructed and put together, the way it is held, the way it is sharpened, the way that it cuts, and so on —before you start cutting the joints. And, of course, this way forward isn't such a chore if you are working with good quality traditional tools. It's a pleasure to hold a tool that has been made with care, a tool that has evolved over two or three hundred years. And just in case you are wondering, we define "traditional" as meaning high-quality tools that were made to be used by craftsmen woodworkers. This has nothing to do with the tools being old—after all, traditional tools are still being made—but rather everything to do with manufacturing specifications. For example, consider four of our planes: One was made in India, one in the USA, one in Germany, and the other in England, and all are modern. The Indian plane is made from folded steel, it has a plastic handle that is too small to hold, the sole is skewed, the blade is made of inferior, bubbled metal, and all in all, it is so awful that it couldn't be used. The American, English, and German planes, on the other hand, are more or less the same good quality planes that the firms have been making for the last 100 years or so. One plane is a useless toy, whereas the other three are top quality traditional tools. And the definition has nothing to do with cost, because more often than not the quality tools are less expensive than the tacky rubbish. And not to worry if you are working on a tight budget, because it's the easiest thing in the world to obtain quality tools at yard sales and flea markets at a fraction of the cost of poor grade new tools. Certainly these secondhand tools will need to be disassembled, sharpened, and tuned, but then, these activities are part and parcel of your learning curve!

All you need do is read through this book, get a good tool and a piece of honest-to-goodness wood, and get started.

At the end of it all you will know how to judge the keeness of a blade by eye. You will be able to use a plane in much the same way as did your folks way back. You will know how and why a bent gouge does what it does. You will be able to cut a joint and shape and fashion a piece of oak. You will be able to sit in a chair of your own making. You will be able to build furniture for the whole house! All are wonderful experiences that should not be missed.

Best of luck.

CHAPTER ONE

The Workshop

The workshop is where it all happens. The size, shape, and structure of the workshop do, of course, depend to a great extent on such factors as where you live, the type of woodworking projects that you have in mind, the available space, and your bank balance, but there are certain fundamentals that are always needed.

Okay, so you might have to start little and then go on to greater things, but no matter, it's important that you know right from the start what it is that you ought to be aiming for.

The following listing and definitions are based on our personal woodworking experiences, pleasures, and needs. For example, we enjoy woodcarving and wood-turning, plus we also enjoy using salvaged wood to make large items like chests. What this all adds up to is a workshop that reflects our specific woodworking interests. It's made from several buildings, with a lot of space set aside for wood. We have a big bench with plenty of natural light, lots of hand tools, and a handful of relatively small machines. That said, if your woodworking interests have to do with building your own yacht, or making musical instruments, or making small wooden boxes, or building all the furniture for your home, or whatever, then your workshop will of course need to be shaped to suit your needs.

The best way to proceed is to read through the following sections, take note of the various fundamentals, and then go your own way.

THE WORKSHOP

When it comes down to it, most of us are limited to one of three or four possible workshop options. We can work in a spare room in the house, we can work in the basement, we can work in the garage, or we can work in a wooden shed out in the garden. We have tried all those places, and for our money, we would go for the garage or the wooden shed in the garden every time. The spare room in the house fails because the noise and the debris make life difficult for the rest of the household, and the basement fails because it's short of natural light and items have to be carried up and down stairs. The garage, on the other hand, is separate from the house and yet convenient, and the wooden workshop in the garden can be sited and sized to suit both the lay of the land and your specific needs.

We have two buildings: the garage where we keep the lathe, the portable planer, the shop-vac, and our growing supply of wood (see 1-1) and the wooden shed in the garden where we have our workbench, scroll saw, drill press, band saw, and all our chests full of hand tools. All in all, we would say that the garage measures about 14 by 20 feet and the shed about 7 by 20 feet. Our thinking behind this arrangement is as follows: Working on the lathe and planing are both noisy and dusty, whereas working at the bench is quiet and relatively clean—shavings rather than dust. By having the bench-work separate from that done on the lathe and the planer, we win on several counts: We are able to limit the dust and debris to one building, and we can work at the bench knowing that it's going to be quiet. When we are set to start a project, we go into the garage work-shop, select a piece of wood from the stockpile, and then run it through the planer or turn it on the lathe. We then clean up the dust with the vacuum, and then move to the workshop in the garden where we complete the final jointing, polishing, or whatever.

Our garden workshop is a beautiful building. It's made of clapboard, with a 1-inch-thick plywood floor, plywood walls on the inside, a door at each end, and windows all along one side at bench height. The windows face southwest. Our bench and work surface run all

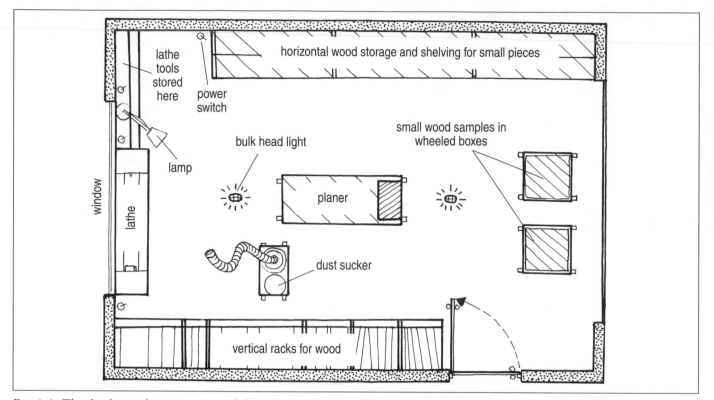

Fig. 1-1. The plan layout for our garage workshop where we keep the dust-making machines.

Labels in figure:
- lathe tools stored here
- power switch
- lamp
- window
- lathe
- horizontal wood storage and shelving for small pieces
- bulk head light
- small wood samples in wheeled boxes
- planer
- dust sucker
- vertical racks for wood

along the window side (see 1-2). What we have, in effect, is a long well-lit corridor. It's not so large that we rattle around, nor so small that we keep bumping into the walls. It's easy to keep warm in the winter and cool in the summer, it's got a huge amount of natural light, and it's got space for a stool and an old armchair. We like the feel of wood underfoot, it's easy to fix shelves and hooks on the wall, and above all, it has a good view of the garden. It's a comfortable working space. The thing to remember here is that you and your tools need more or less the same environment—clean, warm, and dry!

THE WORKBENCH

Next to having the workshop, you must of course have a workbench. The workbench is at the very heart of the American and European woodworking tradition. The workbench must be versatile and yet as firm as a rock. At one and the same time, it mustn't creep or bounce when you are chopping mortises, or rack or twist when you are doing heavy planing. A good workbench must be so heavy and foursquare that it just stays put. If it in any way wobbles, bounces, or creeps, then it is nigh on useless. Of course, as we once did, you can get by with a solid farmhouse kitchen table, the type of solid-as-a-rock kitchen table that our great-grandmothers worked at. If you own such a table, then the chances are you can sell

it as an antique and get yourself a top-of-the-line workbench with the proceeds.

As to what constitutes the perfect workbench—meaning its shape, size, and design—the only thing that most woodworkers will agree on is that the working surface should be more or less level with your wristwatch when you are standing with your arms at your sides. We know this isn't much to go on, but it's a guide. That said, whereas old books suggest that between 28 and 30 inches is a good bench height, we see that current catalogs are selling benches that range between 34 and 35$\frac{1}{2}$ inches in height. The question here is, are woodworkers getting taller? Or are their arms getting shorter?

If you have got yourself a bench with end frames, and it is a bit too high, the best bet is to build a low platform to jack yourself up a little bit higher.

As to the shape and style of the workbench, you will find that there are just about as many "perfect" designs as there are woodworkers. There are benches about 24 inches wide with flat surfaces, there are benches with troughs (see 1-3), there are benches with one, two, or three vises, there are benches with leg vises, and the list goes on. The only thing that woodworkers will agree on is that there is universal disagreement as to what constitutes a good bench. We have a German bench that is 35$\frac{1}{2}$ inches high and 18$\frac{1}{4}$ inches wide from the front

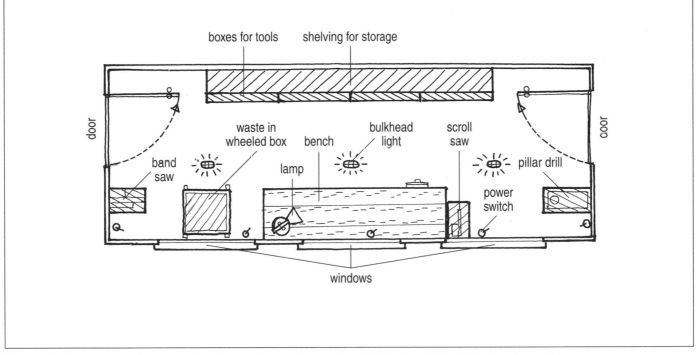

Fig. 1-2. *The plan layout for our garden shed workshop where we have the bench and the relatively quiet machines.*

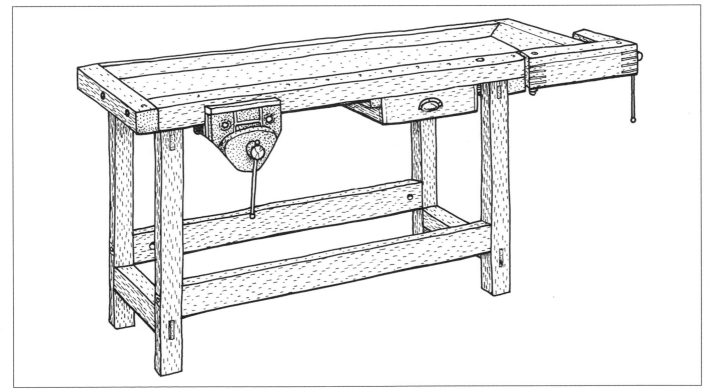

Fig. 1-3. *This particular workbench has an integral tail vise, a pair of sprung steel dogs or stops, a tool well, a good drawer, and a quick-release vise. The end vise provides a clamping force along the length of the bench to enable lengths of timber to be held for planing.*

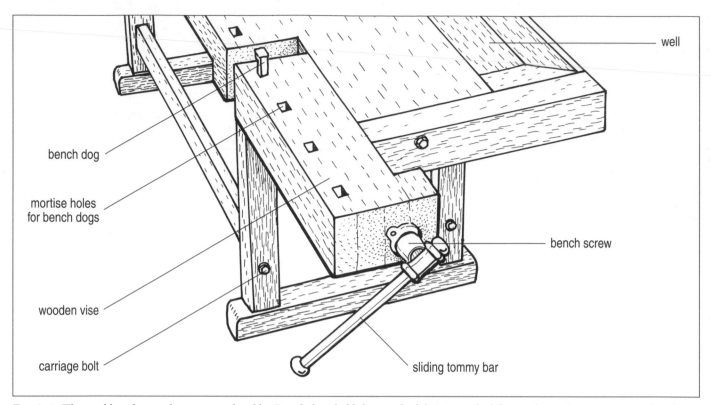

Fig. 1-4. The workbench must be strong and stable. Bench dogs hold the wood while it is worked flat on the surface. Many woodworkers prefer wooden dogs; they say that they are less likely to mark the workpiece, and they are kinder to the tools when slipups occur.

edge to the trough. The trough is 6 inches wide, the table is 90 inches long, and the surface is about 4 inches thick at the edges. It is made of solid beech throughout. It has panel ends, a massive tilt-out drawer for tools, a front vise, and a tail vise, and the surface is mortised for solid steel square-section dogs and stops (see 1-4). We know for a fact that it is currently possible to build such a bench for about $300, with about half the money for the wood and half for the fittings and fixtures that make up the vise.

Though the vise might seem to be an expensive item, it gets a lot of wear so it needs to be strong and foolproof. Basically, there are two types of vises: an all-metal one that you purchase all in one piece (see 1-5) and various bench screws that you use to make your own German- or Scandinavian-type vise.

Lots of woodworkers prefer a vise with a quick-release mechanism, which disengages the main screw to allow the jaw to slide freely in and out. It's a good idea if you need to work swiftly.

WOOD STORAGE

Storage is always something of a problem for the simple reason that wood comes in all manner of lengths and widths. It's important that all the wood is easily accessible; it's no good at all if the piece that you need is so far down in the woodstack that you are going to wear yourself out looking for it. The best layout is to have horizontal racks for boards longer than 6 feet (see 1-6), vertical racks or bays for shorter lengths at, say 3 to 6 feet, shelves for pieces about 1 to 3 feet, and boxes for tagents. We find that wastepieces are something of a problem, because we hate to throw them away. What happens is that we like the look of a certain piece (nearly all the pieces in fact) and put it in a box. And, of course, what inevitably happens is that the workshop is soon cluttered with boxes full of oddends. We think that perhaps the best rule of thumb is to set a few shelves aside for a limited number of pieces, and then you will simply have to add the rest to the winter woodpile.

TOOL STORAGE

First and foremost, tools need to be kept dry. We have found that the best way of storing tools is to keep them in traditional chests and boxes. Certainly, this isn't the most convenient method, and it is a bit of a nuisance having to move things off the boxes to get to the tools, but against that, the tools are protected. We have got five or so chests: one for wooden molding planes, one for chisels and gouges, one for general everyday tools, one for saws, and one for drills and bits. Anything that needs to be hung on the wall gets hung on whittled wooden pegs—no nails, no Peg-Board, and no patent clips or gizmos. If we want another peg on the wall, we simply drill a ¹/₂-inch-diameter hole and whittle another peg to fit. And when the peg gets in the way, we saw it off, leaving the hole ready-plugged.

LIGHT

Light is one of the most important factors in a workshop: too little and you are liable to misread measurements and have accidents; too much and you finish up with hard shadows on the wrong side of tools and dazzle. You need as much natural light as possible, plus lots of backup lamps that you can move around to focus in on problem areas. With the lathe and the workbench, we like to have windows in the front and artificial light coming in from the side. As to the specific type of lights, we think that a good balance of protected bulkhead lights for overhead and flex-arm lights for the side seems about right. We think that two big no-no's are swinging ceiling lights that are going to get broken and flickering florescent lights. Never use florescent lights near the lathe, because the mix of spinning items plus a flickering florescent sometimes causes an unsettling strobe light effect.

As for the surfaces, we have white walls and ceiling in the garage and natural wood in the garden workshop.

VENTILATION

Workshops need good ventilation: not so much that paper leaps off the work surface, but rather a good supply of clean, dry live air. Woodworkers, tools, and wood all benefit if air is allowed to circulate. It discourages the growth of mold on the wood, it stops the tools from getting dank, and it generally helps to

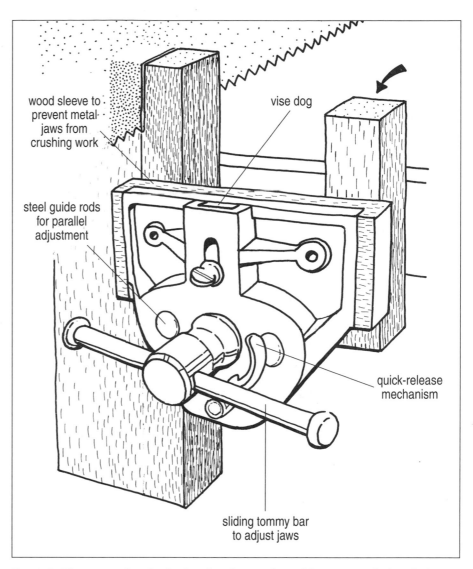

Fig. 1-5. The vise needs to be fitted so that the top edges of the jaws are flush with the surface of the bench. To protect your vise and to prevent twist damage, always balance the load by using a piece of waste wood to fill the vise when only half the width is being used.

keep you and the workshop from smelling of damp and decay. Of course, you can't beat having the doors and windows open, with warm summer air wafting through, but when the winter days are damp and still, and the windows are shut tight, then you need one or more fans. Beware of large metal fans that tinkle and clatter. It's much better to go for a small, silent fan.

HEAT

Heat is something of a problem. We say this because the temperature of the workshop will depend on your activity. If you are standing at the lathe you need more heat, but if you are slogging away ripping down a plank, then summer or winter you might well need to be in your shirtsleeves, with the door open. Of course, it's no problem to regulate the temperature in the summer: All you do is throw the doors and windows open. But in the winter you need some sort of heater. Much depends on your situation—the size of the workshop, its location, and how much time you spend in it. The important factors are immediacy and safety: You must

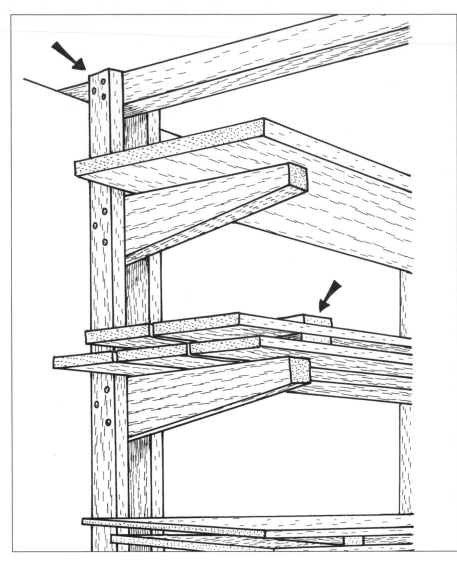

Fig. 1-6. The post-and-spar wood rack can easily be made from salvaged timber. It is hung from the ceiling joists and bolted together. Place stickers between the planks to ensure good circulation of air. Make sure that the stickers are aligned one on top of another.

have the heat when you want it, and it's got to be safe. We think that the two best options are a wood-fired stove and electric wall convector heaters. We find that in our situation we need electric heaters in the garage, so that we can turn them swiftly on and off, and a couple of electric heaters in the garden workshop. We tend to turn the heaters on for starters, and then shed clothes and turn down the heat as the activity heats up. As for safety, much depends on how much dust you make. Dust and naked flames or red hot elements are a very dangerous mix.

POWER

You need power in your workshop. Even if you have in mind only to work with hand tools, you still need power. Precisely how many outlets you need is not so easy to say. All we know is that our woodworking friends are always complaining about the sad lack of power outlets in their workshops. Even if you are working in a small garden shed workshop, and even if you dislike power tools, there will come a time when you need an outlet for a heater, an electric coffeemaker or radio, a piece of studio lighting equipment for taking photographs, an extra light, and so on. My advice is to work out how many outlets you think you will need, and then double the figure.

One thing I can say for sure is that the power outlets must be sited in such a way that there are no trailing cables. If your machines and work surfaces are pushed hard against the wall, then you can have the outlets on the wall, but if you have items in the middle of the room, then either the cables need to be buried in the floor so that the outlets can be sited near the equipment, or the cables need to run overhead.

CHAPTER TWO

Saws

Generically, no matter their size or shape, saws are either ripsaws or crosscut saws. The teeth of a ripsaw are designed to cut in the direction of the grain (see 2-2 and 2-3), whereas crosscut teeth are designed to cut across the grain. All you really need to know is that the many different types, shapes, and sizes of saw have each been designed for a specific task. Or put another way, the trick is not to buy a saw and then sit and wonder what you can do with it, but rather to first identify the need, and then get yourself a saw that does the job.

All the many and various traditional saw types are grouped under one of three headings, or you might say they belong to one of three families. There are *handsaws*, which are used for cutting the wood down into the primary strips and lengths; *backsaws*, which are used for all the secondary cuts, like, for example, cutting joints; and *narrow-bladed saws*, which are used for cutting curves.

The best way forward for a novice is to decide what it is that you want to cut. Do you want to convert large planks? Then you need a handsaw. Do you want to cut joints? Use a backsaw. Do you want to cut curves? In that case you need a narrow-bladed saw. After you have identified your needs is the time to select a specific size and type of saw to suit. The following listing will show you the way.

HANDSAWS: FOR CONVERTING WOOD INTO STRIPS AND LENGTHS

The ability to choose the best saw for the task is at the heart of good woodworking. In essence, there are only two types of saws: those for cutting in the direction of the grain and those for cutting across the grain. No matter what the task may be—sizing the lengths, cutting dovetails, cutting tenons, or whatever—the procedure always breaks down into either cutting with the grain or cutting across the grain. Rip teeth saws are designed to

cut with the grain, so it's plain to see why a small dovetail saw has rip teeth. If you're still confused, then keep reading.

RIPSAW

The first question that you have to ask yourself is, do you need a ripsaw? We say this because nowadays more and more wood is being sold in the sized, planed, and ready-to-use state, so many woodworkers don't use a ripsaw. That said, it's best get yourself a saw with 4 to 5 points to the inch if you have in mind to do a lot of converting—sawing thick wood down the run of the grain—or a finer 7-point saw if you only plan to rip the occasional short piece. As for the length of saw blade, this is best chosen to suit your stature, that is, your height and the length of your arm (see 2-2).

CROSSCUT SAW

You can't get by without one or more crosscut saws. If you are going to cut across the grain—and that's what most woodworking is about—then you need a good quality crosscut saw. As to the number of teeth, the question that you have to ask yourself is, do you want to go fast and furious, and then spend time cleaning up with the plane, or do you want to go for a finer but slower cut? The rule is the fewer the teeth to the inch, the coarser the cut. A good middle-of-the-road choice is a 7- to 8-point for heavy cabinet work, and a 6- to 7-point for more general carpentry.

BACKSAWS: FOR GENERAL BENCHWORK

Backsaws are primary woodworking tools; they are used day in and day out for all the general work and for jointing. This being the case, and we think most professional woodworkers would concur, beginners must invest in the very best quality saws that they can afford. If you are

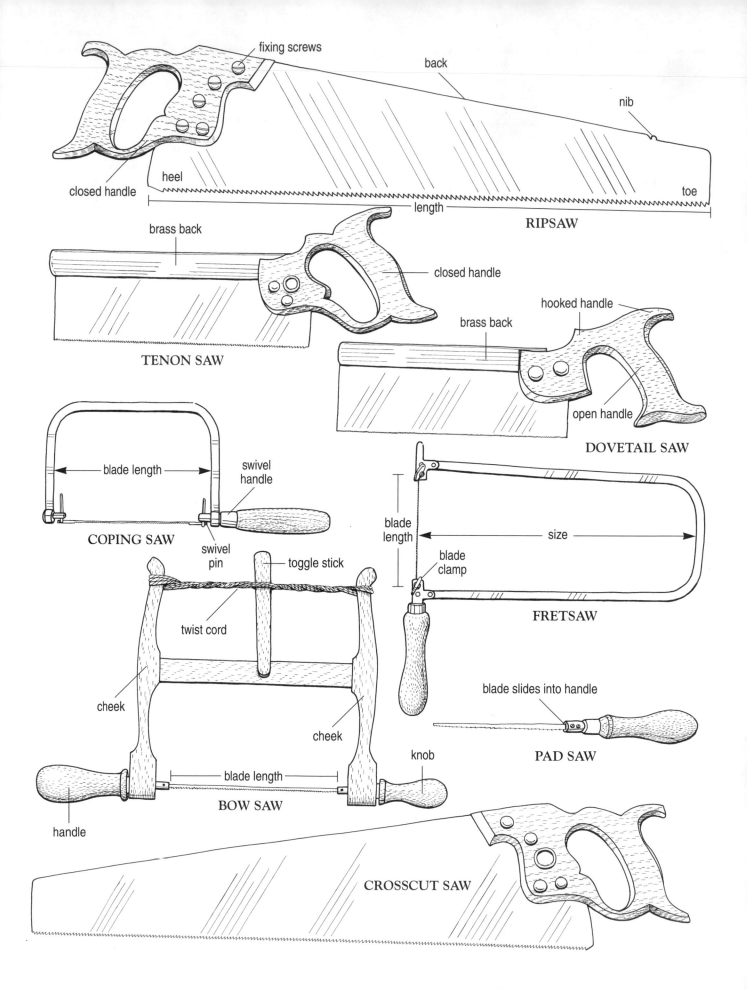

Fig. 2-1. Details of Saws.

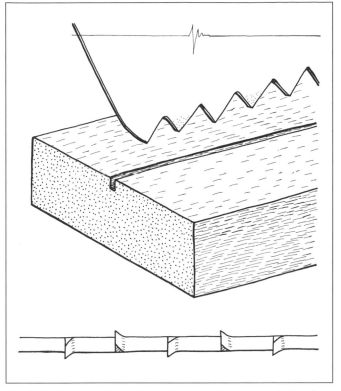

Fig. 2-2. Top, detail showing a close-up of ripsaw teeth plus the shape of the resultant kerf. Note how the chisel-shaped tooth leaves a square-bottomed channel. Bottom, ripsaw teeth are filed straight across, at right angles to the blade, so that each tooth has a chisel-like edge.

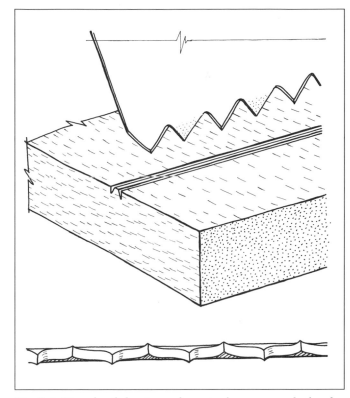

Fig. 2-3. Top, detail showing a close-up of crosscut teeth plus the shape of the resultant kerf. Note how the peaked center crumbles away as the saw descends. Bottom, crosscut teeth are filed at an angle so that the cutting points, or bevels, are on alternate sides of the saw blade.

short of cash, we would recommend that you seek out old tools—the sort of thing that you might find in your grandfather's toolbox—and then spend time bringing them up to snuff.

In general terms, a good quality backsaw will have a brass back, a polished blade that is fully tensioned, tempered, and stiffened, and a well-fitted good-to-hold wooden handle. Though there are many types and sizes of backsaws, some with rip teeth, others with crosscut, and yet others described as half-rip, the average woodworker needs just three straightforward saws: a tenon, a dovetail, and a bead.

TENON SAW

Bearing in mind that of all the saws, the tenon is perhaps going to get the most use, it will pay you to get a top quality tool. Though tenon saws commonly range in blade length from 8 to 14 inches, sometimes even longer at 16 inches, we would go for a 14-inch saw with about 13 points to the inch. Get one with a good solid beech handle that is fixed to the blade with three brass screws.

DOVETAIL SAW

The dovetail saw is the kid brother to the tenon. The difference between the two saws is not so much the length of the blade (it is possible to get a small tenon saw and a large dovetail saw both at 8 inches long) but rather the number of teeth to the inch. Just remember the phrase "fine-and-fancy": If you want to make a fancy joint, then you need a saw that is going to make a fine cut. If your woodworking ambitions involve cutting exhibition joints, then you had best get yourself a top quality dovetail saw with about 18 to 22 points to the inch.

As to why many traditional dovetail saws have an open handle with a hook at the top, we were once told that the open handle allows room for maneuvering when cutting dovetails, while the hook at the top of the handle allows the index finger to be crooked in such a way that it is possible to achieve maximum control with minimum effort. We have given it a lot of thought, and we think it's true to say that the open handle does encourage a more delicate and responsive grip.

BEAD SAW

Bead-type saws are many and varied. There is the brass-backed "gent's" saw with a fine blade and 14 points to the inch, the light backsaw or jeweler's saw with about 24 points to the inch, and many others. Our advice is to stay with your dovetail saw if you aim to cut medium-sized joints, and only get a bead saw if you want to cut the smallest of small dovetails or you like working in miniature.

NARROW-BLADED SAWS: FOR CUTTING CURVES

The rule with curve-cutting saws is the narrower the blade, the quicker or tighter the curve. It follows that the finer the blade, the more complex the frame needed to hold, support, and tension the blade. But then again, there is a limit to the thickness of wood that a very fine bladed saw will cut. What the novice has to figure out is when and why to use one saw instead of another. The good news is that narrow-bladed saws are so inexpensive that most beginners will be well able to get the whole range of saws and compare one to another.

BOW SAW

Though the design of the wooden bow saw looks positively archaic, what with its shaped side pieces or cheeks, twisted cord, toggle stick and all, it is in fact an amazingly satisfactory and versatile tool. The purpose of the frame, of course, is to hold the relatively fragile blade in tension and to prevent it from buckling when the saw is in use. Blade tension is achieved by twisting the cord with the toggle stick so that the top ends of the cheeks are pulled together (see 2-5). The handle and knob are able to rotate in the frame, making it possible to turn the blade through 360 degrees. Note that whereas the two wooden

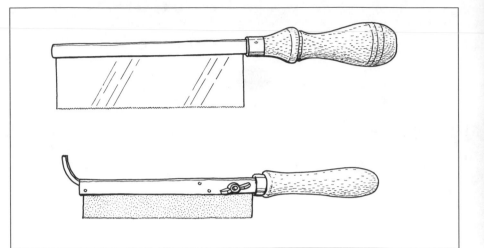

Fig. 2-4. Top, *not all ripsaws are big*. Though the gent's saw is one of the smallest backsaws, it nevertheless has rip teeth designed for cutting down into the grain for fine endgrain joinery. Bottom, *the bead saw, with its finger hook and replaceable blade*, is the smallest of all the backsaws.

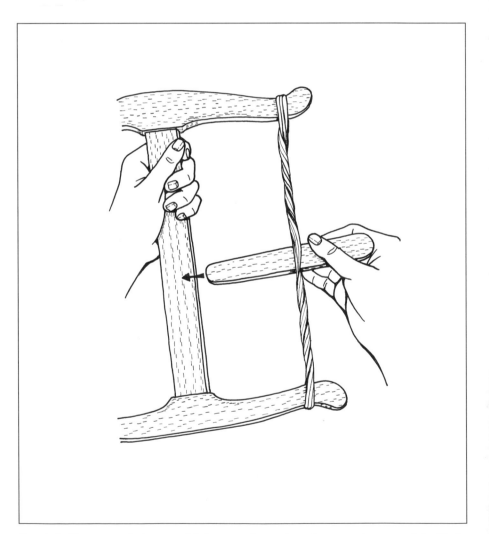

Fig. 2-5. To tension the bow saw blade, turn the toggle stick over and over until the blade "pings" when plucked, and then slide the end of the toggle stick down against the stretcher rail so that the direction of twist holds the stick in place.

handles are in fact usually more or less the same shape and size, the larger one is termed the "handle" and the smaller one the "knob" (see 2-1).

Though it is possible to obtain two or three types of new bow saws, and more than a dozen if you are prepared to buy old saws, we think that the small type of bow or turning saw—one with a blade at 12 inches long —is a very useful all-around tool.

PAD OR KEYHOLE SAW

The keyhole saw is used primarily for cutting small-sized holes in relatively thick wood, such as a keyhole or slot in a solid wood door. The clever thing about this tool is that the tapered soft-tempered coarse-toothed blade is held and supported in the handle in such a way that the user need only withdraw a length of blade to suit the thickness of the wood being worked. As to the question of whether or not the beginner needs such a saw, it really depends on the type of work. All we can say is that although we don't get to use our keyhole saw very often, it is a choice tool for cutting small holes in wide slabs of wood, when the distance between the hole and the edge of the wood renders the bow saw useless.

COPING SAW

The coping saw, with its small U-shaped metal frame and 6-inch-long 14-point blade, is in a good many respects a bow saw in miniature. It is a relatively modern saw that is designed specifically for tasks such as cutting small moldings and trim and cutting holes in thin wood. We find it a particularly useful tool for cutting tight curves in plywood and for clearing the waste between dovetails. If you have a choice, get a coping saw with a wooden handle. In use, the blade is held taut by the tension of the frame and the adjustment of the screw handle, with the ends of the blade being held by swivel pins (see 2-6).

FRETSAW

Though at first sight the fretsaw looks to be no more than an extended version of the coping saw, the small differences in design make it an altogether more useful tool. For example, the 12- to 20-inch depth of the frame means that it can be used a good distance in from the edge of the wood, a particularly useful feature for fine cabinetwork. And because the blades are clamped in the frame rather than fitted with pins, the saw can be fitted with the smallest of small blades, which in turn means that you need drill only the smallest of pilot holes if you want to saw a pierced hole.

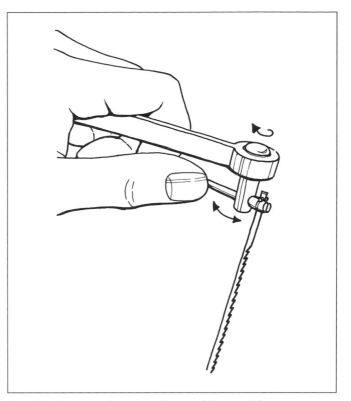

Fig. 2-6. If you need to swing the metal frame of the coping saw aside so that you can cut at a different angle, push on the swivel spigot to turn the blade around on its pivot.

If you are going to get yourself a fretsaw, get the biggest size possible, that is, one with a 20-inch frame or throat.

TIPS ON SELECTING A GOOD SAW

Way back at the end of the nineteenth century, when the American Henry Disston—the largest saw manufacturer in the world—was asked to give guidance on purchasing saws, he gave the following advice and tips:

- In selecting a saw, start by trying the handle for size; make sure that it is a comfortable fit.
- Avoid handles that are made from poor grade wood, because they are liable to shrink, crack, and become loose.
- Try the blade by springing it; it should bend evenly from end to end.
- The blade must not be too heavy in comparison with the teeth.
- A narrow true saw is much better than a wide true saw. The thinner the blade the better.
- The blade should ring clearly when sprung and struck.
- Never be tempted by low cost.

THE ANATOMY AND CUTTING ACTION OF A SAW

The term "saw" refers to the whole range of sheet or strip metal tools that have teeth along one edge. The cutting action involves pushing and pulling rhythmically—with European saws cutting on the "push" stroke and Eastern saws cutting on the "pull." The cut or groove made by the saw is termed the kerf. The thicker the saw blade and the larger the teeth, the faster the cut, and consequently the coarser the kerf. The choice of saw depends on four factors: the type of timber to be cut, the direction of the cut in relationship to the run of the grain, the character of the cut —is it being used in the context of fine benchwork, or general carpentry?—and the speed that you want to make the cut. A good part of traditional woodwork has to do with being able to select the correct saw for the task. In general terms, large teeth are best for softwood, while saws with many small teeth are best for hardwoods. You, therefore, need to appraise the wood, decide how you want to cut in relationship to the run of the grain, determine whether or not you want a fine or a coarse kerf, and then choose your saw accordingly.

RIPSAWS AND CROSSCUTS

There are only two generic types of saws: the ripsaw, which is designed to cut in the direction of the grain, and the crosscut saw, which is de-

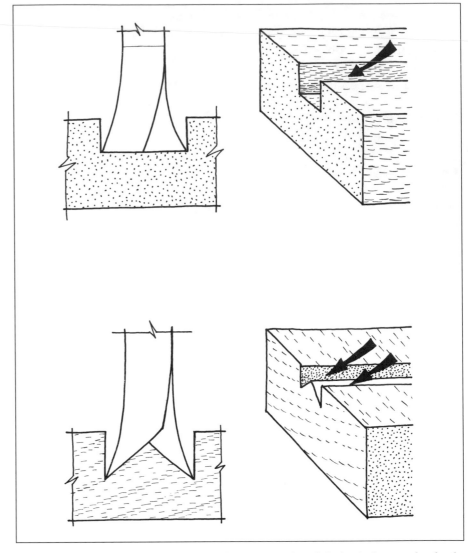

Fig. 2-7. Top left, *cross section through the ripsaw teeth and the kerf, showing the chisel-like action of the teeth.* Top right, *the ripsaw leaves a characteristic square-cut channel.* Bottom left, *cross section through the crosscut saw and the kerf, showing how the teeth slice across the fibers of the grain.* Bottom right, *the crosscut saw leaves a characteristic peaked channel.*

signed to cut across the run of the grain. To put it in terms of a plank of wood, the ripsaw is designed to cut the plank down its length, whereas the crosscut saw is designed to cut the plank across its width.

The best way of understanding how and why the two saw types have evolved is to think what happens when you use a chisel to cut variously with and across the grain. For example, when you cut a trench down a plank, the grain simply rolls up in nice tidy curls. But try to cut

the selfsame trench across the plank, and the grain will splinter and tear. The answer to cutting the trench across the grain is to set the sides of the trench in with stop-cuts before using the chisel. If you now visualize and miniaturize this procedure in terms of saw teeth, then it's easy to understand why the teeth of a ripsaw are shaped like miniature chisels, whereas the teeth of the crosscut are like two knife points set side by side (see 2-7). The teeth of the ripsaw can be likened to a row of chisels that plough up the fibers of the wood, while the teeth of the crosscut can be likened to two rows of side-by-side knives that make two parallel stop-cuts. And just in case you decide to try and get by with only one type of saw, although you can use a crosscut saw to cut in the direction of the wood fibers (it is slow but you will get there in the end), there is no way that you can use a ripsaw to cut across the run of the wood fibers.

SAW TEETH: SIZE, CHARACTER, AND HOW MANY

The size of a saw is defined primarily by the character of the cut it makes: a coarse cut or a fine cut. With the size of the cut being determined by the thickness of the blade, the amount of set to the teeth, and number of teeth to the inch, the rule is the greater the set and the fewer the teeth, the coarser the cut. You might conversely say the smaller the angle of set and the greater the number of teeth, the finer the cut.

When you purchase a saw, you need to bear in mind that saws are variously defined as having TPI or PPI (see 2-8). Although both definitions have to do with the number of teeth to the inch, TPI ("teeth per inch") indicates the number of tooth points if you measure between gullets, whereas PTI ("points per inch") indicates the number of teeth if you measure from point to point. To further confuse things, you have got to remember that a saw described as 8 PPI is identical to one described as 7 TPI.

As for the length of the blade, this is of secondary importance, the choice being made when you have settled on the set and the number of teeth to the inch. So, for example, we see from a current catalog that in the crosscut saw range, you

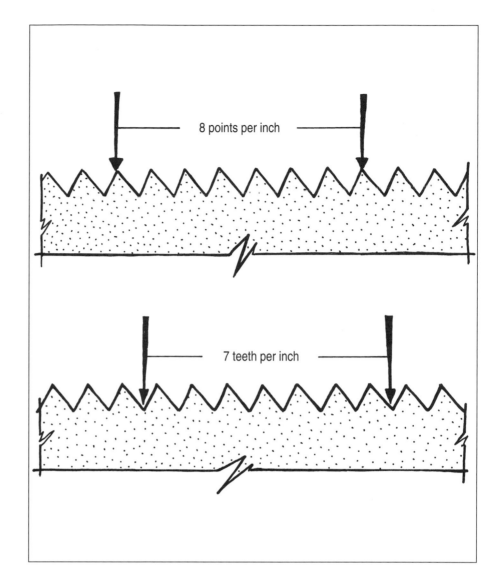

Fig. 2-8. *The number of saw teeth are described either as TPI or PPI. Top, the European PPI system measures the number of "Points Per Inch"; the teeth are counted from point to point. Bottom, the American TPI system measures the number of "Teeth Per Inch"; the teeth are counted from gullet to gullet. Note that though in this instance one system comes up with the number 7, whereas the other system comes up with the number 8, it's plain to see that they are referring to the identical saw.*

have a choice between a pretty coarse-set saw with 7 points to the inch on a 24-inch-long blade and a fine-set saw with 10 points to the inch on a 22-inch-long blade. They are both crosscut saws, but one is going to be pretty fast and furious and leave a relatively wide slot, or kerf, whereas the other is going to be slow going and leave a fine kerf. If you were faced with this choice,

you would have to decide whether you wanted a coarse-toothed saw with few points to the inch and a large angle of set for cutting damp unseasoned wood, or a fine-toothed saw with a lot of teeth to the inch and a small angle of set for cutting crisp and dry hardwood, or both saws. To our way of thinking, since wood is so variable, we would probably go for both saws.

SHARPENING

If you have it in mind to sharpen your saws, then you should start with the biggest, roughest, ripsaw or crosscut saw that you posses; the fewer teeth to the inch the better. (If you are ever faced with sharpening a high-quality small fine-bladed backsaw, you had best take it to a specialist saw doctor.) You need four pieces of equipment: a saw vise, or at least two boards that you can clamp in the bench vise, a flat file, a set of three little triangular section saw files, and a saw set (see 2-9). Saws described by the manufacturers as "hard point" cannot be sharpened. Such saws are intended as throwaways.)

The sharpening procedure is divided into three sequential stages or steps: jointing, fitting, and setting.

JOINTING

If a saw is badly worn, then it needs to be jointed. Jointing, sometimes also called topping, is the procedure of cutting all the teeth down to the same level (see 2-10). Arrange all the tools so that they are comfortably at hand, then take the saw and position it teeth uppermost in the jaws of the vise. Arrange the saw so that the teeth protrude no more than about 1/2 to 3/4 inch and then clamp it tight so that the saw doesn't move or chatter. This done, take the flat file, hold it down on the teeth so that it is a bit like a train sitting on a rail, and then run it away from you along the length of the saw (see 2-11). Repeat this procedure several times until the top of every tooth has been touched.

If the saw is badly worn, then the jointed teeth will need to be reshaped. All you do is take a small triangular file and file across the saw at right angles to the blade so that each and every tooth and gullet have been cut back to the correct size and angle (see 2-12).

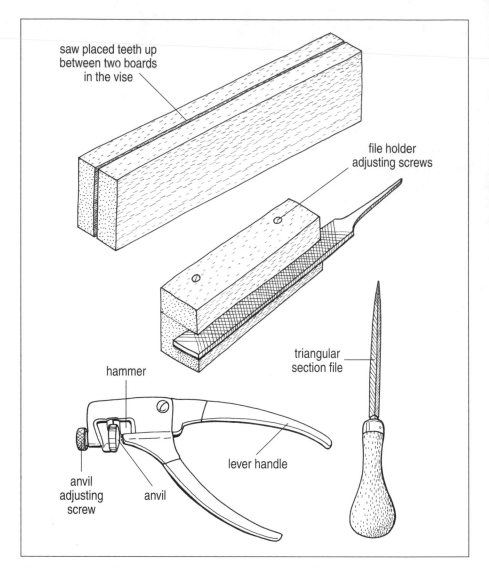

saw placed teeth up between two boards in the vise

file holder adjusting screws

triangular section file

hammer

lever handle

anvil adjusting screw

anvil

Fig. 2-9. You need four pieces of equipment to sharpen and tune a saw: Top, an arrangement of two boards that you can use to grip the saw in the vise; Middle, a flat file held and gripped in a homemade wooden fence cum holder (note that the fence must be at right angles to the face of the file); Bottom right, a triangular section saw file; Bottom left, a patent saw–setting devise.

FITTING

Fitting, sometimes described as filing, is the procedure of filing each tooth so that the burr or cutting edge is on the correct side of the tooth (see 2-13). As the procedures for ripsaws and crosscut saws are slightly different, we will describe one technique and then the other.

Fitting a Ripsaw. Having jointed the saw, and with the saw clamped in the vise as already described, start by having a close look at the teeth (see 2-14). You will see that, unlike a crosscut saw, each tooth is filed straight across, so in effect the tooth is with a burr but without a bevel. This being the case, select a triangular file of proper size, set the file in the gullet nearest the handle end of the saw, hold the file so that it is at right angles to the saw blade, and then make one pass of the file. If you have done it correctly, you will have filed both sides of the gullet, or you might say, one slope of one tooth and one slope of the next tooth in line. Having done the first gullet, skip the next gullet and repeat the procedure in gullet number three. And so you continue down the length of the saw, filing a gullet, skipping one, filing the next one, and so on. When you get to the end of the line, all you do is turn the saw around in the vise, and file all the gullets that you skipped the first time around.

Fitting a Crosscut Saw. Having jointed the saw, and with the saw clamped in the vise as already described (with the handle to your left), have a close look at the teeth. See how each tooth has two cutting edges or bevels, one on one side, and one on the other (see 2-15). When you are ready to start, set the file in the first gullet so that the tooth on the left of the file is leaning toward you. Angle the file around so that it is pointing to the left, or you might say toward the handle and at an angle of 45 to 60 degrees (45 degrees for softwood and 60 degrees for hardwood), and make a single pass. If you have trouble maintaining the correct angle, draw it out on a piece of cardboard and move it along the saw so that you can sight the file down the drawn line. At the end of the stroke, lift the file clear and make a second pass in the same gullet. If you now have a close-up look, you will see that you have cut a bevel on the opposite face of the tooth on the left, and on the near face of the tooth on your right. And so you continue with every other gullet. When you get to the toe end of the blade, turn the saw around in the vise, so that the handle is toward your right, and repeat the procedure in the gullets that you skipped the first time around. The only difference this time is that although the file is still pointing toward the handle, it is in fact pointing toward the right.

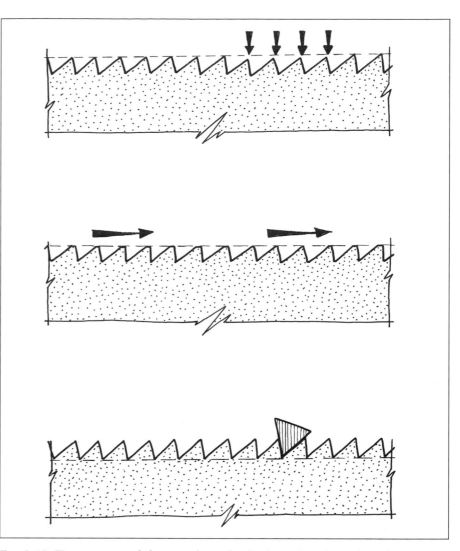

Fig. 2-10. Top, *jointing and shaping only need to be done when the teeth are badly worn and uneven. Put a metal straightedge against the teeth, and if the points fall short, then the teeth need to be jointed and the gullets need to be shaped.* Middle, *gently file the top of the teeth until they are all down to the same level.* Bottom, *reshape each and every tooth by running the triangular file at right angles across the gullet until the shape of the teeth conforms. This reshaping is not to be confused with sharpening proper, that is, when alternate teeth are filed.*

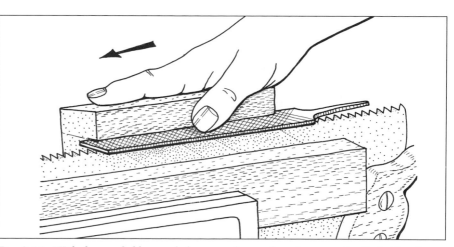

Fig. 2-11. *With the saw held securely between the two boards, grasp the file holder, butt the fence hard up against the side of the saw so that the file rests on top of the teeth, and then very lightly stroke the file along the full length of the saw. If you have done it correctly, every tooth should shine when you sight down along the saw.*

SETTING THE TEETH

Setting is the procedure of bending alternate teeth left and right. The object of the exercise is to create a kerf that is slightly wider than the thickness of the saw (see 2-16) so that when the saw is being used it moves freely without sticking or binding. You need a large set and, consequently, a wide kerf for a saw that is going to be used on damp unseasoned wood, and the smallest of sets and the narrowest of kerfs on a saw that is going to be used on well-seasoned dry hardwood. Though there are any number of ways of bending the teeth, the only foolproof way is to use a patent saw set. All you do is adjust the plier-like tool to the correct setting for your saw, set it on the first tooth in line, and give it a squeeze to bend over the tooth (see 12-17). You do every other tooth on one side of the blade, and then turn the saw around and repeat the procedure with the teeth that you skipped the first time around.

TUNING A SAW

Tuning is best thought of as the sum total of all the procedures that go into creating the perfect tool. Of course the extent and sequence of a first tuning will depend on whether you start out with a new or a secondhand saw, but sooner or later, your saw will not be so shiny and beautiful, and you will have to run through the whole works.

Let's start out on the premise that you have inherited your saws and that they all need bringing to order. The saws are top quality and well used, and they have been sitting in your grandfather's toolbox, in a dry attic, for the last twenty-five years.

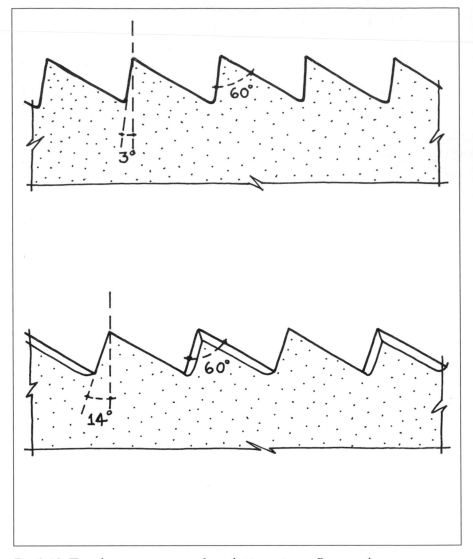

Fig. 2-12. Top, *the correct geometry for reshaping a ripsaw.* Bottom, *the correct geometry for a crosscut saw.*

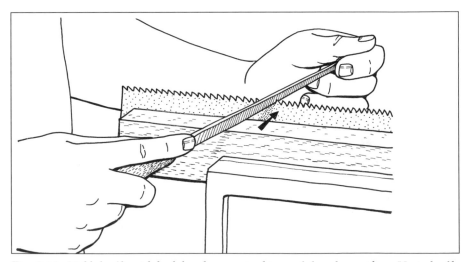

Fig. 2-13. Hold the file with both hands—one pushing and the other guiding. Keep the file level and steady and maintain an even pressure. File alternate teeth, and then turn the saw around and cut the teeth that you missed the first time around.

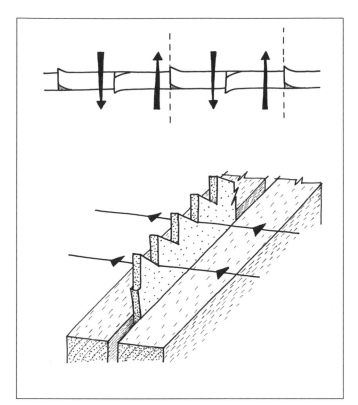

Fig. 2-14. Top, *the 90-degree angle at which the file is held creates a characteristic burr rather than a bevel. Bottom,* hold the *file at 90 degrees to the side of the blade, and then cut alternate teeth.*

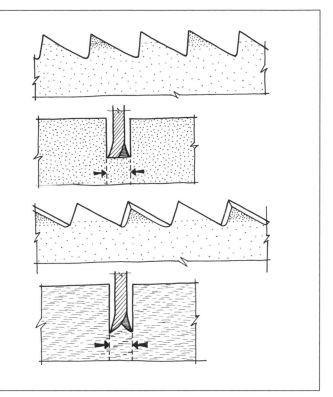

Fig. 2-16. Top, *ripsaw teeth side view.* Upper middle, *ripsaw teeth in cross section.* Lower middle, *crosscut teeth side view.* Bottom, *crosscut teeth in cross section.*

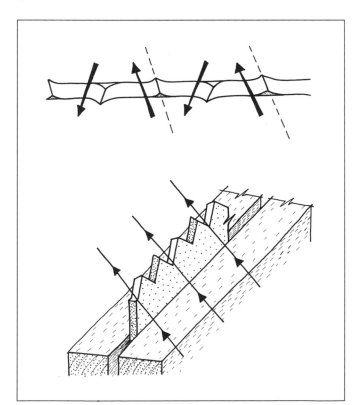

Fig. 2-15. Top, *the angle at which the file is held—60 degrees for hardwood and 45 degrees for softwood—creates a characteristic beveled cutting edge.* Bottom, *the file is held at the selected angle (60 or 45 degrees) and then used to cut alternate teeth.*

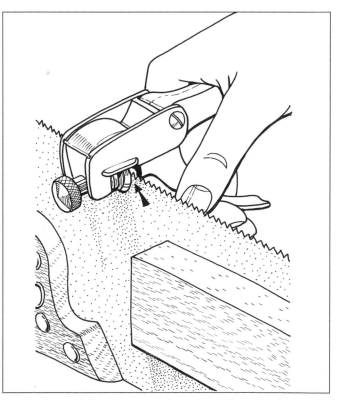

Fig. 2-17. *With the saw-setting pliers adjusted so that the tooth angle matches the original geometry of the saw, the tool is used to bend over individual teeth. Set alternate teeth on one side of the blade, and then flip the blade over and set the teeth that you skipped the first time around.*

STRAIGHTENING OUT A BUCKLE

Have a good long look at each saw. Sight down the length of the blades and make sure they are free from cracks and sharp-angled kinks. A saw with a crack is useless! If a handsaw is very slightly buckled, set it on an anvil or metal plate, with the convex side of the buckle uppermost, and give it a few well-placed blows with a smooth-faced hammer.

If a backsaw is buckled, tap the brass back off the blade, straighten the blade as already described, and then use a hammer and a piece of hardwood to tap the brass spine strip back onto the blade (see 2-18).

If your saw is badly buckled or kinked, it's best to take it to a saw doctor. We say this because it's all too easy for a heavy-handed beginner to overdo the hammering, to the extent that the steel stretches and the buckle gets worse.

OVERHAULING THE HANDLE

Wipe the handle with turpentine to remove the grime and make sure that the handle is free from splits, borers, and rot. If the handle is split, all you do is undo the fixing screws, remove it from the blade, break it apart, clean the break, and glue it back together. If, however, the handle is, say, riddled with borers, then the easiest procedure is to use the old handle as a pattern and to fret out another one (see the Working Drawings at the end of this chapter). If the handle is loose or the blade is rusty, then remove the nuts and bolts, slide the handle off the blade (see 2-19), clean the blade with the finest grade of steel wool, oil the nuts and bolt threads, and then put the whole works back together.

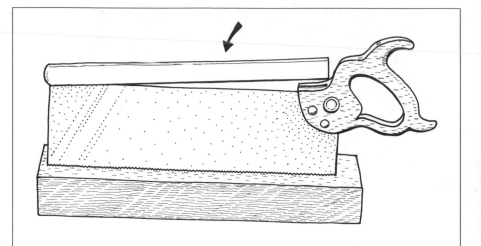

Fig. 2-18. *Once you have achieved a blade that is true, set the blade tooth-edge down on a piece of hardwood and use a hammer to tap the brass spine back on the blade. Go at it nice and easy while being sure not to twist the blade or split the handle.*

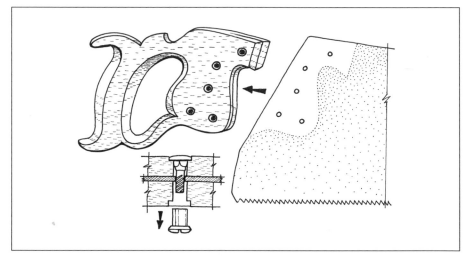

Fig. 2-19. Top and right, *unscrew and remove the bolts and screw fixings, and then very carefully slide the handle off the blade.* Bottom, *cross section showing how the spigoted fixings clamp the handle in place on the blade. A sure sign of a worthless saw is one with a handle that can't be removed from the blade, meaning it is riveted.*

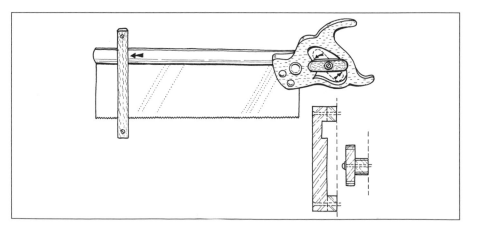

Fig. 2-20. Top, *traditionally, small saws were fitted to the inside lids of toolboxes and to the insides of cupboards by means of small homemade clips and turn buttons. The bridgelike clip is shaped to take the thickness of the blade with its brass back, while the turn button is cut so that it fits inside the closed saw handle.* Bottom right, *side view cross sections showing how the clip and turn-button relate to the surface on which they are fitted.*

CLEANING AND WAXING

When the saw has been variously straightened, jointed, fitted, set, and the handle has been refurbished, all that remains is to give it a final cleaning. If the saw is badly tarnished, start by cleaning the brass with metal polish and rubbing the blade down with a pad of the finest steel wool dipped in a mix of beeswax and turpentine. Finally, give the whole saw a good rub down with a cotton cloth, and it is ready to be used.

STORING

If you have just spent hours getting your saw into good working order, it follows that you will want to store it straight and flat so that it isn't clashing together with a whole heap of other saws. It's best to make a special holder for this purpose (see 2-20; see also the Working Drawings at the end of this chapter).

STANCE AND CONTROL

Though beginners would, by trial and error, eventually discover the best methods of sawing, they would also inevitably pick up one or two bad habits along the way that well might hinder their progress or damage the tools. That said, we believe that the following guidelines will iron out the little wrinkles before they become tears—or do we mean tears?

STARTING THE CUT

Keeping in mind that the first few strokes of a cut set the pace for all that is to follow, the common mistake that most beginners make is that they start the cut at too high an angle, causing the saw to drift off the line. And, of course, when they twist the saw in an effort to compensate and get back to the drawn line, they finish up with a wavy cut.

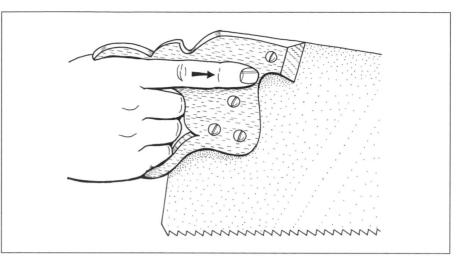

Fig. 2-21. Grasp the handle with the index finger pointing the way and use the extended finger to help brace and control the stroke.

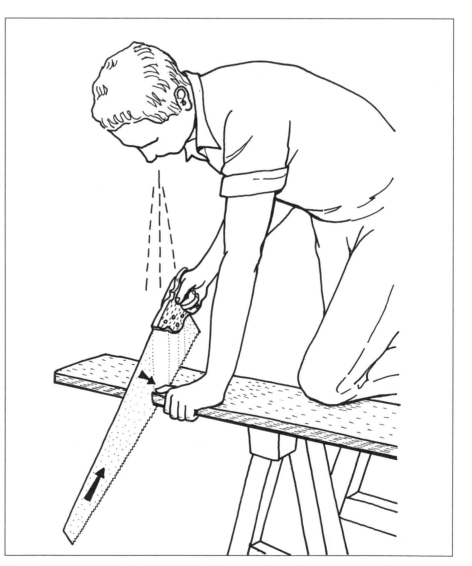

Fig. 2-22. With the thumb of the left hand being used as a fence to position the blade on the line of cut, sight down the blade to make sure that the saw is correctly aligned. If it is, then the blade will look to be no more than a thin black line. When all is correct, establish the cut with a few careful dragging strokes.

The best procedure is as follows: First and foremost you need to hold the saw firmly. Grasp the saw so that the index finger is pointing the way and helping to guide and control the cut (see 2-21). This done, start the cut by setting the saw on the mark, with the left thumbnail on the line to act as a fence, then lower the handle so that you can sight down the blade and check that the saw is correctly aligned and square with the face of the wood. Then make a few careful short dragging strokes (see 2-22).

Once you have squarely entered the wood and have achieved a cut of about 2 to 3 inches long, gradually raise the handle and lengthen the stroke until you reach a point where the blade is at an angle of about 45 degrees to the face of the wood, and the whole length of the blade is being used. You won't go far wrong if you make sure that the back edge of the saw blade, the forearm, the shoulder, and the eye are all aligned and on the same plane as the drawn line.

STANCE AND CONTROL WITH THE RIPSAW

In the context for which the ripsaw is always used—ripping down the grain of a long plank—the best procedure is to start by bridging the plank across a couple of sawhorses at a comfortable height. If all is correct, when you are standing with one knee on the wood and with you shoulders and head over the mark, the distance between your shoulder and the workpiece should allow you to use the full movement and thrust of your arm (see 2-23). Once the saw has entered the wood squarely, you can raise the handle until the 45-degree angle is reached. That said, if the wood is thick and slightly damp, then the best procedure is to raise the handle until the saw is nearly vertical so

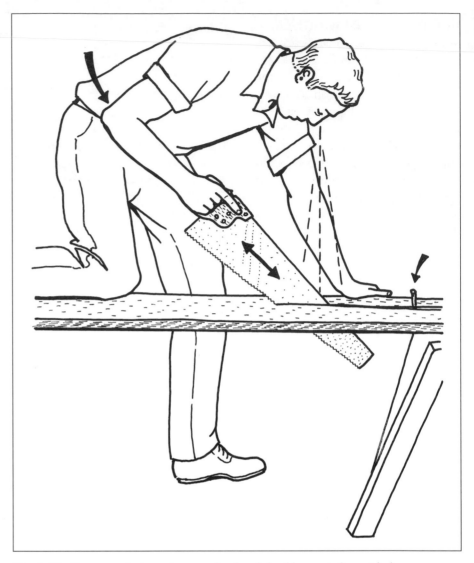

Fig. 2-23. Place your body so that your head and shoulder are in line with the cut; you can sight down the back of the saw, and your arm can deliver a good straight thrust.

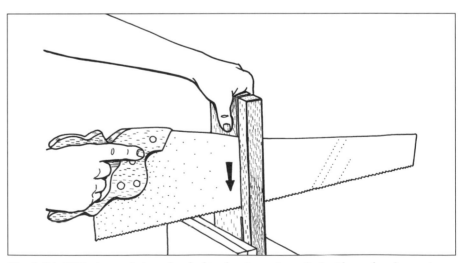

Fig. 2-24. With the workpiece clenched in the vise and steadied with one hand, run the saw halfway down the line of cut, then turn the wood around and rerun from the other end. This way of working prevents the wood from splitting down along the run of the grain.

that there is the smallest amount of wood in contact with the saw blade, keeping to a minimum the wet sawdust that can jam the blade in the kerf.

To rip short lengths, secure the wood in the vise, steady the wood with one hand, and gradually raise the wood as the cut proceeds. To minimize the risk of the wood splitting, flip it over in the vise and run a cut in from the other end (see 2-24). When you are using the ripsaw, you must make allowances for the width of the set and the consequent width of the kerf by positioning the blade well to one side of the mark. Allow about $^3/_{32}$ inch for the width of the kerf.

STANCE AND CONTROL WITH THE CROSSCUT SAW

Though the crosscut saw can be used in conjunction with a sawhorse for the occasional ripping and when you want to take a length off a plank, we would think that, for the most part, the crosscut is used at the bench. Though the overall approach is much the same as for the ripsaw, the crosscut operation requires a minimum of downward pressure. The procedure is as follows: Secure the workpiece with clamps and bench stop (see 2-25), hold the saw with one hand, and steady the workpiece with the other. Set the saw down to the waste side of the mark so that it is clear by about $^1/_8$ inch, position the thumbnail against the side of the saw blade, and drag the saw so as to cut a small notch. Once you have achieved a good length of cut, then settle down into an easy action, keeping the saw at a low angle, and using your arm at full swing— or you might say at full thrust. If you think of your arm as a piston that is pumping through at a nice, easy, rhythmic, and effortless stroke, then you won't go far

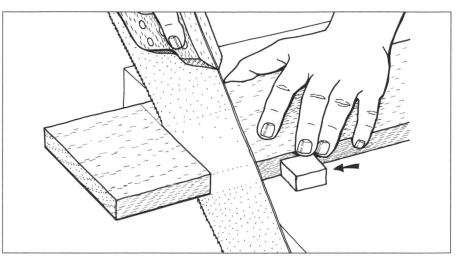

Fig. 2-25. *With the workpiece butted hard up against a bench stop and held securely with a clamp, brace your arm against the workpiece and set the saw to the waste side of the mark.*

Fig. 2-26. *With your legs braced and set apart so that your shoulders are aligned with the direction of the cut, the workbench height should be such that it allows for the full unimpeded swing of the sawing arm.*

wrong. Finally, when you have more or less sawn the board through, cradle your left hand around the workpiece—to take the weight of the wood—and then ease off the sawing pressure and complete the cut. This way of working minimizes the risk of the wood splitting.

STANCE AND CONTROL WITH THE BACKSAW

Backsaws are generally used for benchwork, for cutting all the joints, angles, widths, and lengths that go to make up most woodworking projects. Though the overall stance and control are much the same as that already described for, say, the crosscut saw, the main difference has to do with how the workpiece is held and controlled. There are three main ways of controlling the workpiece: It can be butted hard up against a bench hook or stop (see 2-26), it can be held in the vise (see 2-27), or it can be supported in a miter box (see 2-28).

In action, the saw is held in one hand, with the index finger pointing along the blade or at least curled around the top of the handle, while the other hand firmly holds the workpiece. The object of the exercise is to make absolutely sure that the workpiece stays put. If you allow the workpiece to move or twist, then chances are the resultant joint is going to be a ragged, badly fitting mess.

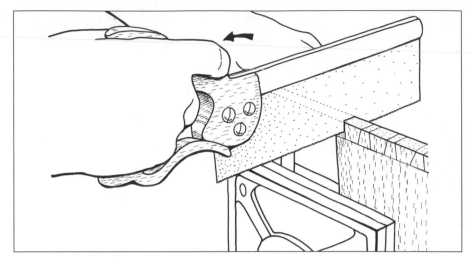

Fig. 2-27. With the workpiece held securely in the vise, curl your index finger around the top "horn" of the handle and use the thumb of the free hand to accurately position the blade to the waste side of the marked line.

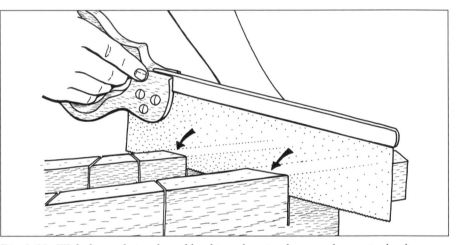

Fig. 2-28. With the workpiece butted hard into the miter box, set the saw in the slots, make sure that the blade is truly aligned (free to move), and then make the cut. It's important that the saw and the miter box are well matched. It's no good if the saw is so tight in the slot that it's actually cutting the box. Always have a piece of scrap wood under the workpiece so that the saw can run through without doing damage to the bottom of the box.

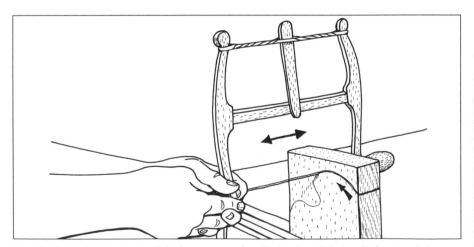

Fig. 2-29. Hold the frame of the bow saw with a double-handed clenched grip, while doing your best to ensure that the saw stretcher and the blade are truly aligned and square with the face of the workpiece. The bow saw is the perfect tool for cutting out curved blanks, which means there is allowance for a good amount of waste between the line of cut and the drawn line.

STANCE AND CONTROL WITH A CURVE-CUTTING SAW

Though it's not possible to state categorically that all curve-cutting saws must be held in a certain way —because, after all, there are so many designs and sizes of saws—it is possible to generalize that all curve-cutting saws have narrow blades. In this context, no matter the saw, the success of the cut hinges on achieving a balance between the speed of the saw and the movement of the wood. We find that the easiest all-around option is to go at a nice and easy pace that allows the timely presentation of the next line of cut to the moving blade. That said, each and every curve-cutting saw needs to be approached in a slightly different way.

For example, the traditional bow saw (see 2-29) is generally best worked with a short firm stroke, either with both hands clasped around the handle or with your hands spread so that there is one on the handle and one on the knob. The coping saw, on the other hand, nearly always requires that both ends of the frame are supported to minimize frame twist and blade breakage (see 2-30). The fretsaw is rather a curious beast, in that it is held in an underhand grip so that it can be operated with a swift joggling action (see 2-31). Unlike most saws, we find that a jigsaw is best worked at a fast and furious pace, with the length of movement being relatively short. The keyhole or pad saw is generally used in such a way that the minimum length of blade needed is withdrawn from the handle. Once again, it is worked with a relatively short fast stroke, with most of the action taking place near the handle (see 2-32).

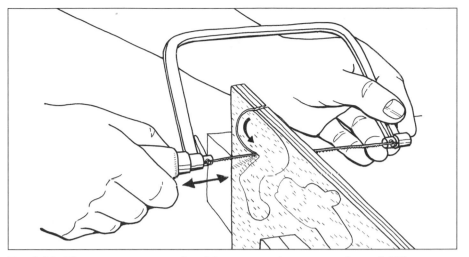

Fig. 2-30. The coping saw is a good tool for cutting tight curves in plywood. When you come to cut a tight angle, increase the rate of the stroke and decrease the amount of pressure, so that you are almost sawing on the spot, and then maneuver the blade in the resultant cut.

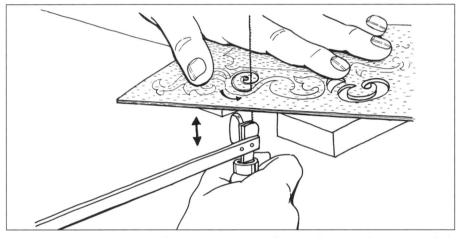

Fig. 2-31. The fretsaw is a good tool for cutting very thin wood. In use the saw is joggled up and down with one hand while the workpiece is held and maneuvered with the other.

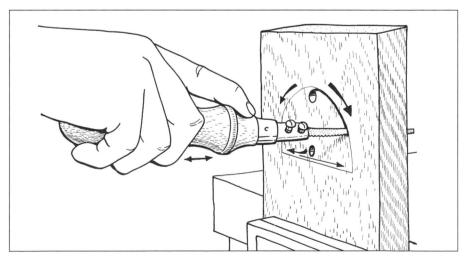

Fig. 2-32. With the smallest possible length of blade being withdrawn from the handle, grasp the handle with one hand and enter the tip of the blade into the drilled pilot hole. Work with a short rapid stroke until the cut is underway, and then use the portion of blade nearest the handle to do the main bulk of the cutting. The sharp corners of the hole are achieved by making two cuts that run into the corner.

SAWING TECHNIQUES: STEP-BY-STEP METHODS

Once you have chosen your saws and gotten them into working order, then comes the wonderful business of using them. We say "wonderful" because, of all the woodworking procedures, sawing is potentially the most exciting and dynamic. Okay, so sawing can be a bit sweaty, and you might well make any number of blunders along the way, but the good news is that once you get it right, it is a very satisfying experience.

The following step-by-step activities will get you started.

CONVERTING A LARGE PLANK WITH A RIPSAW

There is an old saying that goes, "You can rate a woodworker by his horses." It does sound a bit obscure, but what it means, of course, is that you can tell a great deal about a woodworker's skill and methods by his or her sawhorses—their shape, the quality of the joints, the amount of damage, and so on. If you plan to do a lot of ripping with a handsaw, then ideally you need two sawhorses, one of which has been modified so that it has a 1-inch-wide slot along the length of the saddle.

1. Start by arranging the wood so that it is at a comfortable working height. If the plank is wide and long, then the easiest procedure is to bridge it across the horses so that it runs down the length of the slotted horse and across the other horse (see 2-33). Arrange the wood so that you can kneel on it in such a way that your head and shoulder are over the line of cut.

2. When you are happy with the arrangement, take your ripsaw and burnish both sides of the blade with a wax candle. This done, and with the plank supported on the horses as already described, set the saw

Fig. 2-33. Bridge the plank over a couple of sawhorses. The design of these particular horses is rather clever in that one has a slot running down its center for long ripping, whereas the other has a V-notch for tricky small cuts (see the Working Drawings section in this chapter).

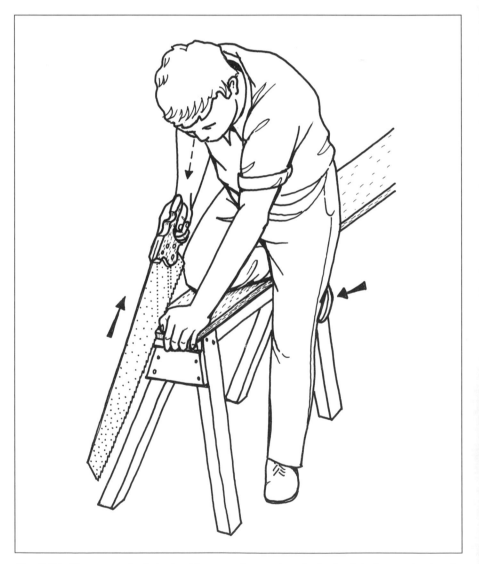

Fig. 2-34. Brace your body by hooking your foot against the back of the leg, and using the nail or knuckle of the thumb as a guide, start the cut with a careful dragging stroke.

down on the end of the plank so that it is well to the waste side of the drawn line. Lower the handle so that the saw blade is at a very low angle, and then take a few short dragging strokes until the cut is started (see 2-34).

3. Having achieved a kerf about a $1/2$ inch long, sight along the length of the blade to make sure that the whole saw is running true to the drawn line, keeping in mind that the first few strokes set the standard of the cut. Lift the handle slightly and increase the length of your stroke.

4. Once the cut is underway, lift the handle until the teeth-to-wood angle is about 45 degrees, and then continue until you are using the full thrust of your arm (see 2-35).

5. As the cut advances, re-arrange the wood so that your saw runs down the slot in the sawhorse. When the saw reaches the end of the slot nearest you, all you do is slide the wood forward until the back of the blade is within about $1/2$ inch of the far end of the slot, and then continue sawing.

SIZING A PLANK ON THE BENCH WITH A CROSSCUT SAW

You have a dozen or so expensive, thick hardwood planks that you have ripped to width, and now you want to cut them down into short lengths. Let's say that the planks are 7 feet long, 4 inches wide, and 2 inches thick, and you want to cut them down into 24-inch lengths. Certainly you could use the sawhorse, and at the final stages of the cut hook your left hand around to retrieve the lengths—that is if the planks were wider and thinner, and the lengths shorter. But in this case, not only is the wood too narrow to be comfortably supported by your knee, but more to the point,

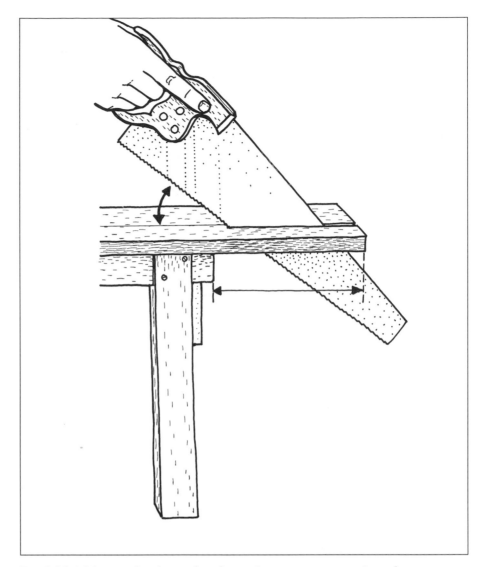

Fig. 2-35. Make sure that the saw has plenty of room to maneuver. Once the cut is underway, raise the saw to a comfortable height and put the full weight of your shoulder behind the stroke. Slide the wood forward as the cut advances.

the need is for precision rather than speed. Apart from a perfectly tuned crosscut saw and a workbench fitted with a vise, you also need to have the use of a bench holdfast and a short bar clamp.

1. Having used a ruler, square, and knife to accurately mark off the lengths, and having allold for the thickness of the saw blade, set your 4-inch-wide plank down across your bench so that the 24-inch-length hangs out over the vise, with the line of cut being will clear of the vise handle. This done, set a couple of blocks in the vise so that

there is one hard up against each side of the plank—like bench stops. Next, swing the holdfast around on the bench so that the pad is on the wood and about 12 inches in from the vise, and then tighten it up. Lastly, bridge the bar clamp over the plank so that it grips the blocks that you have set up in the vise, and tighten it up (see 2-36).

2. When you have achieved the arrangement as described, take your saw and burnish both sides of the blade with a domestic wax candle. This done, hold the 24-inch-length with your left hand, set the blade

down to the waste side of the mark, and use your left thumb as a guide.

3. Bearing in mind that the first inch or so of cut sets the scene for all that is to follow, make a couple of careful dragging strokes to start the kerf. Now, with your eye sighted down the back of the saw and through to the line, take a few short backward and forward strokes until you are on course, and then gradually increase the length of the stroke until you are using the full length of your arm and the full power of your shoulder.

4. When you have more or less cut the length of wood through, slide your left hand along so that it takes the weight of the wood, then decrease the power and length of your stroke and cut the wood through (see 2-37). If you have done it right, you will be left with the wood nicely supported and balanced in your hand, and the sawn face will be clean-cut and complete, with no risk of the wood falling to the floor or torn grain running along the wood.

CUTTING A TENON WITH A TENON SAW

The mortise and tenon joint is one of the most important joints in woodworking. Cutting a two-shoulder tenon with a saw is a primary woodworking technique that needs to be mastered (see 2-38 top). First, you need to set out all the guide lines that make up the design of the joint. For this procedure, usually described as "setting out" or "laying off," you need four tools: a marking gauge for marking with the run of the grain and on the end grain, a small square for marking across the run of the grain, a marking knife, and a ruler.

1. Start by using the square and the marking knife to set in the line of the shoulder. The correct procedure is to butt the handle or stock of

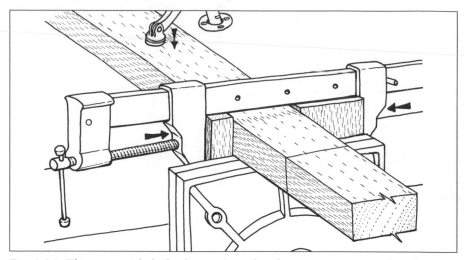

Fig. 2-36. *This setup might look a bit overfussy, but then again, you can at least be sure that the wood is going to stay put. Make sure that the line of cut is well clear of the handle of the vise.*

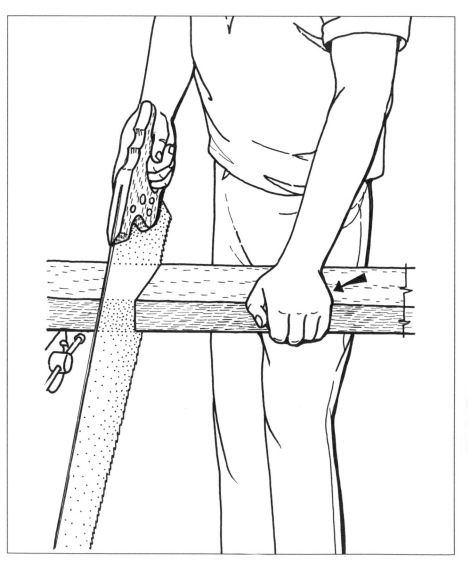

Fig. 2-37. *When the wood is nearly sawn through, make sure that the wood stays at the same level by clenching it between your hand and your thigh. Be ready to take the weight.*

the square hard up against the edge of the workpiece, hold the knife so that the flat side of the blade is running up against the steel arm of the square and the bevel is looking toward the waste side of the joint, and then run a deep cut across the wood. Repeat this procedure on all appropriate faces and edges (see 2-38 middle). With the shoulder line in place, take the marking gauge and run a mark up from the shoulder line and across the end of the wood (see 2-38 bottom).

2. When you have spent time making sure that all the guide lines are perfectly placed, secure the workpiece in the vise at an angle of about 60 degrees, then take the tenon saw and position yourself so that you are standing square to the workpiece and generally comfortable and well braced. Set the blade down on the point of the wood that is farthest away from you—so that it is in the knife cut—and sight down the back of the saw (see 2-39). Now, at one and the same time, run a cut across the end-grain top of the wood and down to the line of the shoulder. Aim to carry the kerf over and down without lifting the saw so that the saw finishes up parallel to the surface of the bench (see the broken line on the illustration). The two golden rules are to go at it nice and easy and to make sure that the saw blade is upright and square with the wood. Reverse the workpiece in the vise and run a cut down to the other shoulder line.

3. Having sawn down at an angle, first on one side and then on the other, you will be left with a triangular area of uncut wood at the bottom of the kerf. Set the wood upright in the vise and saw through the uncut triangle until you are within a whisker of the shoulder line (see 2-40).

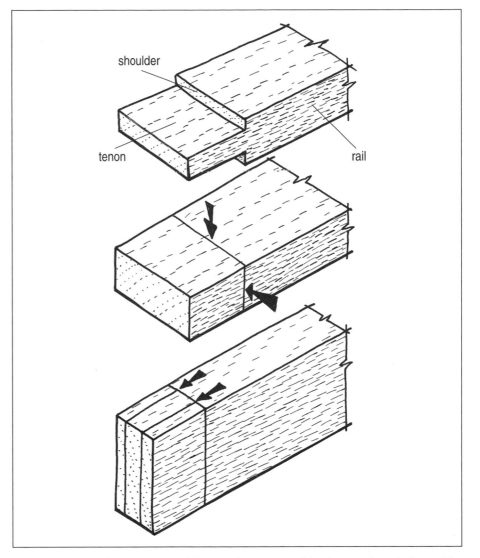

Fig. 2-38. Top, *a basic tenon*. Middle, *use the square and knife to mark in the line of the shoulder*. Bottom, *use the marking gauge to mark from the shoulder line across the end grain of the wood*.

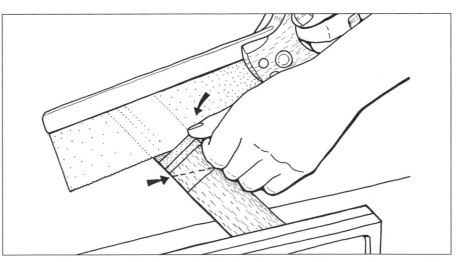

Fig. 2-39. *Use your thumbnail to accurately place the cut, and then saw down to within about $1/16$ inch of the shoulder line, so that the bottom of the kerf is just about parallel to the surface of the bench.*

4. Place the workpiece in the bench hook so that it is braced hard up against the stop. Set the saw about ¹/₁₆ inch to the waste side of the scored line, sight down the back of the blade to make sure that it is square, and then run a saw cut down so that the waste falls away (see 2-41). Finally, use a chisel or shoulder plane to clean out the small corners of waste.

CUTTING THROUGH DOVE-TAILS WITH A DOVETAIL SAW AND A COPING SAW

The dovetail is one of the strongest of all joints; the wedged design is such that it locks and tightens under stress. If you have in mind to make high-class cabinet wares, then you must be able to make a good sound dovetail.

You must decide whether you want to cut the tails or the pins first (see 2-42 top). Though there are two schools of thought as to which ought to be cut first, with some so-called experts declaring that you must do it this or that way, we think that, to a great extent, it's simply a matter of personal choice. We prefer to cut the tails first, for the simple reason that we find it easier to put the "pins" board upright in the vise and then to mark through directly from the "tails" board. You also have to decide whether to cut the tails and the pins overlong and then sand the end grain back or to cut them short and then plane the sides of the boards back. We prefer to cut the pins and tails long.

1. Burnish your saw with candle wax and select, size, and prepare the wood. Start by setting the marking gauge to about ¹/₃₂ inch more than the thickness of your wood, and run a fine line around

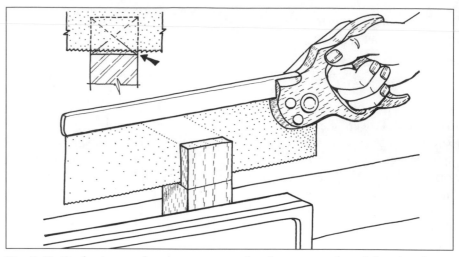

Fig. 2-40. By the time you have sawn at an angle—first on one side and then the other—all the on-view cuts will have been established, and you will have only a little peak of wood at the center that needs to be sawn. Top left, cross section showing how you need to stop the cut short of the shoulder line.

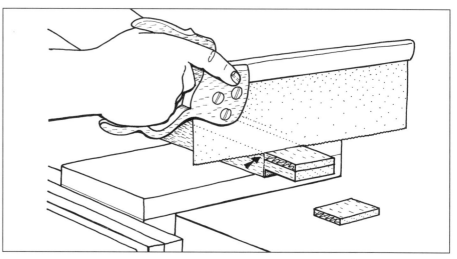

Fig. 2-41. Make sure that the saw is set to the waste side of the shoulder line so as to allow for a small amount of waste to be cut back with the shoulder plane.

the ends of both pieces. Label one board "tails" and the other "pins" (see 2-42 bottom).

2. Use a pencil and the sliding bevel to set out the shape of the tails (see chapter 8, "Primary Marking and Testing Tools"), then shade in the waste between-tail areas that need to be cut away. Secure the wood in the vise at an angle, with one side of the tails being vertical. Take the dovetail saw, set the teeth down on the edge farthest away

from you on the waste side of the drawn line, and then run the kerf toward you, across the end grain, and down to within a whisker of the gauged line. Repeat this cut on one side of every tail, then shift the wood in the vise so that the other side of the tail is vertical, and rerun the cut as already described. It's all easy enough, as long as you don't force the pace and do your best to saw right up to the shoulder line (see 2-43).

3. Flip the workpiece down in the vise and cut away the small pieces of end waste. Once again, be very careful that you hold the saw square and run the cut to the waste side of the drawn line (see 2-44).

4. Use the coping saw to remove the bulk of the waste (see 2-45). This done, set the wood flat down on the bench and use the widest possible bevel-edged chisel to pare back to the gauged line. Being very careful not to undercut the joint, work half the thickness of the wood from one side of the board, and then turn the board over and work the other side.

5. With all the tails nicely cut to size, put the "pins" board in the vise and slide it down so the end grain is slightly above the surface. Now set the "tails" board across the bench with the tails carefully aligned and square on the end grain, clamp it in place, and then use a fine-point knife to transfer the shape of the tails (see 2-46). It's important that the boards are square to each other, so if need be, block up the "tails" board with thin pieces of plywood until a right angle is achieved. Make sure that the scribed lines are hard against the sides of the tails. Use a square to run scored lines down to the shoulder.

6. Finally, having first removed the bulk of the socket waste with the coping saw, as already described, use the bevel-edged chisel to pare back to the gauge line (see 2-47). Be warned: A common mistake made by a lot of beginners at this point is to undercut the socket slightly so as to achieve a tight fit. Certainly this looks fine from the outside, but the problem is, of course, that the resultant little cavity that is hidden away in the joint becomes a weak point that is almost impossible to glue.

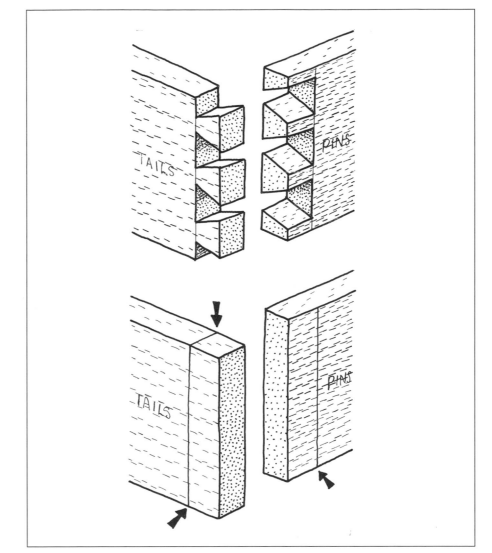

Fig. 2-42. Top, *the two component parts that make up the dovetail joint, with the "pins" on one board and the "tails" on the other. Bottom, having used the marking gauge to mark the ends, label the boards to avoid mix-ups.*

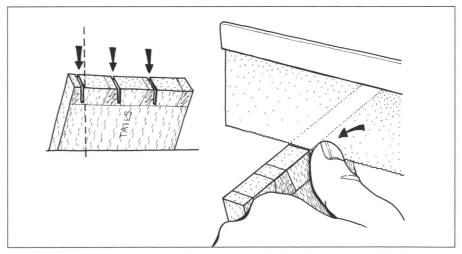

Fig. 2-43. Left, *secure the wood in the vise so that the line of cut is vertical. Right, use the thumb as a fence to guide the saw to the mark. Make sure that the whole width of the kerf is to the waste side of the drawn line.*

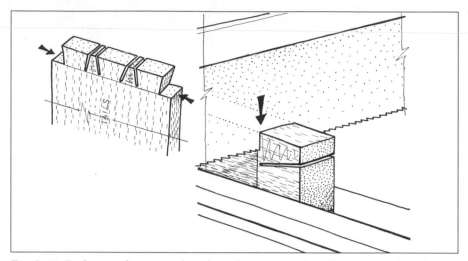

Fig. 2-44. Right, *use the saw to clear the end waste from the tails; saw to within about* ¹/₁₆ *inch of the shoulder line. Left,* use a chisel to pare back to the shoulder line.

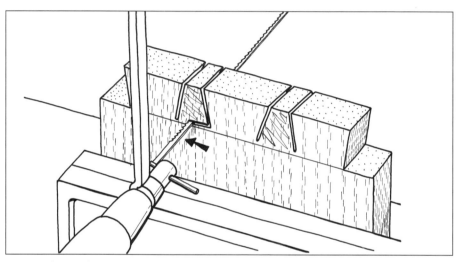

Fig. 2-45. *Use the coping saw to remove the waste from between the pins. Leave a small amount of waste on the shoulder to be cut back with a chisel.*

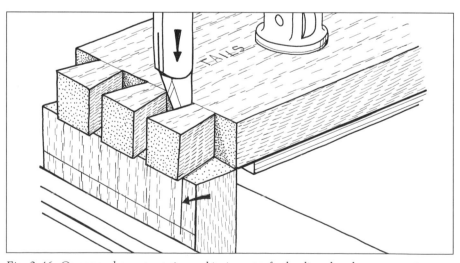

Fig. 2-46. *Once you have spent time achieving a perfectly aligned and square setup, use a knife to swiftly transfer the shape of the tails through to the end grain. Use a square to run the end-grain tail lines down to the shoulder.*

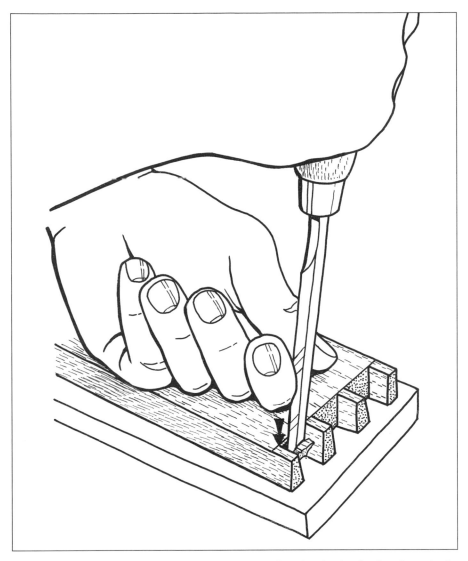

Fig. 2-47. With the workpiece set down on a cutting board, take the chisel and pare back the waste flush to the line of the shoulder, first from one side and then from the other.

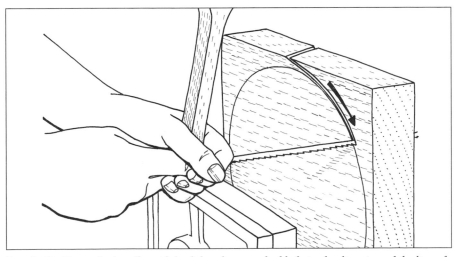

Fig. 2-48. Grasp the handle with both hands, turn the blade in the direction of the line of cut, and swing the frame around slightly so that it is clear of the wood.

CUTTING A LATHE BLANK WITH A BOW SAW

The small bow saw or turning saw is the perfect tool for cutting out curved work in relatively thin-section wood, as with lathe blanks that need to be cut from wood up to, say, 1½ inches thick.

1. Having first made sure that your bow saw is in good shape, set the handles and pins straight with each other, check that the blade is straight to the frame, and tighten up the toggle stick. If you have got it right, the saw blade will ping when plucked. Last but not least, make sure that the teeth of the blade are raked or looking away from the large handle (not the small knob).

2. With the circle drawn out on the wood, secure the workpiece in the vise in such a way that it is supported as close as possible to the start of cut, and the grain is running from side to side. Now, take up the saw with both hands clenching the handle, and stand with your feet astride. It's important that you feel well braced and comfortable.

3. When you are happy with your stance, start the cut by sawing straight down toward the right-hand quarter of the circle so that the cut hits the drawn circle at about 12 o'clock. Use both hands and work with a nice and easy rhythmic stroke—no sudden twist, just an even stroke (see 2-48).

4. Once you reach the drawn circle, then swing the frame of the saw slightly to the right, realign the teeth, and carry on sawing. When you reach the point where the bench is in the way, all you do is slacken off the vise and reposition the wood. Of course, much will depend on the size of your saw, the size of the disc, and the standard of finish that you require, but aim to stay about ⅛ inch to the waste side of the drawn line.

5. And so you continue, sawing a little, putting a small amount of sideward pressure on the saw, and generally repositioning the wood in the vise. It's all pretty easy, as long as you continuously maneuver both the saw and the wood so that the blade is always presented with the line of next cut, and the cut is running in the direction of the grain (see 2-49).

CUTTING A CAT DOOR WITH A PAD SAW

The pad or keyhole saw is designed primarily to cut holes that are too far in from the edge of the wood for the bow saw to reach. Though this saw is a very useful little tool, it is also a tool that is sadly misunderstood. The problem has to do with the fact that the blade slides in and out of the handle. The beginner usually pulls all 12 to 16 inches of blade from the handle, and then happily sets to work trying to use the full length. What happens then is that the rather soft blade kinks and bends. The blade can easily be straightened, but from then on, it tends to bend in the same spot. So always try to use the portion of the blade nearest the handle and withdraw no more of the blade from the handle than is necessary for a short stroke.

1. When you have drawn out the shape of the cat door on the wood of a solid wood door, start by boring out four starter holes. If you can use something larger than a 1-inch-diameter bit, then so much the better. Have the holes set slightly to the waste side of the drawn line—one in the middle of each straight side of the square (see 2-50).

2. Draw about 3 to 4 inches of the blade out of the handle and tighten up the two holding screws. Being careful to work well to the waste side of the drawn line, enter

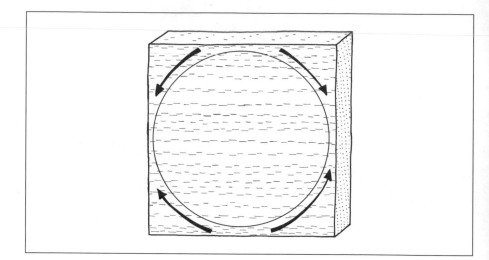

Fig. 2-49. You will find the going much easier if you saw in the direction of the grain, that is, from high to low grain.

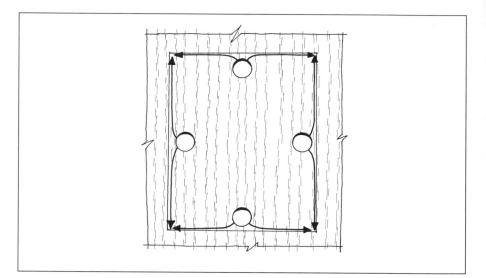

Fig. 2-50. Diagram showing the drilled pilot holes and how best to achieve sharp clean-cut corners. The small peaks of waste between the holes and the drawn line can be cut back with a plane or chisel.

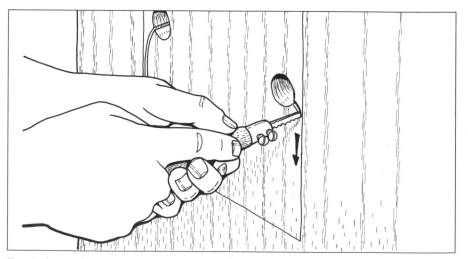

Fig. 2-51. Hold the saw with both hands and make short strokes while trying to use the portion of the blade nearest to the handle.

the blade in one of the holes and start the cut with a series of fast short strokes. Run a curved kerf in toward the nearest straight side, and then head for the nearest corner (see 2-51). Finally, when you have made eight such saw cuts, all you do is tidy up with a paring chisel or a small plane, and the task is done.

CUTTING A COPING WITH A COPING SAW

Although the coping saw is a first-choice tool for all manner of small curve-cutting tasks, it is of course perfect for the task for which it was designed, namely, for cutting a coping joint (see 2-52). And just in case you don't know, a coped joint, also known as a scribing joint, fits two lengths of identical molding together at an inside corner, as with baseboards, picture rails, and ceiling covings. In inside angles where the end grain is hidden, a coped joint is more quickly and easily accomplished than a mitered one.

1. Let's say that you are cutting two baseboards to meet in a corner, where the molded face of the wood is on the inside angle. First, cut both boards to the full length, so that they both butt hard up into the corner angle.

2. With both boards cut to size, take a length of waste molding, and transfer the profile to the back face of one board length, so that the back face of the molding is flush with the end of the wood (see 2-53).

3. Finally, make sure that the blade is well tensioned and fitted so that the teeth point away from the handle, and then set to work sawing the profile. The best procedure is to have the molding secured at an angle in the vise or clamped securely so that it overhangs a bench top. Hold the saw square to the workpiece and work with an easy

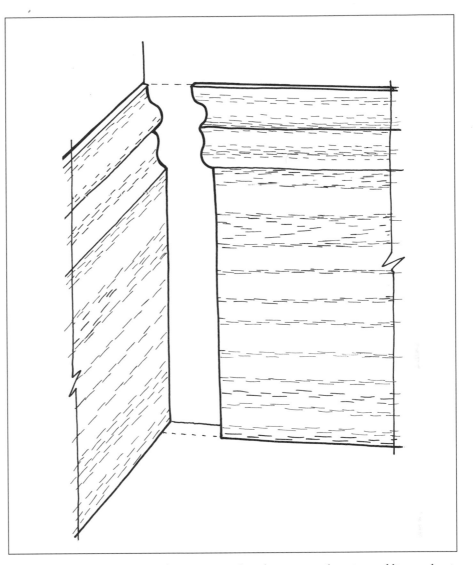

Fig. 2-52. The coping, or coped, joint is a swift and easy way of cutting molding so that it fits an inside 90-degree corner. The board on the left is cut off at right angles so that it fits hard up into the corner, while the end of the board on the right is shaped to fit the molding, which means, in effect, that you only have to spend time on one board.

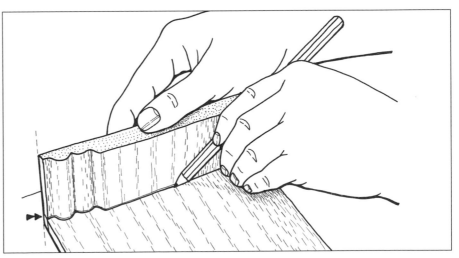

Fig. 2-53. Use a waste piece to transfer the shape of the molding to the back of the board so that the molded profile is a flush fit with the end of the board.

steady stroke. Don't bear down hard or force the pace, and do be sure to run the cut slightly to the waste side of the drawn line (see 2-54).

CUTTING A PROFILE IN THIN WOOD WITH A FRETSAW

The classic fretwork saw is a first-choice tool for cutting curved profiles in thin section wood. If you have in mind to make toys in, say, 1/8-inch-thick plywood, or you want to try your hand at inlay or marquetry, then this is the best hand tool for the task. As to the size and grade of the blades, they are about 5 inches long, with some blades being so fine that they will pass through a pinhole. And, of course, the finer the blade, the finer the cut. With the blade being fitted so that the teeth point or rake toward the handle, this saw is ideally used in conjunction with a V-table, sometimes known as a "bird's-mouth" sawing table.

1. Having marked out the design on the wood and fitted the cutting table in the vise or clamped it to the bench—depending upon its design—set the workpiece on the table so that the design is uppermost. There are two points to bear in mind before you start. The saw will be cutting on the downstroke, and the point of cut always needs to be as close as possible to the apex of the V of the table (2-55).

2. When you are ready to cut, hold the saw in one hand with the frame uppermost, so that the handle is at right angles to the cutting table; press the workpiece firmly down on the V-table with the other hand, and then work the saw with a rapid up-and-down movement. The trick is not to follow the drawn line with the saw, but rather to keep the saw joggling up and down on the spot while you maneuverer the workpiece, so that the blade is always fed with the line of next cut (see 2-56).

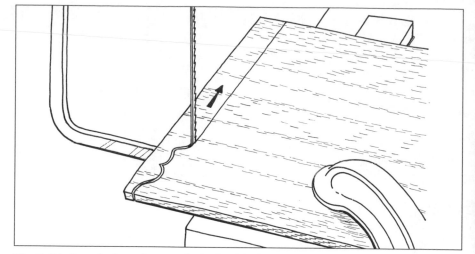

Fig. 2-54. Run the line of cut on the back of the board so that the sawn end is at right angles to the face of the board.

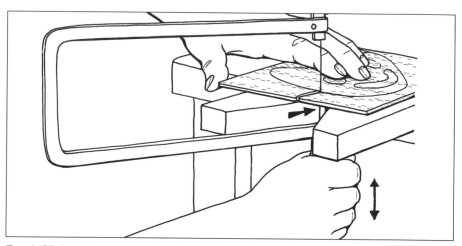

Fig. 2-55. Maximum support is achieved by working as close as possible to the apex of the V. Keep the saw joggling up and down on the spot and maneuver the wood so that the saw is presented with the line of next cut.

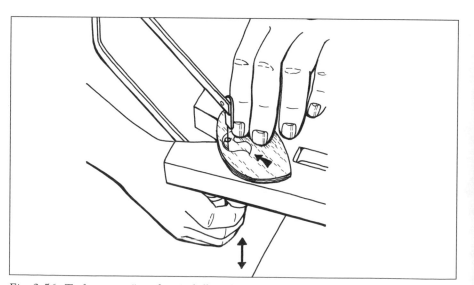

Fig. 2-56. To fret out a "window," drill a pilot hole through the waste, unhitch one end of the saw blade and pass it through the hole, rehitch and tension the blade, and proceed with the cut as already described.

Sawing Project 1: Bench Hook

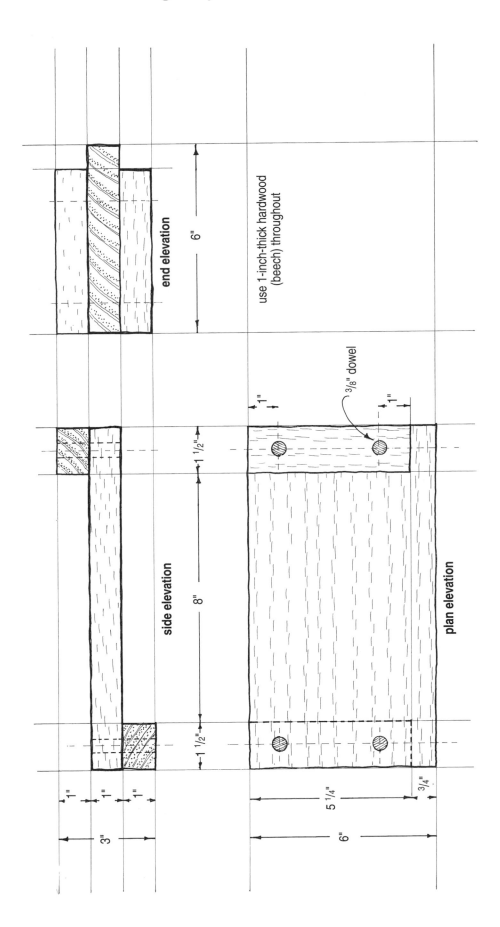

end elevation

6"

use 1-inch-thick hardwood (beech) throughout

3/8" dowel

side elevation

8"

1 1/2"

1 1/2"

1"

1"

plan elevation

1"

1"

1"

3"

5 1/4"

6"

3/4"

Sawing Project 2: Bird's-Mouth Cutting Board

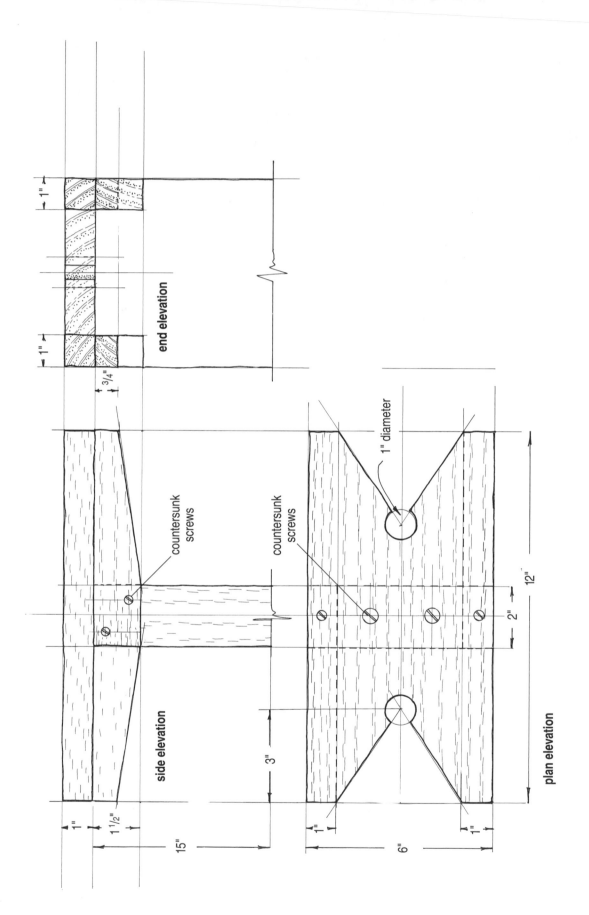

1"

3/4"

1"

end elevation

1" diameter

countersunk
screws

countersunk
screws

12"

2"

side elevation

3"

1"

1 1/2"

15"

1"

1"

6"

plan elevation

Sawing Project 3: Saw Vise

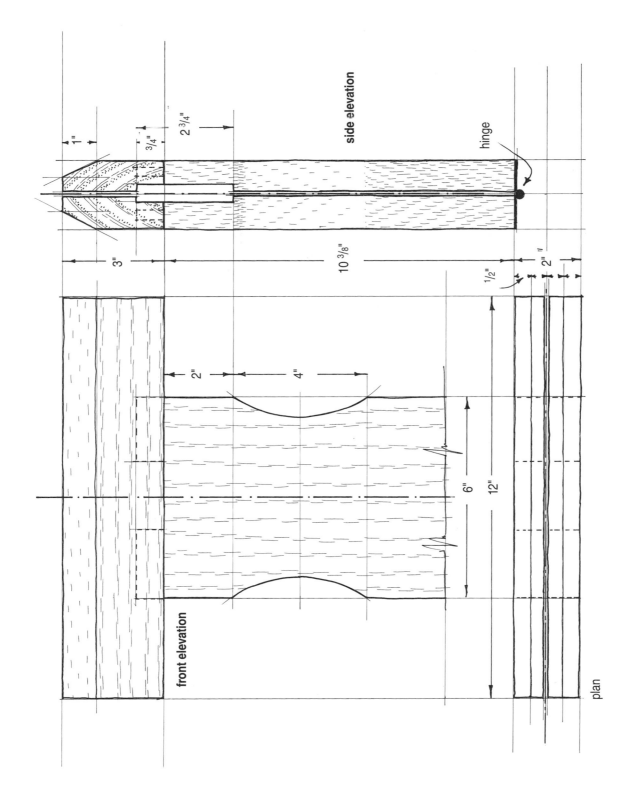

side elevation

hinge

1"

3/4"

2 3/4"

3"

10 3/8"

1/2"

2"

2"

4"

6"

12"

front elevation

plan

Sawing Project 4: Toolbox Saw Clip

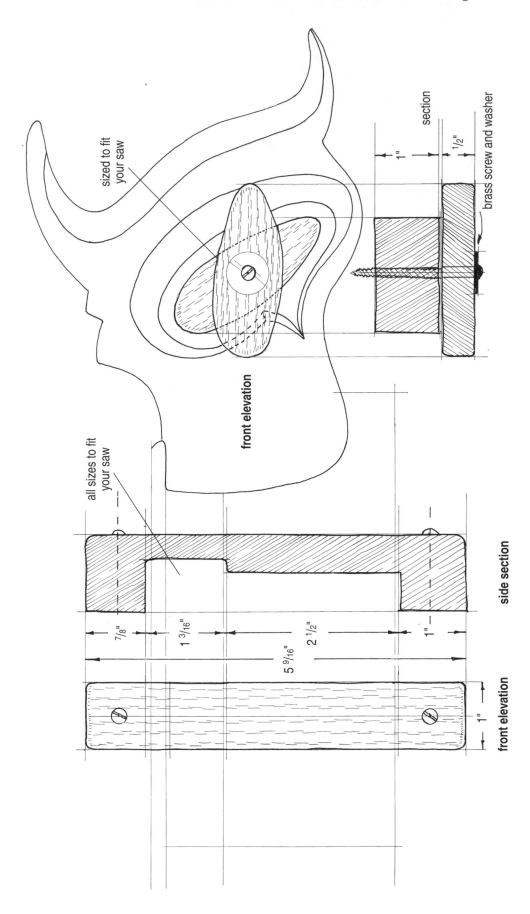

sized to fit your saw

section

1"

1/2"

brass screw and washer

front elevation

all sizes to fit your saw

7/8"

1 3/16"

2 1/2"

5 9/16"

1"

1"

side section

front elevation

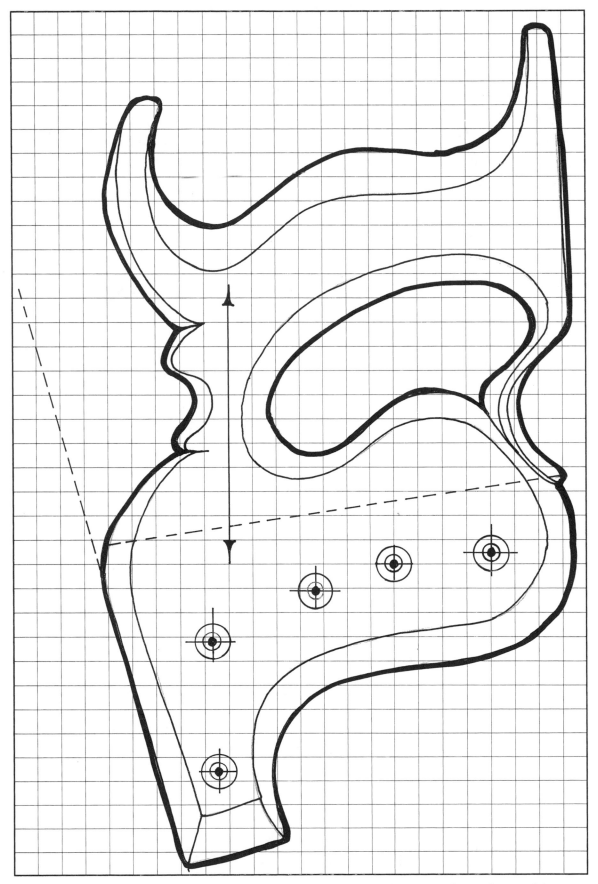

Ripsaw handle, circa 1900. The scale is 4 grid squares to 1 inch. Note that the arrow indicates the run of the grain.
Use 1-inch-thick cherry or beech.

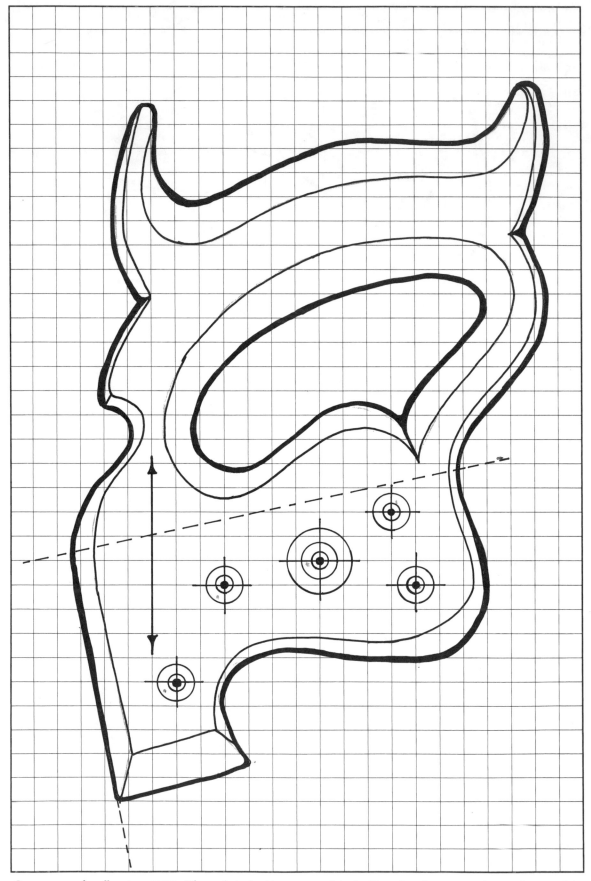

Crosscut saw handle, circa 1910. The scale is 4 grid squares to 1 inch. Note that the arrow indicates the run of the grain. Use 1-inch-thick cherry or beech.

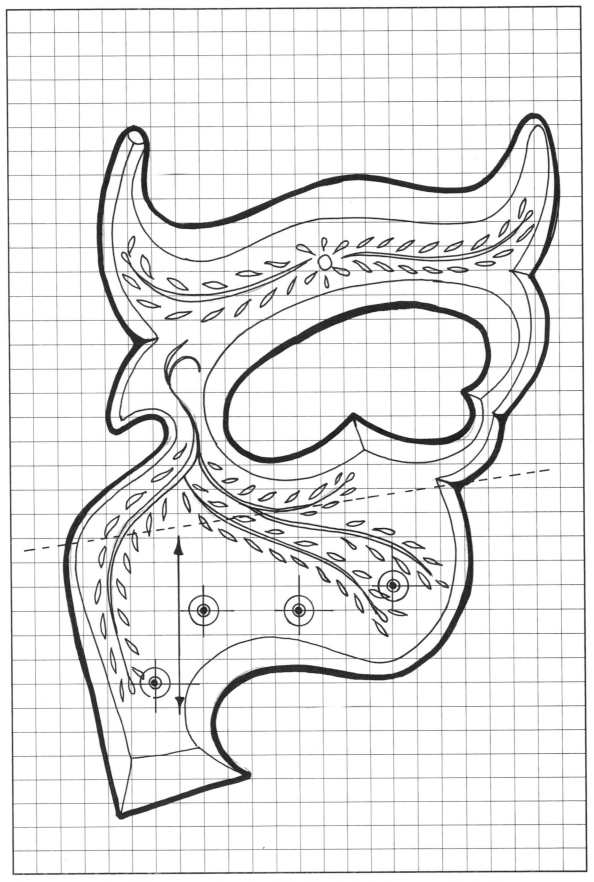

Crosscut saw handle with decorative carving, circa 1900. The scale is 4 grid squares to 1 inch. Note that the arrow indicates the run of the grain. Use 1-inch-thick cherry or beech.

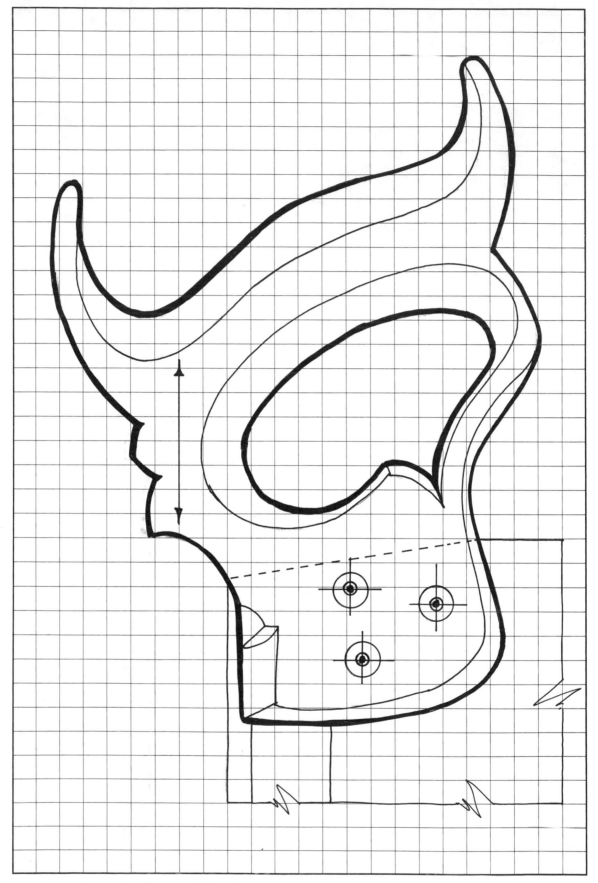

Backsaw with closed handle, circa 1920s. The scale is 4 grid squares to 1 inch. Note that the arrow indicates the run of the grain. Use 1-inch-thick cherry or beech.

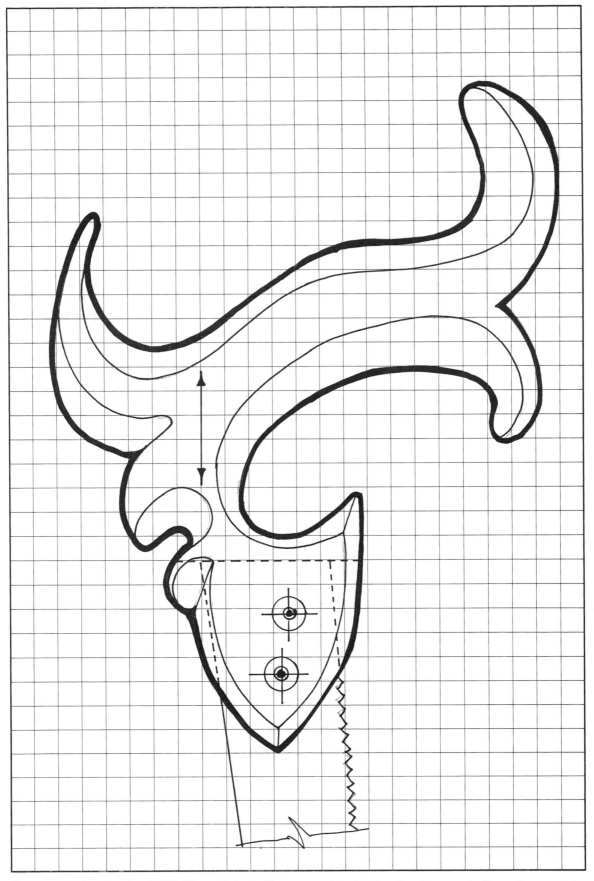

Compass saw handle, circa 1900. The scale is 4 grid squares to 1 inch. Note that the arrow indicates the run of the grain. Use 1-inch-thick cherry or beech.

Sawing Project 6: Sawhorse

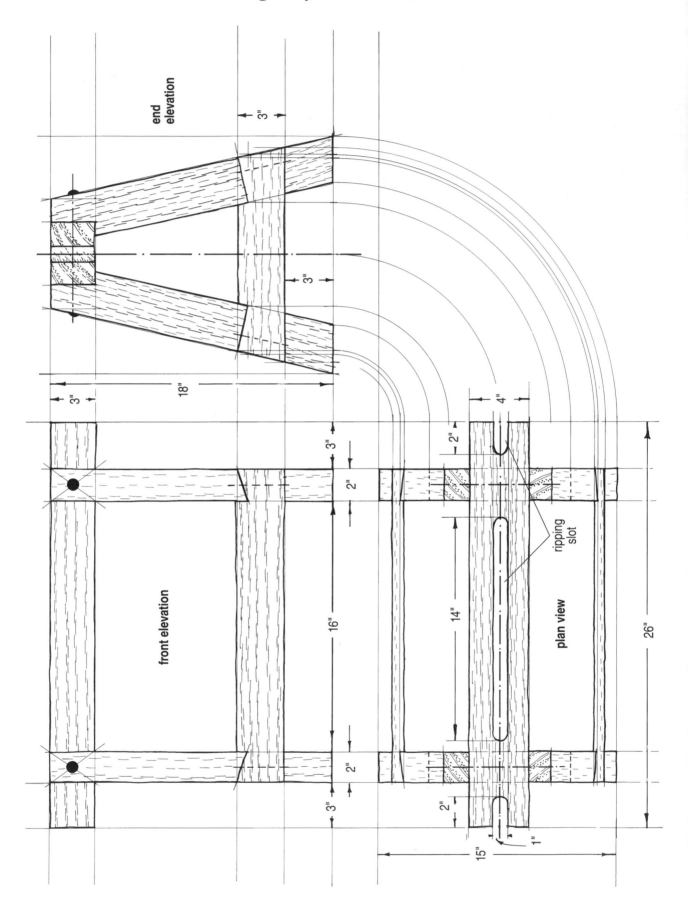

end elevation

3"

3"

18"

3"

front elevation

16"

3"

2"

3"

2"

4"

2"

ripping slot

14"

plan view

26"

2"

15"

1"

CHAPTER THREE

Planes

Woodworkers need planes. No matter the size and character of the piece of woodwork or the woodworker's approach to the craft, the sawn wood invariably needs to be first planed square, then planed smooth, and then variously planed so that squared up component parts fit, slide, and slot together. Planes are needed just about every step of the way. Even prepared wood, or wood that has been through your planer, needs to be hand planed.

If you are a raw beginner, rather than purchasing a plane and then guessing at its function, identify your need, and then get yourself a specific plane that is designed for that task.

If we forget for the moment that wood can be purchased ready planed, and that some planes are designed to perform more than one task, you can take it that there are at least ten primary procedures that need in some way or other to be worked with a plane. This is not to say that each and every project will require all ten procedures, or that you will need to use ten different planes—but it's possible. For example, the edge of the sawn wood needs to be jointed, or you might say, planed true; the flat face or sides need to be planed smooth; the end grain needs to be planed square and true; all these procedures are necessary just to achieve the basic board. And, of course, when it comes to making the joints, the various rabbets need to be planed, grooves need to be planed, moldings need to be planed, rounds and hollows need to be planed, the joints need to be trimmed and tidied up with one or more planes, convex and concave curves need to be planed, and so on.

There has recently been a huge revival of interest in using a new generation of wooden planes. Sometimes rather misleadingly described as "transitional" planes, the modern wooden plane not only has all the easy adjustments that you would expect to find on a metallic plane, but better yet, the engineered lignum vitae sole is by its very nature self-lubricating. Many craftsmen prefer using wooden planes. They claim that the new wooden planes with their "Primus" adjustments can be more easily adjusted and tuned than the metal planes. And some of the modern wooden planes are in themselves beautiful works of art.

So there you go. As if the notion of needing ten or more planes isn't daunting enough, you will also have to decide whether or not to opt for using wooden planes or metal planes.

Exciting isn't it?

BENCH PLANES: FOR CONVERTING SAWN WOOD INTO SMOOTH TRUE SECTIONS
On account of their use at the workbench, there are four planes that have commonly come to be described as bench planes. Taking them in order of sequential usage, they are the scrub, the jack, the jointer or trying plane, and the smoothing or smooth plane.

SCRUB PLANE
Made in wood or metal, the scrub plane, sometimes called a roughing or scud plane, or even a cow plane, is designed specifically for removing a large amount of wood swiftly (see 3-2). Though the electric planer has to a great extent negated the need for the scrub plane, there are still occasions when it's much easier to use the scrub plane to swiftly reduce the thickness of a plank than it is to set up the electric planer. If you are working in a situation where power isn't readily available—say in a boatyard or in the woods—then a scrub plane is a very useful tool. In shape and form it's much the same as a smoothing plane, the only real difference being that the shape of the blade at the cutting edge is generously rounded at the corners. In use, the scrub plane swiftly removes the wood by cutting deep furrows or "hoggings" (see 3-3).

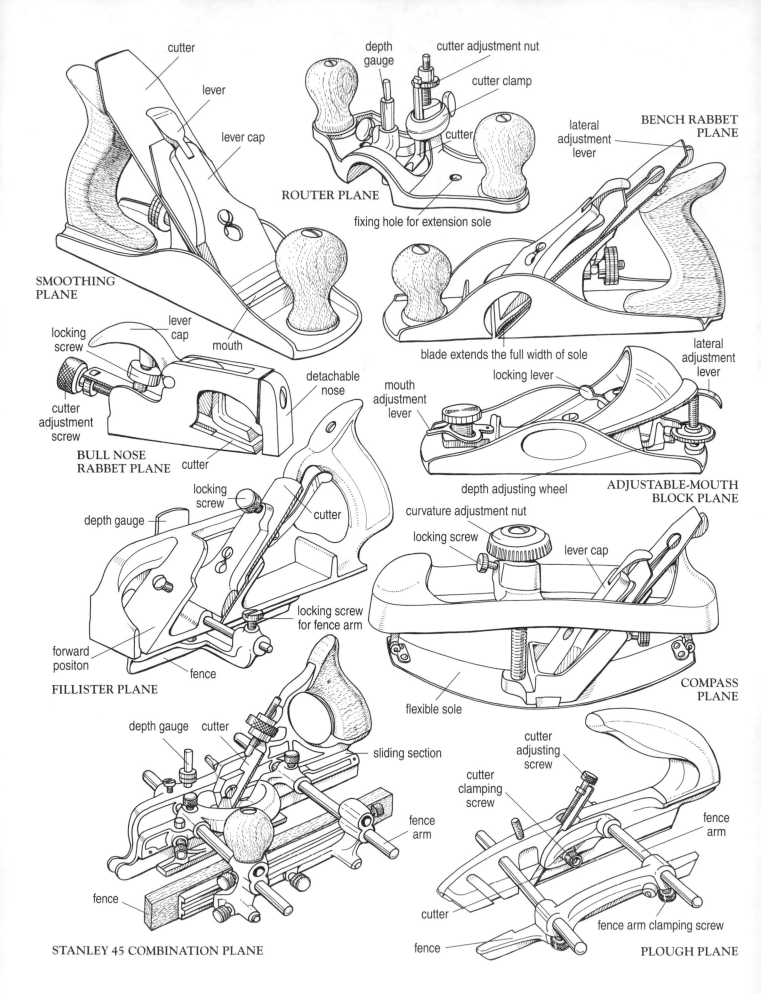

Fig. 3-1. Metallic planes.

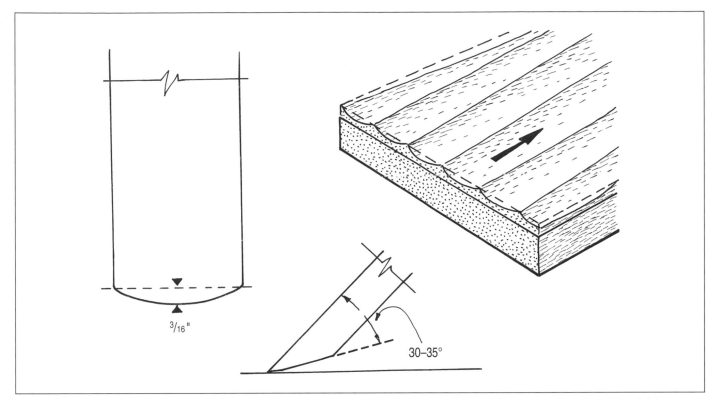

Fig. 3-3. Left, *the cutting edge of the scrub plane blade is generously rounded.* Right, *the waste is removed as deep furrows.* Old-time woodworkers described this procedure as "hogging." Bottom, *the primary angle of the bevel needs to be ground to 30 to 35 degrees—a larger angle than usual—so that the edge is strong.*

JACK PLANE

Made in wood or metal, the jack plane, sometimes also called a fore plane, at 14 to 15 inches long, is used primarily for cleaning and squaring sawn wood. It is used before the smoothing plane for planing sawn timber to size and for planing faces and edges. With a cutting iron that is slightly convex so as to prevent the corners from digging in, and with a long sole to bridge small lumps and bumps, this is the plane to use when you want to prepare sawn stock (see 3-4).

JOINTER OR TRYING PLANE

Made in wood or metal, the jointer or trying plane, at 22 inches long, is the choice tool for truing up the edges of boards prior to jointing them edge to edge. In spite of its length, the jointer or trying plane is a good plane to hold and handle. The long sole allows the plane to ride over dips, rather than fall into them (see 3-5). In use, the long sole requires that you walk the plane along the entire length of the board at a single pass.

SMOOTHING PLANE

Once the sawn wood has been cleaned up with the jack plane, and the edge has been leveled true with the jointer or trying plane, then comes the time to use the aptly named smoothing plane (see 3-1 and 3-2) to bring the face of the board to a supersmooth finish. Though this plane has in many ways become the beginner's one-choice tool—a tool to be used in place of just about all the other bench planes—it was originally designed to be used specifically for the final finishing and smoothing. Prior to use, the cutting iron must first be honed so that the corners are very slightly rounded, and then it is mounted and set so that it is perfectly square with the bottom of the sole. The iron must be set for the lightest of light cuts so that the shavings are paper-thin and the full width of the mouth (see 3-6).

SPECIAL-PURPOSE PLANES: FOR ALL THE SECONDARY WORK

BLOCK PLANE

Made in wood or metal, the block plane gets its name from the time when it was used for smoothing the end-grain surfaces of butcher blocks. Just to confuse matters, the block plane is also sometimes described as being a small bench plane. No matter its classification, the block plane (see 3-1 and 3-2), with its short body at about 6 to 7 inches long, and with the cutter set so that the bevel is uppermost, is the ideal plane for trimming

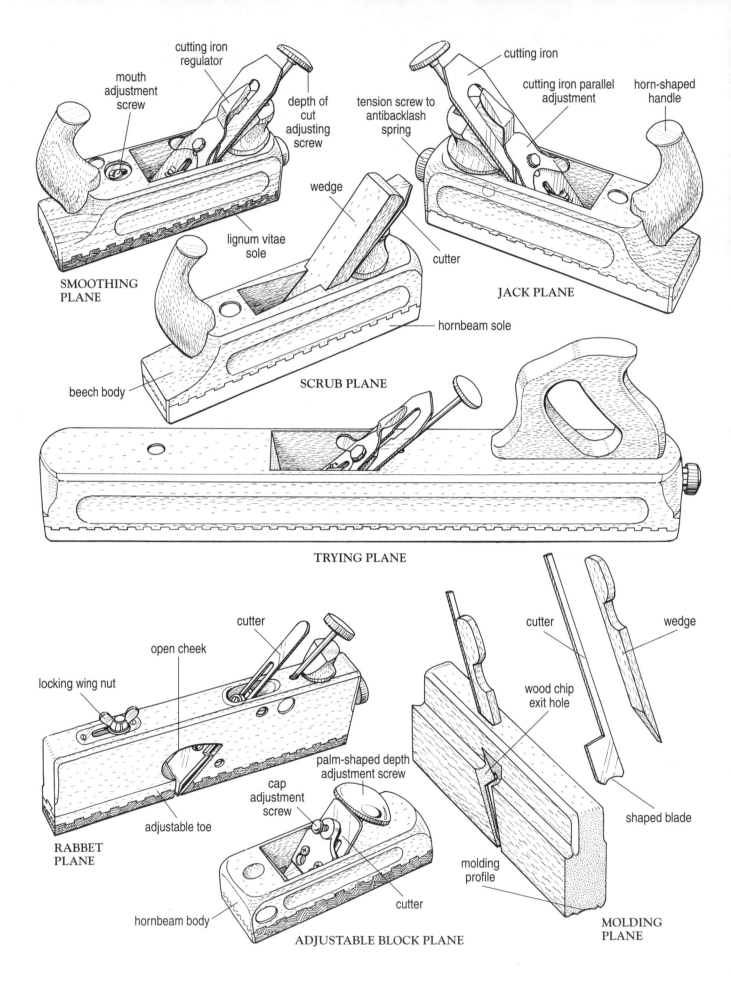

cutting iron
regulator

mouth
adjustment
screw

depth of
cut
adjusting
screw

cutting iron

cutting iron parallel
adjustment

horn-shaped
handle

tension screw to
antibacklash
spring

wedge

cutter

SMOOTHING
PLANE

lignum vitae
sole

JACK PLANE

beech body

hornbeam sole

SCRUB PLANE

TRYING PLANE

cutter

open cheek

locking wing nut

palm-shaped depth
adjustment screw

cutter

wedge

wood chip
exit hole

cap
adjustment
screw

adjustable toe

shaped blade

RABBET
PLANE

cutter

molding
profile

hornbeam body

ADJUSTABLE BLOCK PLANE

MOLDING
PLANE

Fig. 3-2. Modern wooden planes.

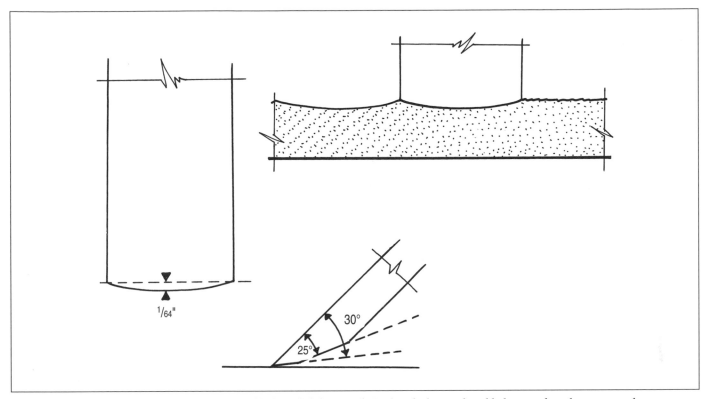

Fig. 3-4. Left, the cutting edge of the Jack plane blade is slightly curved. Right, the heavy-duty blade is used to clean up rough-sawn wood. Bottom, note the primary angle of 25 degrees and the secondary angle at 30 degrees.

and tidying up. The low angle of the blade and the narrowness of the mouth make it particularly useful for planing end grain (see 3-7).

METALLIC BENCH RABBET PLANE
The metallic bench rabbet plane—sometimes called a coach maker's rabbet—is much the same as the smoothing and jack planes, the only difference being that the blade extends the full width of the sole (see 3-1). The size and weight of the plane allows it to be used for cutting large-scale rabbets such as those for in joinery and house building. In use, a batten is clamped to the workpiece to act as a fence, and then during the cut, the plane is pressed hard up against the workpiece.

METALLIC RABBET FILLISTER PLANE
Though beginners are often confused by this plane—the name sounds a bit fancy—all you have to remember is that when the rabbet plane is fitted with a fence, it is generally known as a fillister. Though there are all manner of fillister types, our preference is for the all-metal plane known as a "duplex" or "bullnose fillister" (see 3-8). This plane has two seatings for the cutting iron: one for normal cuts and the other placed near the front of the sole for bullnose work.

METALLIC DADO PLANE
A groove is a channel that runs with the grain, whereas a dado or housing is a channel that runs across the grain (see 3-9 left). Dado planes are much the same as grooving planes, apart from the fact that they are sold in dedicated sizes. So, for example, dado planes are sold in graded sizes such as $1/4$ inch, $3/8$ inch, $1/2$ inch, and so on, right up to 1 inch. Dado planes can be easily recognized by two simple facts: The cutter is usually set at a skewed angle to the sole, and there are two scribes set in front of the blade and at each side of the body. The scribes are designed to prepare the way by slicing across the fibers of the wood. Nowadays, while it is still possible to buy old sets of dado planes, most woodworkers go for the easier option of using a combination plane. They simply remove the fence and set both scribes in the "down" position (see 3-9 right).

METALLIC SHOULDER PLANE
With its sole and sides being accurately machined so that they are at perfect right angles to each other, and with the cutting iron being set at a low angle, this is the perfect tool for trimming and cleaning shoulders and rabbets. Though there are any number of shoulder plane types, our advice is to get a shoulder plane that has a

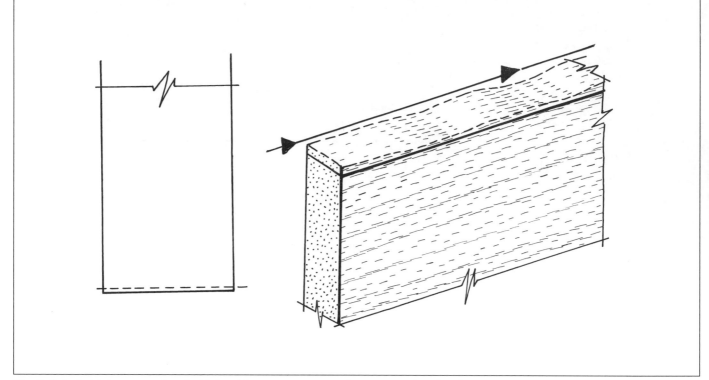

Fig. 3-5. Left, *it's important that the blade of the jointer or trying plane is ground so that the cutting edge is perfectly square with the side, that is, so that the corners are at 90 degrees.* Right, *the long sole allows the plane to ride over dips and hollows.*

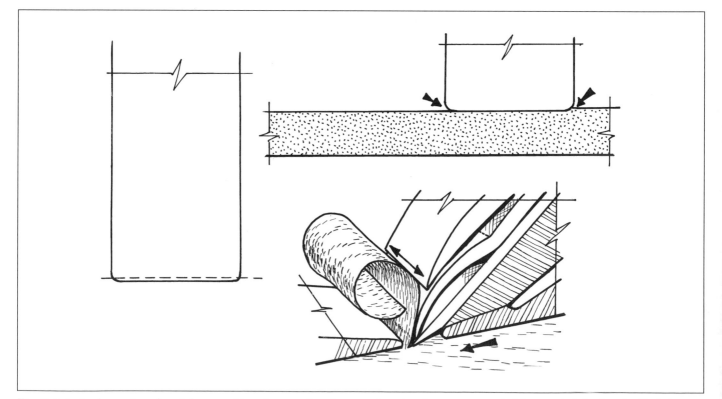

Fig. 3-6. Left, *the cutting edge of the smoothing plane needs to be ground so that the corners are slightly rounded.* Right, *the blade leaves a smooth cut—no ridges or dips.* Bottom, *the resultant shavings are paper-thin and the full width of the mouth.*

screw adjustment for the cutter (see 3-1). If you have in mind to do a lot of fine work, then you are most certainly going to need a shoulder plane.

METALLIC BULLNOSE PLANE

Though bullnose planes have much the same body shape as the shoulder planes—some with wooden wedges and others with screw adjustments—the main difference has to do with the size of the body and the way the cutter is set nearer to the front. The bullnose is designed to plane close up to a right angle, as with, say, a stopped rabbet or the stop at the end of a closed housing channel. Some bullnose planes are designed so that they can be swiftly converted into a chisel plane (see 3-1).

METALLIC GROOVING PLANE

Known variously as plough planes, grooving planes, dado planes, and many other names besides, the grooving plane is used, as the name so aptly suggests, for cutting grooves and rabbets. These planes are divided into two primary groups: the plough (or plow) planes that are used to cut grooves with the run of the grain (see 3-1 bottom right) and the dado or trenching planes that are used to cut grooves across the run of the grain. The main difference between the two groups is that the dado planes have spurs or scribes that slice across the grain in advance of the cutter. As with many of the other plane types, there are all kinds of grooving planes that have been designed to be used in very specific situations. For example, there are planes designed to cut a groove of a fixed width and depth, planes with a selection of cutters able to cut various groove widths, planes designed to

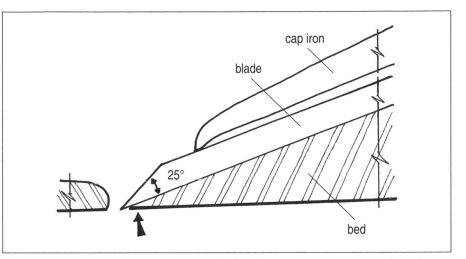

Fig. 3-7. The block plane cutter is set with the bevel uppermost so that the back of the blade is well supported almost down to the cutting edge.

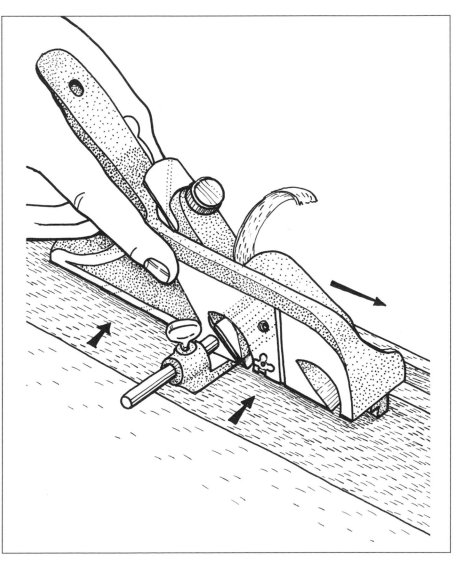

Fig. 3-8. The metallic rabbet plane is characterized by having two seatings for the cutting iron: one for normal cuts and the other placed near the front of the sole for bullnose work.

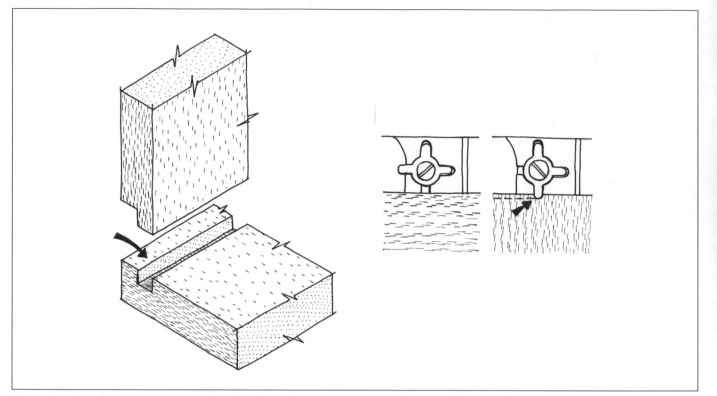

Fig. 3-9. Left, *a dado or housing is specifically a channel that runs across the direction of the grain*. Right, *the scribe, spur, or cutter is set in the "up" position for working with the grain and "down" when working across the grain. The function of the cutter is to prepare the way by slicing across the fibers of the grain.*

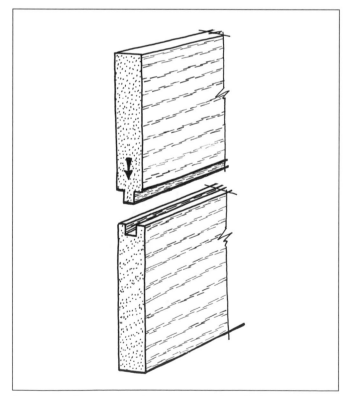

Fig. 3-10. *The tongue-and-groove cut on board edges makes for a strong edge-to-edge joint, with the tongue fitting into the groove.*

cut grooves around the inside edge of wooden barrels, and so on.

METALLIC TONGUE-AND-GROOVE PLANES

Tongue-and-groove planes or matching planes are designed for cutting matching tongues and grooves on the edges of boards. Though wooden tongue-and-groove planes were once sold in sized matching pairs—one plane to cut the groove and the other to cut the tongue (see 3-10)—these have to a great extent been superseded by all-metal combination type planes that are able to cut both the tongue and the groove. Our plane, an old Stanley 49, has a brilliantly simple function that allows the fence to be pivoted around: one way around for cutting tongues and the other way around for cutting grooves.

METALLIC COMPASS PLANE

The compass or circular plane is used to work convex and concave surfaces, like the edges of round tables or the cyma-curved edges of shelves. The modern all-metal compass plane is a beautiful tool (see 3-1). In use, all you do is wind the curvature screw until the flexible sole takes on the curve of the workpiece, and then get on with the job—much the same as with other planes. The cutter, cap, and cap iron unit are identical to those used on most bench planes.

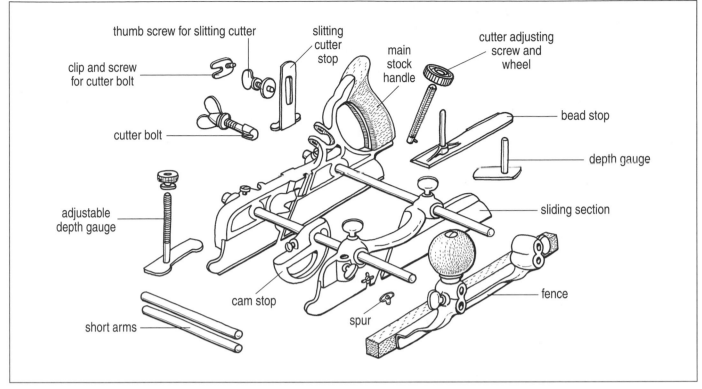

thumb screw for slitting cutter

slitting cutter stop

main stock handle

cutter adjusting screw and wheel

clip and screw for cutter bolt

cutter bolt

bead stop

depth gauge

adjustable depth gauge

sliding section

cam stop

fence

short arms

spur

Fig. 3-11. A disassembled Stanley 45 multicombination plane.

METALLIC SIDE RABBET PLANE

The combination side rabbet plane (see 3-12), for both left- and right-handed working, is designed for such tasks as cleaning up the walls of rabbets, increasing the width of straight-sided grooves, and tidying up the undercut walls of dovetailed channels. Some side rabbet planes have a function that allows the front to be removed so that they can be used for cutting hard into tight corners.

METALLIC COMBINATION AND MULTIPLANES

Multiplanes, sometimes called combination or universal planes, depending on size and type, are planes that are capable of performing a whole range of tasks. Cutting spurs in the body of the plane, a sliding section, an adjustable fence, a depth gauge, plus thirty or more different blades make this one of the most versatile planes ever made. Multiplanes can cut just about everything from beads, reeds, grooves, channels, and dado housings, to tongues, rabbets, slits, rounds, hollows, and all kinds of moldings besides. They can even make cuts that are beyond electric routers. Certainly, these planes are a bit tricky to set and tune, but they are great fun to use. If your enjoyment has to do with the pure pleasure of working with hand tools, rather than with the need to

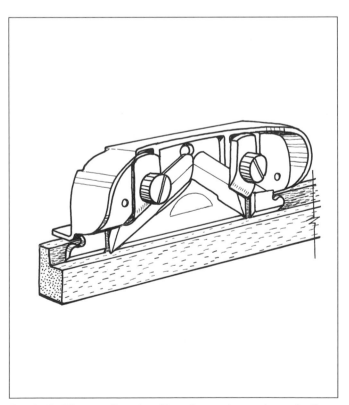

Fig. 3-12. The metallic side rabbet plane is designed specifically for cleaning up the sides of rabbets, grooves, and channels. It's a good plane for cabinetmakers.

get the job done at a fast and furious speed, then you most certainly need to get yourself a combination multiplane (see 3-11). We use a Stanley 45, a beautiful tool that is good to handle and hold, and altogether efficient (see 3-1 bottom left).

CLASSIC WOODEN MOLDING PLANES

Wooden molding planes (see 3-2) were traditionally used to produce all the many and varied moldings or profiles that were used to decorate furniture and architecture, such as the trim around doors and windows and the strips that embellish furniture and interiors. With each type, shape, and size of molding being produced by its own dedicated plane, traditional woodworkers would have needed whole sets and series of molding planes in graduated sizes. A specialized craftsman might well have needed a set of twenty-four "hollows" for cutting round profiles, a matching set of twenty-four "rounds" for cutting concave sections, a set of twelve "coves," a set of twelve "ovolos," and so on, for "ogee," "astragal," and all the other traditional profile forms.

The soles and cutters of molding planes are, in shape, the reverse of the molding that they are intended to cut (see 3-13). As with most traditional wooden planes, the cutters are held in place with wooden wedges.

THE ANATOMY OF A METALLIC BENCH PLANE

The term "bench plane" refers to the range of metal and wooden planes that are most frequently used at the bench, that is, at the primary stage to convert sawn timber into prepared stock. Taken in order of size, from large to small, there are the trying or jointing plane, the jack plane, the smoothing plane, and one or two other not much-used planes, like the scrub and the toothed plane.

All modern metallic bench planes have a lever cam and screw adjustment mechanism that replaces the wooden wedge seen in older planes. This mechanism, known as the Bailey patent, was developed in the United States in the last quarter of the nineteenth century by Leonard Bailey. Most metal bench planes are now fitted with the Bailey mechanism, so they all have more or less the same design and construction (see 3-14).

If you want to learn the anatomy of your bench plane, our advice is to set it on a table and take it apart with a screwdriver.

The following listing describes and defines the parts of the metallic bench plane in the natural order that the plane is disassembled.

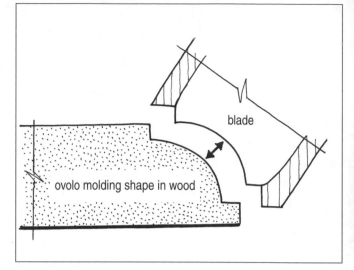

blade

ovolo molding shape in wood

Fig. 3-13. The sole and cutter of a molding plane are the reverse of the resultant molding. Rather contrarily, some molding planes like "hollows" and "rounds" are named after the shape of the plane, rather than the mark they make. So, for example, if you want to cut a round profile, you use a "hollow" plane, and if you want to cut a hollow profile, then you use a "round" plane. Odd isn't it?

LEVER CAP

The function of the lever cap is to hold the cap iron and cutter assembly hard up against the frog. To remove the lever cap, place the plane on its side, pull the lock forward to release the pressure, and then lift the cap up and out.

CAP IRON AND CUTTER

With the lever cap removed, you will see that the cap iron and cutter unit is made up of three component parts: the cutter blade or plane iron, the cap iron or back iron, and a large threaded screw. The function of the cap iron is twofold: It stops the blade from flexing and chattering, and it breaks the shavings into chips as they curl up and out of the mouth. To remove and disassemble the cap iron and cutter unit without damaging the cutter edge, you lift the two-iron unit up and out, loosen the screw, move the blade forward so that the cutting edge is well clear, then swing the blade at right angles to the cap iron, and finally, slide the cap iron along the blade until the head of the screw slips through the hole at the end of the slot (see 3-15).

Okay, so our description of how to remove the cutter sounds a bit fussy, but if you don't do it this way, and instead you simply undo the screw and drag the blade clear, then the chances are you will damage the edge of the blade or cut your fingers. You have been warned!

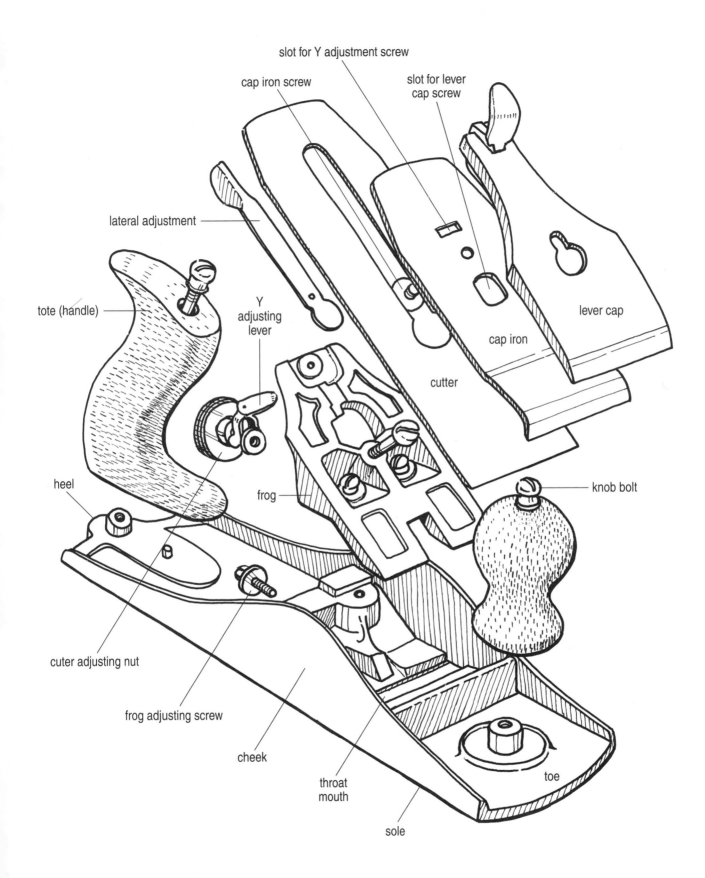

slot for Y adjustment screw

cap iron screw

slot for lever
cap screw

lateral adjustment

Y
adjusting
lever

tote (handle)

lever cap

cap iron

cutter

heel

frog

knob bolt

cuter adjusting nut

frog adjusting screw

cheek

throat
mouth

toe

sole

Fig. 3-14. A disassembled Bailey patent metallic bench plane.

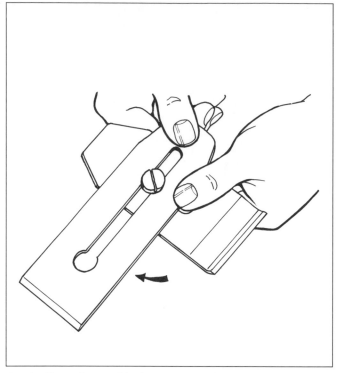

Fig. 3-15. To disassemble the cap iron and cutter, slacken the screw, move the blade forward so that the cutting edge is well clear of the cap iron, swivel the cutter around so the two components are at right angles to each other, and finally, slide the cap iron along the blade until the holding screw slips through the hole at the end of the slot.

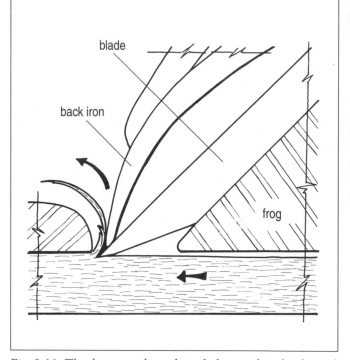

Fig. 3-16. The shaving curls up through the mouth and is directed toward, and broken off by, the cap iron. It is important that the cap iron is a close fit to the blade so that the shaving doesn't try to force its way between the two.

FROG ASSEMBLY

Once the cap iron and cutter are out of the way, you will be presented with the heart of the plane, the wedge-shaped assembly known as the "frog." The function of the frog is threefold: It holds the blade at the correct angle, it provides support on which the lateral lever is pivoted, and it can be slid backward and forward to govern the size of the throat. To move the frog, you simply loosen the two setscrews, and then adjust the single screw that is positioned just below the large knurled brass wheel at the back of the frog.

LATERAL LEVER

The function of the lateral lever is to tilt the blade from side to side so that the cutting edge of the bevel is aligned parallel with the mouth. If you set the cap iron and cutter assembly back in place on the frog, you will see that side-to-side movement is achieved by means of the little disc at the bottom end of the lever pushing against the sides of the slot that runs up the middle of the cutter or blade.

BODY AND SOLE

Once you have removed the lever cap, the double irons, and the frog complete with its various screws and levers,

you will be left with the body of the plane complete with the wooden front knob and back handle or tote. Unscrew the handle and knob, and put them to one side. You now have what is termed the "body" of the plane. With the whole body being made of cast iron, the various elements or features are named after parts of the human body. The front end is termed the "toe," the back end the "heel," the flat sides are the "cheeks," the whole underside is the "sole," and the slot that runs across the sole is termed the "mouth." To reassemble the plane, see the section below entitled "Tuning a Bench Plane."

THE CUTTING ACTION OF A METALLIC BENCH PLANE

If you look very closely at a metallic bench plane in action, you will see that the shaving is equal to, or as thick as, the amount by which the cutter projects through the mouth. The rule of thumb is the greater the projection of the cutter through the sole, the heavier the cut and the thicker the shaving.

If you could somehow or other focus in on a cross section of the plane in action, you would see that with the cutter iron set bevel down, when the cutting edge shaves or slices into the surface of the workpiece, the shaving curls up through the mouth. If you now look closely at the shaving, you will see that when it comes up through the mouth, it gets directed toward and broken off by, the cap iron (see 3-16). Without the cap iron, the shavings would pile up under the wedge or lever cap and jam the throat.

If you play around with various positions of the cap iron in relation to the cutter, you will see that the closer the cap iron is to the cutter edge, the sooner the shavings are broken, and the less risk of the wood splitting or tearing. Bear in mind that softwood is more likely to curl out as whole shavings than hardwood. The very general rule of thumb is the harder the wood, the closer the set between the cap iron and the cutter.

THE ANATOMY OF A MODERN WOODEN BENCH PLANE

As far as we can see, all modern wooden planes, at least the ones that we see currently on sale in the United States and England, are made in Germany by a company called E. C. Emmerich—E.C.E. We have looked long and hard for other modern wooden planes being made now, and they are nowhere to be found. So when we use the term "modern wooden planes," we are referring to planes made by E.C.E. in Germany.

Although modern wooden planes are fitted with traditional wedges and trigger cams, which are sound means of holding the cutter securely and at the correct angle, the top-of-the-line wooden bench planes are fitted with a patented mechanism known as the "Primus Adjustment System," or simply as "Primus." Although the Primus system is completely different from the Bailey mechanism seen on most metallic planes, many woodworkers claim that it is capable of a finer, more positive action. They claim that the Primus adjustment, with its tension rod and spring, not only makes it possible to positively regulate the depth of cut—a thing that's not easy to do on a metallic plane—but better yet, also does away with the annoying backlash movement and wobble that is found on some metallic planes. Some woodworkers claim that the Primus system is revolutionary!

The best way to learn about your modern wooden plane is to take it apart (see 3-17). Though the following listing specifically describes and defines the various parts of the top-of-the-line Improved Primus Smooth Plane in the natural order that the plane would be disassembled, you can take it that the jack and the trying planes are much the same in design and form.

TENSION SCREW, ROD, SPRING, AND KNOB

The tension screw, rod, spring, and knob mechanism is at the heart of the Primus system. The function of the spring-loaded tension rod is to pull the blade assembly hard back against the throat so that the blade sits firmly

without chattering. To remove the mechanism, you start by undoing the depth adjustment screw a couple of turns. Undo and remove the large black tension screw nut. Next, you remove the washer and the spring, and then, at one and the same time, you lift the double blade up out of the throat and push and turn the tension rod forward so that the rod cross pin slips out of its seating. Lastly, you draw the tension rod back out of the hole at the heel.

REGULATOR

With the tension rod out of the way, you will see that the regulator is bolted on the cap iron and cutter unit so that it is able to swivel from side to side. The function of the regulator is to correct the lateral adjustment of the blade unit. It does this by levering on the inside of the body cavity in such a way that it eases the blade from side to side. To remove the regulator, you simply undo the regulator pivot bolt (see 3-17).

CAP IRON AND CUTTER

Having removed the regulator, you will be left with the cap iron and cutter unit. Be careful how you handle the cutter, because it is honed and ready for use. To remove the cap iron, you simply slacken the two setscrew bolts (see 3-17) and slide the cap back along the cutter slot until it drops free.

ADJUSTING SCREW

With the whole blade assembly removed from the throat of the plane, you will be left with the "depth adjustment" screw running down through the handle. To remove the screw, turn it counterclockwise until it comes free. If you now play around with the tension rod, you will see that the adjustment screw functions by screwing down through a captive nut toggle to push on the humped part of the tension rod.

ADJUSTABLE TOE

The Improved Primus Smooth Plane is unique among bench planes in having an adjustable toe plate that controls the size of the mouth. The idea is that as the part of the sole in front of the blade acts as the primary chip breaker, so the smaller the mouth, or the closer the toe is to the cutter, the more effective the breaker. To remove the toe plate, all you do is undo the screw between the horn and the throat so that the toe block falls free.

BODY AND SOLE

Once you have removed the Primus unit, the double blade, and all the various screws and bolts, you will be left with the body of the plane complete with the handle and the tote. As with the metallic bench planes, the

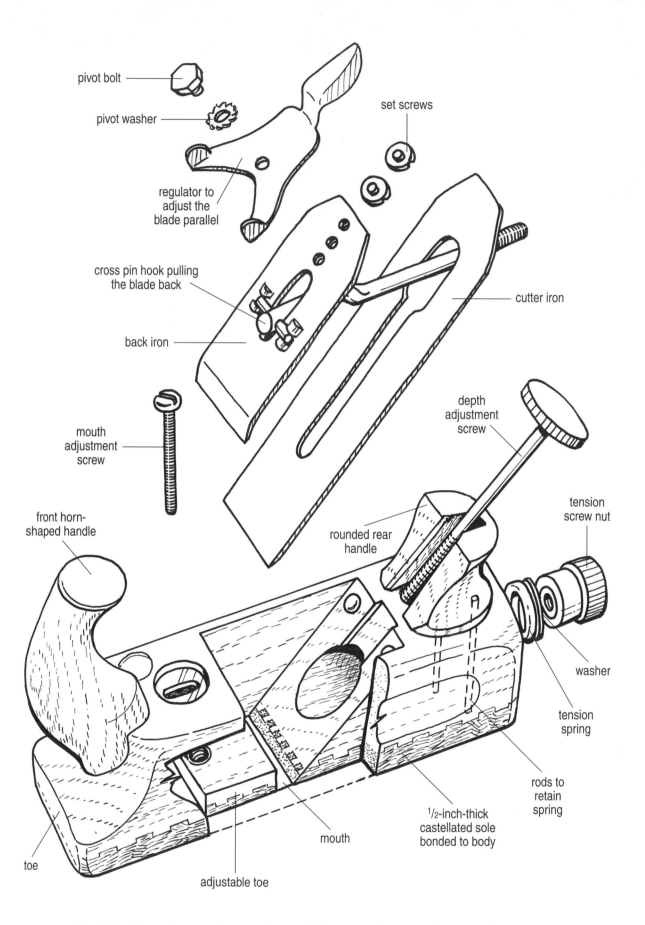

pivot bolt

pivot washer

set screws

regulator to
adjust the
blade parallel

cross pin hook pulling
the blade back

cutter iron

back iron

depth
adjustment
screw

mouth
adjustment
screw

tension
screw nut

front horn-
shaped handle

rounded rear
handle

washer

tension
spring

rods to
retain
spring

½-inch-thick
castellated sole
bonded to body

mouth

toe

adjustable toe

Fig. 3-17. The modern wooden plane disassembled showing the patented "Primus" blade adjustment.

various elements that make up the body of the plane are named, for the most part, after parts of the human body. The front is the "toe," the back is the "heel," the sides are the "cheeks," the cavity is the "throat," the base is the "sole," and the slot in the base is the "mouth."

The front handle is horn shaped, an age-old design used in traditional preindustrial plane forms. The design of the handle is so comfortable to grasp that it makes for an easy arm and wrist thrusting action. The turned and shaped tote perfectly fits the palm of the hand, making it possible to put the full weight of your shoulder and arm behind the thrust.

The body is made from American cherry and the sole from Central American lignum vitae. Lignum vitae is the closest-grained wood known. It is only slightly lighter than iron, and its spiral grain gives it enormous strength and crush resistance.

THE CUTTING ACTION OF A MODERN WOODEN BENCH PLANE

While the modern wooden bench plane is used in the same way as the metallic bench plane, with the cutter iron set bevel down and the shavings running up through the mouth to be broken off by the cap iron, the cutting action is in many ways quite different. For example, whereas the wooden plane is slightly lighter in weight than the metallic plane, it is also slightly bulkier. Whereas the metallic plane is gripped at the front knob and grasped at the tote, the wooden plane is grasped at the front horn, and clasped and pushed at the tote (see 3-18).

Although the setting action is much the same as on the metal plane—a lever adjusts lateral movement of the blade and an adjusting

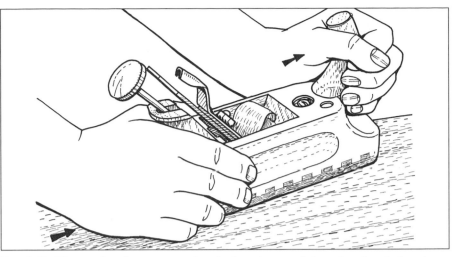

Fig. 3-18. The wooden plane is grasped at the front horn and clasped and pushed at the tote. The shape of the tote and the back of the plane are such that they comfortably butt into the palm or heel of the hand.

screw runs the double blade in and out—the Primus action is quite unlike the Bailey action. The Primus depth-of-cut control is instant and positive. The moment you turn the screw, the blade starts to move; there is no waiting for contact.

The lignum vitae sole bleeds an oily resin when it is warmed and rubbed, a quality that makes it perfectly suited for its task.

SHARPENING THE BENCH PLANE CUTTER

Working with a wooden or metallic bench plane is a truly pleasurable experience; it's quiet, efficient, and swift—but only if the cutter iron is sharp! A plane with a dull cutter is a horror; it's almost impossible to control, it leaves an unpleasant finish, and using it is altogether hard and sweaty work.

The sharpening procedure consists of three sequential steps or stages:
- Grinding on a stone wheel.
- Honing or whetting on an oil- or waterstone.
- Stropping on a leather.

GRINDING
Ideally, the edges of plane irons need to be shaped according to the

work at hand. For example, for rough hogging the edge needs to be slightly rounded, for general surface planing the edge needs to be rounded at the corners, and for jointing the edge needs to be ground square (see 3-19 left). If you intend doing a lot of planing, it's a good idea to get yourself a couple of spare blades so that you always have a blade shape to suit your needs. If you have only one bench plane, then it's best to grind the iron so that the edge is straight with the corners slightly rounded. The cutting edge must always be at right angles to the sides (see 3-19 right).

You only really need to grind the iron if the edge has been badly ground or damaged. You don't need to grind new plane irons unless you want to change the profile. You can sharpen irons many times on the whetstone before they need to be reground. Just keep in mind that a bad grinder can ruin the blade by overheating, by getting the edge out of square, by changing the bevel, and so on. There are any number of pitfalls. Grinding needs to be done with extreme care and caution, or not at all.

Though grinding may look to be relatively safe, it is in actual fact extremely hazardous. The main dangers have to do with the wheel shattering and with pieces of hot metal flying up in your face. Always read the manufacturer's warnings, always wear eye protection, and keep the guards in place. *Never leave kids alone with the machine!*

The Grinding Stone. As to the question of the grindstone, you should never use an engineer's high-speed bench grinder. The problem with the fast stone is that, by its very nature, it is very difficult to stop the blade from overheating, even when it is frequently dipped in water. When steel overheats to the extent that it turns blue, the steel becomes soft and useless.

Instead, use a slow-speed wheel with water running on the stone. You will find that the shape and flow of the water as it streams down the stone and over the iron is a good indicator of your sharpening progress. The water will flow and skip over the iron when the bevel is in close contact with the stone, and it will run under the iron when there is a gap between the cutting edge and the stone.

In order to grind a plane iron on a traditional grindstone, the surface of the stone must be true. A traditional stone is a sensitive item. If you leave it standing in water it goes soft, if you leave it in the sun it goes hard, and if you leave it standing out in water in the frost, then it might well crack.

The Grinding Procedure. You have set yourself up with a traditional slow-speed, sitting-in-water radial stone—one that rotates toward you—and you have read all the manufacturer's warnings and you are ready to go. Start by checking the shape of the iron at its edge. If there are any nicks or chips, then the edge must be squared off.

To square the blade, support it on the tool rest so that the flat face

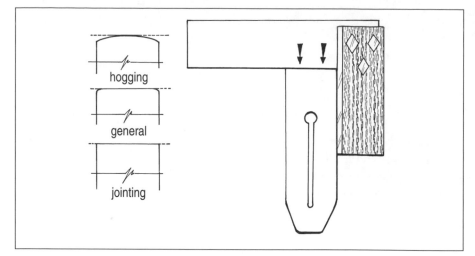

Fig. 3-19. Left, *plane irons are ground differently according to their intended function— for hogging, for smoothing, or for jointing. Some old-timers had one plane and a selection of cutters.* Right, *use a square to check that the cutting edge is at right angles to the side of the blade.*

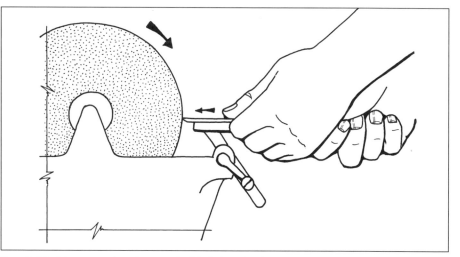

Fig. 3-20. *To square the edge, set the blade bevel-side down on the rest so that it is square with the stone. Advance and stroke the blade from side to side across the face of the stone.*

is uppermost, and pass it gently from side to side until you have achieved a cutting edge that is straight and free from nicks (see 3-20). If you want to grind an iron for a hogging plane or grind off the corners for a smoothing plane, then follow through the same procedure as already described and adjust the curve of the blade to suit.

To grind the bevel, adjust the tool rest so that it is set to an angle of 25 degrees (see 3-21 left). Rest the bevel of the blade on the stone, hold it steady, and then repeatedly

pass it from left to right (see 3-21 right). You won't go far wrong if you hold the iron firmly and if you make sure that the blade is held square, with both edges being at equal pressure. Every now and then along the way, hold the blade up so that the light strikes across the bevel and check to see if any of the old bevel remains. The old bevel or "flat" will reveal itself as a strip of reflected light. Continue grinding a little, holding the blade up to the light, grinding a little more, and so on until the job is done. Finally, you can check the bevel angle off against the correct angle that is marked on the cap iron of most planes.

HONING OR WHETTING

Though the cutting edge left by the grindstone is pretty keen, it is still a bit too rough for use. The iron needs to be honed. Honing is the procedure of rubbing the plane iron on an oilstone, waterstone, or diamond whetstone until the cutting faces are established and fully burnished. As to the question of which type of stone is best, there are pros and cons for each and every type. We personally prefer to use an oilstone, perhaps for no other reason than we were given a set of high-quality stones. You need two grades of whetstones—medium and fine.

Having dribbled a small amount of light engine oil on the medium stone—or water if it's a waterstone—start the honing procedure by setting the back of the blade absolutely flat on the stone (see 3-22). Hold the iron with one hand and apply downward pressure with the fingers of the other hand. Rub the iron to and fro along the length of the stone until the surface of the steel has been honed to a bright shiny finish. When you can see that the surface is good and burnished, rerun the procedure on the fine-grade stone.

When you come to honing the bevel, you must be aware that the bevel is in fact made up of two faces: the primary bevel and the secondary bevel—sometimes referred to as the microbevel (see 3-23 left). Start by honing the primary bevel. Having dribbled a couple more drops of oil on the stone, turn the iron over so that the bevel is looking at the stone, and then set the iron down on the stone so that the heel of the bevel is in contact. Hold the iron firmly down, raise

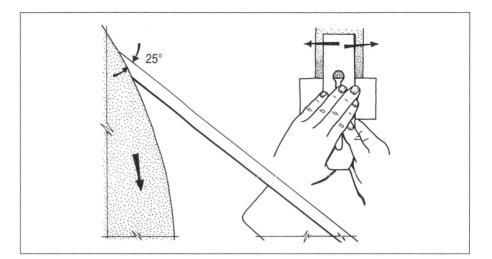

Fig. 3-21. Left, *to grind the bevel, adjust the tool rest so that the blade makes contact at an angle of 25 degrees.* Right, *with one hand holding and guiding and the other pressing down, pass the blade from side to side across the face of the stone.*

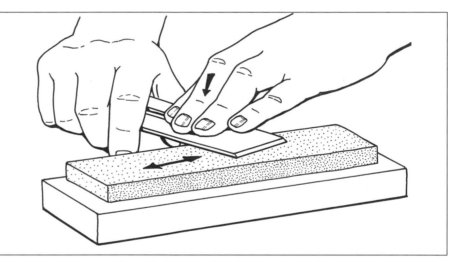

Fig. 3-22. *To clean and burnish the back of the blade, grasp the iron with one hand and lightly press down with the spread fingers of the other hand so that the whole back of the blade is in contact. Work the blade up and down the length of the stone.*

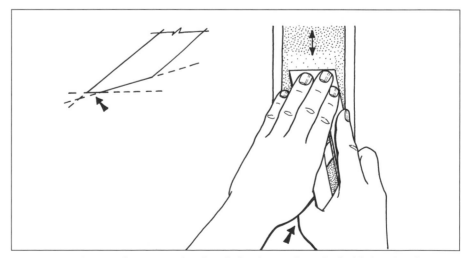

Fig. 3-23. Left, *once the primary bevel angle has been achieved, the blade is lifted a few degrees so that there is a secondary or micro-bevel along the leading edge.* Right, *the secondary bevel not only allows for greater clearance between the back of the blade and the frog, it also extends the life of the blade by minimizing the amount of metal that is removed during honing. Think about it!*

the end until the full width of the bevel is in contact, and then maintain the angle and repeatedly push and pull the iron along the length of the stone (see 3-23). If you are doing it right, that is, if the bevel is in full contact and at the 25-degree primary bevel angle, you will see a bead of oil or water bubble out across the full width of the blade. Repeat this procedure on the fine stone. If you are not happy about how to find and maintain the 25-degree angle or you simply prefer using gizmos, there are any number of foolproof jigs and guides that can be used for holding the blade at the correct angle.

To hone the secondary bevel, set the iron down on the stone at the 25-degree angle so that the primary bevel is in full contact, then raise the iron another 5 degrees or so and hone as already described. If you have done it correctly, when you hold the iron up to the light, the secondary bevel will reveal itself as a thin strip of light that runs along the cutting edge. Finally, polish the back of the iron on the fine stone to remove the burr.

STROPPING

Stropping is the final stage in the sharpening sequence. A strop is a piece of leather impregnated with a fine abrasive. In use, you smear the finest abrasive paste over the leather—something like silicon carbide is just fine —and then you work the iron in much the same way as when honing on the whetstone. The only difference this time around is that you always drag the iron; you never push. First, drag the bevel along the strop, and then turn the iron over, so that the back is flat on the strop, and polish the back.

> SPECIAL TIP: If and when you want to sharpen a shaped blade, say, for a molding plane or maybe a multiplane, you follow much the same procedures as already described, only you use little shaped slips, rather than grinding stones and flat bench stones. Sharpening a shaped blade is more akin to sharpening wood-carving gouges (see chapter 5).

THE ANATOMY AND CUTTING ACTION OF SPECIAL PLANES

The best way of understanding the anatomy and cutting action of all the so-called special planes is to realize that they are all modifications on the basic bench plane theme. So, for example, the simple block plane is no more than a standard plane that has been developed to perform a specific function. No doubt sometime in the dim and distant past, when some now long-forgotten

woodworker wanted a plane that he could hold in one hand and use for working end grain, he looked at the smoothing plane, decided that the iron was pitched too high and the body was too heavy, and then made his own small version. He reduced the size of the body so that it could be held in one hand, he lowered the pitch of the cutter so that it would slice across end grain, he turned the blade over so that the bevel was uppermost, he did away with the cap iron, and so on. And so it is with all the other special planes; because they are all planes that have evolved to perform specific tasks, they have all manner of shape, form, and function peculiarities that are unique to themselves.

Although in broad general terms it's easy to see that the anatomy and cutting action of the special planes are much the same as for the bench planes, you do have to be aware that each and every special plane might well need singular consideration when it comes to sharpening and setting up. For example, whereas the bench plane iron is ground to a primary bevel angle of 25 degrees and bedded bevel-side down at a frog angle of 45 degrees, the block plane blade, on the other hand, is ground to a bevel angle of 25 degrees and bedded bevel-side up at a frog angle of 12 to 20 degrees. All this adds up to the simple fact that when working with special planes, you must always have a good look at the way the cutting iron is ground and bedded before you start disassembling and making modifications.

TUNING A BENCH PLANE

All planes, wooden or metallic, new or old, need to be tuned before you can use them. Though we describe how to tune an old much-used metallic bench plane, you can take it that much the same procedure can be followed for most planes.

The procedure is as follows: You have completely disassembled your plane (see 3-14), the cutter iron has been ground, honed, and stropped, and you are generally anxious to have the plane back together and up and running. The process of cleaning the plane and putting it together and making sure that it is in perfect working order is usually referred to as "tuning."

Take the iron body and check it over for such problems as chips and cracks. Make sure that the wooden knob and tote are secure and the screws are tight. See to it that the bedding for the frog is clean and free from resin. If need be, take a small amount of turpentine and a brush and clean out all the crannies in and around the frog seating. Make sure that the lip that leads down to the mouth is clean.

Take the frog unit and undo and remove the brass adjusting nut. Clean the threads with turpentine and make sure that the Y-shaped unit is able to move freely on its pivot fixing (see 3-24). Clean away the buildup of dust from under the lateral lever and dribble a few drops of fine machine oil under its pivot so that it's free moving. While you are at it, clean the two frog setscrews and the frog adjustment screw. When you arc happy that all is correct and as described, dribble a small amount of oil on the frog seating and screw it back in place on the body.

Having adjusted the frog so that the mouth is at a size to suit—a wide mouth for roughing and a narrow mouth for fine work—then carefully tighten up the two setscrews. Don't overdo the tightening; make it just enough to grip the frog.

Take the two plane irons (the cutter and the cap) and slide them together so as to avoid damaging the newly sharpened bevel. The best procedure is as follows (see 3-25):

- Hold the cutting iron bevel-side down and place the cap iron across and at right angles.
- Locate the cap iron screw in the hole of the cutter, and still holding it at right angles, slide the cap iron down toward the other end of the slot.
- Swing the cap iron around so that it is aligned and on top of the cutter iron.
- Slide the cap iron toward the bevel, set it in place, and tighten the screw.

The recommended spacings between the edge of the cap iron and the edge of the cutter are as follows: for rough work, $1/32$–$1/16$ inch; for fine finishing, $1/64$ inch; for hardwood, as close as possible.

When you have tightened the screw, take what is now the double

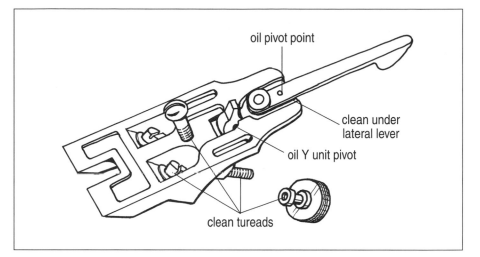

Fig. 3-24. *Having removed the whole frog unit, undo and remove the large adjusting nut and clean and oil all the moving parts. Be sure to remove the buildup of wood dust between the lateral lever and the body of the frog.*

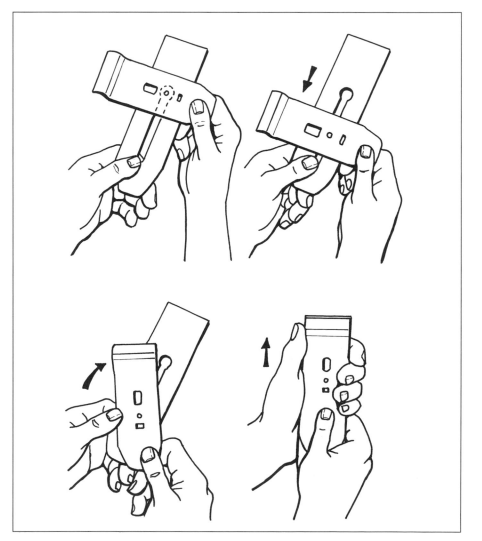

Fig. 3-25. Top left, *set the unit so that the cutter iron is bevel-side down, set the cap at right angles to the cutter (like a cross), and locate the cap iron screw in the hole at the end of the slot.* Top right, *slide the cap iron down toward the end of the slot.* Bottom left, *swing the cap iron around and align it with the cutter.* Bottom right, *slide the cap iron toward the bevel end of the cutter, set the distance, and tighten up the fixing screw.*

iron and set it bevel-side down in the throat of the plane. See to it that the small square hole on the cap iron is located on the end of the Y adjustment lever, and the roller on the end of the lateral lever is located in the cutter iron slot. When you are sure that the iron is well bedded down on the frog, take the lever cap and snap it in place. If need be, adjust the lever cap screw for a firm fit.

Turn the plane over so that the sole is uppermost and the toe is looking toward you, and sight down the plane (see 3-26). Very carefully adjust the brass nut until the blade projects through the mouth and reveals itself as a thin dark line that is parallel to the mouth. If the blade projects a little too much at the left or right, adjust the lateral lever accordingly (see 3-27).

When you think that the blade setting is just so, try it out on a piece of scrap wood. Take several trial cuts. If the resultant shavings are too heavy or too light, adjust the brass wheel accordingly. Many beginners misunderstand the range of adjustments and just settle for the first setting that takes a cut. Having sharpened the cutter as described, they fail to realize that finetuning is made up from a mix of four adjustments (see 3-28): the position of the frog on the sole, the position of the cap iron on the cutter, the position of the lateral lever, and the position of the double iron within the throat. The rule is a fine-set cap iron and a fine mouth for a fine shaving and a wide-set cap iron and a wide mouth for a coarse shaving.

HINTS ON PLANE TUNING
To find out if your plane needs tuning, make a pass over a piece of scrap wood, and then inspect the surface of the wood. If there are chatter marks, then it is likely that

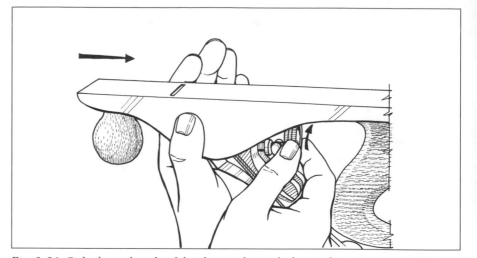

Fig. 3-26. *Sight down the sole of the plane and turn the brass adjusting screw until the blade just shows itself through the mouth.*

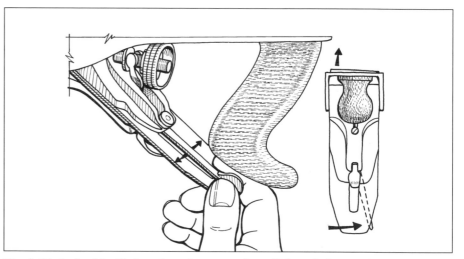

Fig. 3-27. *Left, if the blade is skewed as it reveals itself through the mouth, that is, if it is out of lateral alignment, make adjustments by moving the lateral lever. Right, when the lever is pushed to the right, then the left corner of the blade will reveal itself, and vice versa.*

the blade is set too deep. If the surface is unmarked, then the cutter needs to be set lower. If the surface of the wood is scored, then the blade is set so that one corner is lower than the other. If this is the case, hold the plane upside down so that you can sight down the sole, and then move the lateral lever so that the offending blade corner tilts back into the mouth. Continue until the visible part of the cutter edge shows itself against the mouth slot as a thin parallel line. If the

blade is fine set, and yet the shaving is still heavy and coarse, make the mouth smaller by moving the whole frog unit ever-so-slightly forward.

To adjust a wooden-wedged molding plane, sight down the sole of the plane so that the nose of the plane is looking at you, and advance the iron by lightly tapping the end of the tang with a small large-faced hammer. To withdraw the iron, very lightly tap the heel of the stock, meaning the back end of

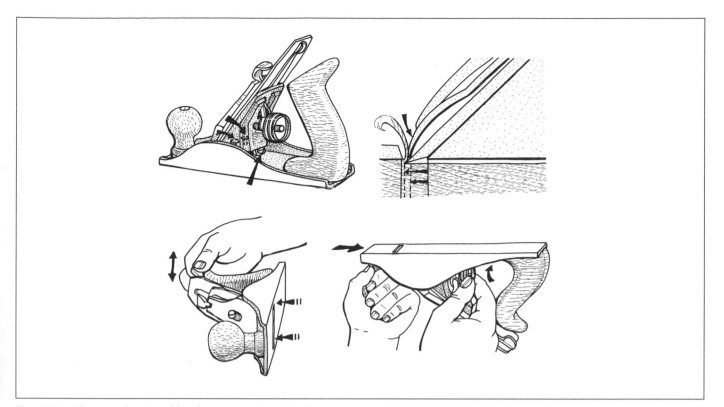

Fig. 3-28. *There are four possible adjustments: Top left,* the position of the frog can be moved backward or forward so as to make the mouth slot bigger or smaller. *Top right,* the position of the cap iron on the cutter can be adjusted to suit the nature of the wood. *Bottom left,* the lateral position of the cutter, that is, the squareness of the cutting edge in relation to the sole, can be adjusted. *Bottom right,* the position of the double iron within the throat can be advanced or withdrawn according to the desired depth of cut.

the plane. Make lateral adjustments by tapping the sides of the tang. Never hit the sole and never use the peen end of the hammer.

STANCE AND CONTROL

Planes are designed to be used with both hands, with the workpiece being held securely in the vise. Even the block plane, which is sometimes used with one hand, is best used with two hands. Good control is vital. It's no good resting the workpiece on a couple of chairs or trying to do it on the floor; you must have a workbench. The workbench is at the heart of planing. It would be false economy—foolish even—to set yourself up with a beautiful well-tuned plane and then try to cut costs by working on a wobbly kitchen table. You must have a good bench.

At last! You have a good firm bench fitted out with a large vise, you have a selection of top quality planes all sharpened and tuned, you have some choice wood, and you are ready to go. The guides on stance and control will help you on your way.

STANCE AND CONTROL WITH A BENCH PLANE

Bench planes are designed to be held and used with both hands, the left hand wrapped around the knob and the right hand clasped around the tote or handle. With the workpiece held in the vise or butted up against a stop, you need to be standing to the left of the workpiece, with your feet well braced and with your body positioned so that you can put the full weight and the power of your shoulders and body behind the thrust of the cut (see 3-29). Of course, much depends on the task at hand and the particular plane being used, but the working action is generally as follows: Brace your feet, hold the plane firmly in both hands, set the plane down on the wood, put a good amount of downward pressure on the plane, and then make the first forward stroke. At the end of the stroke, lift the plane off the wood—don't drag it back—and then rerun the procedure. If you are working a long length of wood, if, say, you are jointing the edge of a long board, then the only difference is that you might well need to walk the plane along the length of the wood. The secret of success is

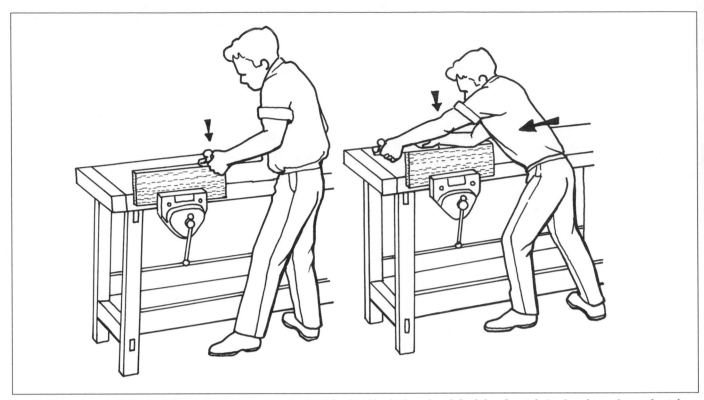

Fig. 3-29. Left, *stand directly behind the workpiece, with the right shoulder high and with both legs braced.* Right, *thrust forward, with the full power of the shoulder behind the stroke, and with the body weight balanced and braced by the left leg.*

not to jerk or rush the task, but rather to make a series of firm positive strokes. You must not let your mind or the plane wander off course. Set the plane down on the wood and make the stroke. Try to imagine that you are cutting a dip or hollow; begin each stroke by pressing down slightly on the front knob and end each stroke by pressing down on the tote or handle.

When surfacing, hold the plane in line with the grain, twist it at a slight angle, and then thrust the plane forward at that angle so as to make a skewed shearing cut. You will find that a shearing angle leaves a smoother, cleaner cut.

When you are using a smoothing plane to true an edge, secure the workpiece in the vise and increase pressure at the front of the plane by pressing down with the thumb, while at the same time using your fingers as a fence or guide. You will find that this hold keeps the plane square and on route (see 3-30).

When you have finished using your plane, set it down on its side so that the cutting edge is on view. Never bang the plane sole down on the bench. Some finicky woodworkers even go to the extent of winding the blade up when they have finished, and others undo the lever cap and remove the cutting iron.

STANCE AND CONTROL WITH A BLOCK PLANE

In many ways, the block plane is the woodworker's no-nonsense, highly versatile friend. It can be held and used in both hands—just like a bench plane; it can be held and used in one hand (see 3-31) for planing tricky corners and chamfers; it can be used on end grain (see 3-32); it can be used horizontally or vertically; and in fact, it can even be worked with a pulling stroke.

When you are using the block plane, you should hold it firmly in one hand, with the back of the lever cap cupped against the ball of your palm, and then, if need be, you should apply additional pressure to the stroke by cross-clasping and pressing down with the other hand; that is, put one hand on top of the other.

Many beginners fail dismally with the block plane, because they go at it rather casually, thinking that it's simply a one-handed tool. Okay, so it's fine to use the block plane in one hand when you are trimming the inside of a cupboard door, or the end of a molding, or whatever, but for the most part, you not only need to work with both hands, but perhaps more to the point, you also need to get the weight and thrust of both arms and shoulders behind the stroke.

To our way of thinking, the block plane is best tuned and set so that it makes the very finest cut. We enjoy using the block plane to make shearing cuts, that is, slicing cuts with the plane running forward at a slight angle. The shearing cut not only reduces the amount of sweat and effort, but more than that, it leaves the end grain smooth and polished (see 3-33). Some woodworkers are so "at one" with the block plane that they use it to remove marks left by other planes and to bring a surface to a perfect burnished finish.

STANCE AND CONTROL WITH GROOVING AND RABBET PLANES

Grooving planes and rabbet planes —or you might say planes with fences—need special consideration when it comes to the question of stance and control. If a plane has a fence, then it needs to be managed with both hands, with the workpiece being held securely and in such a way that there is enough room for the fence to slide alongside the workpiece. The problem is that although the workpiece needs to be clamped to the workbench, it must be fixed in such a way that the plane can be used without it being obstructed by the bench or the clamps. Or put another way, the fence must be able to hang over and slide along the edge of the workpiece without the bottom of the fence or your knuckles banging into the clamps.

The setup is pretty straightforward when you are running a groove or a rabbet along a wide board, because there is plenty of room for the clamps and the plane. But when you are working a narrow strip, you have to figure out a means of holding the wood so that the area to be worked is free and unencumbered. In such instances,

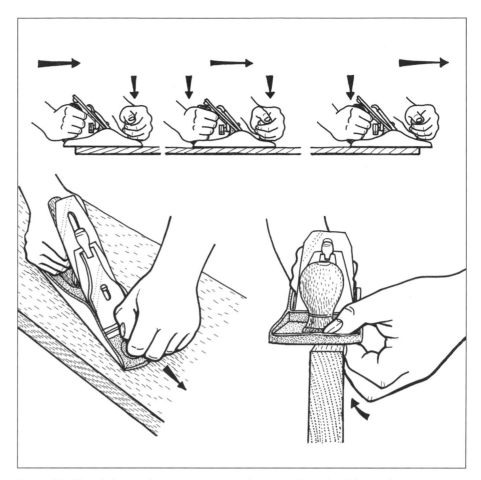

Fig. 3-30. Top, left to right, *to prevent rounding over the ends of the workpiece, press down on the front of the plane at the start of the stroke, have the pressure evenly applied throughout the stroke, and move the pressure to the back of the plane as the plane leaves the wood. It helps if you try to imagine that you are planing out a large dip or hollow. Bottom left, when planing a board in the direction of the grain, hold the plane at a slight angle so that you make a skewed cut. Bottom right, when planing an edge, apply pressure with the thumb while at the same time pushing the fingers against the workpiece, so that the fingers are used like a fence.*

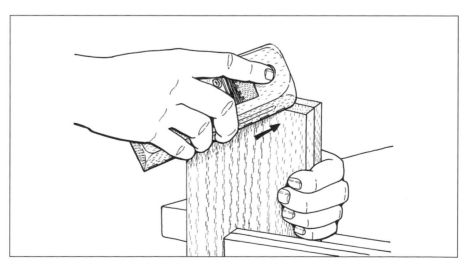

Fig. 3-31. *The block plane is ideal for working small corners and chamfers. The plane is best held and used at a skewed angle. The illustrations show a modern wooden plane being used.*

the best way forward is to butt the workpiece against a bench stop or dog so that about ¼ inch of the edge overhangs the edge of the bench (see 3-34). The wood can then be held with a clamp or pins. If the wood is so narrow that the clamp is in the way, then you might well need to work one end and then reclamp before working the other end.

If the rabbet is wide, then it often pays to work it in two stages. First you run a plowed groove to mark the far side of the rabbet, and then you finish off by clearing the waste between the groove and the edge.

Grooving and rabbeting planes are always held and maneuvered with both hands; one hand supplies the thrust and makes sure that the plane is held upright and square, while the other hand pushes sideways so that the plane's fence is held hard up against the workpiece or, as in this instance, the plane is held hard up against a pinned batten fence (see 3-35). A mistake that a good many beginners make when running grooves and rabbets is that they have the blade set coarse, and they fail to hold the fence flat and hard up against the workpiece. What happens is that they finish up with a rough skewed cut that can't be fixed.

The correct procedure is to have the iron set for the very finest of fine skimming cuts, and to pay particular attention throughout the stroke to the relationship between the fence and the workpiece.

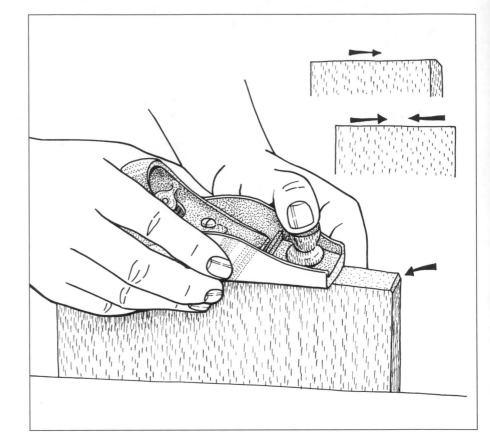

Fig. 3-32. To prevent the grain from splitting off, you can do one of three things: Top, you can clamp a piece of waste on the exit side so that it splits rather than the workpiece. Middle, you can work from side to middle. Bottom, you can use a chisel to cut a slight bevel on the exit side of the stroke.

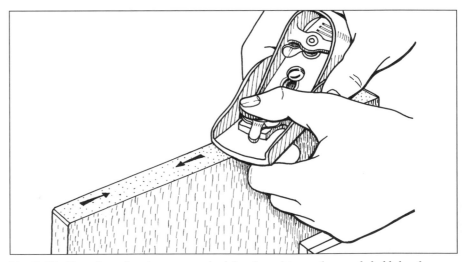

Fig. 3-33. To make a shearing cut, use both hands to drive and control, hold the plane at a skewed angle to the run of the grain, and work from side to center, so as to prevent exit damage.

STANCE AND CONTROL WITH A SHOULDER PLANE

Because shoulder planes are designed for running extremely accurate cuts on short grain and for general trimming, it is important that the body of the plane can "shoot through" without hindrance. The plane is designed to run both on its sole and on its cheeks. In action, the plane is held and maneuvered either in one hand, while the other hand is used either to apply pressure from the side (see 3-36) so as to keep the plane in hard contact with the wood, or to brace the workpiece (see 3-37). Though there is a danger that "running through" a shoulder might result in grain split at the end of the run, this can be mostly avoided by superfine sharpening and honing of the bevel, by having the cutter set to microfineness, and by making sure that the workpiece is held absolutely still. If you have doubts about the "shooting through" approach, then you can run the plane most of the way across the shoulder, and then reverse the plane and come in from the other side.

If you are new to woodworking and are looking to get a shoulder plane, keep in mind that the blade must be set as low as possible—meaning at the lowest possible angle—and that it's best to get a plane that has an adjustable mouth. Note when you disassemble the plane that the cutter is set bevel-side uppermost, and in such a way that it is supported close up to the cutting edge so as to minimize chatter.

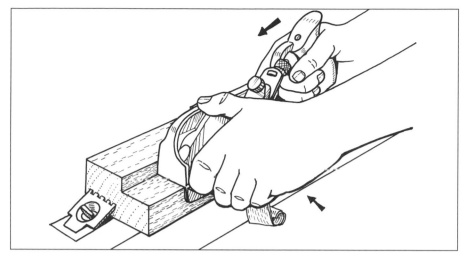

Fig. 3-34. With the workpiece butted against a bench stop or dog so that its edge slightly overhangs the edge of the bench, secure it with a clamp. Work from the far end of the wood and then back up, and continue until the depth stop is reached and the plane ceases to cut. If you are using the fillister plane as shown, then make sure that the cutter is in the normal position, that is, at the middle.

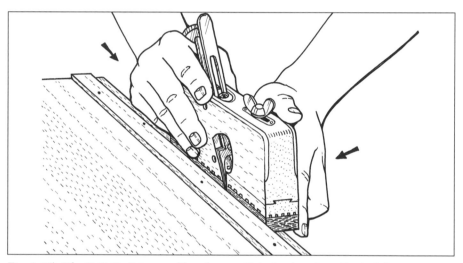

Fig. 3-35. The E.C.E. Primus rabbet plane at 11 inches long is well suited for cutting long through rabbets in hardwood. Note how, with this plane, the mouth can be adjusted by moving the toe.

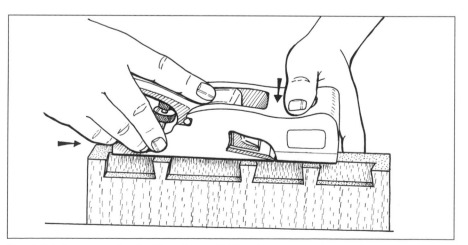

Fig. 3-36. In action, the shoulder plane is held and maneuvered in one hand while the other hand is used to apply pressure. In the situation shown, you would have to be extra careful not to split off the sides of the sockets.

STANCE AND CONTROL WITH A BULLNOSE PLANE

The bullnose plane is a beautifully adaptable tool; it can be used for trimming in all kinds of tight and awkward situations, and for all manner of varied tasks. The one drawback is that although the short nose allows the cutter to remove shavings close up to the stop, the lack of nose also makes the plane a little tricky to use. The problem is that the short nose all too often results in the cutter digging in and doing damage. The best way of controlling the plane is to go for short tight strokes, with your hand applying a small amount of extra pressure to the back of the plane (see 3-38). If you are using the plane to, say, cut a delicate stopped chamfer, then a good approach is to push and guide the plane with one hand, while pressing down on the front of the plane with the two fingers of the other hand. This allows you to make a steady even run while ensuring that the sole of the plane stays in contact with the wood.

STANCE AND CONTROL WITH A ROUTER PLANE

Being a sort of cross between a plane and a spokeshave, the router plane is quite different from all the other planes, in that it is held and used with both hands gripping side knobs. To put it another way, you might say that the hands are set symmetrically one at each side, so that the pressure is entirely equal. Though we have read that the metal router is worked on the pull stroke, and though there is no doubting that it can be used in this way, it is best to work with a steady forward thrusting and skimming action (see 3-39).

Since the working action has to do with pushing down and forward, it is vital that the workpiece be well supported. The easiest control pro-

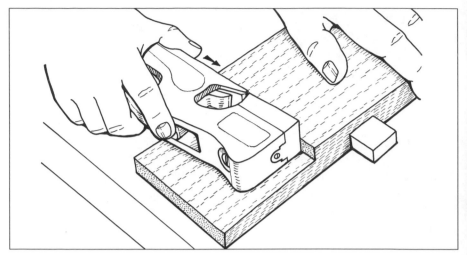

Fig. 3-37. In this instance, the shoulder plane is held and maneuvered with one hand while the other hand is braced against the workpiece. If you have a choice, always go for the shoulder plane that has the lowest cutter angle.

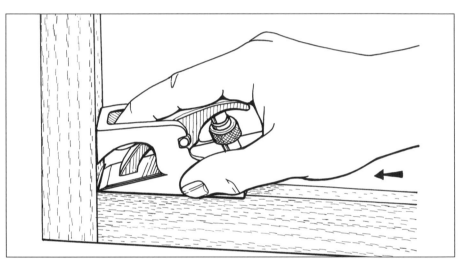

Fig. 3-38. The bullnose chisel plane is used to trim in tight and awkward situations. Work with tight short strokes while applying a small amount of extra pressure to the back of the plane.

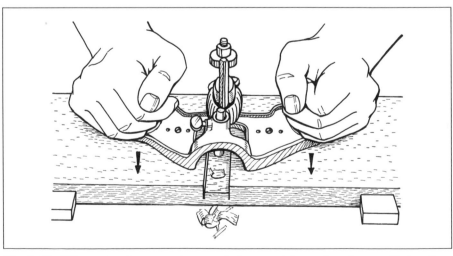

Fig. 3-39. When using the router plane, push down and forward on the two side handles so that the blade travels evenly between the two presawn lines.

cedure is to set the workpiece down flat on the bench so that it is butted hard up against a couple of stops, and then secure it with clamps or a holdfast. The knobs of the router are placed in such a way that maximum pressure and thrust are obtained with minimum effort. The working action is as follows: Grip both knobs, set the router blade down between the sawn lines so that the cutter is fractionally lower than the surface of the wood, and then proceed with a delicate but firm backward and forward stroke. As you cut deeper and deeper, lower the blade by making quarter turns of the adjustment screw.

PLANING TECHNIQUES: STEP-BY-STEP METHODS

So far you have chosen your planes and brought them into good working order. You have sharpened the cutters, oiled the moving parts, and burnished the soles with candle wax; the metal surfaces are gleaming and shining, and the wooden bodies and handles are all aglow. Each and every plane is tuned to perfection. You have chosen your wood with care, the bench setup has been well considered, and you are aching to go.

What else is there to say except that working wood with a well-tuned plane is like no other activity! We wish you well.

The following step-by-step activities will guide you. You might well see that, from one activity to another, we suggest the use of different planes and procedures—sometimes different ones for similar tasks. This is not to say that you should use different planes for like procedures, or that we can't make up our minds as to the best approach, or that we are being contradictory. Instead, we are intentionally presenting you with a broad range of possible alternatives. The idea is

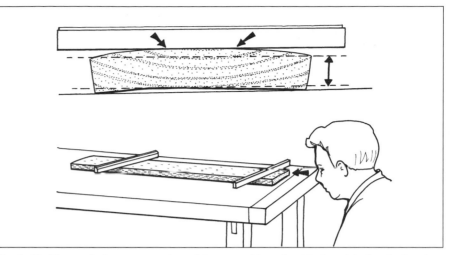

Fig. 3-40. Top, *end view cross section of the cupped board, with the stick clearly showing the high spots. The dotted lines show the usable thickness of the board after it has been planed.* Bottom, *set the rods parallel to each other and bridged across the width of the board. If, when you sight across the sticks, they are level, then it follows that the board is true, not twisted, along its length.*

that you should experiment with the various tools and techniques, and then find your own way—the way that works best for you.

FACING A BOARD WITH A METALLIC JOINTER PLANE

You have a well-seasoned sawn pine board free from knots and splits, but slightly cupped, and you want to plane it so that it has one fair face. The reason why you're using a jointer plane rather than a smoother is beautifully simple: Whereas the short smooth plane tends to fall into the dips and hollows and slices off everything in its path, the longer heavier jointer plane rides over hollows and slices off only the "hills."

1. Start by setting the cupped board down on a level surface so that the convex side is uppermost. Sight down the board to establish whether or not it is also twisted (see 3-40), generally check by eye and feel to identify the high spots, and then mark the high spots with a soft lead pencil.

2. With the high spots on one side clearly marked, set the board down on the bench so that the

high spots are uppermost, and spend time working out how it is going to be held securely. If you have a bench fitted with a tail vise, you can grip the board between a couple of bench stops and the vise; otherwise, an arrangement of a batten nailed to the bench, plus a bench holdfast, works just fine.

3. When you are happy with the way the wood is held down, position the cap iron or chip breaker of the jointer about $1/16$ inch away from the cutter edge, and set the blade for a fine to medium cut. Make sure that the cutting edge is parallel to the mouth.

4. When all is ready and as described, start at the far end of the board and run the jointer in a series of skimming cuts that angle across the width (see 3-41). If the wood cuts up rough, then try planing at a slightly different angle or approach the grain from the opposite direction. When you have sliced off the penciled high spots, tilt the plane over on its side and use the edge of the plane to sight down the board. If need be, pencil in more high spots. Continue skimming, sighting, and marking, until you have

what you consider is a fair surface. Mark the finished side so as to avoid confusion.

THICKNESSING WITH A WOODEN SMOOTHING PLANE

Thicknessing is the procedure of taking a board that has a single fair face and planing the second face so that it is flat and parallel to the first face, and at a thickness to suit. Though ordinarily we would use a jointer plane for planing both faces of a board, as described in the above project, there are many woodworkers who have only a 9-inch smoothing plane. This project is for them.

1. Set the marking gauge to the required thickness, position the gauge fence on the fair side of the board, and run a line around the edges and ends of the board (see 3-42 top).

2. Flip the board over so that it is fair-face down, and butt it at an angle against a stop. Take a metal straightedge like a square, set it across the board, and sight down the board to test how much needs to be planed off (see 3-42 bottom). If you have already planed off the high-center face on the other side of the board, then the second face will probably be dipped or cupped at the center, or you might say high along the edges. Mark all the high spots with a soft lead pencil.

3. Position the board fair-face down on the bench and hard up against the stops, adjust the cutter for the very lightest of skimming cuts, and have a trial pass along the run of the grain. If you fail to make a cut, or the blade scores along one side, make adjustments by winding down the cutter and shifting the lateral lever. The tuning and first-cut procedure usually goes something like this: Make a pass, sight down the sole and wind down the cutter some, make another pass,

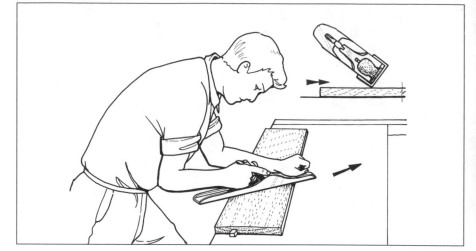

Fig. 3-41. Left, *starting at the far end of the board, make cuts at an angle to the run of the grain.* Right, *tilt the plane on its side and test for high spots by sighting between the edge of the plane and the workpiece.*

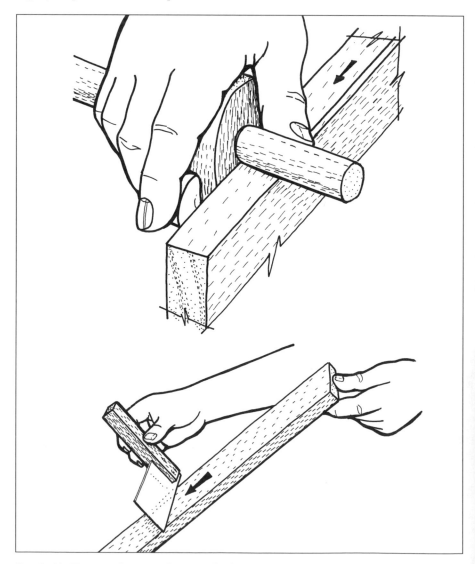

Fig. 3-42. Top, *set the gauge fence on the fair side of the board and score lines around the edges.* Bottom, *to test for general unevenness, hold the square across the workpiece and sight down the board. If all is well, the band of light that shines under the straight edge will be straight and parallel.*

sight down the sole and adjust the lateral lever some, and so on, until you are making the perfect cut.

You have the choice of going for lots of light skimming cuts or for fewer cuts that are heavier and coarser; it's best to go for lots of light cuts. Though whisper-thin cuts might well appear to be a good deal slower than coarse ones, we have a feeling that by the end of the day, thin cuts have gotten the job done faster. And, of course, lighter cuts are not only easier on the muscles, but better yet, they also leave a smoother surface. That said, there are times when you'll be bursting with energy and the wood is so easygoing that you'll enjoy building up a sweat. If in doubt, try both methods and see how it goes.

4. When you have achieved what you consider is a fair cut, start at the far end of the board and plane off the high spots (see 3-43). Work with a slanting shearing action, all the while backing up toward the near end. Skim the edges of the board down to the scribed mark, and then clear the center.

5. To test for flatness, stand so that the board is between you and the main light source, set a metal straightedge across the width of the board, and then look for light showing under the straightedge— like light showing under a door. Or if your prefer, close your eyes and run your hands across the wood.

EDGING WITH A METALLIC JOINTING PLANE

"Jointing" is the term given to the procedure of planing the edge of a board straight, true, and square. Sometimes all you need is a true edge like, for example, the edge of a table, and at other times you need a matched pair of edges on two boards. The procedure of jointing a pair of boards, with a view to gluing them edge to edge, is called edge

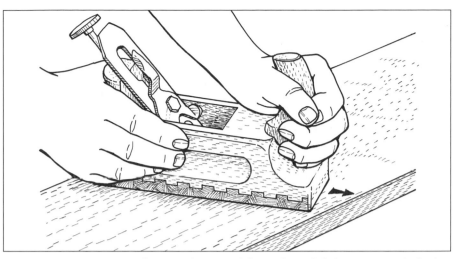

Fig. 3-43. Put pressure on the toe at the start of the stroke and shift pressure to the heel at the finish. Always try to plane in the same direction as the grain as it emerges at the surface. If you have doubts, then see how the grain runs out at the side edge.

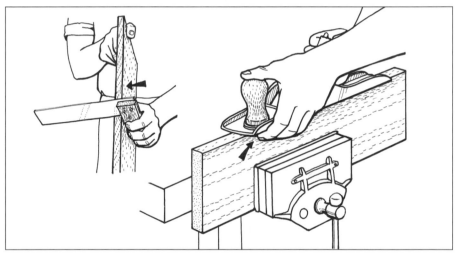

Fig. 3-44. Left, check with a square and mark any high spots with a soft-pencil. Right, apply pressure with your thumb while using your fingers as a fence or guide, and use the other hand to supply forward thrust.

jointing. Some woodworkers prefer to joint the edges of a board before they smooth the side faces; others like to smooth a side face, an edge, the other side, and then the last edge; and yet other woodworkers like to smooth both faces and then finish up with the edges. It doesn't really matter as long as you finish up with a board that is true, square, fair faced, and unbruised. In this project we're going to plane the edges last.

1. When you have achieved a board that is beautifully flat and true on both side faces, then comes

the not-so-easy task of planing the edges straight and square. Since the object of the exercise is to plane off the peaks so that the edge runs true with the deepest hollow, you first need to identify the dips and hollows along the edge. Set the board at eye level and use a square to sight along the edge to be worked (see 3-44 left). Identify all the high spots—or you might say the peaks—and shade them with a soft-lead pencil or chalk.

2. When you have identified the high spots that need to be planed off, secure the board in the jaws of

a muffled vise, and set to work with the jointer plane. In general terms, the procedure is as follows: First plane off the individual peaks, and then finish up with a couple of through strokes. Tune your jointer plane for a fine skimming cut. Set the plane down on the wood and do no more than skim off the pencil marks (see 3-44 right). Take another sighting, mark the high spots, and then plane off the pencil marks as before.

3. Let's say that at the first sighting you identified two peaks, and that you have repeatedly marked and planed as described. You will have noticed that as the planing proceeds and the peaks get lower, so the two shavings have gotten longer. Continue the procedure until the two shavings more or less add up to the full length of the board being worked.

4. When the point is reached where the two peaks have disappeared and the shaving is more or less continuous, get ready for the final pass. Take another sighting, test the edge for squareness, rest the toe of the plane on the work, and then take a series of through passes until you achieve a single continuous unbroken shaving that is as wide as the edge and as long as the board. Finally, if another sighting shows that the edge is true, level along its length and at right angles to the side faces, and the job is done.

SHEARING END GRAIN WITH A MODERN WOODEN BLOCK PLANE

Though the block plane is, for the most part, the perfect tool for working end grain on hardwood, it sometimes happens that when the plane is being used straight on, the grain tears out and the end of the board presents a surface that is rough and pitted. When this happens, no amount of sanding will

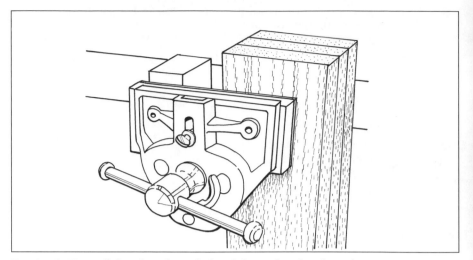

Fig. 3-45. Have all three boards stacked and clamped so that the end grain is uppermost. Note how the waste piece at the other side of the vise screw relieves "twist" pressure on the mechanism.

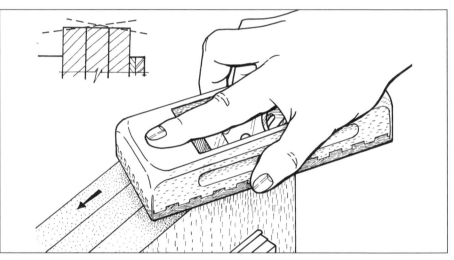

Fig. 3-46. Right, hold the plane at an angle and work with a forward shearing stroke. Top left, the combined thickness of the three layers helps to ensure that the plane and the resultant cut are level and true.

prepare the surface for gluing, varnishing, or whatever. The good news is that the whole problem can easily be avoided by using a technique known as "end-grain shearing" or "shear-planing." Shearing is particularly useful when you are looking to make a presentation piece, that is, when the end grain is on show and you have to make a batch of similar pieces.

1. Having tuned your block plane to perfection, set the three pieces of wood to be worked in the vise, with the end-grain face uppermost. You should end up with a sort of sandwich with the workpiece at the center and with all three pieces showing end grain (see 3-45).

2. Use a soft-lead pencil to mark across the whole end-grain face and use a set square to test for squareness.

3. Set the block plane fair and square on the surface to be worked, just as if you were going to plane it straight on, and then turn the plane slightly at a skewed angle (see 3-46). Grip the plane firmly and make the first shearing pass. If you are using the plane at the correct shearing angle, the wood will

be left so smooth and burnished that it will not need sanding.

4. The pencil marks will show you whether or not you are holding the sole of the plane square with the board. If the plane is square, all the pencil will be skimmed off; if not, then the remaining pencil marks will show you just how much the plane is being tilted out of true.

SHOOTING END GRAIN WITH A METALLIC SMOOTHING PLANE

The shooting board is a jig used in conjunction with a plane for squaring up the edges and ends of small component parts. The ordinary shooting board is no more than two pieces of board set together like a step so that the top step supports the workpiece and the lower step acts as a run for the plane. This design has a flaw, however, because only a small part of the plane's cutting edge is used. The "oblique" or "ramp" shooting board, on the other hand, is especially useful, because not only does the full width of the plane blade get used, but better still, the design also results in the plane making a shearing or slicing cut.

You can use just about any plane for shooting, as long as it's big enough for the task at hand, and as long as the sides or cheeks of the plane are ground at perfect right angles to the sole.

1. Having made your "ramp" shooting board (see the projects at the end of this chapter), tuned your bench plane for the very finest cut, and burnished the sides and sole with candle wax, clamp the shooting board in the bench vise, and generally get ready for the action (see 3-47). If you are a raw beginner, then it's a good idea at this stage to play around with the plane and the shooting board so that you can see how the whole setup works.

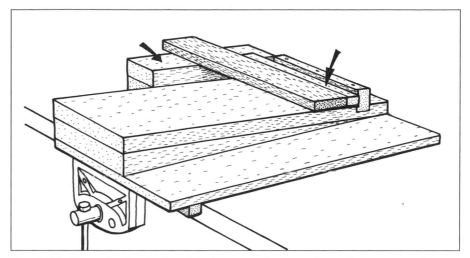

Fig. 3-47. Clamp the shooting board in the vise and arrange the workpiece across the board and butt it hard up against the stop. Note how there is a waste piece between the stop and the workpiece, and another piece to ensure that the workpiece is held level.

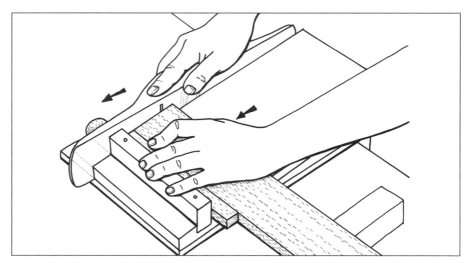

Fig. 3-48. Having waxed both the plane and the board, set the plane on its side, clench the workpiece against the stop, and run the plane down the ramp.

2. Set a scrap of waste wood against the stop and butt the workpiece hard up against the waste so that the workpiece and the waste both overhang by no more than about $^1/_{32}$ inch. Then set the plane down on its side so that the blade is facing toward the workpiece.

3. With one hand gripping and holding the workpiece against the stop, and with the other hand holding the plane hard up against the side of the ramp, slide the plane backward and forward in its track (see 3-48). You will see that the angle of the wood on its ramp plus the weight of the plane in its run results in the shavings peeling away to reveal an end-grain surface that is burnished and nigh on finished. Continue the process, easing the wood out slightly, until you achieve a perfectly square-cut and burnished end-grain surface.

CUTTING A CROSS-GRAIN RABBET WITH A METALLIC FILLISTER RABBET PLANE

The procedure for cutting a rabbet that goes across the run of the grain is much the same as cutting a rabbet that goes with the grain, apart from the fact that the spur or scribe comes into play. If you look at the side of your metal plane, you will see that the spur is set between the cutter and the depth gauge in such a way that it is in line with and in front of the blade. On both the Stanley and Record planes, the spur is in the shape of a three-spoked wheel that is set in a four-spoked recess. The idea is that you have one of the three spurs set in the "down" position when you are working across the grain (see 3-49). The function of the spur—sometimes also called a cutter or nicker —is to prepare the way for the blade by slicing across the fibers of the grain.

1. Let's say that you want to cut a rabbet across the end of a board at 1-inch wide and $^1/_2$-inch deep. Having first tuned your rabbet fillister so that it takes the very finest cut, undo the little setscrew and turn the spur around in its recess so that the cutter is in the "down" position. Make sure that the flat face of the spur is flush with the side of the plane so that the spur bevel is looking toward the underside of the sole. Take a ruler and very carefully set the depth gauge to $^1/_2$ inch and the fence to 1 inch (see 3-50). Don't forget to burnish the sole, fence, and depth gauge with some candle wax.

2. Clamp the board to the bench so that the end to be rabbeted is overhanging by about 1 inch. Clamp a small piece of waste to the far side of the board so that the plane can run off without splitting the grain.

3. Hold the plane level so that the fence is pressed hard up against the wood, and take an even, well-considered stroke (see 3-51). As when cutting a groove, start on the far side of the board, on the farthest end of the cut, and work backward. Don't rush or try to force the pace; just make sure that every stroke

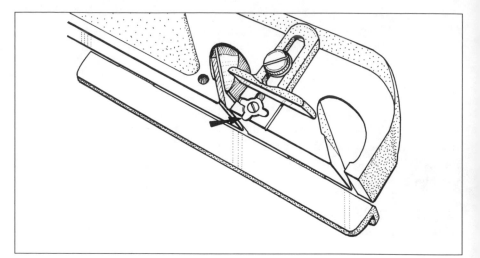

Fig. 3-49. Set one or other of the three spur arms in the "down" position. (Note that when you sharpen the spur—it's done in a few moments with a fine file—make sure that you work over a clean bench; if you drop the spur on the floor, then it's as good as lost.)

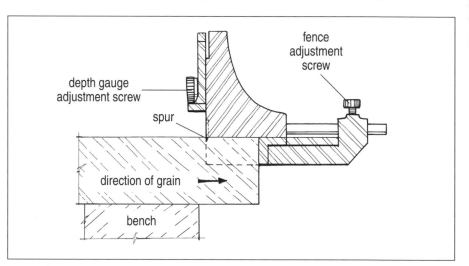

Fig. 3-50. A cross-section view through the fillister plane and the workpiece showing the position of the fence and the depth stop, and the way the spur cuts across the run of the grain.

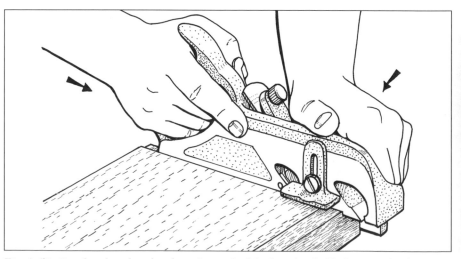

Fig. 3-51. One hand pushes the plane forward while the other holds down-and-side pressure so that the fence is in contact.

counts. Continue pushing the fence hard up against the wood and taking cuts, until the shavings stop coming and the depth stop reaches the surface of the wood.

CUTTING A DEEP DADO OR HOUSING WITH A COMBINATION PLANE

You are working with a $1^3/4$-inch-thick board, you want to cut a dado that is $1/2$ inch wide and $3/4$ inch deep, and you are using one of the common plough or combination-type planes.

1. Remove the fence and the depth stop from the plane and fit the $1/2$-inch-wide cutter. Set both scribes or spurs in the down position (see 3-52), and burnish the sole and the side of the main stock runner and the sliding section runner.

2. Mark the position of the dado or housing, clamp the board to the bench, and clamp or pin a $1/8$-inch-thick strip of hardboard to one side of the dado to act as a guide. While you are at it, clamp a $1^3/4$-inch-thick scrap to the far side of the workpiece to prevent exit splintering (see 3-53). Use a marking gauge to set out the depth of the dado on the waste piece. (An alternative to using a waste piece to prevent exit splintering is to use a chisel to slice off the edge of the board to the depth of the dado.)

3. Set the plane to the far side of the board and drag it toward you so that the two scribes make their marks. Then make repeated passes until the depth of the dado is such that the piece of hardboard begins to get in the way (see 3-54), say, when the groove is down to about $1/4$ inch. At this point, remove the guide strip.

4. Continue making passes until the cutter reaches its natural depth, and the shoulder on the mainstock begins to act as a depth stop. At this point, wind the cutter down a frac-

tion so that it projects beyond the bottom of the runners, and continue planing as before. If you have a close-up look at the plane in action, you will see that the body of the plane is now resting on the surface in such a way that the bottom of the runners are out of contact with the bottom of the dado channel.

5. Continue making a couple of passes, winding down the cutter a whisker, then taking another couple of passes, winding down slightly more until the $3/4$-inch depth has been reached.

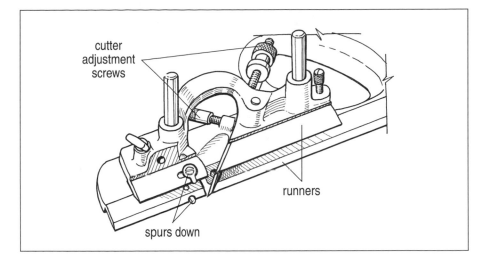

Fig. 3-52. Fit the $1/2$-inch-wide chisel cutter and set both spurs in the "down" position. Make sure that the runners are set flush with the sides of the cutter.

cutter adjustment screws

runners

spurs down

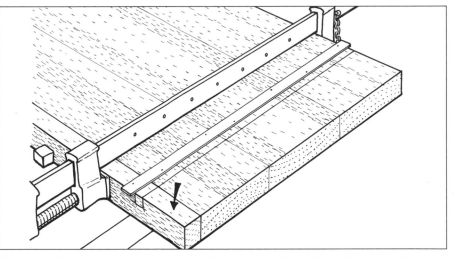

Fig. 3-53. The setup for cutting a deep dado or housing. Note the hardboard guide strip and the waste piece clamped to the far side that prevents exit splintering.

WORKING WITH A CLASSIC WOODEN "SPRUNG" MOLDING PLANE

Traditional wooden molding planes can be divided into two groups: those made to the Continental pattern, which are designed to be held and used upright, and those made to the English and American pattern, which are designed to be held and used at an angle. The English and American planes that are used at an angle are described as being "sprung." Sprung planes are much easier to use because the canted

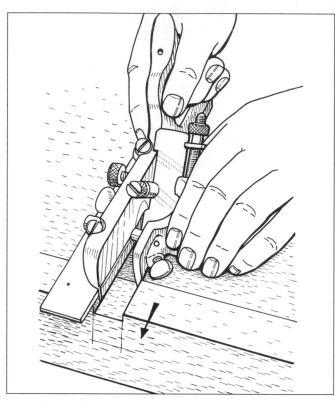

Fig. 3-54. Make repeated passes until the body of the plane touches the hardboard strip; then remove the strip and gradually lower the blade.

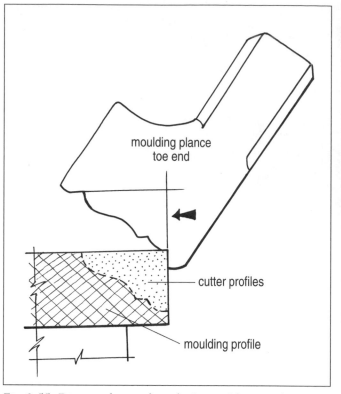

Fig. 3-55. Diagram showing how the "spring" lines on the toe of the molding plane relate to the cutter and the side of the workpiece.

angle requires only downward pressure, whereas the Continental upright planes require the user to apply pressure both from above and into the side.

Make sure when you have chosen your plane that it is of the English or American "sprung" type. If you look closely, you will see that most sprung planes have "spring" lines marked on their toes (see 3-55). (The fun thing about old woodworking tools is that there are no absolutes. For example, the moment we say that a certain molding plane can be identified by "spring" lines on the toe, we see that just occasionally some planes have the marks on their heels, and others have no marks at all!)

1. Secure the workpiece face up on the bench so that about 1 inch of the left-hand edge overhangs. Hold the plane at a canted angle and set it down on the corner or arris of the board nearest to you so that the fence is in contact with the wood.

2. Check that the guide lines on the toe of the plane are correctly aligned, and then grip the toe, push against the heel, and walk the plane from one end of the board to the other (see 3-56).

3. Continue starting at the end of the board nearest you, setting the plane down on the workpiece, checking the angle of spring, and walking the plane along the length of the wood until the molding is complete, or

until the stop at the top of the plane's profile rides on the surface of the wood.

CUTTING A DOUBLE-BEAD RETURN WITH A STANLEY 45 MULTIPLANE

To our way of thinking, of all the fancy do-it-all planes, the old Stanley 45 multi- or combination plane is one of the most exciting to use. This plane has all the qualities that make planing such good fun: It is beautifully engineered, it has lots of moving parts that need to be carefully tuned, it has a fine range of cutters, it does a good job, and it never lets us down. If you are a beginner to woodworking, then you can take it from us, the Stanley 45 is worth a whole pile of routers!

Though the Stanley 45 went out of production sometime at the beginning of the 1960s, they are still available secondhand. If you can't find a Stanley, then try for the look-a-like old Record 405.

The double-bead return is a feature that is used to decorate the edges of tabletops, box lids, and the like. The double bead is in fact made up from three bead cuts: an edge-return bead with offset fillets, a face bead that runs in with the edge bead, and a center bead with a quirk at each side (see 3-57 top). In this project we are using a $3/4$-inch-thick board.

1. Having selected a ³/₄-inch-thick board that is smooth grained and free from knots and splits, have a good long look and choose the best edge. Make sure that the face and edge to be worked are completely free from knots.

2. Fit the Stanley 45 with the ¹/₂-inch bead cutter—number 27—and set the plane up to make a simple bead on the front edge of the board. Set the plane's fence so that the bead is slightly offset from center, which will make the quirk on the face side of the board the smaller of the two (3-57).

SPECIAL TIP: By "setting the plane up" we mean all the little tuning procedures that are necessary with a complex plane of this type. In this instance, you fit the cutter in the slot, slide the middle section over so that the cutter is contained, and then make fine adjustments until the sole runners or skates are perfectly aligned with the sides of the cutter. You then adjust the fence, the depth stop, and the depth of the cutter.

If you are a raw beginner to woodworking or you are the proud new owner of a Stanley 45, then it's a good idea, prior to this project, to practice the various planing procedures on some scrap wood. Generally play around with the cutters and the setting of the fence until you know what's what.

3. With the board secured edge-up in the vise, start by planing a single bead along the edge of the board (see 3-58).

4. When you are happy with the shape and depth of the first bead, set the board best face uppermost on the bench so that the beaded edge is overhanging, and then ad-

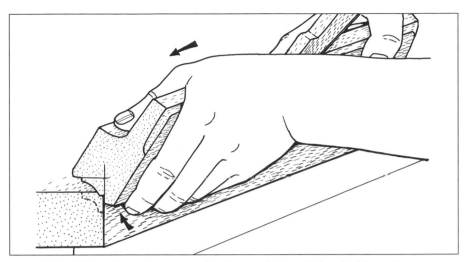

Fig. 3-56. Hold, push, and maneuver the plane with the right hand while at the same time pushing in from the side and guiding with the left hand. Use the fingers of the left hand as a brace and fence.

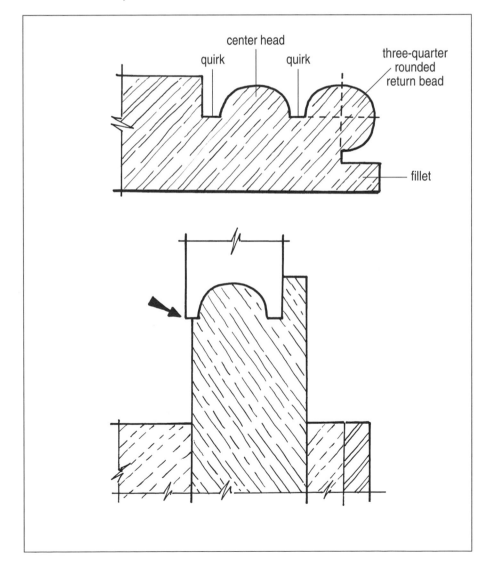

Fig. 3-57. Top, the completed double-bead return in cross section. Bottom, start by cutting the edge bead; note how the bead is slightly offset so that the quirk on the face side of the board is the smaller of the two—almost a half-quirk.

just the fence and run a second bead on the face of the board. If you have done it correctly, the two beads, one on the edge and the other on the face, will have linked up to make the decorative feature known as a "three-quarter rounded return bead" (see 3-59 left).

5. To make the third bead cut, adjust the fence so that the plane's left-hand runner is located in the surface bead's quirk or trench, and then run the second face bead alongside the first (see 3-59 right).

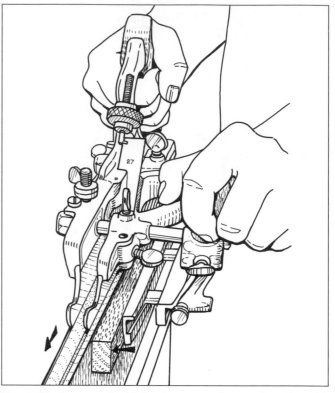

Fig. 3-58. Cutting a double bead return with a Stanley 45. Hold and push the main stock handle with the right hand while using the left hand to push the fence hard up against the workpiece.

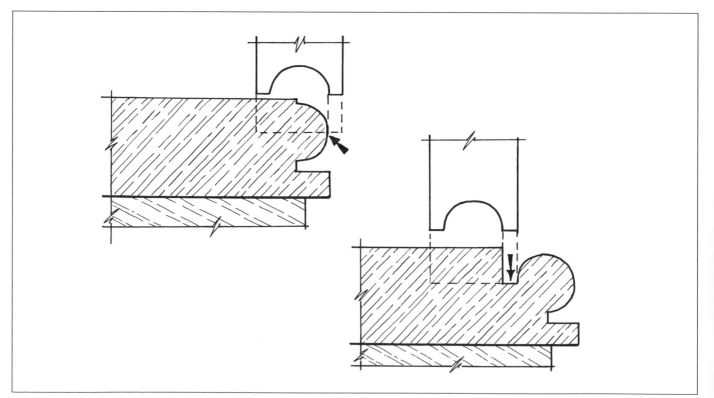

Fig. 3-59. Left, *secure the wood flat on the bench and set the cutter and fence for completing the return bead. Make sure that the cutter doesn't bite into the side of the first bead.* Right, *set the cutter in the quirk, adjust the fence accordingly, and then run the third bead as already described.*

Planing Project 1: Ramp Shooting Board

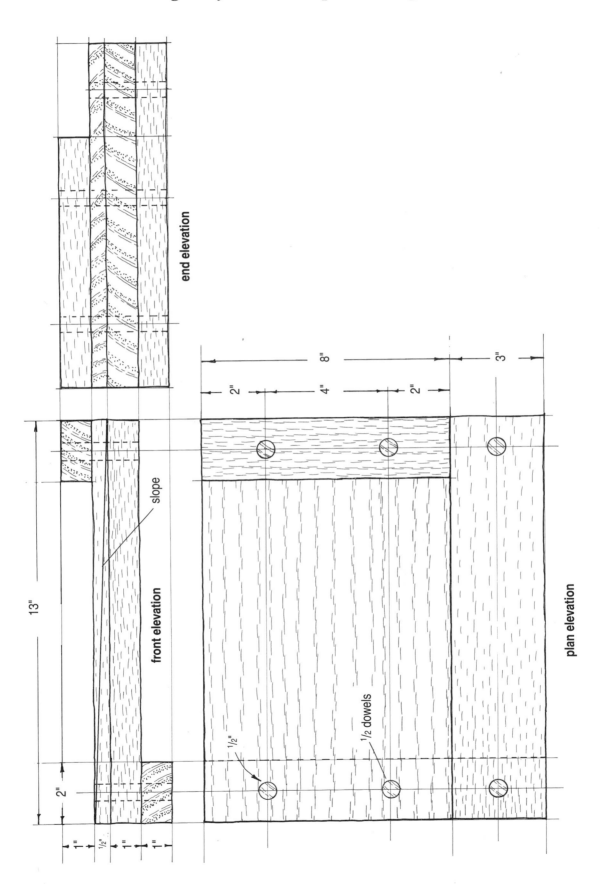

end elevation

front elevation

plan elevation

slope

13"

2"

1" ½" 1" 1"

8"

2" 4" 2"

3"

½"

½ dowels

Planning Project 2: Miter Shooting Board

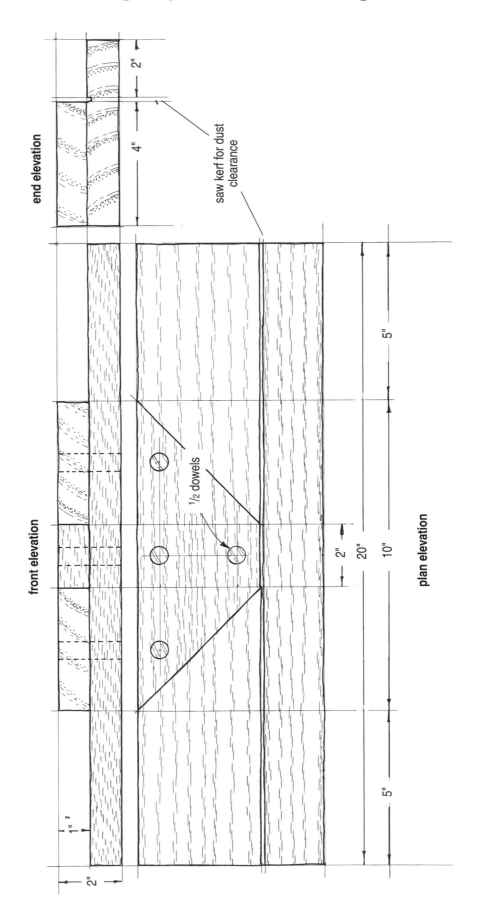

end elevation

2"

4"

saw kerf for dust clearance

front elevation

½ dowels

2"

20"

10"

5"

5"

1"

2"

plan elevation

CHAPTER FOUR

Joinery and Cabinet Chisels

The chisel, in many ways, is one of the most basic woodworking tools. It is no more than a rectangular-section steel blade that is ground to a sharp edge at one end and fitted into a wooden handle at the other. It is also one of the oldest tools, one of the most widely used, and one of the most multifarious. Although there are no more than three traditional basic chisel forms—meaning the way the blade is set in the handle; when it comes to specific usage and the shape of the handle and blade, there are dozens and dozens of chisels with many and varied shapes, sizes, and uses. And we're not talking about woodcarving or woodturning chisels and gouges here (they are dealt with in another section), we're just referring to the chisels that are used for joinery, framing, cabinetmaking, and general woodworking. And just in case you are a beginner and wondering, a chisel makes a straight mark when the blade is stabbed down into wood. A gouge, on the other hand, makes a mark shaped more like a "C" or a "U."

WHAT CHISEL TO USE AND WHEN
Woodworkers need a good range of chisels to suit the various operations involved in general everyday woodworking (see 4-1). There are many kinds to choose from, everything from massive chisels for heaving, chopping, and framing, to delicate chisels for paring and skimming. There are chisels designed for carpenters, for cabinetmakers, for framers, and so on.

Because chisels are potentially very dangerous, it is always a good idea to keep them covered when not in use to protect you from accidental contact and to protect the fragile beveled edges from damage.

If you are a beginner, the following listing will help you define your needs.

FIRMER CHISEL
The firmer, sometimes known simply as a "wood chisel," is designed for general-purpose everyday work. With its fairly heavy parallel-sided blade, its shoulder and bolster, and its tang fitting for the handle, it is strong enough to withstand being driven with a mallet. Some older heavier firmers are fitted with socket handles. They are commonly obtainable in sizes from 1/8 inch to 2 inches.

AMERICAN FRAMING CHISEL
Though these chisels are usually termed "American," they are described in English nineteenth-century catalogs simply as "heavy-duty socket framing chisels." This chisel, which has a heavily beveled or canted back and a heavy socketed handle bound with an iron hoop, is the perfect tool for heavy framing tasks like cutting deep mortises, and for general heavy carpentry.

ENGLISH BRUZZ CHISEL
Known variously over the last three hundred years or so as a "buzz iron," a "wheel maker's buzzet," a "burze," and one or two other local names besides, the bruzz is a massive angle-sectioned chisel that is designed specifically for cleaning out the corners of deep holes. Currently, in the United States at least, the chisel is most commonly known as a socket corner chisel.

The in-cannel bevel—the bevel on the inside of the angle—ensures that the sides of the chisel are able to cut clean and flush with the inside face of a hole. The short stubby iron-bound handle is set into the socketed blade so that the tool can be heavily pounded without fear of the handle splitting. If you have in mind to frame up an oak house or build your own boat, then this is the tool to use.

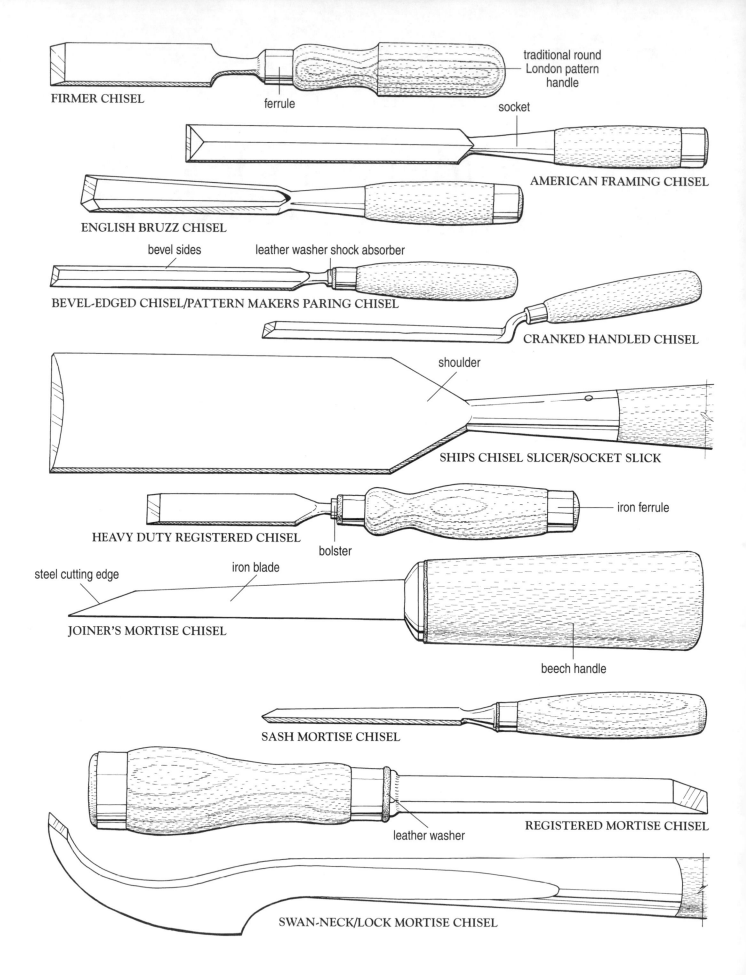

FIRMER CHISEL

traditional round
London pattern
handle

ferrule

socket

AMERICAN FRAMING CHISEL

ENGLISH BRUZZ CHISEL

bevel sides

leather washer shock absorber

BEVEL-EDGED CHISEL/PATTERN MAKERS PARING CHISEL

CRANKED HANDLED CHISEL

shoulder

SHIPS CHISEL SLICER/SOCKET SLICK

iron ferrule

HEAVY DUTY REGISTERED CHISEL

bolster

steel cutting edge

iron blade

JOINER'S MORTISE CHISEL

beech handle

SASH MORTISE CHISEL

REGISTERED MORTISE CHISEL

leather washer

SWAN-NECK/LOCK MORTISE CHISEL

Fig. 4-1. Joinery and cabinet chisels.

SHIPS CHISEL

Known in England as a "slicer," and in the USA as a "socket slick," this chisel has a blade up to about 3 inches wide and 10 to 24 inches long and a shaped pommel handle socketed into the blade. This tool was traditionally used to clean up large rough-hewn surfaces that needed to be smooth, but not so smooth that they needed to be planed. The handle is kinked out at a slight angle from the blade to allow space between the user's fingers and the workpiece.

BEVEL-EDGED CHISEL

Sometimes called a "bevel-edged paring chisel," or "patternmaker's paring chisel," this chisel has a long thin blade about 9 inches long and a handle that is fitted onto a shouldered and bolstered tang. There is sometimes a leather washer between the bolster and the handle. There are two types of bevel-edged chisels: the "beveled firmer" that is used for cleaning up dovetails and the like, and the "beveled paring chisel" with a longer blade at about 8 to 9 inches that is used specifically for cleaning up long dado housing grooves and channels. Sometimes the handles of paring chisels are cranked or offset at an angle of about 15 degrees—like a trowel—to make it easier to clean out a long deep channel.

EXTRA HEAVY CHISEL

Usually known as a "heavy duty registered chisel," this tool is designed for really rough treatment. The extra thick blade is thick and flat in cross section; a leather washer between the bolster and the handle acts as a shock absorber, and steel ferrules on both ends of the handle prevent the wood from splitting. These chisels are used primarily for general chopping and mortising. As to why they are known as "registered" chisels, the most likely explanation has something to do with some long-expired copyright or registered patent.

JOINER'S MORTISE CHISEL

As the name suggests, this chisel is used for cutting mortises. The traditional joiner's mortise is a rather curious tool with a massively thick blade, an oval bolster, a huge oval handle, and a thick leather washer fitted between the bolster and the handle. Though the handle looks to be almost too heavy and cumbersome to hold, it is in fact the ideal tool for heavy work.

If you are looking to buy one of these chisels secondhand, there are two points that you have to watch out for. First, it's important that the handle is free from splits, and second, the larger oval bolster must be bigger than the tang hole. Or put another way, if the bolster looks as if it is being forced into the tang hole, then it's likely that the handle is about to split.

SASH MORTISE CHISEL

A smaller version of the joiner's mortise chisel, the sash mortise is used for lighter work and for working with softwood. While it gets used for much the same work as the joiner's mortise, the handle shape has evolved quite differently, with most handles being turned and fitted with a ferrule just above the bolster. Currently, one or two American catalogs describe these chisels as "deep-mortise chisels."

REGISTERED MORTISE CHISEL

Although in just about every respect, the registered mortise chisel is the same as the traditional firmer, the handle of the registered type has an iron ferrule at each end. This chisel is designed to be used in conjunction with a mallet.

SWAN-NECK LOCK MORTISE CHISEL

The swan-neck mortise chisel, sometimes also known as a "heavy lock" mortise, is a tool designed specifically for cutting deep mortises in the edges of doors. An old woodworker told us that he called it a "swan-necked bank" mortise chisel because he used it for setting the locks in bank doors. He said that the curved blade allowed him to lever out the waste from the bottom of deep mortise slots when he was cutting through the ends of tenoned rails.

THE ANATOMY OF A CHISEL

Although it seems true that a chisel is no more than a wooden handle and a steel blade with one or two little bits and pieces in between, one look through a catalog will soon confirm that there are any number of blade and handle types, in all manner of sizes and shapes. If you aim to be a woodworker par excellence, then it is important that you can confidently determine why and when you should use one combination of blade and handle rather than another. And just in case you don't like the "par excellence" bit, the fact of the matter is that the correct tool gets the job done swifter and with less aggravation then the wrong tool.

HANDLE

Though in essence there are two types of traditional wooden handles—those for a tang fitting and those for sockets (see 4-2)—we see from one old catalog that, in the joinery section alone, there are at least sixteen variations on the two-type theme. The difference has to do not only with traditional shape and function, but also with quality. So, for example, while you may well have decided that your chisel needs an octagonal section handle with a ferrule and a tang hole, you also have the choice between a "best," a "plain," and a "common".

In most cases this choice has to do with the degree or the complexity of the turning, the type of wood used, and whether the ferrule is made from steel or brass. So, for example, while the "common" handle might be made from beech and fitted with a black steel ferrule, and the "plain" handle made of beech and have a bright steel ferrule, the "best" handle will most certainly be made from boxwood or perhaps rosewood, with the ferrule made from brass. All that said, the listings in modern catalogs are a bit on the slender side, but you can still obtain a wide choice of handles.

FERRULE

A ferrule is a ring or hoop that is driven onto or clenched around the handle. There are two types: those fitted at the tang hole end of the handle and those fitted around the butt or pommel end (see 4-3 top). The function of the tang hole ferrule is to stop the handle from splitting when the chisel is pushed or struck. It's plain to see (and this is born out by some inferior chisels) that a tanged chisel handle without a ferrule is likely to split. The socketed handle needs no ferrule, because the handle is being pushed into a socket, rather than the other way around.

The iron hoop or ring at the butt end of the handle tells you that the handle is designed to be struck with a mallet. The idea is, of course, that the ring will reduce the chance of the handle mushrooming or splitting. You must avoid so-called bargain chisels that have ferrules made from thin tinplate; they are liable to swiftly rust and split.

LEATHER SHOCK ABSORBER

There are two ways that a layer of leather is used to absorb shock. On the tanged chisel, a leather washer is set between the handle and the

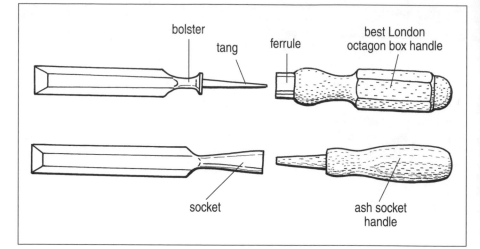

Fig. 4-2. Top, *a tanged chisel*. Bottom, *a socketed chisel*.

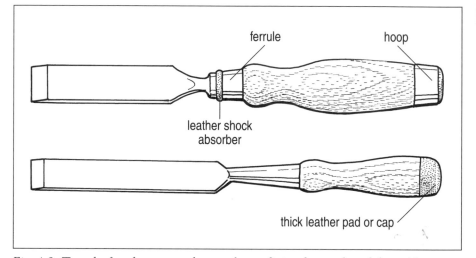

Fig. 4-3. Top, *the ferrule prevents the tang from splitting the wood, and the end hoop prevents the end of the handle from mushrooming when it is struck with a mallet.* Bottom, *with the socket chisel, the leather washer shock absorber is built into the top end of the handle.*

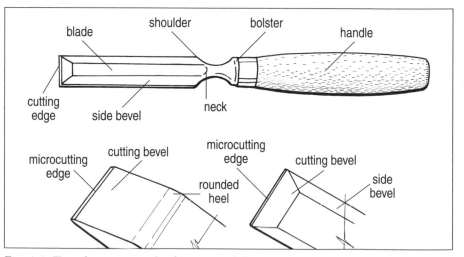

Fig. 4-4. Top, *the anatomy of a classic tanged chisel.* Bottom left, *the bevel and microcutting edge on a mortise blade.* Bottom right, *the bevels and microcutting edge on a bevel-sided blade.*

bolster, whereas on the socketed chisel the washer—actually more a thick layer or pad—is fitted at the butt or pommel end of the handle (see 4-3). Either way, the leather dulls the jarring action of severe mallet blows, and so makes the activity more comfortable.

TANG
The tang is the pointed bit of metal that runs from the bolster up into the handle. Traditionally, chisels have evolved into two distinct types: those with a tang and those with a socket (see 4-2).

SOCKET
On a socketed chisel (see 4-2), the handle fits into rather than over the metal part that goes to make the blade. It's something of a mystery why some chisels have evolved with tangs and others with sockets. However, if we were to take two identical-sized mortise chisels, one with a tang and the other with a socket, and use them both to destruction by repeated severe blows with a mallet, we believe that the handle on the socketed chisel would last longer. Overall, we would say that socketed chisels are more suited to heavy work than those fitted with tangs. That said, it's interesting to note that traditionally some of the biggest chisels are fitted with tangs.

BOLSTER
The bolster is the splayed part at the top of the blade (see 4-4 top) where the metal spreads to meet the handle. The bolster not only prevents the tang from running into and splitting the handle, it also spreads the load and acts as a cushion or reinforcing pad. If you are offered a bargain tool that lacks a bolster, back off and keep on looking.

SHOULDER AND NECK
The shoulder is the curved part of the chisel that runs from the side edge to the neck before the metal spreads to become the bolster.

BLADE
The blade is the usable part of the chisel, that is, the part that runs from the cutting edge to the shoulder. The length of the blade indicates the quality and the life expectancy of the tool.

SIDE BEVEL
The side bevel is the edge or side of the blade on bevel-edged chisels that runs down from the shoulder to the cutting edge. The beveled edge allows you to work into the tightest corners without binding the edge of the chisel.

CUTTING BEVEL
The cutting bevel, sometimes termed the "ground bevel" or "cannel" or even the "bezel," is the part of the blade that is ground at an angle to form the primary cutting angle (see 4-4 bottom left). Unlike a plane iron or even a carving gouge, the cutting bevel on a good many chisels—especially mortise chisels—is ground so that the heel is slightly rounded. The function of the curved heel is to ensure that the blade easily slides in and out of deep mortise holes.

CUTTING EDGE
The cutting edge is the secondary angle or micro-angle at which the cutting bevel is honed (see 4-4 bottom right). If you hold a perfectly ground and honed chisel up to the light, you will see that the cutting edge reveals itself as a thin strip of reflected light that runs across the width of the beveled angle.

THE CUTTING ACTION OF A CHISEL
Basically, there are only two ways that a chisel can be handled. It can be supported in one hand and pushed with the other, or it can be held in one hand and struck with a mallet. It is nevertheless a tool that has an infinite number of nuances or shades of use. For example, the chisel can be held flat on the workpiece, with the bevel uppermost, and then used as a fine paring or skimming tool. It can be used with a slicing skewed action on end grain. It can be held upright like a dagger and stabbed down. It can be used like a miniplane. It can be used in conjunction with a mallet to cut a mortise, and so on.

Although it is a combination of the size and shape of the chisel and the angle of the bevel, that to some extent decides the character of the cut, the ultimate success of the cutting action depends on how specifically the chisel approaches the grain. Let's say you have a chisel and a board (see 4-5).

- You can set the blade flat down on the face of the board and slice along in the direction of the grain, in which case the wood will offer minimum resistance and the grain will roll up as a controlled ribbon or shaving (see 4-5 top left).
- You can set the blade flat down on the face of the board and slice across the run of the grain, in which case the wood will offer medium resistance and the grain will come up as broken slivers (see 4-5 top right).
- You can set the blade upright and at right angles to the grain and stab directly down into the face of the board, in which case the wood will offer some resistance, but nevertheless the cutting edge will slice across the run of the grain causing the

wood to crumble (see 4-5 middle left).

- You can align the blade with the grain and stab directly down into the face of the board, in which case the wood will offer minimum resistance and the cutting edge will force its way between the fibers of the grain, splitting the wood (see 4-5 middle right).
- You can run the blade directly into the end grain, in which case the blade will follow the grain and split the wood (see 4-5 bottom).

To sum up, you always need to control the cutting action of the chisel either by judiciously approaching the grain, or by setting in stop-cuts to limit the length of the cut.

SHARPENING THE CHISEL

Using a good sharp chisel is a truly delightful experience. To feel the chisel as it shears, slices, chops, and skims through the wood is one of the highs of woodworking. On the other hand, a blunt dull chisel is a horror!

If you are a nervous beginner wondering whether or not you are going to make the grade, take it from us—at least half the battle is won if you keep your chisels razor-sharp.

The sharpening procedure is managed in three sequential stages:

- Grinding on a slow wheel or bench grinder.
- Honing or whetting on an oil- or waterstone.
- Stropping on a leather.

Although the whole procedure of achieving a keen edge is generally and correctly described as "sharpening," there is some confusion because woodworkers tend to use the term "sharpening" to describe only the procedure of using

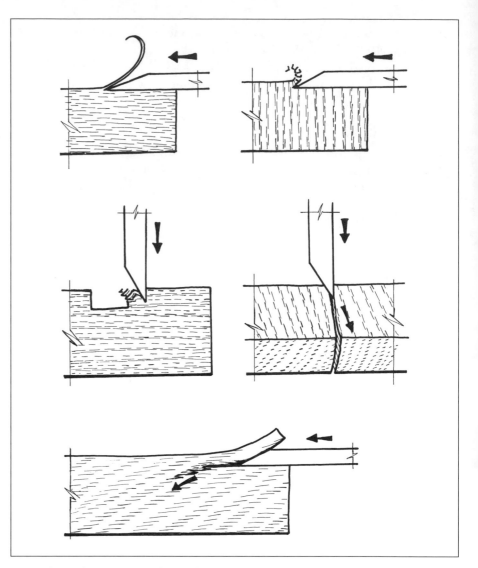

Fig. 4-5. Top left, *cutting in line with the run of the grain results in a fine curled shaving.* Top right, *cutting directly across the grain results in a crumbled roll of waste.* Middle left, *stabbing directly down across the grain results in the waste splitting and crumbling away.* Middle right, *stabbing directly down along the run of the grain results in the wood splitting.* Bottom, *making a low cut into the end grain results in the wood splitting.*

the oilstone. To avoid confusion, we use the term "whetting" or "honing" for the oilstone stage.

GRINDING

Using the grinding stone is the first stage in the sharpening procedure. Here you square off the leading edge if it is in any way damaged, and then establish the angle of the primary bevel. Though in theory the angle at which the bevel is ground should vary according to

the job at hand and the type and character of the wood being used, most woodworkers opt for having one use-for-everything mortise chisel that is ground with a middle-of-the-road angle between 25 and 30 degrees. You also have to be aware that although a chisel with a fine-angled bevel will cut more swiftly than a large-angled one, the trade-off is that the fine bevel will be more fragile. That said, the various types of chisels do most certainly need to be ground at different angles. For example, the bevel-edged paring chisel needs an angle of about 20 degrees, the firmer needs an angle of about 25 degrees, and the heavy mortise-type chisel needs an angle of about 30 degrees (see 4-6). We use the word "about" advisedly, because it doesn't matter too much if the angles run a little over- or under-size.

The Grinding Procedure. While we would always advocate using a traditional low-speed, large-wheel grindstone, as described in the chapter on planing, we understand that a good many woodworkers have no option but to use a high-speed bench grinder. This section is for them. So if you want to know how to use your large stone, look to the planing chapter.

High-speed bench grinders are potentially very dangerous; they need to be used with extreme care. Having first studied the instructions for your particular machine, the primary safety rules are as follows:

- Never work on the side face of the wheel.
- Always wear goggles or better still a full face mask.
- Never try to sharpen a naked-tanged chisel, that is, one with the handle removed.
- Never work with a wheel that you suspect might be chipped or cracked or otherwise damaged.
- Never let your children stand alongside you as you use the grinder, and never leave them alone in the workshop while the machine is switched on.

Although we think it's a great idea for you to be working alongside your kids, you do have to be aware of all the dangers. To our way of thinking, a grinder is a big problem, simply because it spits out splinters of metal, and it is at eye level with the kids!

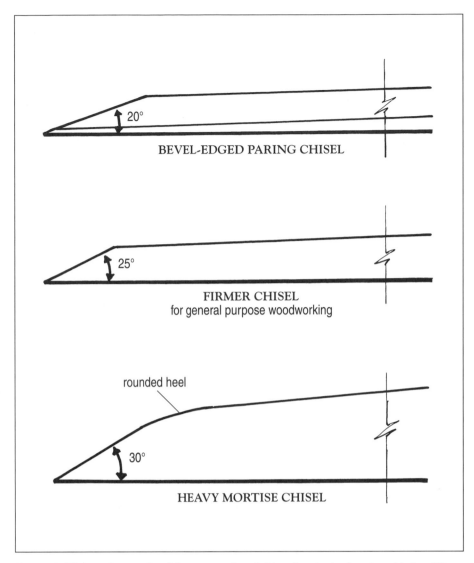

Fig. 4-6. *The grinding angle of the primary bevel:* Top, *bevel-edged paring chisel at 20 degrees.* Middle, *firmer—general-purpose chisel at 25 degrees.* Bottom, *heavy-duty mortise chisel at 30 degrees.*

Grinding the Edge Square. Start by giving your chisel a good going over. Make sure that the handle is sound, the blade is free from cracks and bends, and so on. Study the cutting edge and assess whether or not you need to grind it back. If it is dull edged but free from chips, then you can skip the grinding stage.

Okay, let's say that your chisel is slightly chipped. With the grinder fitted with a fine-grit wheel, adjust the tool rest so that it is horizontal at 3 o'clock, then set the chisel down flat on the tool rest so that the bevel is uppermost (see 4-7 top). With a can of water nearby, and not forgetting to move the chisel from side to side to avoid overheating and bluing the steel, gently advance the chisel and grind it back to a good edge. It's all pretty easy, and all over in a few seconds. The secret is to be swift, keep moving, and on no account let the

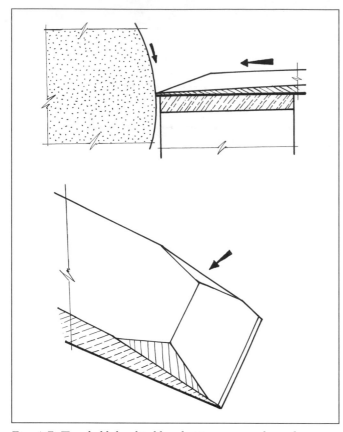

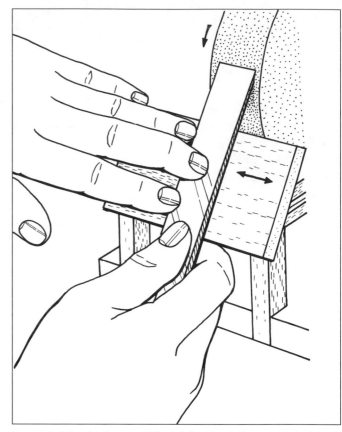

Fig. 4-7. Top, *hold the chisel bevel uppermost on the tool rest so that the sides of the chisel are at right angles to the face of the stone; advance the chisel to make contact with the stone, and then move it from side to side. Bottom, grinding the corners off stops the tool from binding when it is being used in tight areas.*

Fig. 4-8. *Use the fingers of the left hand to lightly press the bevel on the wheel while using the forefinger of the right hand held against the rest to act as a guide and stop.*

chisel overheat. If you do feel that the chisel is getting too hot, then all you do is dunk, or you might say quench, it in water to cool it down.

Chisels are sometimes ground off at the corners so that they can be used in tight corners without the edges of the chisel damaging the joint (see 4-7 bottom).

Grinding the Primary Bevel. When you have achieved what you consider is a good square edge on your chisel, adjust the tool rest so that it is at the appropriate angle—let's say 20 degreess; then turn the chisel over so that the bevel is in contact with the wheel, and rerun the procedure in much the same way as already described. The only difference this time around is that you advance the chisel, lightly press the bevel on the wheel, and then come off and quench the chisel in the water all in a few moments (see 4-8). Continue to advance, press, quench, and inspect until you have a bevel of the correct length and angle. The metal always needs to be cool and wet. So if at any time the water dries off, back off and give the tool another dip.

Whereas most chisels are simply ground to the appropriate angle, which maintains a sharp angle at the end or heel of the bevel, the large mortise chisel needs to be ground so that the heel is rounded (see 4-6). The idea is that when the chisel is being used to a cut a deep mortise, the rounded heel allows the chisel to slide and roll smoothly in and out of the hole.

HONING OR WHETTING
Having ground the bevel to a good primary angle, start by arranging your fine and medium stones so that they are at a comfortable height. As to the question of whether to use an oil- or a waterstone, it makes no difference as long as the stone is flat and clean.

The sequence of events is as follows:
- Backing off to remove the burr left by grinding.
- Polishing the primary bevel.
- Honing the secondary or microbevel.
- Final backing off.

The procedure is simple; all you do is set the back of the chisel down on the finest stone, press it down hard with your fingers, and then polish the back (see 4-9). Next, move to the medium stone, turn the chisel over so that the full width and depth of the bevel are in contact with the stone, and polish away the rough surface left by the grinder (see 4-10). Now, having returned to the finest stone, start with the bevel in full contact, then raise the handle a few degrees so a bead of oil or water oozes out from in front of the bevel, and then drag the tool firmly back toward you (see 4-11). Come to a standstill just before you get to the end of the stone, and lift the chisel clear. On no account should you run the chisel off the end of the stone or flip the chisel up in a curve. Rerun the dragging until you achieve the desired microangle, and until you can feel a slight burr at the back of the blade. If you are at all unhappy about trying to hold the blade at certain angles, there are a number of foolproof bevel guides on the market that make the job easy. Because of their size, mortise chisels occasionally need to have the sides rubbed before taking off the burr (see 4-12). Finally, turn the blade over so that the back of the blade is down flat on the stone, and back off to remove the fine burr. As to the question of just how sharp is sharp, you can skip the traditional blood-and-guts methods of trying to shave your arm or pare your thumbnail; simply make a paring cut on a piece of end-grain waste, and see how you do.

STROPPING

Stropping is the final stage in the sharpening sequence. A strop is a thick piece of leather fixed to a board so that the rough side of the leather is outermost. Prior to

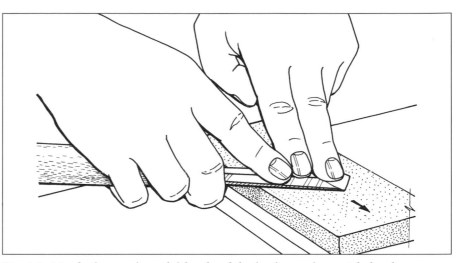

Fig. 4-9. Use the fingers of your left hand and the forefinger of your right hand to press the blade down onto the surface of the fine stone. The whole width of the back of the blade needs to be in contact.

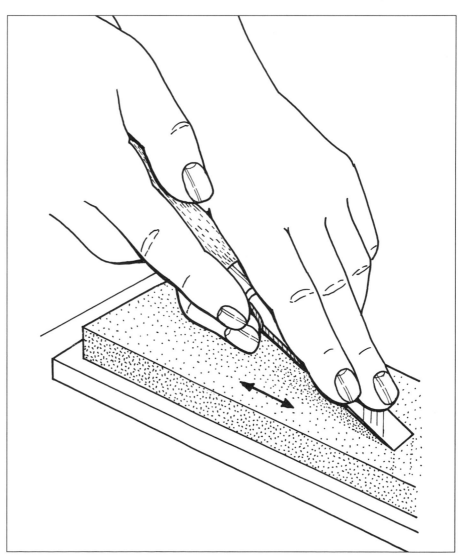

Fig. 4-10. Hook the thumb of your left hand around the chisel while using the fingers to keep the bevel in contact with the medium stone.

stropping, the leather is charged or dressed with a mix of light oil and a fine abrasive powder such as emery. Stropping won't do anything at all for a blunt chisel, but it will make a sharp edge even sharper. The procedure can be done in a moment. All you do is dribble a small amount of fine oil on the charged strop, and then drag and stroke the chisel bevel across the strop in much the same way as already described for honing (see 4-13). And just as with honing, you finish up by turning the chisel blade over so that the bevel is uppermost, and buffing off the back to remove the fine burr.

TUNING A CHISEL

Though you can't tune a chisel in the same way as you can a plane because there aren't any moving parts to oil and maintain, you can tune a chisel in the sense of making sure that the tool is in good condition.

It's a good idea to start every new project by tuning your chisels. The tuning procedure not only gets the chisels into shape, but it also may help you to think through the potential problems of the task ahead.

With each and every chisel, check the handle and make sure that it isn't loose or split, sight down the blade to make sure that it's straight, look at the bevel and make sure that it hasn't been chipped, and occasionally clean the handle with turpentine, and wipe the blade over with oil. Don't make a big thing of the tuning, but get into the habit of doing it at the start of a project. And of course, if a chisel is chipped, then you will need to fix it.

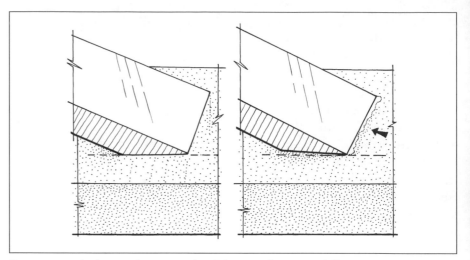

Fig. 4-11. Left, *first set the primary bevel down so that it is in full contact.* Right, *raise the handle slightly until you see a thin bead of oil or water ooze out in front of the cutting edge.*

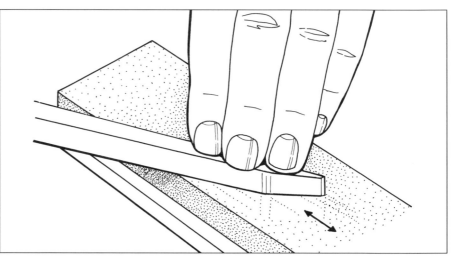

Fig. 4-12. *To maintain the flat sides of the mortise chisel, rub them side-face down on the stone. Do this before you take off the burr.*

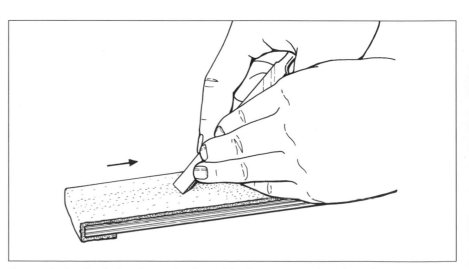

Fig. 4-13. *Stroke the bevel over the charged leather strop; work with a delicate dragging action.*

STANCE AND CONTROL

While it is generally accepted that woodworking is made up of the three primary skills of working with the plane, working with the saw, and working with the chisel, it sometimes happens that the essential skill of using the chisel is overlooked, or you might say overshadowed, by the other two. As we see it, beginners tend to think that whereas planing and sawing skills need to be learned and practiced, chiseling skills can somehow or other be picked up along the way. The problem is that their failure to get good at using the chisel all too often results in the project going awry.

In joinery and cabinetmaking, chisel work can be broken down into three activities: horizontal push paring or skimming, vertical thrust or stab paring, and vertical mortising with a mallet. The good news is that all we are talking about here is stance and grip, or you might say power and control. You have to be standing well braced and balanced, you have to be holding the chisel so that your hands are both guiding and providing the push, you have to be using your energy to best effect, and you must be ready to pull back if your feel the chisel running out of control.

HORIZONTAL PARING

With the workpiece held either down flat on the bench or in the vise, take the chisel in your right hand so that the handle is butted into your palm and stretch the index finger so that it is extended in line with the blade. Cradle the blade with the left hand so that the thumb is on top of the blade, and the fingers are on the underside. Line the chisel up so that there is a straight line that runs from your elbow to the cutting edge. Now stand so that your feet are apart and

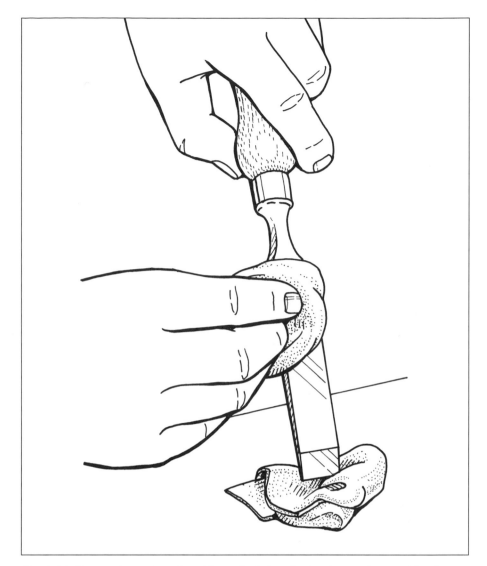

Fig. 4-14. Protect the cutting edge with a soft cloth and wipe the metal over with a fine-grade oil; something like sewing machine oil is just fine.

well braced, and rock the top of your body slightly so that the blade does the cutting (see 4-15). There are occasions—for example, when you are working in small tight areas across end grain—when you will need to hold the chisel low down on the blade. In this situation, you hold and pivot the blade with your left-hand thumb, which presses the chisel down flat on the workpiece, while you advance and swivel the blade with the fingers of the right hand. The swiveling shearing action is controlled by the index finger of the right hand being extended along the edge of the

blade. The interesting thing about this approach is that the handle doesn't really get to be held, and the chisel is used more as a small bullnose plane (see 4-16).

No doubt you will adjust the stance somewhat to suit your own particular way of working. The important thing is that while your shoulder is behind the thrust, your body needs to be well balanced so that you are totally in control and ready to brake and pull back if you feel the cutting edge running away. The secret of good paring has to do with taking the finest of skimming cuts, while putting a lot of power behind the stroke. If you think of yourself as a big powerful machine that is rocking backward and forward so that the chisel is always horizontal, then you won't go far wrong.

VERTICAL PARING

With the workpiece well supported on the bench, take up the chisel as if it were a dagger—with your fingers wrapped around the handle and your thumb pressing down on the handle. Now, rest your left-hand knuckles down on the workpiece so that the side of the index finger is acting like a stop or fence, and then set the cutting edge of the chisel down on the mark with the back of the blade pressed against your index finger. Bring your left thumb around to grip the blade. Stand with your feet apart and well braced, with your right shoulder over the top of the chisel handle. Lastly, lock your upper body so that your arm and the chisel more or less make a triangle (see 4-17). The cut is now made by rocking your body so that the line of force runs from your shoulder and down through the chisel. Once again, the best way of working is to think of your body as a slow-moving super-powerful machine that is going to make an inexorable stroke.

VERTICAL MORTISING WITH A MALLET

The first thing to say here is that a hand-cut mortise does not need to be partially bored prior to working with a chisel. Clearing the waste with a drill is not, as some beginners suspect, a swift and easy short-cut method of getting the job done, but rather just the opposite; it's a surefire way of making a mistake. What usually happens is that the holes get to be drilled too big so that they go over the line, and then

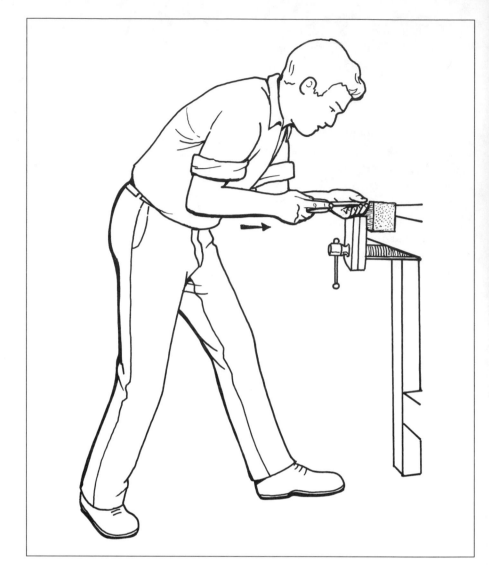

Fig. 4-15. Position yourself so that a straight line runs from your elbow to the tool.

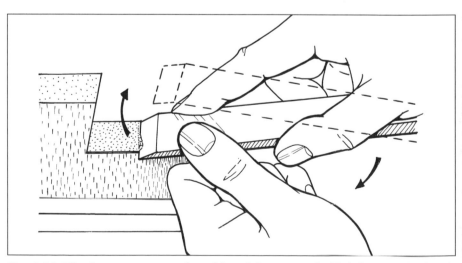

Fig. 4-16. The shearing action is achieved by tightly pivoting the blade between the thumb and forefinger of the left hand while swiveling the tool from side to side.

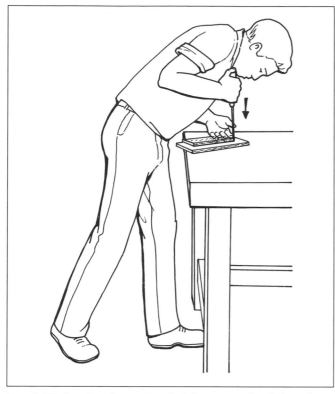

Fig. 4-17. *Stand with your feet slightly apart and well braced, and work with a tight stabbing action so that your shoulder is more or less touching the thumb of the stabbing hand.*

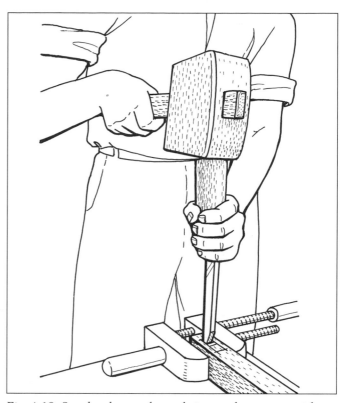

Fig. 4-18. *Stand end-on to the workpiece so that you can sight down the length of the mortise. Hold the chisel upright and give the handle a smart tap with the mallet. Note the use of a clamp to help prevent the wood from splitting down the length of the grain.*

once drilled, the holes keep directing the chisel off course.

With the workpiece clearly marked out, support it on the workbench so that it's going to stay put. You might try, if possible, to site the workpiece directly over one of the bench legs so as to lessen vibration. If you are working a large deep mortise with a heavy chisel, grasp the chisel firmly in your left hand and use the fingers of your right hand to place the cutting edge on the mark. Take the mallet in your right hand, brace your legs, take a sighting to make sure that the chisel is vertical, and then give the chisel a smart, not too heavy, blow (see 4-18). Continue repeatedly setting the chisel on the mark and giving the handle a sharp tap until the job is done.

If you are working with a much lighter chisel, and you want to place the cutting edge precisely on the mark, take the chisel in your left hand and turn it around so that you are looking at the back of the blade. Now hold it low down on the blade, with your fingers spread and hooked and with your thumb pushing hard against the back (see 4-19). If you have got it right, you will be able to hold the tool in a perfectly balanced grip, and in such a way that you can slide your fingers down the blade and precisely set the cutting edge on the mark.

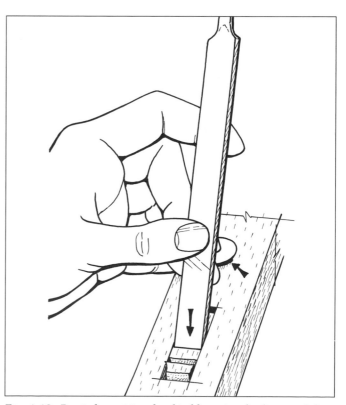

Fig. 4-19. *Precisely position the chisel by using the fingers of the left hand to pivot against the workpiece.*

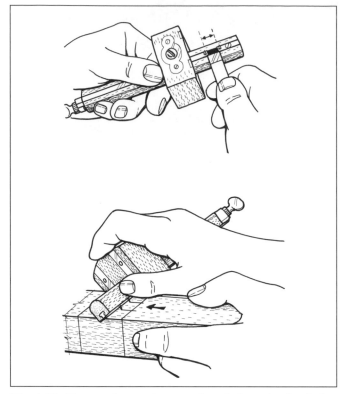

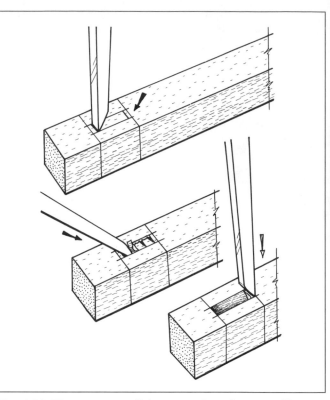

Fig. 4-20. Top, *set the mortise gauge directly from the chisel; the points must be the same distance apart as the width of the chisel.* Bottom, *use the gauge to scribe parallel lines between the squared lines.*

Fig. 4-21. Top, *start a small distance in from the squared lines.* Middle, *clear away the resultant chips of waste and repeat the procedure.* Bottom, *make well-placed plunge cuts to pare the waste back to the squared lines.*

CHISELING TECHNIQUES

You have searched through the tool catalogs, explored the old tool shops and flea markets, and persuaded your aged grandfather to let you dip into his toolbox; now, at long last, you have got yourself a really good selection of top quality chisels. You have polished the handles with beeswax, and you have ground, whetted, and stropped each and every chisel to razor-sharp perfection. The workbench has been swept clean, the projects have been planed, the wood has been marked out, and you are ready to go. Let the following step-by-step activities and procedures be your guide.

As with sawing, planing, and all the rest, you will most certainly see that from one activity to another, we suggest alternative procedures—sometimes almost contradictory ones. The idea is that you should experiment with the various tools and techniques, and then go for the way that works best for you.

CHOPPING OUT A BLIND MORTISE WITH A SASH MORTISE CHISEL

Of all the woodworking activities, beginners are always attracted by the notion of cutting really crisp joints. In truth, jointmaking is central to good woodworking, and

of course, central to becoming a skilled jointmaker is learning how to cut a swift mortise.

1. Having first used the plane to smooth the wood and the square to run guide lines around the wood, take the mortise gauge and set it directly from your chisel (see 4-20 top).

2. Use the gauge to run parallel lines on one face of the wood (see 4-20 bottom).

3. With the guide lines in place, clamp the wood down flat on the bench so that the mortise can be approached from end and side. Starting a small way in from the end of the marked box, turn the chisel around so that the bevel is looking toward the middle of the mortise, set the chisel down square and vertical, and give the handle a well-placed blow (see 4-21 top).

4. Having made the first cut, repeat the procedure at $1/4$-inch intervals, stopping short about $1/8$-inch clear of the end of the marked box. Use the chisel to clear out all the chips (see 4-21 middle).

5. Repeat the procedure again and again until the mortise is at the required depth. Clean the bottom of the recess so that the corners are free from debris. When this point is reached, take the chisel and make a single hand-driven plunge to cut the dubbed over ends back to the mark (see 4-21 bottom).

PARING A HALF-LAP WITH A BEVEL-EDGED CHISEL

Short channels, short dadoes, and half-laps are all best cut and cleared with a beveling chisel using the technique that we've always known as "horizontal peak paring."

1. With the wood well secured to the bench, and with sides of the lap having been set in with saw cuts that run down to the gauged line, take a paring chisel that is about two-thirds the width of the lap, and pare in from one side. Tip the chisel alternately left and right as you go so that you are left with a peak of waste (see 4-22). When you have pared in from one side, turn the wood around and rerun the procedure from the other side.

2. Having pared in from both sides so that you are left with a little roof-shaped peak of waste, take the chisel, tilt the handle down somewhat, and then pare the peak down to the gauge line. Repeat this procedure on both sides until the waste looks to be a flat pyramid shape (see 4-23 top).

3. Finally, hold the chisel absolutely horizontal and skim the peak off the waste first from one side and then from the other (see 4-23 bottom). When you are within a whisker of the mark, make smaller and smaller passes until you split the gauge line.

CHOPPING A DEEP THROUGH MORTISE WITH A CLASSIC OVAL CHISEL

Of all the chiseling skills, cutting a deep mortise must rate pretty high on the "most feared" scale. Okay, so it is something of a make-or-break joint, but there is no magical method; it is no more or less than a skill that needs to be worked at.

There are just about as many ways of cutting a deep mortise as there are woodworkers. Most woodworkers, however, would agree you

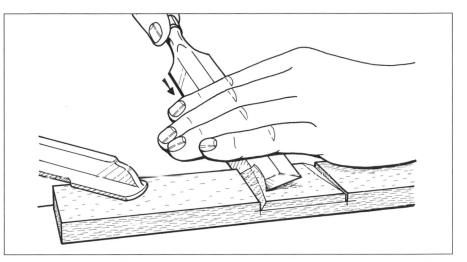

Fig. 4-22. Repeatedly skim to the left and the right to leave a central peak of waste. Skim down to the middle of the gauged line on one side of the wood, and then turn the wood around and rerun the procedure from the other side.

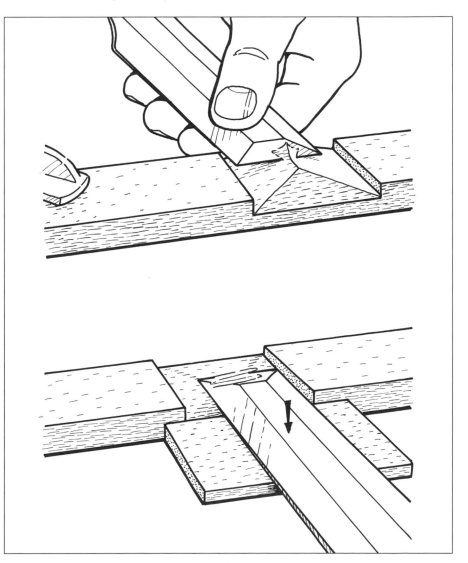

Fig. 4-23. Top, with chisel handle held at a slightly cocked or low angle, pare away the waste first from one side and then from the other. If you are doing it right, you will be left with a little pyramid of waste. Bottom, hold the chisel absolutely level so that the back of the blade is pushed hard down on the block of supporting waste, and remove the waste with a series of slightly skewed skimming cuts.

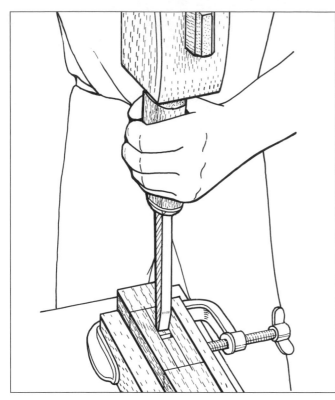

Fig. 4-24. *Having cut a V-shaped chip from the center of the marked box, make a succession of carefully placed deeper and deeper cuts to finish up just short of the squared line. Note the use of the C-clamp to help prevent the wood from splitting.*

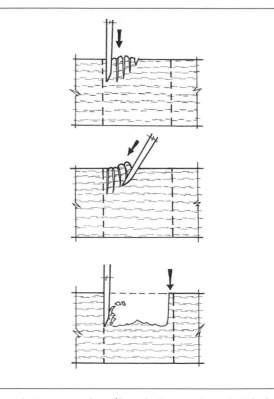

Fig. 4-25. Top, *stop about* $^1/_8$ *inch short of the end of the box. Middle,* angle the chisel so as to chip out the waste. Bottom, *use a vertical plunge cut to pare the bruised edges back to the squared lines.*

should leave cleaning up the ends until the chips have been levered out. The reason is that if you clean up the ends and then start levering, the chances are the levering will do damage to the finished end.

1. Having set the joint out on both faces of the wood with a square and mortise gauge, set the wood down on the bench so that it is directly over one of the legs and secure with a clamp or holdfast.

2. Start by cutting a small V-shaped chip from the center of the marked box with the chisel. Turn the chisel around so that the bevel is looking at the center and you are looking at the back of the blade (see 4-24), and then make a succession of deeper and deeper cuts or drives toward the end of the box nearest you. Stop about $^1/_8$ inch short of the end of the box (see 4-25 top).

3. With the cuts running deeper and deeper, angle the chisel down and dig out the chips of waste (see 4-25 middle). When the waste is out of the way, turn the chisel around so that the bevel is looking at the center and clear the other end of the mortise in precisely the same way as already described. Having cleared about half the depth of the mortise and trimmed the ends, set the back of the blade carefully on the mark and finish off with a single cut (see 4-25 bottom). Do this on both ends.

4. Finally, when you are happy with the mortise on one side, turn the wood over and repeat the procedure in from the other side.

MAKING A THROUGH DOVETAIL WITH A BEVEL-EDGED CHISEL

If you want to make dovetails, then you have got to bone up on your chisel paring skills. As to whether you cut the pins before the tails, or the other way around, there are points in favor of both ways of working. However, for this project, we're going to cut the tails first. (For details on sawing, see "Step-by-Step Methods" in chapter 2).

The best approach to working dovetails is a somewhat contentious issue. Although we always advise beginners to try a whole range of methods, and then to go for the one that works, there are times when a certain technique is quite simply wrong. For example, some woodworkers advocate undercutting the end grain at the bottom of the sockets; they say that it results in a close fit. Okay, so undercutting does most certainly leave the finished joint looking good and tight, but the sad fact is that the undercut results in a weak internal fit. The problem is that the hidden cavity within the joint gets filled with either glue or fresh air. This tech-

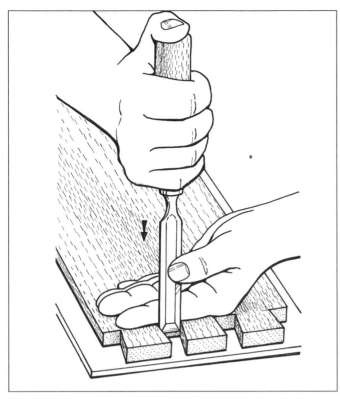

Fig. 4-26. *Position and steady the blade with one hand while at the same time thrusting downward with the other hand. Pare about halfway through the thickness of the wood, and then repeat the procedure from the other side.*

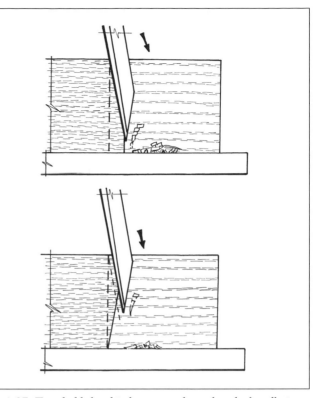

Fig. 4-27. Top, *hold the chisel at an angle so that the handle is canted away from the end, and then pare back to the gauged line.* Bottom, *when you have pared back to the gauged line, turn the board over and repeat the sequence on the other side. Go at it nice and slowly so that the last cut splits the gauged line.*

nique is wrong because the integrity of the joint is sacrificed for the sake of cosmetic good looks!

1. Having first set out the shape of the tails, start by shading in the areas of waste that need to be cut away. This done, set the wood in the vise and use a fine dovetail saw to cut down to the waste side of the drawn line. Do this on the tail angle at each side of every tail. While the saw is at hand, turn the wood around in the vise so that the side edge is uppermost, and clear the half-pin waste. Cut about $1/8$ inch to the waste side of the gauged line.

2. When you have achieved all the cuts, take the coping saw and remove the small area of waste between the tails by sliding the coping saw blade down the kerf and swiftly joggling and rotating the blade so as to run a cut about $1/8$ inch to the waste side of the gauged line.

3. With the bulk of the waste out of the way, set the board down flat on the bench so that it is resting on a piece of waste, and use the widest possible bevel-edged chisel to pare down to the gauged line. The procedure is as follows: Hold the chisel in a stabbing grip, set the blade down on the edge of the waste, tilt the handle back so that the blade is running forward slightly, and then pare down half the waste (see 4-26). Continue making paring cuts and backing up until you split the

gauge line with the last cut (see 4-27). When you have finished paring from one side, then all you do is turn the board over and rerun the paring from the other side (see 4-27 bottom).

4. By the time you have angled back the chisel and pared in from both sides of the board, you should be left with a little peak of waste between each of the pins. Set the board upright in the vise so that the gauge line is horizontal, and then hold the chisel horizontal and pare across until the end-grain face of the socket is flat and square (see 4-28).

5. To cut the pins, use a marking knife to transfer the shape of the tails to the end of the pins' board, use the square to run the lines down to the gauged line, and then saw and pare away the waste as already described.

CUTTING A LAP OR DRAWER DOVETAIL WITH A BEVEL-EDGED CHISEL

The lap or drawer dovetail, sometimes also called the secret dovetail or even the half-blind dovetail, is as the name suggests, the joint most commonly used in drawer making to connect the front of the drawer to the sides. The terms "lap," "half-blind," and "secret" refer to the way one member laps over another in such a way that

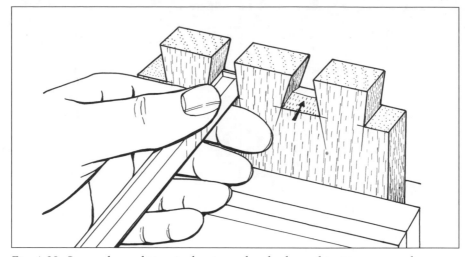

Fig. 4-28. *Secure the workpiece in the vise so that the dovetail is uppermost, and use a series of finer and finer skimming cuts to pare the waste back to the gauged line. Do NOT (as some woodworkers advise) undercut the waste.*

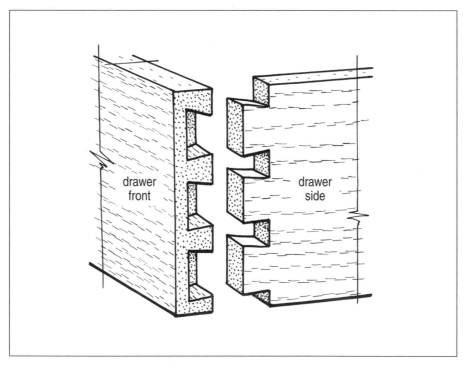

drawer front

drawer side

Fig. 4-29. *Lap dovetails are good joint used in drawer making; the pins and sockets are lapped so that the joint can't be seen on the front face.*

the pins and sockets are hidden or blind on one face (see 4-29).

1. The front board of the drawer should be 1 inch thick and the sides $^5/_8$ inch thick. Set out the joint in the way described for the common through dovetail. The preliminary setup uses the same gauge setting on the front ends as for the sides of the drawer. It's important that the gauge line on the inside face of the drawer front match the thickness of the drawer side (see 4-30). Shade in the areas so that there is no doubting the waste that needs to be cut away.

2. Having marked the "tails" out on the inside face of the $^3/_4$-inch-thick drawer side and shaded in the waste, secure the board upright in the vise, and clear the waste with the saw, as already described for the through dovetail. Rerun this procedure on the other drawer side.

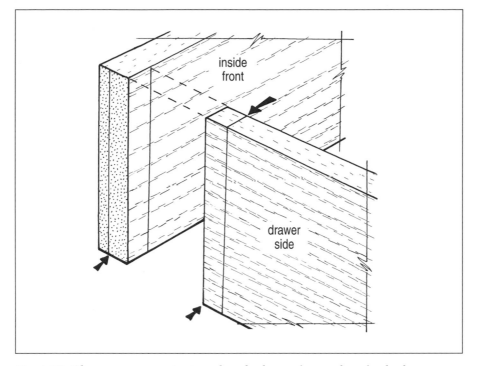

Fig. 4-30. The same gauge setting is used on the drawer front ends as for the drawer sides. The gauge line on the inside of the drawer front relates to the thickness of the drawer side.

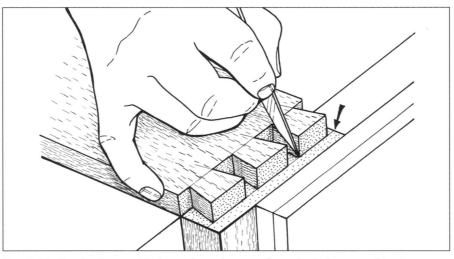

Fig. 4-31. Set the drawer side dovetails on the gauge line, check that everything is square, and then mark through using the tails as a template.

3. With the tails cut and worked on the drawer sides, set the drawer front upright in the vise. Make sure that the alignment with the gauged line is exact, and then, using the tails as a pattern, scribe the shape of the pins (see 4-31). Do this on both ends of the drawer front.

Make sure that the inside face is looking toward the bench.

4. With the shape of the pins set out on the ends of the board, take the square and extend lines from the pins down through the gauged line on the inside of the drawer front. Do this on both ends.

5. With all the guide lines in place, and with the drawer front turned around in the vise so that the inside face is outermost, take the dovetail saw and run cuts down to the waste side of the drawn lines so that they run across the angle of the inside edge (see 4-32).

6. With the drawer front board clamped down with the inside face uppermost, take the chisel and clear the waste with alternate cuts. The procedure goes as follows: Set the chisel down just ahead of the gauge line so that the chisel is vertical and the bevel is looking away from the line, and tap down with the mallet (see 4-33 top); now, tilt the chisel down so that the handle is over the end, and tap into the initial cut so that a small wedge of waste pops out (see 4-33 middle). Repeat this procedure a couple of times until there is a wedge-shaped hole.

7. When you are about one-third the way down into the waste, flip the chisel over so that it is horizontal, set the cutting edge about one-third down on the end grain and tap in so that the waste pops out (see 4-33 bottom).

8. Rerun the sequence—vertical and chop, tilt and tap, horizontal and tap—until you are within a whisker of the gauge line, and then use both vertical and horizontal paring cuts to take the tails and sockets to a clean finish. Do your best to split the gauged lines, and on no account undercut the end of the socket.

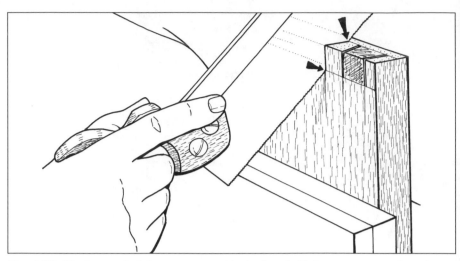

Fig. 4-32. Having marked the waste to avoid mistakes, hold the saw at an angle and run a kerf down to the gauged lines. It's important that the saw cuts are completely to the waste side of the drawn lines.

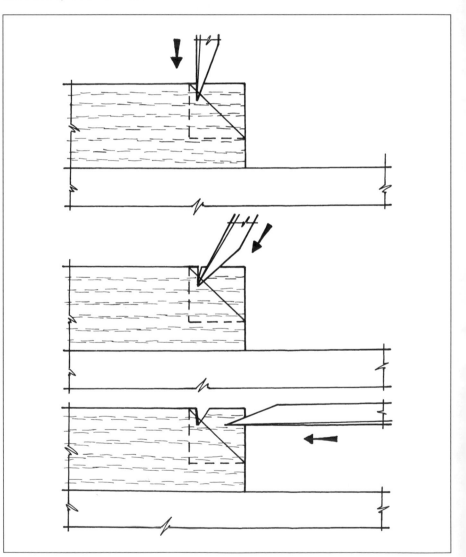

Fig. 4-33. Top, hold the chisel at right angles so that the bevel is looking toward the end of the wood, and tap down with the mallet. Middle, tilt the chisel over and tap with the mallet so that a small wedge of waste falls away. Bottom, turn the chisel over so that the bevel is uppermost, and cut horizontally into the end grain to remove about one-third of the waste. Repeat the procedure until you are down to the mark.

Chiseling Project 1: Oilstone Box

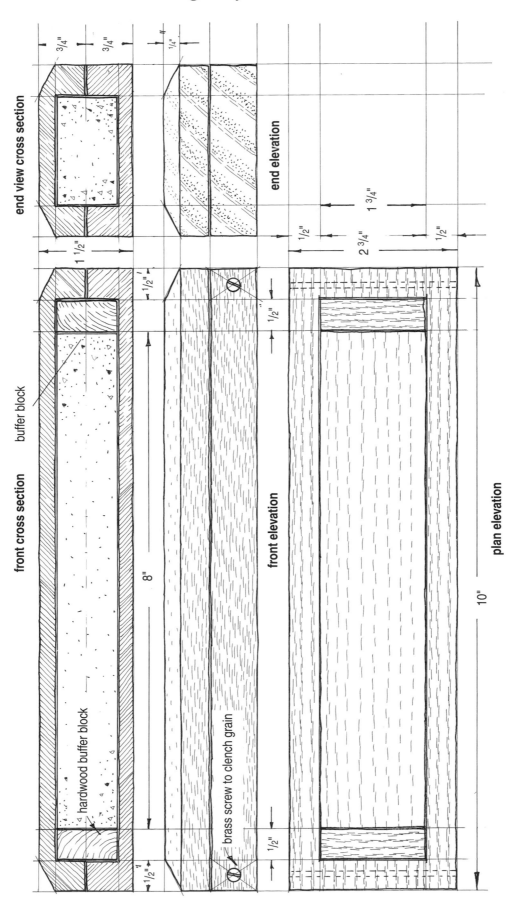

end view cross section

end elevation

front cross section

buffer block

hardwood buffer block

front elevation

brass screw to clench grain

plan elevation

3/4"

3/4"

1/4"

1 3/4"

1/2"

2 3/4"

1/2"

1 1/2"

1/2"

1/2"

8"

1/2"

1/2"

10"

Chiseling Project 2: Gallows Shelf Bracket

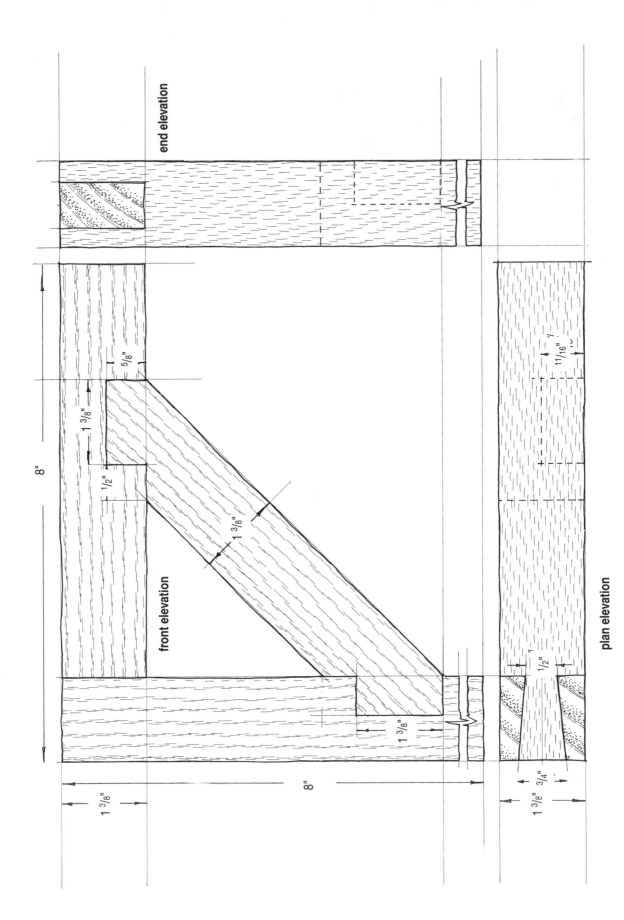

end elevation

plan elevation

front elevation

5/8"

1 3/8"

1/2"

8"

1 3/8"

11/16"

1/2"

1 3/8"

8"

1 3/8"

1 3/8"

3/4"

CHAPTER FIVE

Woodcarving Chisels and Gouges

Woodcarving is a unique woodworking activity that never ceases to fill us with joy and awe. One moment an unpromising lump of wood is taking up space in our workshop—a branch cut from an old apple tree, a chunk of driftwood dragged up from the beach, a piece of pine salvaged from a demolition site—and the next moment, we have a bowl, a duck decoy, a figure, a water dipper, or some other beautiful object to have and to hold.

We are not those carvers who much enjoy working with noisy dust-making tools like chain saws. For us, the fun of the craft has to do with the silent pleasure of working with gouges and chisels. We enjoy handling the chisels and gouges, tuning them, seeing how sharp we can get them, and feeling the way each and every tool perfectly performs its task. Woodcarving is exciting!

WHAT WOODCARVING CHISEL OR GOUGE TO USE AND WHEN

One thing that tends to put beginners off is the fact that there are so many tools to choose from. For example, in a batch of current catalogs you can find at least a thousand different gouges and chisels, all with curious names and puzzling code numbers. Even so, woodcarving is so exhilarating and rewarding that it really pays to get to know and understand the tools.

So there you go. If you are a nervous and confused beginner who is really looking to come to grips with the craft, then the following listings and definitions have been designed to guide you on your way.

STRAIGHT SQUARE CHISEL

A straight square chisel is straight along its length and straight or flat in cross section. The term "square" refers to the fact that the cutting edge is at right angles to the

side. The woodcarving straight chisel is much the same as the joinery chisel, the main difference being that the carving chisel is thinner in cross section, with the cutting edge having a bevel on both sides of the blade. In use, the straight chisel is held and pushed or held and tapped with a mallet. The straight blade results in the energy or thrust going straight down the blade. It is generally used for tasks like setting-in straight lines, cleaning up wide shallow recesses, and lettering.

STRAIGHT SKEW CHISEL

The straight skew chisel is identical in all respects to the straight square chisel except that the cutting edge is at an acute skewed angle to the side of the blade. Mostly, skewed chisels are ground at an angle of about 25 degrees. The skewed cutting edge allows the carver to dig away in small tight corners.

STRAIGHT SQUARE GOUGE

Though the straight square gouge has many of the characteristics of the straight chisel, including a straight blade and a cutting edge that is at right angles, it is also quite different in having a blade that is hollow in cross section. Straight gouges are sold in a whole range of width sizes—$1/16$ inch through $1^1/2$ inches— with each width also sold in a different size sweep or curve. When you want to purchase a gouge, first decide on the width that you need, and then think about the depth of the profile or sweep (see 5-2).

BENT OR CURVED TOOLS

Bent or curved chisels and gouges are identical to their straight brothers and sisters in all respects except that the blades are bent in a low curve along their lengths. As to why you might need a bent or curved tool, consider this scenario. You are quite happy carving away

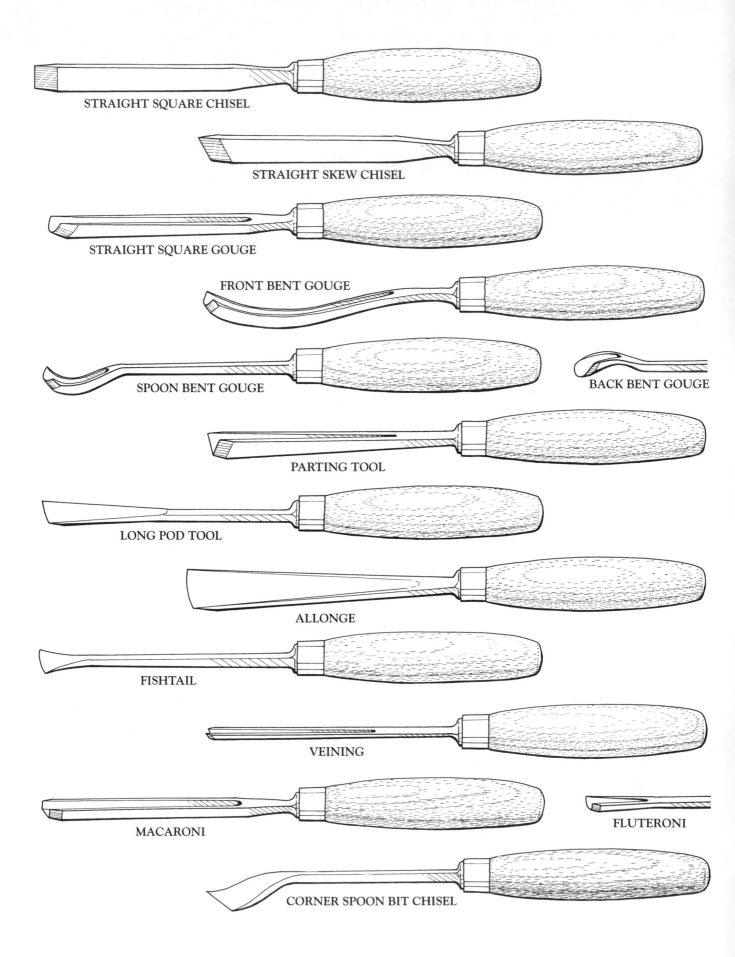

STRAIGHT SQUARE CHISEL

STRAIGHT SKEW CHISEL

STRAIGHT SQUARE GOUGE

FRONT BENT GOUGE

SPOON BENT GOUGE

BACK BENT GOUGE

PARTING TOOL

LONG POD TOOL

ALLONGE

FISHTAIL

VEINING

MACARONI

FLUTERONI

CORNER SPOON BIT CHISEL

Fig. 5-1. Woodcarving chisels and gouges.

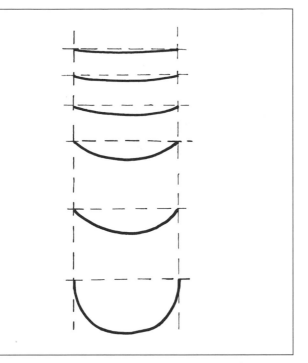

Fig. 5-2. Straight square gouges are made in a range of cutting edge profiles or sweeps. Within each tool width, there is a range of sweep depths.

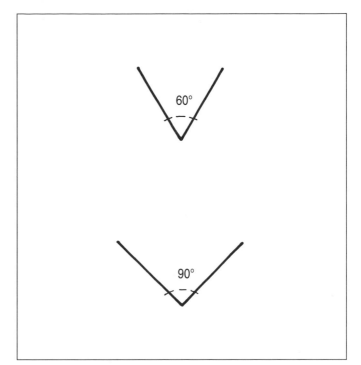

Fig. 5-3. Parting tools are commonly found in two angles: 60 degrees and 90 degrees.

with, say, a 1/4-inch-wide shallow sweep straight gouge, and then one day, the character of the carving is such that you can't get the straight blade into a deep undercut or hole. So what do you do? Get a bent or curved version of the selfsame straight gouge, one that allows you to scoop the blade into the hole, bowl, or hollow.

FRONT BENT OR SPOON TOOLS

Front bent and spoon bent (or spoon bit) chisels and gouges have the same characteristics as their straight or bent relatives; the only difference is that the end of the blade is bent or spoon shaped. The spoon shape allows the tool to be used for deeply recessed details and for acute curves. So you might need three gouges, all at 1/4 inch wide, and all making the same cut or sweep, except that one is straight, one is curved, and the other is spoon bent. In general terms, it's fair to say that the deeper and more complex your carving, the more bent and curved tools you will need.

BACK BENT GOUGES

Back bent gouges are identical to spoon bent ones except that the spoon shape is bent backward rather than forward. Though generally this tool has limited use, it is good for carving beadings and flutings that run in a curve over a shoulder.

PARTING TOOLS

Parting tools, also known as V-tools, are defined as chisels for the plain and simple reason that when they are stabbed into wood, the cut marks are straight sided. Made in two or three different angles (see 5-3) and in sizes that range from 1/16 through 1 inch, this is the perfect tool for tasks like outlining, cutting sharp-edged grooves or furrows, finishing corners, lettering, and chip carving.

LONG POD TOOLS

Long pod chisels and gouges are sometimes known as "grounding" tools because they are used for finishing and skimming areas of low ground, that is, areas that have been lowered, or you might say recessed. In shape, the blade is angled back from the cutting edge, the idea being that in use, the cutting edge can be sheared from left and right without the blade width getting in the way.

ALLONGE TOOLS

Though allonge chisels and gouges are very much like pods, they differ in that the blade flares out from the bolster, rather than from the shank. The tapered blade of this design makes it easier to get into difficult areas, and it also directs the energy straight to the cut.

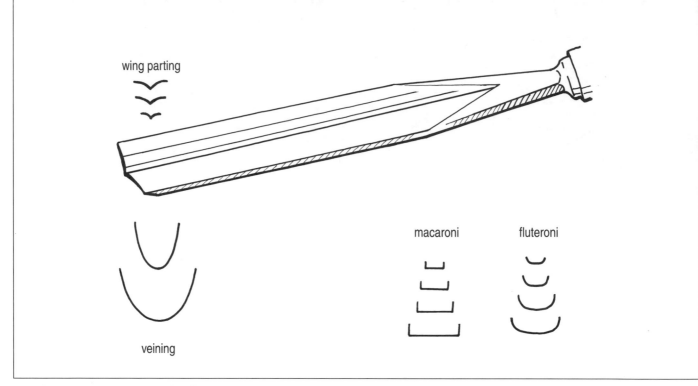

Fig. 5-4. Top, *wing parting tool and cross-sectional shape*. Bottom left, *cross-sectional shape of a veiner gouge*. Bottom right, *cross-sectional shapes of macaroni and fluteroni gouges*.

FISHTAIL TOOLS

Fishtail chisels and gouges are used for light finishing, for lettering, and for general skimming and modeling. The flared fishtail shape of the blade allows the carver to choose between using the full width of the blade or using one corner of the tail. In many ways, this tool can be used like a skewed tool, with the two corners of the tail making it suitable for both left- and right-handed use.

WING PARTING TOOLS

The wing parting tool gets its name from the mark made when the blade is stabbed down into the wood; it is very much like a sketch of a bird in flight at a distance (see 5-4 top). Though wing-parting tools are seldom needed, they are the perfect tool for carving details like drapery and linen folds.

VEINING TOOLS

The veiner gouge is used, as the name suggests, for cutting fine deep U-section channels and grooves (see 5-4 bottom left). This gouge is designed to perform very specific tasks like detailing, lettering, and the like. Some carvers use the veiner for setting-in rather than, say, a V-tool.

MACARONI AND FLUTERONI TOOLS

Macaroni and fluteroni gouges are used for finishing the sides of deep recesses. In essence, these gouges are wider than they are deep (see 5-4 bottom right). The fluteroni is a particularly good tool for cutting trenches that have rounded sides, and for modeling leaf and stem details. If you want to carve large details such as acanthus leaves, swags, and the like, then chances are you will find a straight fluteroni very useful.

THE ANATOMY OF WOODCARVING CHISELS AND GOUGES

There is a simple answer to the oft-asked question, What is the difference between a chisel and gouge? If the tool makes a curved mark like a C or a U when it is stabbed down into wood, then it is a gouge. If, on the other hand, it makes a straight mark when stabbed into the wood, or at least a mark that is made up of straight lines, like a V, then it is a chisel.

The shape of the stabbed cut describes in cross-sectional width the shape of the usable part of the blade. All the prefix names, like "straight," "bent," and "spoon," do no more than describe and define the shape of the blade along its usable length. So, for example, although a ³/₄-inch-wide straight gouge, a ³/₄-inch-wide

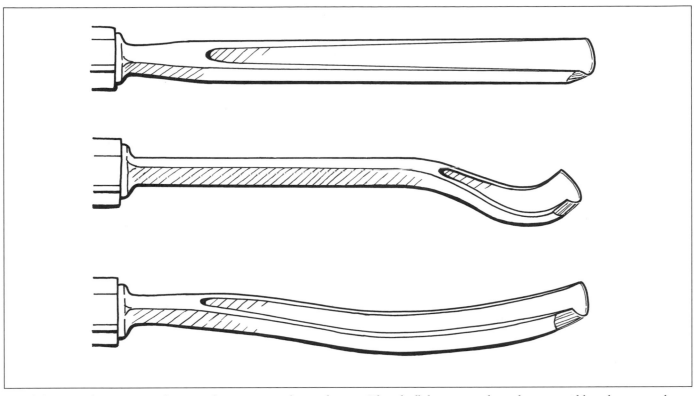

Fig. 5-5. Top to bottom, straight gouge, bent gouge, and curved gouge. Though all three gouges have the same width and sweep at the cutting edge, they are all different in shape along the lengths of their blades. It is this shape that leads to the tool being called straight, bent, or curved.

bent gouge, and a ³/₄-inch-wide curved gouge (see 5-5) all make the same mark when stabbed into the wood, they are quite different in shape along the lengths of their blades. A good memory aid is to think of your index finger; if you push the tip down into a soft surface, it will always make the same mark, no matter if the finger is straight, curved, or bent. And just as you bend and curve your finger to get to difficult-to-reach items, so with a gouge, you need straight, curved, and bent variations to make difficult-to-reach cuts.

The next question that beginners ask is, What does "sweep" mean? Sweep refers to the precise shape or curve of the gouge blade in cross section. So, for example, although two straight gouges might both be ¹/₂-inch-wide across the horns of the curve—meaning across the top of the U—one might be almost flat in cross section and the other a deep scooped U-shape. The shape of this curve is termed the sweep (see 5-2).

Since 1880 or thereabouts, the sweep or cutting edge shape of all gouges has been described and defined by a "Sheffield list" number. By this system all gouges of the same cross-sectional profile or sweep, irrespective of width, have the same number. On the face of it, this is a nice tidy system, because it's not so difficult to remember that a certain "family" of gouges is defined as being,

say, a number 06. The different manufacturers have complicated matters by adding their own prefix numbers to the Sheffield list numbers. So 06 becomes 5006 or even 3706, or whatever.

Gouges are traditionally sold in two ranges: "ladies'" or "amateurs'" and "professionals'." All this usually means is that the professionals' tools are longer, and the ladies' or amateurs' tools are shorter and shinier. The rather out-dated idea is that women or amateurs have smaller more delicate hands than professionals!

Last, but not least, gouges are sold as either "black iron" or "straw ground," meaning either black as they come from the forge or bright and shiny as they come from the buffing machine.

Our advice is to forget about the numbers and specifications for the moment. Instead, study the following definitions and descriptions, decide on the sort of profile of gouge that you need, and then walk into a store and select the tool of your choice.

There are all sorts of variations on the basic chisel and gouge theme, with all the component parts that go to make up the tool coming in many shapes, sizes, and standards.

The following breakdown will help you in your choice.

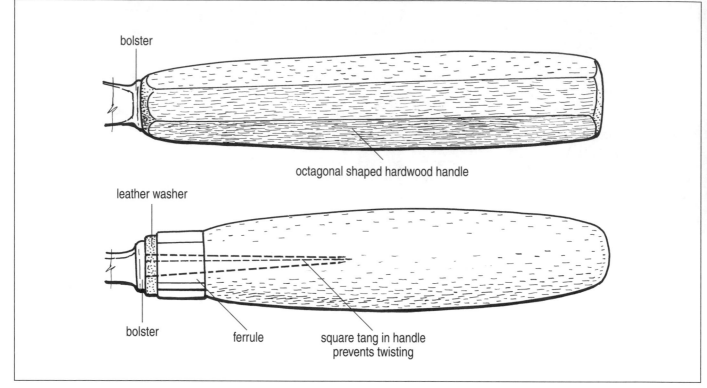

Fig. 5-6. Top, *the traditional octagonal handle not only provides a more positive grip, but it also stops the tool from rolling about on the bench.* Bottom, *large straight tools that are used with a mallet need to have a leather washer to absorb the shock, and a ferrule to prevent the handle from splitting.*

HANDLE

While in essence, woodcarving chisel and gouge handles are much the same shape as the handles for, say, joinery chisels and woodturning tools, it's fair to say, that woodcarvers are generally more concerned about how the handle feels in the hand, meaning its weight, shape, and texture. Up until about the 1920s, the woodcarver almost invariably used hand-cut unferruled handles that were tapered and roughly hexagonal or octagonal in cross section. From around that date up until the present day, most English and American manufacturers have favored fitting their tools with turned handles. No doubt the change had to do with the fact that, from about that date, tools have been mass produced in factories rather than made by small workshops. And, of course, it's easier and cheaper to make turned handles. That said, the problem with turned handles is that although a whole array of identical highly varnished rosewood or beech handles does look impressive, it's much better in practice if each and every handle is different. (What with most woodcarvers having anything from twenty to a hundred different gouge types and sizes, it's vital that they can recognize each one at a glance. The good news is that certain German and Swiss manufacturers sell handles that are octagonal in shape and unpolished (see 5-6 top). We tend to use turned boxwood handles and

the traditional hand-cut octagonal handles, always unvarnished, or at least sealed rather than varnished.

One English manufacturer sells carving chisels and gouges that are fitted with turned and varnished handles, with each and every handle having a large transfer label. The problem is that after a few hours use, the label on the handle breaks down and becomes a sticky mess that has to be removed. There is no doubting the superb quality of the tools, but the labels are an ill-considered nuisance.

FERRULE

The ferrule is a ring or hoop driven onto or clenched around the handle of some woodcarving tools. Whereas most of the traditional octagonal and hexagonal knife-cut handles were without ferrules, most of the modern turned handles are fitted with them (see 5-6 bottom). Although the function of the ferrule is to bind the handle together and so stop the tang from splitting the wood, it seems to us that hand-cut handles are none the worse for not having ferrules.

LEATHER SHOCK ABSORBER

Though not all woodcarving tools are fitted with leather washer shock absorbers (see 5-6 bottom), we think it a distinct advantage that the larger-sized straight tools

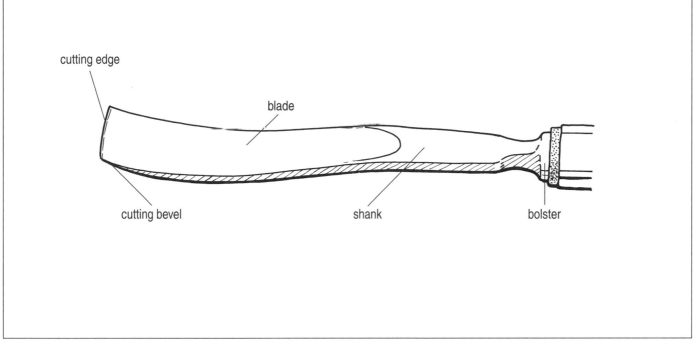

cutting edge

blade

cutting bevel

shank

bolster

Fig. 5-7. The business end of the gouge.

designed to be struck with a mallet have a leather washer between the bolster and the handle. The idea is that the leather dulls the jarring action of severe mallet blows, and makes the activity that much more comfortable. On a couple of old gouges that we have—both made by Addis Sheffield sometime between 1870 and 1944—you can see that the leather washer also functions as a sort of filler between the back of the uneven hand-forged bolster and the end of the uneven hand-cut octagonal handle. Without the washer, there would be a gap.

TANG

The tang is the pointed bit of metal that runs from the bolster up into the handle. The square section shape of the tang prevents it from moving and twisting in the handle. Unlike joinery chisels that have evolved into two distinct types—those with a tang and those with a socket—woodcarving chisels and gouges are always tanged (see 5-6 bottom).

BOLSTER

As with the joinery chisels, the bolster of a woodcarving chisel or gouge is the splayed part at the top of the blade where the metal spreads to meet the handle. The bolster not only prevents the tang from running into and splitting the handle, it also spreads the load and acts as a

cushioning pad (see 5-6). It was quite common in the past for good quality small-sized carving tools to be without a bolster, with the blade running in line through the shank and onto the tang.

BLADE

The blade of the woodcarving chisel or gouge is the usable part running from the cutting edge to the shank (see 5-7). Although it could be said of a joinery chisel that the length of the blade equates with the quality and the life expectancy of the tool, and so the joiner will search around for a tool with the longest blade length, this is not so with a woodcarving tool. The length of the blade of a carving chisel or gouge might necessarily be only a small part of the total length of the tool. For example, the spoon part of a spoon gouge is the essence of the tool, the part of the gouge that does the work, but the usable part of the spoon might only be a $1/2$ inch or so long.

Because the blades of woodcarving chisels and gouges are relatively expensive to produce, it is all the more important that the blade be of top quality. Most woodcarvers would agree that a top quality blade needs to be forged and finished to provide a good balance, and carefully ground and sharpened at the cutting edge, with the inside sweep being very finely ground so as to facilitate easy sharpening.

CUTTING BEVEL

The cutting bevel of a woodcarving chisel or gouge is the part of the blade that is ground to form the primary cutting angle. The cutting bevel of a woodcarving chisel can be likened to that on a joinery chisel, but the bevel on a wood-carving gouge is very different in that it wraps around the convex side of the sweep (see 5-7). The woodcarving gouge is also different in that the blade also has a micro-bevel on the inside.

CUTTING EDGE

As with the joinery chisel, the cutting edge of a woodcarving chisel or gouge is the secondary angle or microangle at which the cutting bevel is honed. If you hold a perfectly ground and honed chisel or gouge up to the light, you will see that the cutting edge reveals itself as the thin strip of reflected light that runs across the width of the beveled angle.

THE CUTTING ACTION OF A WOODCARVING TOOL

On the face of it, there are only two ways that a woodcarving chisel or gouge can be held and handled: It can be held and guided with one hand and pushed with the other (see 5-8), or it can be held in one hand and struck with a mallet (see 5-9). But the gouge in particular is a tool that has a countless number of uses. Much depends on the type and the shape of the particular gouge; but overall, it can be held in one hand and struck with a mallet, it can be held in one hand and pushed, it can be used with a scoop-ing action like a spoon (see 5-10 left), it can be stabbed straight down to create a stop-cut (see 5-10 right), it can be pushed straight down and skewed on the spot, it can be used at a very shallow paring angle, and so on (see 5-11).

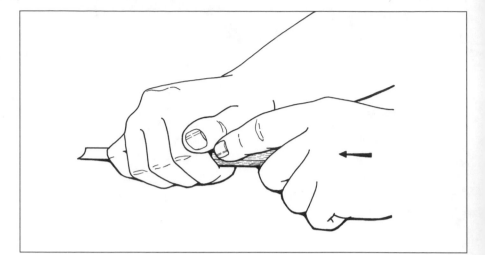

Fig. 5-8. *One hand guides and controls the blade while the other supplies the directional thrust.*

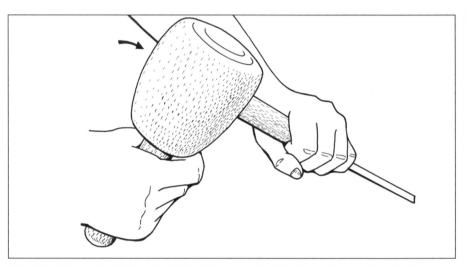

Fig. 5-9. *The tool is held and guided with one hand while the mallet supplies the thrust.*

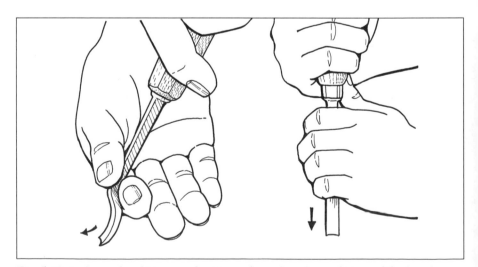

Fig. 5-10. Left, *one hand pivots and supports the tool on the workpiece while the other hand levers and thrusts. Right, the hands are linked to stabilize the downward thrust.*

To a great extent, the success of the cut depends on five particulars:

- The shape of the tool.
- The choice of wood.
- The depth of the carving.
- How the workpiece is secured.
- How the tool approaches the grain.

Grain direction is paramount. In very general terms, it is much easier to cut across the run of the grain than with it; such tasks as roughing and grounding are worked across the grain (see 5-12 top). Modeling end grain is best achieved with a slicing downward and sideways skewing cut (see 5-12 bottom). Designs made up of lines that are curved present problems, because with most cuts, the gouge will be cutting both with and at an angle to the grain. And just to make it a bit more complicated, when a gouge is being used to cut a groove that runs in a curve across the grain, one side of the gouge will cut with the run of the grain and the other side of the gouge against it. Put another way, one side of the groove will be clean and smooth, and the other rough and ragged (see 5-13).

Inasmuch as woodcarving is all about how best to remove the waste wood, woodcarvers spend most of their time making decisions as to which chisel or gouge to use for such and such a stroke or cut. The main problem faced by the carver is how to achieve a groove in a carved design without doing damage to the surface that is to remain. To put it another way, if you set the chisel down on the drawn line and give it a tap with a mallet, the chances are that the force of the tool cutting into the wood will cause the grain to splinter and split on the design side of the line, or the cutting edge of the tool will be damaged. The solution is simple.

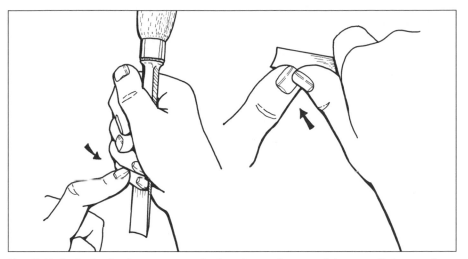

Fig. 5-11. Left, the forefinger acts as a brake when making a tightly controlled vertical shearing cut. Right, brace the thumbs for a shallow paring cut.

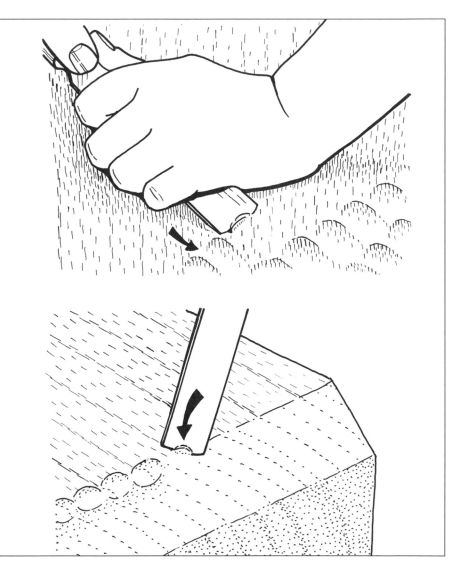

Fig. 5-12. Top, work across and at an angle to the run of the grain, with the tool held at a low angle. Bottom, use a sideways slicing or skewed cut to remove end grain.

Most relief carved designs are outlined by a procedure known as
"setting-in." All you do is run a preliminary groove or trench slightly
to the waste side of the drawn line,
and then set in the drawn line with
a straight-down stop-cut (see 5-14).
What happens is that the initial
groove provides a space for the
wood that will be displaced and
keeps the back of the tool from
being forced against the wood that
is to remain.

At this point, it is probably best
for us to stop talking about specific
cutting actions. It is enough to
know that each and every cut needs
to be carefully considered in the
context of the grain. We're not
ducking the issue, but rather we will
be more specific about the com-
plexities of woodcarving in the
"Step-By-Step Methods" section toward the end of this chapter.

SHARPENING WOOD-CARVING CHISELS AND GOUGES

When we're telling beginners all
about the joys and jubilations of
woodcarving, the pure pleasures of
the activity, and the wonderful feeling when the wood cuts crisp and
clean, we always add, "but only if
your tools are razor-sharp."

There is nothing quite so miserable and frustrating as trying to
cut wood with blunt tools.

Beginners usually find the
sharpening sequences rather confusing, and they are so eager to get on
with the carving proper that they
push the sharpening procedure to
the back of their minds and just
hope it will go away. To make matters worse, a good many new chisels
and gouges are sold as "ground but
requiring final honing," meaning essentially that they are less than
sharp when new—blunt even!

Since the only way into carving is to work with correctly sharp-

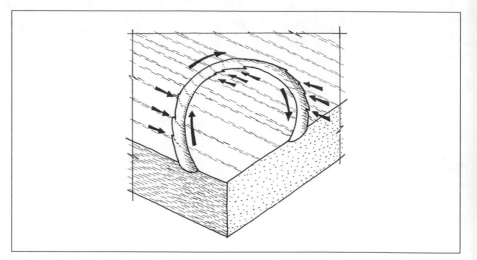

Fig. 5-13. *This shows how a line that curves across the grain will be ragged and smooth on different sides of the cut, depending on how the tool approached the grain. This problem can be approached by working the various points on both sides of the trench in different directions so that you are always cutting with the run of the grain.*

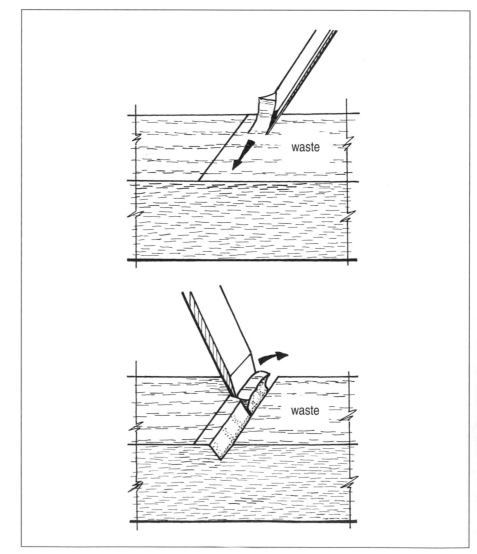

Fig. 5-14. Top, *to avoid bruising and crushing the wood, relieve the pressure by first cutting a trench to the waste side of the drawn line. Bottom, chop downward so that the waste spreads and crumbles into the trench.*

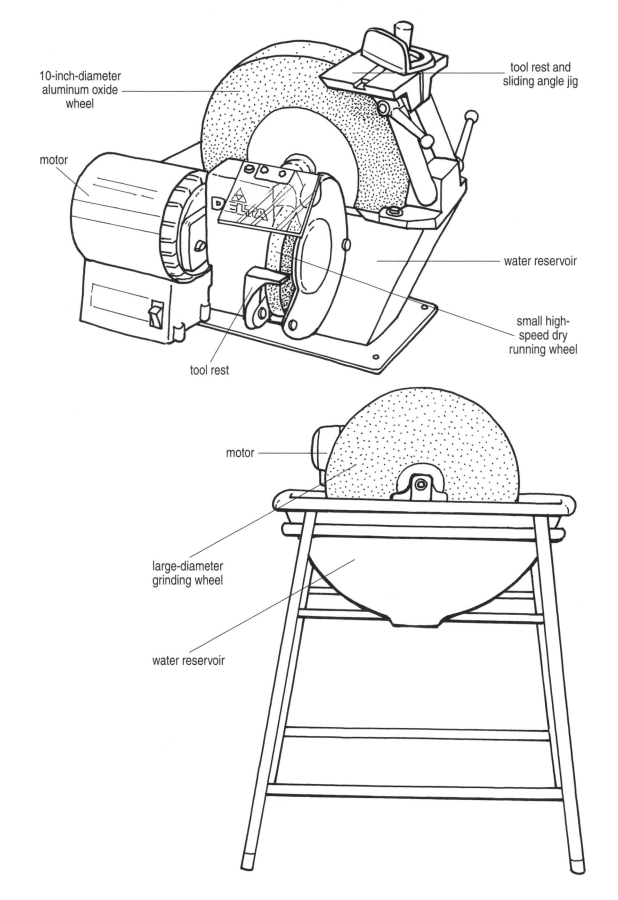

10-inch-diameter
aluminum oxide
wheel

tool rest and
sliding angle jig

motor

water reservoir

small high-
speed dry
running wheel

tool rest

motor

large-diameter
grinding wheel

water reservoir

Fig. 5-15. Top, *the state-of-the-art Delta Universal wet and dry grinder.* Bottom, *the traditional floor-standing wet grinder with a stone about 18 to 24 inches in diameter. This is our first-choice grinder, a really good easy-to-use machine that does the job without doing damage to the tools.*

ened tools, it follows that you have no other choice than to learn and master the correct sharpening procedures. We find that the best approach to sharpening is summed up by the little motto "a little and often." What this amounts to, in effect, is a burst of carving, spending a minute or so honing and stropping, then carving some more, going back to the honing, and so on. Using this approach, you get to stand back and see the workpiece afresh; your back, arm, and eye muscles get a rest; the tools get sharpened; and the project swings along. We find that this approach is much better than trying to work for hours and hours on end, with the tools getting ever blunter, and then stopping for hours trying to get the tools sharp again. However, another carver we know says that it's much better not to stop work to sharpen the tools. Much better, he decides, to leave all the sharpening until the end of the job, when you have nothing much else to do. He says that sharpening breaks his concentration. Well, we agree to disagree. Perhaps you ought to try both ways, and then choose the one that works for you.

The sharpening procedure is managed in three sequential stages:
- Grinding on a slow wheel or bench grinder.
- Honing or whetting on an oil- or waterstone.
- Stropping on a leather.

GRINDING
Although using the grindstone is the first stage in the sharpening procedure, unless you have just dropped the gouge and chipped it, or you have obtained a secondhand tool that has been neglected, you can skip the grinding and go straight on to honing. Remember that grinding removes a lot of very expensive metal!

Whereas we would concede that you can just about use a high-speed bench grinder for bringing joinery chisels to order—it's in no way as good as a large slow-spin waterwheel, but it will do; never try to grind your woodcarving chisels and gouges on a dry bench grinder! If you do, the chances are you will draw the temper out of the tool and ruin the shape of the blade. You have got to use either one of the old-fashioned large wheel grinders (see 5-15), or one of the new slow-speed, small wheel, wet grinders that are now coming on the market.

You can skip the grindstone altogether and do the grinding on a coarse bench stone. It must be borne in mind, though, that whereas grinding a chipped gouge on a wheel takes moments, the same procedure might take an hour or more on a bench stone.

Grinding a woodcarving chisel is much the same as grinding a joinery chisel (described in the last chapter) except that the woodcarving chisel usually needs to have equal bevels on both sides of the blade. The only other difference is that some woodcarvers round over the heel and grind away the corners or thickness at one side so that the chisel can be used in tight corners (see 5-16 bottom left).

It's not so easy to generalize about grinding a gouge, because there are so many shapes and sizes, but in general terms, the two bevels—the outer bevel and the inner microbevel, should make a combined angle of about 30 degrees (see 5-16 bottom center). The procedure is as follows:
- Take the gouge in one hand and set the back of the gouge down on the tool rest.
- Spread the fingers of the free hand, and depending on the size and shape of the tool, set them down on top of the blade or grasp the blades.
- Lift the handle until the bevel is in full contact with the wheel, and then roll the handle from side to side so that the entire bevel comes into contact (see 5-16 right). Make sure that there is plenty of water running over the stone, don't remove more metal than you have to, and be careful not to overtwist the blade to the extent that you round over the corners.

Because the whole grinding procedure is usually finished in a few moments, it might be a good idea if you are a raw beginner to search the flea markets for old inexpensive used and abused gouges, and then use them to perfect your technique. You never know, you might become so proficient that you can buy all your gouges secondhand.

HONING OR WHETTING WOODCARVING CHISELS AND GOUGES
Having ground the bevel to a good primary angle of about 15 degrees, set your fine and medium stones so that they are at a comfortable height, and arrange the shaped slips so that they are comfortably at hand (see 5-17). If you are using an oilstone, then have plenty of fine oil and rags on hand.

While the procedure for honing a woodcarving chisel is much the same as for sharpening a joinery chisel, the sequence of events for honing a gouge is different and somewhat more complicated. There are at least four ways of honing the primary outside bevel of a gouge:
- You can run the tool backward and forward along the stone while rolling the blade so that the whole bevel comes into contact.
- You can do the above procedure except that you run the gouge in a figure-eight pattern on the stone.

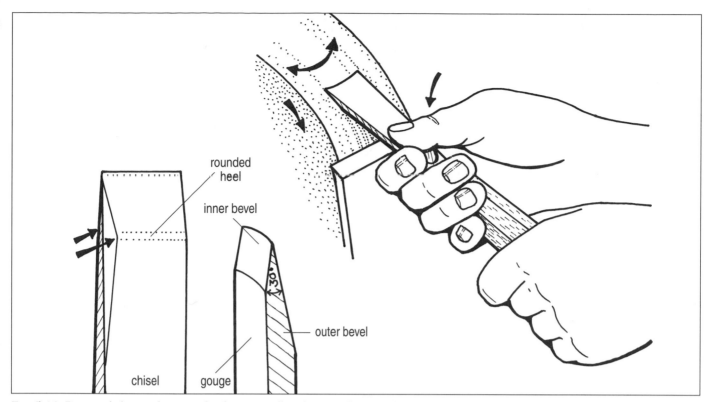

Fig. 5-16. Bottom left, *woodcarving chisels are usually—but not always—sharpened with equal bevels on both sides of the blade. The heel is rounded slightly, and the sharp angles are removed at both corners on one side. Bottom center,* the gouge has two bevels, the main *outer bevel and a smaller inner bevel, that add up to a combined angle of about 30 degrees. Some woodcarvers put microbevels on both primary bevels. Right,* apply pressure with your thumb and twist the handle so that every part of the bevel makes contact.

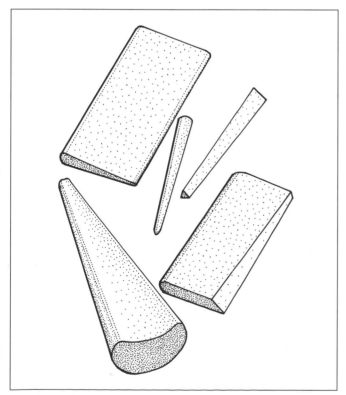

Fig. 5-17. *Shaped slipstones are used to whet gouges and V-parting tools. Starting at* the top and going clockwise, *the slips are rounded edge, tapered point, tapered triangle, multiform, and cone. Our first-choice slips are the tapered points and the cone.*

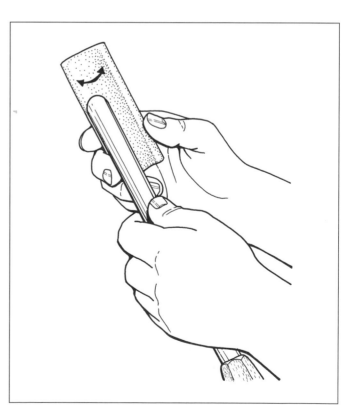

Fig. 5-18. *Our preferred method for whetting or honing is as follows: With the tool held up to the light, roll the tool while at the same time rubbing the stone up and down. Assess your progress by looking at the strip of light that shows between the bevel and the stone.*

- You can hold the tool at right angles to the stone so that the handle is sticking out at the side, and then move and roll the bevel along the length of the stone.
- You can hold the tool up to the light and stroke the stone against the bevel while at the same time rolling the tool (see 5-18).

Having tried all four techniques, we prefer the holding-up-to-the-light method for the simple reason that not only is it easy to maintain the angle of the stone, but better yet, the light shining off the bevel lets you know if you are making a mistake.

When you have achieved the primary bevel, tilt the tool or the stone, depending upon your method, and hone the micro-bevel. Once you have honed or whetted the outside micro-bevel, then you need to use a shaped stone or slip to put a micro-bevel on the inside cutting edge. Select a slipstone of a suitable shape and size, dribble some oil on the stone, and then stroke it through the inside edge (see 5-19). Our favorite slipstone is a little pencil-sized, cone-shaped slip about 3 inches long. In use, you grip the slip between the thumb and middle finger of your left hand, and then vigorously stroke it up and down the inside bevel of the gouge. To hone the inside bevel of a spoon bit gouge, use the same slip, only this time around, simply rest the slip in the spoon and then twirl it rapidly.

STROPPING

Stropping is the procedure of removing the fine burr or wire that is left by honing. While the overall procedure for stropping woodcarving chisels and gouges is much the same as for honing, the difference comes when you need to strop the insides of the gouges. Though you

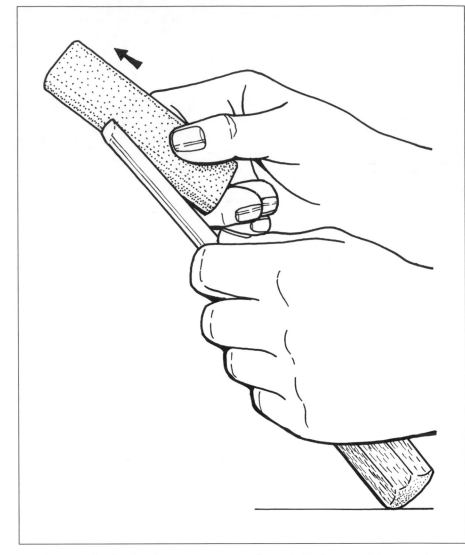

Fig. 5-19. *Find a slip that fits into your gouge, then rub the slip up and down on the inside curve. Slightly roll both the tool and the slip to make contact with the whole inside edge.*

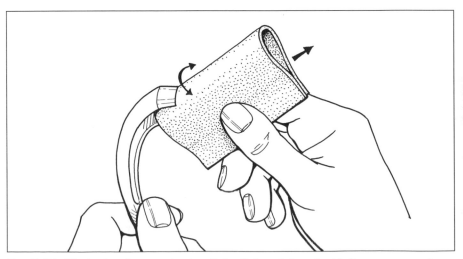

Fig. 5-20. *The leather for stropping is rolled, oiled, and dusted with fine crocus powder, and then stroked against the inside bevel. Continue until you have removed the burr or wire.*

can buy all sorts of little gizmos and gadgets that are good for stropping gouges, the easiest method is to fold over an old leather belt so that the roll fits inside the curve of the gouge, dribble some light oil on the leather, dust a small amount of fine crocus powder on the oil, and then buff the bevel (see 5-20). You can either stroke the strop in the gouge or stroke the gouge against the strop; it makes no difference as long as you don't run the cutting edge into the leather.

Test for sharpness by cutting across the grain of a piece of hardwood; the resultant cut should be smooth and burnished with a clean entry and exit.

TUNING WOODCARVING CHISELS AND GOUGES

We once heard it said that the act of tuning a woodcarving chisel or gouge is at the very root of good woodcarving, and that correct tuning is a great mystery. But we think that successful tuning has more to do with effort and methodical approach than with anything else.

Tuning is defined as bringing the tools into good working condition. There is no denying that the cutting edge needs to be razor-sharp, but there is more to the tool than the cutting edge. We know an old woodcarver who, when he uses a new tool, spends time stripping the varnish off the handle, rubbing the handle with vegetable oil, and burnishing the back of the blade, the shank, and the ferrule to a high-shine finish. He believes that the plain wood handle is more comfortable to hold, that the oil hardens his hands and seals the wood, and that the burnished metal makes for a swifter easier cut. As for the ferrule, he is right on target when he says that lots of new chisels and gouges have sharp-edged ferrules that can do damage to the hands.

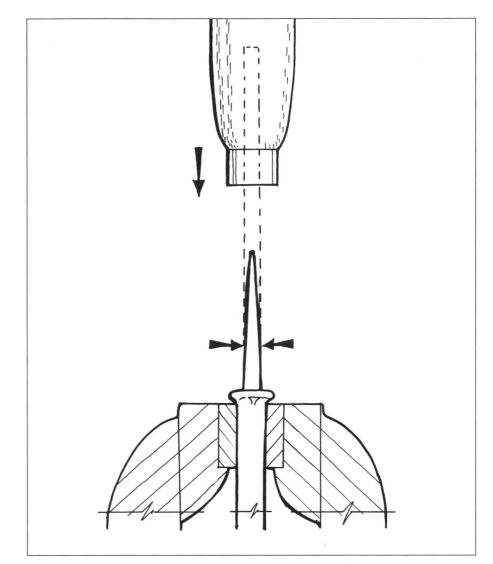

Fig. 5-21. Having first clamped the blade in a muffled vise, measure the thickness of the tang at a point about $1/2$ inch from the bolster and drill a hole in the handle accordingly. Drive the ferruled handle onto the tang.

The tuning procedures are as follows:

- Make sure that the cutting edge is ground to the desired bevel and free from nicks.
- Hone and strop the bevel.
- Make sure that the handle fits your hand and is comfortable to hold. If need be, reshape or replace it (see 5-21).
- If you have hot sweaty hands, then remove the high-gloss finish from the handle.
- Burnish the blade, shank, and ferrule.
- Make sure that you store the tuned tool in a roll or at least so that it can't bump and bash against other tools.

STANCE AND CONTROL WITH WOODCARVING CHISELS AND GOUGES

It's not so easy to break up the activities of woodcarving into clearly defined movements or approaches. Much depends on the size of the carving, the type and size of the carving tool being used, the stage of the carving at which the tool is being used, and the way the workpiece is being secured. In general, you must be comfortable with the height of the bench; make sure that you aren't stretching or bending. The workpiece must be held securely so that the energy from the cutting thrust isn't wasted (see 5-22 and 5-23).

The best that we can do is to give you a few basic tips on stance, technique, and control, and then you can take it from there.

RELIEF CARVING: WASTING OR LOWERING THE GROUND

Relief carving is the act of cutting away the waste from around a feature to leave it standing in relief. The area around the feature is termed the "ground." With the workpiece secured flat on the bench, and with the drawn line having first been outlined with a V-section cut that runs slightly to the waste side of the line, the waste is cleared with straight and bent tools. Use a straight shallow sweep gouge for starters, and then finish up with a bent shallow sweep gouge, or a bent chisel. Because you need to regulate the stroke so that it doesn't run out of control and into the design, hold and push the tool with one hand, with the other hand wrapped around the tool and ready to brake (see 5-24).

Let's say that you are right-handed. If you are doing it correctly, the tool handle will be butted against your palm so that the index finger is pointing down the length of the blade. The fingers of the left hand should be wrapped around the length of the blade so that the thumb of the left hand is braced against the handle. Your thumbnails should be more or less touching. In action, the two hands should be under tension, with the whole setup looking almost as if you are trying to break the tool in half. Working in this way, the tool is held at a low flat angle in your right hand, with the strength and weight of your right shoulder being put behind the

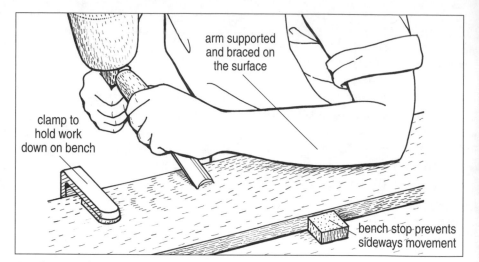

Fig. 5-22. *Make sure that the workpiece is at a good comfortable working height. Use a holdfast or clamp to secure the work, and a bench stop on the opposite side to absorb the force of the tool thrust.*

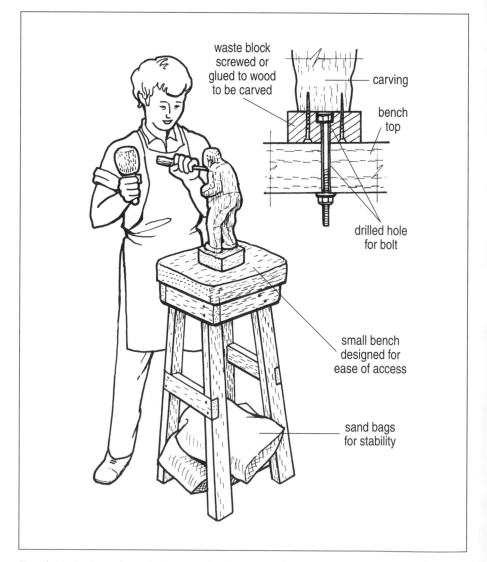

Fig. 5-23. Left, *sculptural pieces need to be mounted securely, either in carver's chops, with a pull-down belt, or in this instance, with a homemade bench screw. Work at a comfortable height, with the bench stabilized with sandbags. Right, the captive bolt runs down through the waste block and on through the top of the bench.*

thrust, while at the same time your left hand is guiding and fine-tuning the thrust. In effect, control is achieved by pushing the tool with one hand and pulling and braking with the other.

RELIEF CARVING: SETTING-IN

Having outlined the design with a V-trench and lowered the waste ground, now comes the procedure known as "setting-in." The object of the exercise is to precisely define the edge of the design, and by so doing, to control subsequent low-angled skimming cuts when the lowered ground is being modeled or cleaned up. If you think of the design feature as being an island with cliffs all around, and the lowered waste as the sea, then the task of setting-in defines the shoreline of the island.

Depending upon the size, shape, and depth of the island, setting-in is achieved by selecting a straight tool, setting the tool vertically on the drawn line so that the handle is canted back over the design, and then either tapping with a mallet or pushing down (see 5-25). If you opt for using both hands, then the stance is much akin to paring. Of course, if the island is straight sided like a square, then you can use chisels; otherwise, you need to select one or the other of your straight gouges that best fits the profile of the curve.

RELIEF CARVING: BOASTING

Boasting is the term used to describe the procedure of roughing out the design to be left in relief and bringing the lowered ground to order. In essence, you take a gouge of a size and sweep to match the design, and then grasp and push the handle with one hand while the other hand wraps around the blade

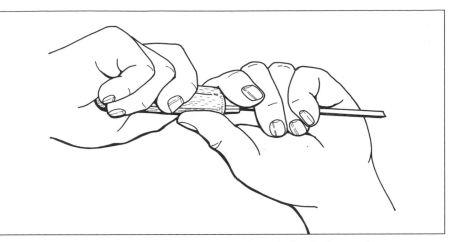

Fig. 5-24. A woodworm's-eye view of the underside of the hands showing how a strong, controlled, fully braced grip, with maximum control over the tool, is achieved by having one hand pushing and supplying the thrust while the other hand guides and maneuvers the blade.

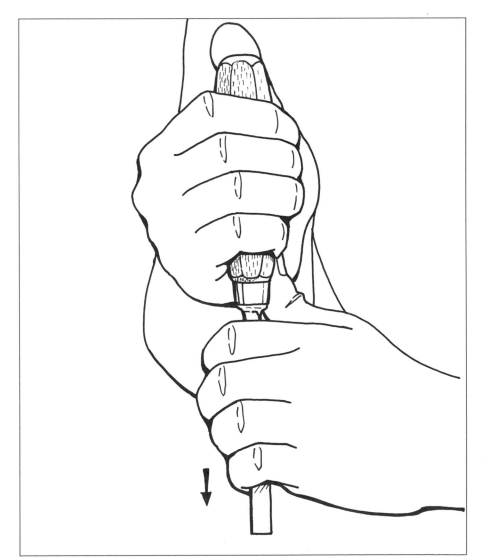

Fig. 5-25. To make a vertical or near-vertical paring or setting-in cut, grasp the tool in a stabbing hold with the thumb on top of the handle, wrap the fingers of the other hand around the blade, and set the thumb on the ferrule so that it is touching the other hand. The stabbing hand supplies the thrust while the other hand guides the cutting edge to the mark.

to exert downward and braking pressure (see 5-26). Control is achieved by the push-pull interplay between the two hands.

MODELING

Modeling is the procedure of shaping the roughed out surfaces so that they match up with the picture you have in your mind. Because of the nature of the exercise, modeling usually has to do with choosing the correct size, shape, and type of tool, and then using it to variously cut in, over, and around the run of the grain. The task of modeling involves using progressively smaller and smaller tools to make increasingly smaller cuts, and it is also a task that requires decisions as to the choice of the tool and the direction of the stroke. Modeling is done almost exclusively with both hands on the tool (see 5-27), rather than using a mallet. There is no way that we can generalize as to your approach, other than to say that as you get nearer to the finish, your tools need to be sharper and the strokes more considered.

MALLET WORK

Mallet work is best thought of as a sort of ongoing pecking (see 5-28) rather than as a series of single blows. Choose a mallet that is not so heavy as to be tiring, hold it nice and loosely, and then deliver lots of swift lively taps. All along the way, keep both the tool and the mallet moving rhythmically so that you are always approaching the grain and the design to best effect.

STRAIGHT STRONG CUTS

A good part of the time—perhaps even most of the time—the woodcarver is involved in using a straight tool to deliver an uncomplicated two-handed cut. So in grounding, boasting, and modeling, the carver takes a straight tool, butts the end

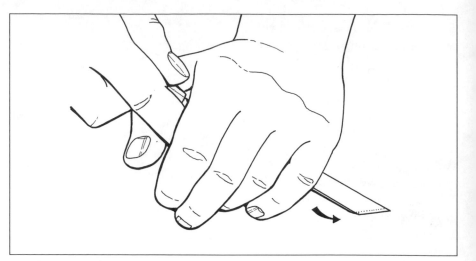

Fig. 5-26. To make sliding paring cuts at a low angle, set the handle into the palm of one hand and wrap the fingers of the other hand around the blade. Good control is achieved by having the two hands linked.

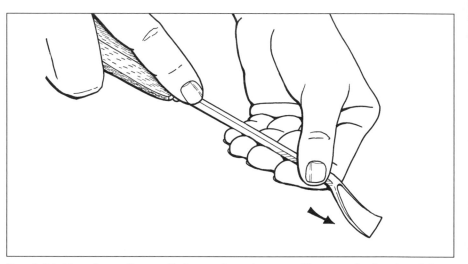

Fig. 5-27. To make small controlled cuts, the tool is pivoted between the thumb and the fingers while at the same time the handle is levered downward. It's important that the pivoting hand is braced on the workpiece.

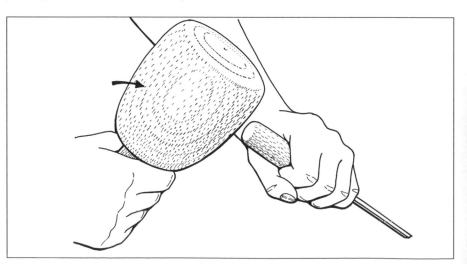

Fig. 5-28. To remove the wood fast from large areas, set the cutting edge on the mark and strike the handle with a series of light pecking taps. Keep both the blade and the mallet moving so that the whole activity is lively and responsive.

of the handle into the palm, wraps the fingers of the other hand around the tool, and then puts his or her shoulder behind the cut (see 5-29). When a cut is described as "straight" or "straight-and-strong," it refers not to a working stage or method, but rather to the grip and stance.

SPOON SCOOPING

In our experience, spoon scooping, or using a spoon tool to scoop out a deep hollow, is the technique that trips up most beginners. It's not that they are nervous of the tool—just the opposite; they like the shape and feel of a spoon bent gouge. Rather, they make the mistake of trying to dig too deeply and too strongly.

Bearing in mind that spoon tools are relatively delicate, with slender shanks and small bowls, it follows that rarely, if ever, should the tool be driven with a mallet. We mostly use two cuts: a delicate scooping cut, where the tool is held in one hand and worked with a small paddling action so that it pivots over the other hand; and a hold-down cut for digging out relatively large amounts of wood, where the blade is held down on the stroke so that the full curve of the spoon slides in and out of the hole (see 5-30).

WOODCARVING CHISEL AND GOUGE TECHNIQUES: STEP-BY-STEP METHODS

You have collected your chisels and gouges, you have a bench, you have a little stockpile of carefully selected pieces of wood—perhaps a small piece of box, a length of cherry or plum, and a host of other treasures—and now at last you are anxious to give it a try.

Be patient, don't try to rush to the finish, and don't give up after the first mishap. The following

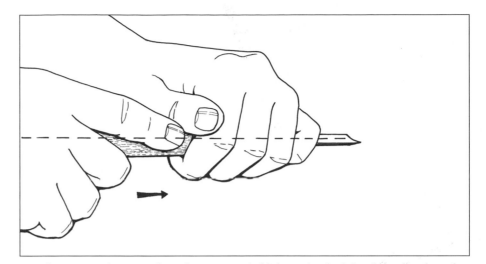

Fig. 5-29. To make a straight and strong cut, hold the tool in both hands so that the index finger is running down the length of the tool, and so that both hands are touching. If you are doing it right, the elbow and forearm will be set in a straight line with the cutting edge so that the thrust is direct and on target.

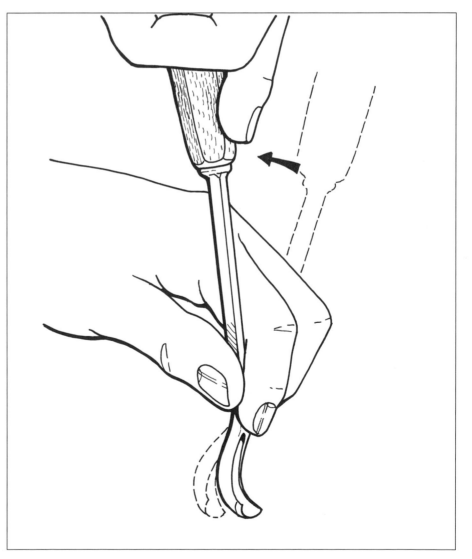

Fig. 5-30. To make small paring cuts in a tight recess, put the cutting edge on the mark, grip the blade between thumb and fingers, and then paddle the handle with the other hand.

projects aren't intended to be complete in themselves; they are no more than exercises, but they will show you the way. The idea is to get some experience with setting-in, modeling, and all the rest, and then you can go on to greater things.

OUTLINING AND SETTING-IN A RELIEF CARVING WITH A V-TOOL AND STRAIGHT GOUGE

Of all the activities in relief woodcarving, beginners are frightened away by the notion of outlining and setting-in. They perceive the tasks as being both tricky and tedious. Certainly it can be both difficult and boring if it's done badly, but in actual fact it's no more or less than a stage that needs to be worked at slowly and methodically. The time and effort put in at the outlining and setting-in stage will set the scene for all that is to come.

When working with the V-tool, always make sure that the bottom of the V is kept in the bottom of the trench; avoid twisting the tool on its side. Don't try to dig too deeply and always be ready to modify your approach to suit the changing run of the grain.

1. Having drawn the design out on the wood, and secured the panel to the bench with a holdfast or with turnbuckles or clamps, take a straight V-tool and cut a V-section trench about $1/8$ inch to the waste side of the drawn line (see 5-31). Work with a strong push-pull-and-hold stroke, that is, with the handle butted hard up into the palm of one hand, and with the fingers of the other hand wrapped around the tool.

2. Once the outlining is finished and the V-trench is in place, get ready to set-in. With one side of the V-cut being slightly to the waste side of the drawn line, study the line and make decisions as to the

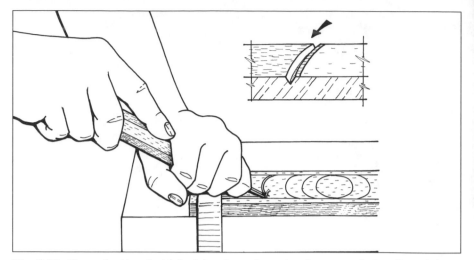

Fig. 5-31. *Grasp the V-tool with both hands, with one hand gripping the handle and the other guiding the blade. For maximum control, have the pad of the hand supported on the workpiece so that the two hands are braced. Top, cut a V-section trench about $1/8$ inch to the waste side of the drawn line.*

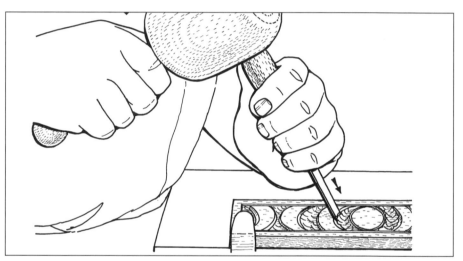

Fig. 5-32. *Set the cutting edge on the line, lean the handle over the design, and give the handle a lively tap. The angling of the handle avoids the risk of undercutting.*

tools that you are going to use. For example, if the line runs straight and then curved, you might select a straight chisel and a couple of small width shallow sweep gouges.

3. The setting-in procedure goes as follows: Set the cutting edge down on the drawn line, cant the handle back over the design, and then push or tap with a mallet (see 5-32) so that the walls of the design are cut cleanly—like a cliff face that angles down to the sea. On no account should the cliff be undercut.

4. If you want to finish up with a ground that is at a lower level than

the bottom of the V-cut trench, then repeatedly use a gouge to angle the waste into the trench, and slice down with setting-in cuts until the desired level is reached (see 5-33).

WASTING AND GROUNDING A RELIEF CARVING WITH STRAIGHT, BENT, AND SPOON TOOLS

Having established the shape of the design and the depth of the lowered ground by outlining and setting-in, then comes the tricky task of lowering the waste. Although this task can be done with various power tools from a pillar drill to a router, we prefer to stay away from noisy dust-making machines and use traditional tools and techniques. There are two ways that you can lower the ground: You can chip it out by chopping straight down across the run of the grain and then levering, or you can scoop and skim. Let's say that we are going for the chopping technique.

1. With the waste clearly defined, position the cutting edge of a shallow curve straight gouge on the waste wood a small way out from the design so that the convex face is looking toward the waste, and the curve is set across the run of the grain.

2. Take the mallet and give the gouge a smart tap to drive the gouge to a depth of about ⅛ inch (see 5-34). If the gouge is well placed, the small amount of waste between the inside curve of the blade and the design will crumble away. Continue this technique around and away from the design, in rows and lines, so that the waste crumbles away. It's all pretty easy as long as you keep the cuts close together, and you don't cut too deep. If you are going at it correctly, the waste will break away with a minimum of levering.

3. Having chipped off the waste layer by layer so that the whole ground area has been roughed out, then comes the most enjoyable task of leveling the lowered ground. This is the stage when you at last will feel as though you are getting somewhere. Study the lowered ground and decide on the best tool for the job. You might, for example, use a dogleg chisel to finish a flat-based recess (see 5-35 left), or if the side clearance is limited, then you could perhaps use a fishtail gouge (see 5-35 right). If there is a large area of relatively shallow waste, you

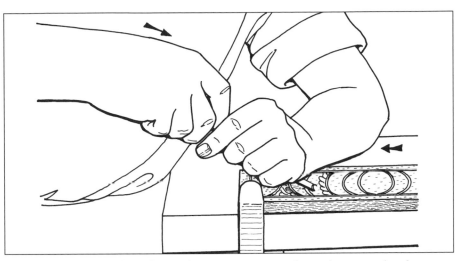

Fig. 5-33. *Hold the tool at a low angle, rest your arm on the workpiece, and make a series of shallow down in-and-out sweeping cuts, all the while backing up from the V-trench. The two-hands-linked arrangement enables you to brake the stroke if you feel the tool running out of control.*

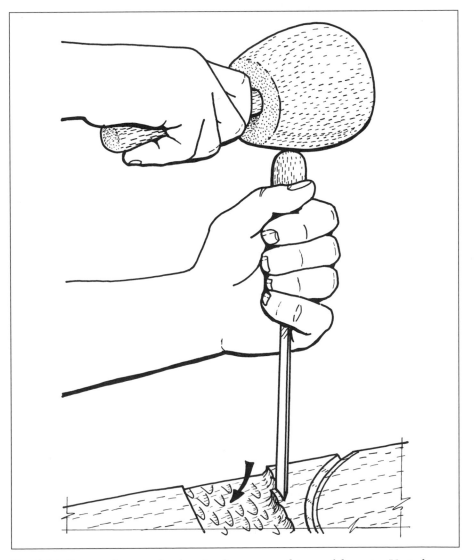

Fig. 5-34. *Remove the waste by chopping down across the run of the grain. Keep the cuts close together so that the grain crumbles away.*

can use a shallow curve straight gouge or maybe a shallow curve bent gouge, but if the ground is deep and tight, then you will need to use one or other of your shallow curve spoon bent gouges. Let's say that the area of lowered ground is both deep and restricted.

4. There are two ways of using a spoon bent gouge: You can scoop and twist, as you might spoon out a hard-boiled egg, or you can hold the tool more or less upright and braced against the fingers of the other hand, with the handle kept at a constant angle so that the gouge is pushed across the surface (see 5-36). Though your approach will depend on the hardness of the wood and the amount of space, you should always be working with a light skimming touch—no deep digging or levering against fragile edges.

MODELING A RELIEF CARVING WITH STRAIGHT, BENT, AND SPOON TOOLS

Having completed the more mechanical procedures of outlining, setting-in, and lowering, then comes the scary but challenging stage of modeling—scary because, although it is fun and exciting, it is also a time when you can make a mistake. You can always mend mistakes to a certain extent, but you may feel a bit miserable and defeated if you are left with a mend. You can make it good with glue and pegs so that it's nigh on impossible to see, but the trouble is that you know it's there. The answer is, of course, to work at it with careful consideration and confidence.

1. When you have a clear picture in your mind's eye of the forms and the texture that you want to model, then start by working around the raised design, roughing off the sharp edges. Using a shallow-curve straight gouge (see 5-37 left),

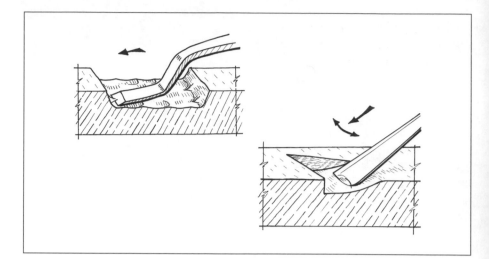

Fig. 5-35. Left, *use the dogleg chisel with a sliding sideways paring or skimming action. Right, use the fishtail with a slight rocking action. The corners of the tool will enable you to get into tight corners.*

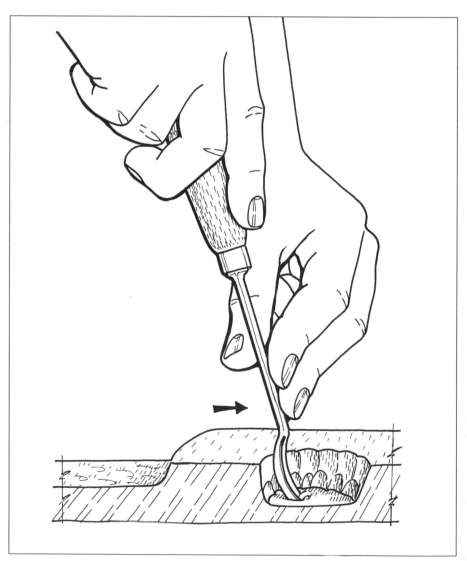

Fig. 5-36. Hold the bent gouge with both hands, push forward while at the same time adjusting the angle until the cutting edge begins to bite, and then stay with that same angle for the rest of the stroke.

cut from high to low wood, that is, from the top face of the design down to the bottom of the V-cut or ground.

2. When you have roughed out the form, you will have to use whatever tool best fits the profile. Use a shallow curve bent gouge for long low inside curves (see 5-37 bottom), a shallow curve straight gouge for the full outside curves, and one or the other of the spoon gouges for the tighter inside curves. A skew tool is particularly useful for tight corners (see 5-37 right). You won't go wrong if you work with increasingly smaller cuts, all the while making sure that you avoid cutting into the end grain. And if the tool cuts up rough, then either change tack and approach the grain from another direction or give the tool a few strokes on the stone and strop.

3. As to the final degree of finish, abrasives are unnecessary. Of course, there are times when an area needs to be very smooth, but even then, the smooth surface can be achieved by using a razor sharp tool of the correct sweep, followed up by a good shaving with a kidney scraper.

CARVING INCISED LETTER FORMS WITH STRAIGHT CHISELS AND GOUGES

First and foremost, it must be said that although it is relatively easy to cut and carve individual letters, it is extremely difficult to carve whole words. The difficulty has to do with carving letters that are well balanced, well proportioned, and well spaced with respect to one another.

As to style, there is no denying that classical Roman and Greek letter forms are incredibly beautiful, but the design is unforgiving. The spacing between neighboring letters, and between the words, must be absolutely right; there is no such

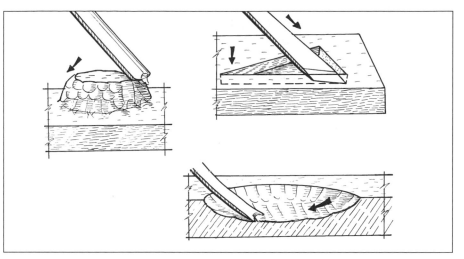

Fig. 5-37. Left, *use a straight gouge with a slightly rocking paring cut*. Bottom, *use a shallow sweep bent gouge with a scooping paring cut*. Right, *use the skewed chisel to slice the waste from tight corners.*

thing as almost. For this reason, you can always opt for more friendly letter forms, those that allow for fancy flourishes and more leeway in spacing. If something jars, simply enlarge a serif or extend a tail. Keep in mind that if your gouge slips, or an upright is less that straight, or a curve less than smooth, it's something that you have to live with. The best way to proceed is to look through books and magazines until you find a style of lettering that suits your needs.

Though it is possible to cut letters in any wood, hardwoods are usually the best choice. Choose close- and even-grained hardwoods that are free from knots, splits, wild grain, and oozy sap. Beech, cherry, oak, sycamore, and maple are all good choices.

1. When you have decided on the order of letters and what it is that you want to decorate (it might be anything from a furniture panel to a bread board), trace the shape of the item on facing paper. Decide where you want the letters to be and how big you want them, and then set out parallel lines of the proper height on the tracing paper. Having drawn the alphabet to size on a sheet of cardboard or thick

paper, trace off the letters so that they fit within your parallel lines. It's not easy. You will almost certainly have to rub out or adjust some letters, try different spacings, and so on.

2. When you are happy with the shape of the letters and the spacing between letters and words, flip the tracing over and use a soft pencil to rework the back of the traced lines. Next, having drawn guidelines on the wood, tape the tracing in place on the workpiece and use a hard pencil or a ballpoint pen to press-transfer the letters through to the wood. Use a ruler if necessary (see 5-38).

3. Having press-transferred the letters onto the wood and reworked the lines so that they are clear, secure the wood at a good working height. Then use a chisel to lightly score down the center of each element that makes up the first letter in line. For example, an "L" has two elements, an "R" has three elements, an "E" has four elements, and so on.

4. Let's say that the first letter is an "R." With the center lines in place, take a $3/8$- or $1/2$-inch chisel and sink a stop-cut into the center line that makes the upright stem.

Sink the cut to a depth of the envisaged V-trench, and stop short about ¼ inch from the top and bottom ends of the stem (see 5-39).

5. With a small skew chisel, run little Y-shaped cuts into the serif (see 5-40 left), and then slice out the resultant triangular pockets (see 5-40 center). This done, go back to using the ½-inch chisel and work from end to end of the stem, running slanting cuts into the stop-cut to form a V-trench (see 5-40 right).

6. When you come to cutting the curved parts of the R, follow through the same procedures already described, only this time around, use gouges that fit the curves, rather than chisels.

Keep in mind that there are some interesting design possibilities where wide and narrow cuts intersect (see the arrows on 5-40 right).

CARVING A BOWL WITH STRAIGHT AND BENT GOUGES

1. You want a circular bowl about 10 inches in diameter and about 3 to 4 inches deep. Having chosen your slab of easy-to-carve wood—something like cherry—pencil label one face "top" and the other "foot." Use a compass to draw the shape of the bowl on the "top," and cut the blank out on the band saw or with a large bow saw.

2. Draw the thickness of the rim on the "top," and run a hole about 2 inches in diameter down into the top center so that it stops about ¾ inch short of the other side of the wood. If the slab is, say, 3½ inches thick, then run in the hole in to a depth of about 2¾ inches.

3. Secure the slab "top" face up on the bench with a bench hook and stops, then work around the drilled hole with a shallow-weep straight gouge and a mallet, cutting away the sharp corners of waste. Work round the drilled pilot hole,

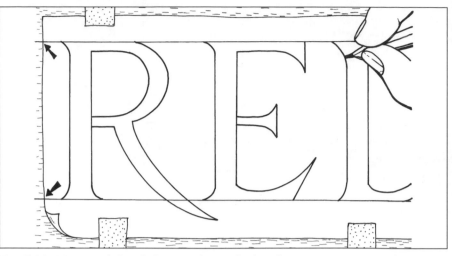

Fig. 5-38. Having ruled guide lines on the wood, align the tracing, secure it with pieces of masking tape, and press-transfer the letters onto the wood.

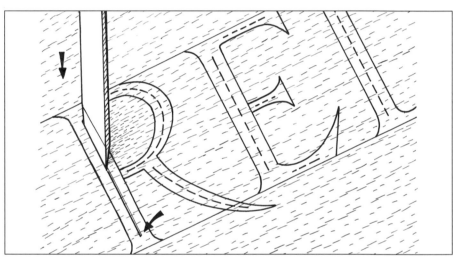

Fig. 5-39. Stab directly down along the center of the various strokes that go to make up the letters, but stop short at each end of the stroke when you come to the serifs.

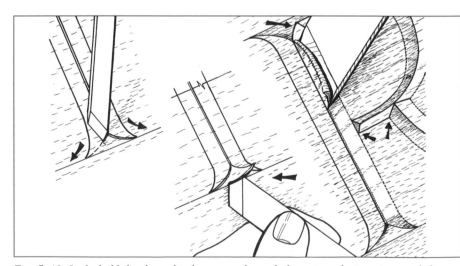

Fig. 5-40. Left, hold the skew chisel at an angle, stab down into the junction, and slice along toward the corner of the serif. Do this for both corners of each serif. Center, to complete the serif, set the tool at an angle and slice in from the end of the serif so that the chip of waste falls away. Right, slice the waste from each side of the initial cut; aim for a total angle of about 55 degrees.

all the while backing up toward the line of the rim and getting deeper (see 5-41). As the hole gets deeper, change to whatever tools get the job done most efficiently. For example, you might change from using a 1/2-inch-wide shallow-curve straight gouge to using a 1/2-inch-wide shallow-curve bent gouge (See 5-42). The important thing is that the curved or bent gouge will reach areas that are inaccessible to a straight tool.

Leave the rim till last so that it won't get bruised when you are carving the inside.

4. When you are happy with the inside shape of the bowl, turn the workpiece over so that the "foot" is uppermost, and set to work carving the outside shape. This time, start at the outside edge and back up toward the center (see 5-43) using the shallow-curve straight chisels for the whole procedure.

5. When you have roughed out the shape of the outside of the bowl, change to your widest shallow-curve gouge. Run the gouge strokes down and around in a spiral shape from the inside rim toward the inside bottom of the bowl and from the outside foot down and around toward the outside rim.

Finally, carve the lip of the rim with the straight gouge, and finish it with a scraper.

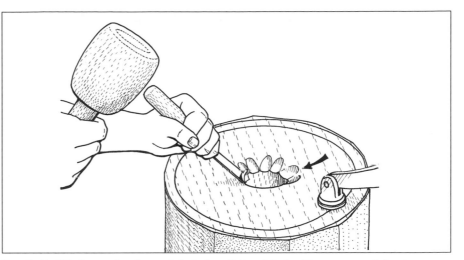

Fig. 5-41. Work round and round the hole, all the while backing up toward the rim. Clear the waste layer by layer.

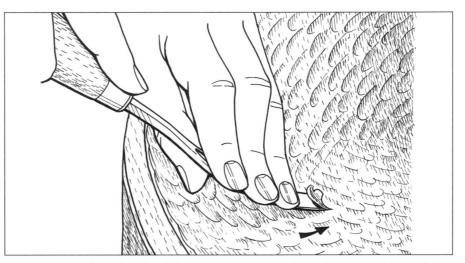

Fig. 5-42. Push the tool with a slight scooping action, all the while running the cuts down and around at a spiraling angle toward the bottom of the bowl.

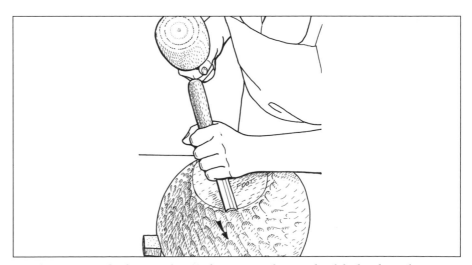

Fig. 5-43. Repeat the down-and-around cutting on the outside of the bowl, working in a spiraling angle that backs up from the rim to the foot.

Woodcarving Project 1: Woodcarving Bench

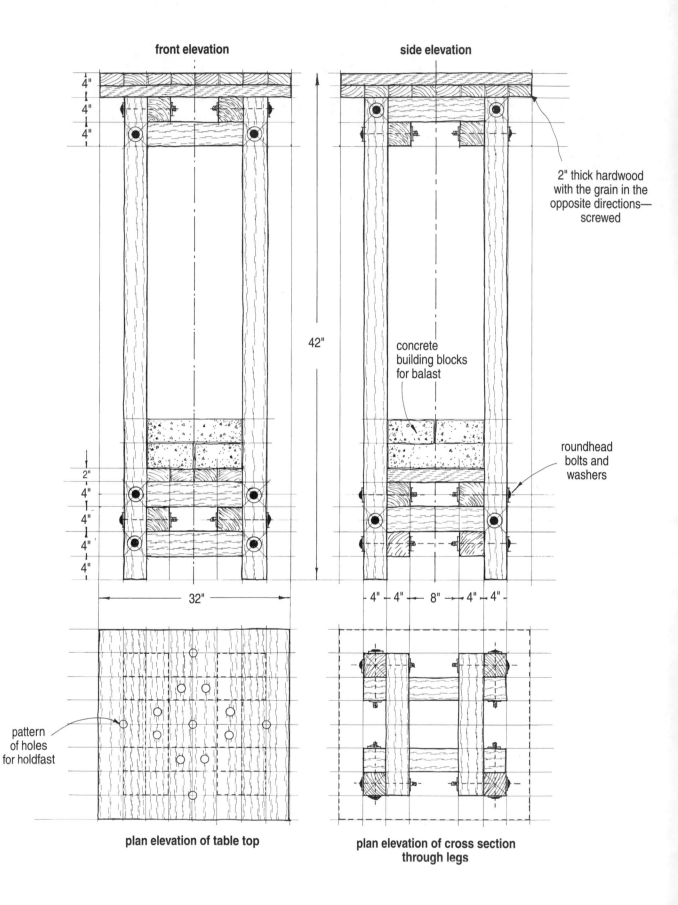

front elevation

side elevation

4"
4"
4"

42"

2"
4"
4"
4"
4"

32"

2" thick hardwood
with the grain in the
opposite directions—
screwed

concrete
building blocks
for balast

roundhead
bolts and
washers

4" — 4" — 8" — 4" — 4"

pattern
of holes
for holdfast

plan elevation of table top

**plan elevation of cross section
through legs**

Woodcarving Project 2: Woodcarver's Cleat

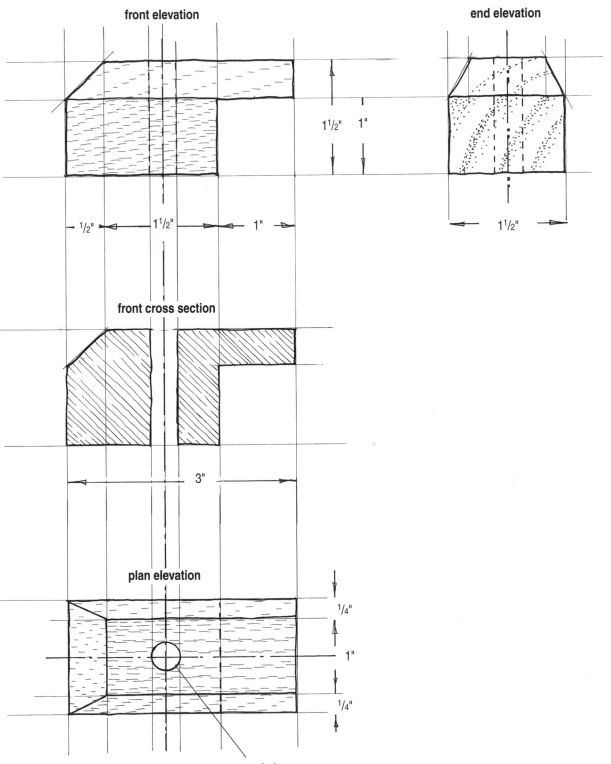

front elevation

end elevation

1¹/₂"   1"

¹/₂"   1¹/₂"   1"

1¹/₂"

front cross section

3"

plan elevation

¹/₄"

1"

¹/₄"

screw hole

Woodcarving Project 3: Woodcarver's Bridge Hold-Down

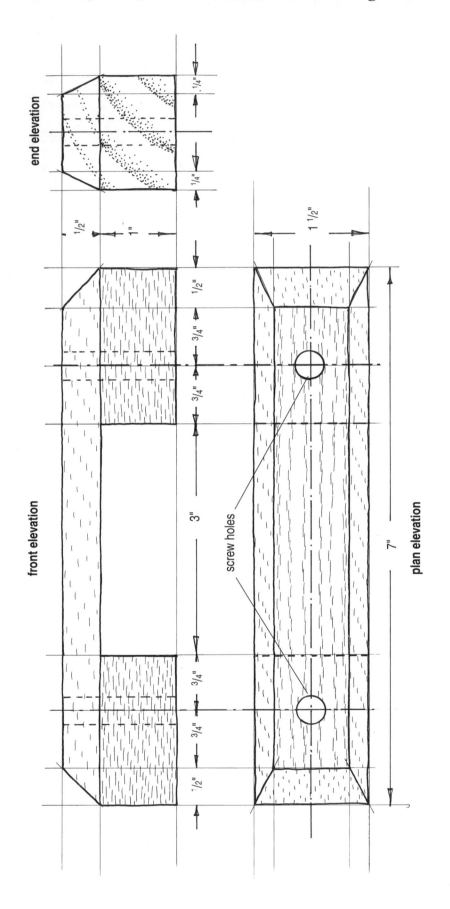

end elevation

1/4"

1/4"

1/2"

1"

1 1/2"

1/2"

3/4"

3/4"

3"

screw holes

front elevation

3/4"

3/4"

1/2"

7"

plan elevation

CHAPTER SIX

Woodturning Chisels, Gouges, and Scrapers

Woodturning is an almost magical woodworking activity that transforms the most unpromising pieces of wood into all manner of bowls, spindles, discs, and spheres; it is also the one area of woodworking that beginners most shy away from. Perhaps this reluctance has something to do with the relatively high initial cost of the lathe, or maybe it is linked to the commonly held perception that the lathe is somehow or other inherently dangerous or unpredictable. Then again, it could be that the lathe is simply too large for the average end-of-garage workshop.

There is no getting away from the fact, though, that woodturning is an essential part of the total woodworking experience. If you have ambitions to become a good woodworker, and to do furniture making, toy making, woodcarving, or the like, then woodturning is as much a pivotal activity as, say, sawing and planing. Woodturning is just another woodworking skill that needs to be learned and mastered.

Okay, so woodturning is dynamic and, yes, there is an element of not quite knowing what you're going to end up with, but that's what makes it so exciting!

As to the common perception that woodturning is dangerous, we've got a feeling that perhaps more than anything else, this has to do with the fact that lots of beginners start out with so-called beginners' lathes and badly designed "bargain" tools. They start by turning on little low-powered "clip-on" lathes and using unsuitable short-handled tools, and before you can say "tools breaking" and "workpiece flying off," they have a catastrophic experience that dulls their eagerness.

All this means that you can't start with a cheapo lathe and a few tools, and then expect to buy bigger, better, and more expensive as your skills and needs grow. If you have ambitions to become a woodturner, then you must start off with a well-designed lathe and a range of carefully selected tools. There is no other way!

As for the lathe, you will find all you need to know in the chapter on woodworking machines. In the mean time, the following tool listings and definitions will put you on the right road.

WHAT WOODTURNING TOOL TO USE, AND WHEN

If most beginners understand the essential difference between a joinery chisel and a cabinet scraper—it's plain to see that a chisel cuts with a slicing action, whereas a scraper cuts with a dragging action; why do so many rely on the scraper to do just about every task? Why spend dusty hours with a woodturning scraper scratching a spindle to shape, when it can be done in minutes with a chisel? if you don't understand the difference between a woodturning chisel and a woodturning scraper then the following entries should be key reading.

LONG-AND-STRONG SQUARE CHISEL

Though, on the face of it, the classic long-and-strong woodturning chisel looks much the same as a straight woodcarving chisel (see 6-1), it is, in fact, a quite different tool. With a blade at about $1/4$ inch thick, $1^1/4$ to 2 inches wide, and 9 to 10 inches long, and with a 10- to 13-inch-long handle, a good turning chisel might well measure out at a massive 19 to 23 inches long. The turning chisel has two equal flat bevels, one on each side of the blade, that add up to the total cutting edge angle of about 30 degrees. In essence, the turning chisel is used as a planing or finishing tool. Currently, square chisels seem to be falling from favor, because they can only be obtained from specialist suppliers.

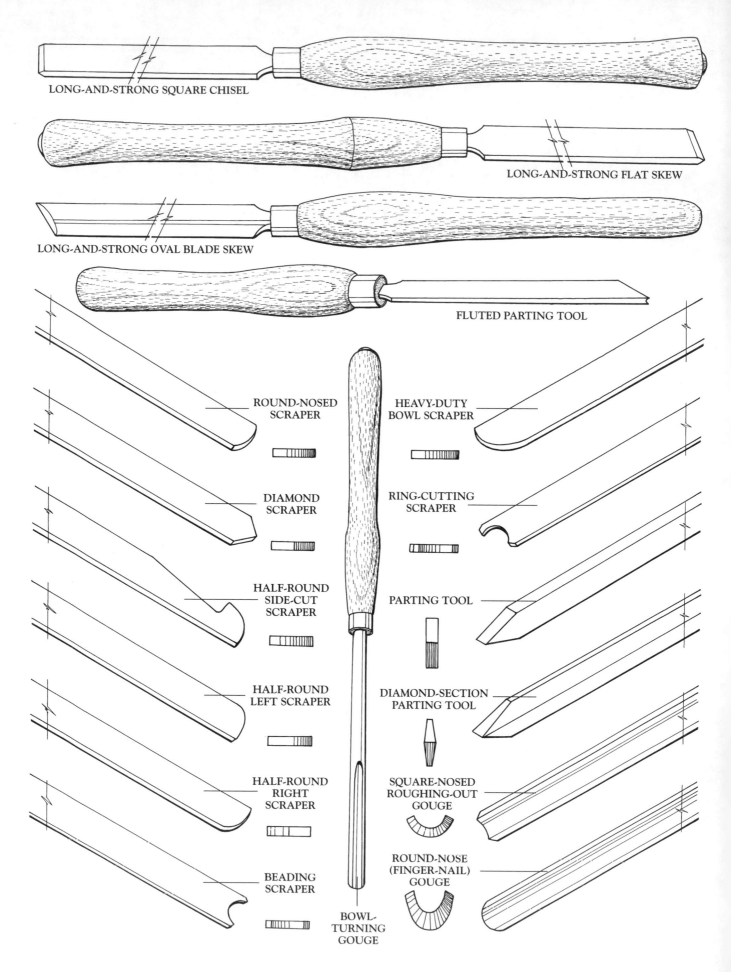

LONG-AND-STRONG SQUARE CHISEL

LONG-AND-STRONG FLAT SKEW

LONG-AND-STRONG OVAL BLADE SKEW

FLUTED PARTING TOOL

ROUND-NOSED
SCRAPER

HEAVY-DUTY
BOWL SCRAPER

DIAMOND
SCRAPER

RING-CUTTING
SCRAPER

HALF-ROUND
SIDE-CUT
SCRAPER

PARTING TOOL

HALF-ROUND
LEFT SCRAPER

DIAMOND-SECTION
PARTING TOOL

HALF-ROUND
RIGHT
SCRAPER

SQUARE-NOSED
ROUGHING-OUT
GOUGE

BEADING
SCRAPER

ROUND-NOSE
(FINGER-NAIL)
GOUGE

BOWL-
TURNING
GOUGE

Fig. 6-1. Woodturning tools.

TRADITIONAL LONG-AND-STRONG FLAT-BLADED SKEW CHISEL

A flat-bladed skew chisel, sometimes called a "long-cornered" chisel, is the primary tool for smoothing or planing convex cylindrical surfaces, making V-section cuts, cleaning end grain, and general finishing between centers. It is, in effect, a straight-bladed chisel that has been ground so that it has two points—one acute and long, and the other obtuse and short; in many ways, it is two tools for the price of one. Most woodturners go for the skew chisel with a skewed angle of about 70 degrees, with two equal bevels of about $12\frac{1}{2}$ to 15 degrees that add up to a total bevel angle between 25 and 30 degrees. As with the square chisel, the blade of the skew needs to be at least $\frac{1}{4}$ inch thick. Though the skew chisel is something of a tricky tool to control, when it has been mastered, it is capable of shearing the wood down to a perfect finish. In action, the skew chisel tends to come into its own when the blade is cutting over the top of the workpiece with the handle held high so that the bevel is more or less rubbing on the workpiece. The shearing cut is achieved with the bevel pressed down on the top of the workpiece, with the short point leading the way, and with the direction of the cut always being on the level or heading downhill. The larger the diameter of the workpiece, the larger the skew chisel.

MODERN OVAL-BLADED SKEW CHISEL

The oval-bladed skew chisel has all the characteristics of its traditional skew chisel brother and more. It is a relatively modern tool that has been designed specifically to overcome the "digging in" problems that are inherent with skew chisels that are rectangular in cross section. So where professional turners once spent time grinding away the corners of a rectangular-section chisel so that it was rounded at the short edge of the skew, they now have the option of getting a tool that starts out being nicely rounded or oval on one or both edges.

SCRAPERS

The scraper, as the name rightly suggests, is a tool that works with a scraping action, rather than a shearing action. With a blade at about $\frac{3}{8}$ inch thick and between $\frac{1}{2}$ and $1\frac{1}{2}$ inches wide, the scraper is made in a variety of profiles, with the cutting edge ground to a single bevel at an angle of about 60–80 degrees. In action, the blade is positioned flat-face down on the rest, with the cutting edge—the top face of the tool—held just about level with the axis or center-of-spin of the workpiece. Though a scraper is a wonderfully easy tool to use for cutting concave shapes, moldings, bowls, and the like, the resultant form tends to look less finished than a form turned with a gouge or a chisel. One old-time woodturner describes a scraped surface as looking "worried and sore."

An old woodturning catalog, dated about 1900 describes a set of a hundred or so scrapers; one dated 1997 describes a set of eight scrapers. Way back at the end of the nineteenth century, when woodturning was a popular "gentleman's" hobby, it may have been that the fashion was to use scrapers rather than chisels and gouges. If you have in mind to do fancy turnings like goblets and such, a set of scrapers that includes such profiles as a "round nose," a "diamond," a "half-round side cut," a "half-round left," and a "half-round right" is likely to be very helpful.

Beginners often make the mistake of going for the easy but disappointing option of using the scraper for just about everything. The correct procedure is to do most of the work with the gouge, and then, if need be, to finish with one or other of the scrapers. So just as a furniture maker might clear the rough with the plane and finish with the cabinet scraper, so the woodturner clears the rough with the gouge and sometimes finishes with the scraper. I say "sometimes" because there are woodturners who hardly, if ever, use scrapers.

BEADING SCRAPER

The beading scraper is a tool designed specifically to cut decorative perfect-every-time beads or half rounds on spindles. Once again, this tool is sometimes spurned by professionals as being "not quite kosher" because of the perfect-every-time aspect, which all too often does result in turnings that lack character. Or to put it another way, there is a great deal of pleasure in seeing the slightly different and individual curve details of a pair of candlesticks, a pair of spindles, or other "matched" items.

HEAVY-DUTY BOWL SCRAPERS

With a single beveled edge ground to an angle of 40 to 80 degrees, and with the body of the blade being up to $1\frac{1}{2}$ inches wide and $\frac{3}{8}$ inch thick, these are swift short-cut tools that are used for cleaning out the inside shape of large bowls.

RING-CUTTING SCRAPERS

The ring-cutting scraper is a tool that has been designed for the very specific task of cutting captive rings. Coming either in sets of "lefts" and "rights," or as a single tool that is beveled on both sides, this tool very neatly performs the otherwise tricky task of cutting a "trick" ring that is part and parcel of the turning, like captive rings on goblets, and captive rings on babies' rattles. Once again, although these easy to use, perfect-every-time tools are great fun, they do somewhat remove the challenge of the task. We prefer to use the point of a skew chisel or grind our own ring-cutting tools.

PARTING TOOL
The parting tool—sometimes called a parting "chisel"—is designed for parting off work, for making V-grooves, and for generally making straight in-and-out cuts. In action, the tool is set on edge on the tool rest, advanced until the bevel is in contact and resting on the wood, and then the handle is raised until the cutting edge begins to bite.

DIAMOND-SECTION PARTING TOOL
Many woodturners prefer to use the diamond-section parting tool for the simple reason that whereas the standard tool sometimes burns and binds when it is used for cutting slots, the shape of the diamond tool allows some clearance for the sides of the tool.

FLUTED PARTING TOOL
This tool has a flute or shallow round channel along the bottom edge. Unlike the traditional parting tool, this tool is ground to a skew point, making the sides of the flute section like two scribes or cutters. In use, the cutters lead the way and scribe at either side before the body of the tool cuts the channel. All this adds up to a finish that is exceptionally crisp and clean.

SQUARE-NOSED ROUGHING GOUGE
The square-nosed round-section roughing gouge is the perfect tool for removing lots of wood fast. The square-nosed tool tends to be used for working between centers, when the wood is being roughed to shape or swiftly sized. In action, the round section and the square end allow the gouge to be rolled from side to side in such a way that the cutting edge is always in contact. Or put another way, the round section allows the tool to be pivoted on its back and at different angles. When you look through the catalogs, you will see that such gouges are sold as "spindle" gouges and "bowl" gouges, with the main difference between the two being the cross-section shape of the blade.

LONG-AND-STRONG ROUND-NOSED GOUGE
The long-and-strong round-nosed or fingernail gouge is, in many ways, the jack-of-all trades tool for creating bowls and spindles. The round section and the absence of corners lessen the risk of the tool digging in and doing damage. In fact, the round nose is so easy to manage that some woodturners advocate that beginners start

off using the round-nosed gouge for just about all their roughing out and shaping tasks, and then gradually change over to using the square-nosed gouge when they better understand what they are doing.

BOWL-TURNING GOUGE
The design of the deep-fluted bowl gouge, made from solid round-section bar, makes it the perfect tool for turning bowls. It is capable of very heavy deep cuts. The tool is used on its side, at 15 to 20 degrees off vertical, so that the flute is pointing in the direction of the cut. In use, the bevel is rubbed on the workpiece to leave a finish that is uniquely smooth and even.

THE ANATOMY OF WOODTURNING CHISELS, GOUGES, AND SCRAPERS
Although a woodturning chisel can be defined as a tool with a bevel on both sides of the blade, a gouge as a C- or U-section tool that has a single bevel running around the convex side of the blade, and a scraper as a tool that has a single bevel, it's important to note that there are many different classes or types of chisels, gouges, and scrapers (see 6-1), all with different functions.

The anatomy of chisels and scrapers is easily understood in terms of shape and structure of the cutting edge. The chisel is rectangular in cross section, it has two bevels, and it is held with one edge in contact with the tool rest; the scraper is rectangular in cross section, it has a single bevel, and it is held with the back of the blade being in contact with the rest.

There is some confusion about the different gouges—not about the shape of the cutting edge—but, rather, with the length and cross section of the blade and the terms applied to it.

There are three terms applied to gouges that beginners find confusing: "HSS," "flute," and "long and strong."

HIGH-SPEED STEEL
The makers of HSS tools, or tools made from high-speed steel, claim that they will not only keep a sharpened edge about six times longer than carbon steel, but will also resist "bluing" when they are being ground. That said, while an HSS tool does most certainly stay sharper longer, because it has been tempered throughout to a uniform hardness, when it does become blunt, it is that much more difficult to grind and sharpen.

In current catalogs, HSS tools are coming down in price to the extent that it is becoming more and more difficult to obtain tools made from carbon steel.

FLUTES

The flute is the gulley that runs down the inside face of a gouge blade. In many ways, it is the shape of the blade and flute in cross section that defines the gouge and allows it to do what it does. There are three types of woodturning gouges, each with a different flute profile: the bowl gouge, the roughing gouge, and the spindle or coving gouge (see 6-2). The bowl gouge has a deep U-section flute with a thickened keel at the bottom of the U; the roughing gouge has a more shallow section and the metal is the same thickness throughout; the spindle gouge is a much flatter C in cross section.

LONG AND STRONG

Long-and-strong gouges, sometimes described as L&S gouges, are extra heavy and solid gouges that are stronger and longer in length and in cross section than regular tools. Such gouges are used almost exclusively for turning bowls. The long-and-strong section allows the turner to push the tool without fear of the tool failing or chattering. The extra length of the blade and handle allows for maximum leverage and control.

HANDLE

Even though woodturning tools are sold with handles, there has always been a tradition among woodturners to knock off the factory-made handles and turn their own. The idea is, of course, that the turner can show off her or his skills by making custom handles. That said, it is a fact that the length and weight of the handle really do need to vary in relation to the height of the turner. Some woodturners like to fit their long-and-strong tools with handles that are extra long and weighted at the end (see 6-3). One turner that we know even goes to the trouble of filling the ends of his long-and-strong handles with lead shot to give them extra stability. Handles are made from strong straight-grained woods like beech, ash, sycamore, box, and maple—almost any wood that is strong along the length of the grain.

FERRULE

As with woodcarving gouges and joinery chisels, the function of the ferrule on a woodturning tool is to contain the handle so that it doesn't split. It's plain to see that if you were to use a tool without a ferrule, the strain put on the blade would almost certainly cause the tang or shank to lever and split out of the handle (see 6-3).

Many catalogs offer ferrules for sale, so if you want to make your own handles and fit your own ferrules, you must be clear in your own mind as to your needs. You can choose between "solid brass" or "brassed" ferrules, that is, steel ferrules that have been coated with brass, or

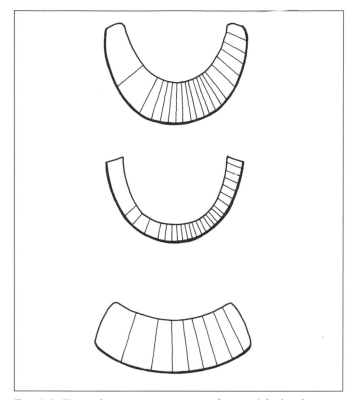

Fig. 6-2. Top to bottom, *cross-section shapes of the bowl gouge, roughing gouge, and spindle gouge.*

ferrules made from plumbers' copper pipe offcuts, stainless steel ferrules, or the like. We don't think that it matters too much, as long as the ferrule is strong and fitting for its task—no sharp edges or rust. Stay away from "brassed" tube ferrules that are made from a folded and rolled steel pipe that is covered with a thin sheet of brass. The brass peels off over time as a thin razor-sharp sheet, and the steel can pull apart at the seam.

TANG

Although it's true to say that all woodturning tools have a tang, in the sense that the blade runs back into the handle, it's also a fact that the tang on most modern woodturning tools is no more that a continuation of the steel section that makes up the blade. For example, on the long-and-strong gouge, the round section bar runs straight back into the handle (see 6-3), and the tang on the roughing gouge is formed by grinding the U-section to shape.

Woodturning chisels, gouges, and scrapers never have bolsters or leather washers. If you look through the catalogs, you will see that although the blades of chisels, scrapers, and roughing gouges might have shoulders that curve into the shank, and the bowl gouge might have a round section that runs straight to the shank, not one of them has a bolster. The shank always runs straight through the ferrule and into the handle.

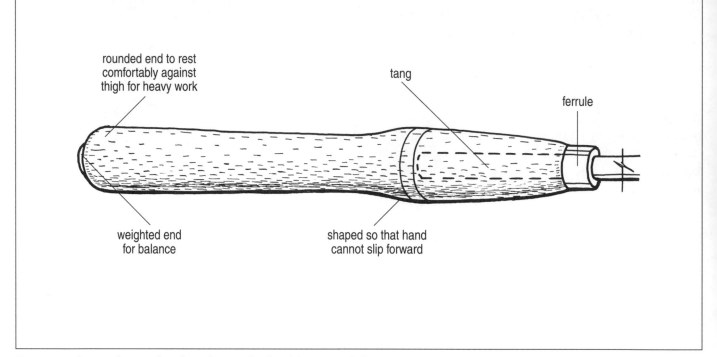

rounded end to rest
comfortably against
thigh for heavy work

tang

ferrule

weighted end
for balance

shaped so that hand
cannot slip forward

Fig. 6-3. A long-and-strong handle with a weighted end for counterbalance.

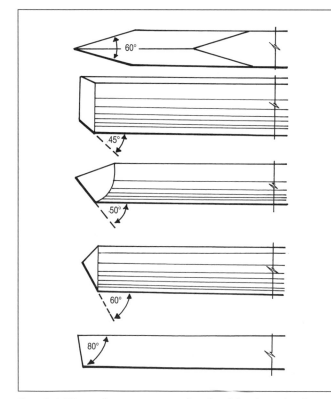

Fig. 6-4. Top to bottom, *cutting bevels of the skew chisel, roughing gouge, spindle gouge, deep bowl gouge, and scraper. Many turners will prefer alternate angles.*

CUTTING BEVEL

Most joinery and woodcarving chisels and gouges are ground to a primary bevel and then honed to a secondary micro-bevel. Woodturning tools are uniquely different in that they are honed on the primary bevel; there is no secondary bevel.

As to the shape of the bevel, most woodturners would agree that many new woodturning tools are ground with overly long and slender bevels that are somewhat dangerous to use. This being the case, many new woodturning tools need to be reground. Ideally, square chisels are ground to an angle of 40 degrees, skew chisels to 30 degrees, gouges to 40 to 50 degrees, deep bowl gouges to 60 degrees, and scrapers to about 80 degrees (see 6-4).

THE CUTTING ACTION OF WOODTURNING TOOLS

Unlike most other woodworking activities, where the woodworker drives or pushes the chisels and gouges forward into the wood, woodturning involves turning the wood against the tool.

Because the three basic woodturning tools vary so in shape and use, it is easier to consider them separately.

CUTTING ACTION OF THE CHISEL

The chisel is primarily used to "plane" the wood. In action the chisel is first set edge down on the rest so that the bevel rubs at a canted angle on the workpiece; the fingers of the free hand press down on the blade, the handle is lifted until the cutting edge begins to bite, and then the tool is traversed along the wood. If you are doing it correctly, only the leading part of the cutting edge will be in contact with the wood. (see 6-5). Whereas beginners tend to think that it is the amount of downward pressure applied by the left hand that governs the cut, it is in fact the angle at which the cutting edge is held that does most of the work. Another point to bear in mind is that planing can only take place when the chisel is, as it were, run downhill, from high to low wood.

CUTTING ACTION OF THE GOUGE

The main difference between the cutting action of the gouge and that of the chisel obviously has to do with the fact that the gouge has a bevel running right around the profile of the blade. The shaped blade enables the turner to roll the tool along the rest while keeping the cutting edge always up to the workpiece.

The primary cutting action of all three gouge types is the same. Of course, each is used differently —turning between centers is very different from turning a bowl—but it is fair to say that the action at the point of cut is much the same in all three.

The cutting action for clearing the waste with a roughing gouge is as follows: Set the gouge down on the tool rest so that the flute is looking to the left, lift the handle until the bevel is in contact and

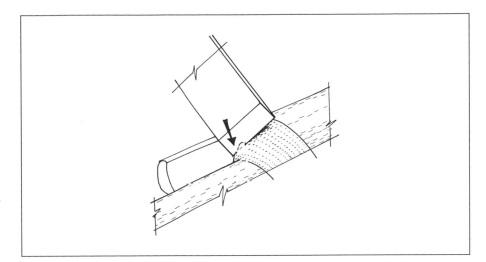

Fig. 6-5. Cutting action of the chisel correctly showing that only part of the blade is in contact with the wood. Always work from high to low wood.

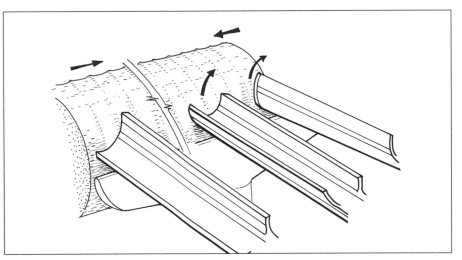

Fig. 6-6. Hold the gouge so that the flute is looking to the left and traverse along the workpiece toward the right. When you reach the tailstock end, roll the gouge over so that the flute is looking to the right, and traverse toward the left. Always travel away from the flute.

the cutting edge begins to bite, and then slowly move the tool from left to right along the rest (see 6-6). When you get to the far right of the workpiece, set the gouge down so that the flute is looking to the right, and then move to the left. When you have cleared the rough and achieved a round section, set the gouge down on the rest so that the flute is looking to the sky, raise the handle slightly until the cutting edge begins to bit, and then traverse the wood. Although this time around you could hold the gouge in

the same position, it makes better sense to roll the blade slightly so that the whole curve of the bevel gets to be used. If you are doing it right, the waste will curl off as an even-width ribbon.

CUTTING ACTION OF THE SCRAPER

Perhaps for the simple reason that they are so easy and safe to manage, scrapers are the favored tools of many beginners. Most experienced woodturners would agree, however, that scrapers tend to reduce the whole activity to an inefficient dusty business of abrading rather than cutting. It's a bit like carving; who would scrape and scour a bowl into shape when it could be done so much more cleanly and crisply with a gouge? And so it is with woodturning. Try to keep your scraping to the minimum.

In action, the tool rest is positioned close to the workpiece, the scraper is held down flat on the tool rest, with the bevel-side down (see 6-7), the fingers of the free hand are pressed down on the blade, and then the tool is advanced and traversed. It is the burred edge of the turning scraper that does the work.

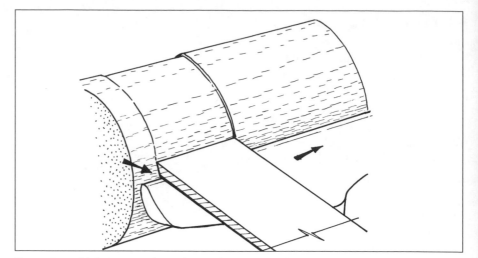

Fig. 6-7. Hold the scraper down flat on the rest and advance into the workpiece; the burred edge does the cutting.

SHARPENING WOODTURNING TOOLS

As with tools for woodcarving and general woodworking, woodturning tools need to be sharp. The sharpening procedure for woodturning tools is somewhat different than for carving tools, in that most turners go for a single bevel, using the tool straight from the grinding wheel. They grind and hone in one swift operation, a speedy on, off, and away, one-stop method known as "grind-honing." There's no need for the bench oilstone.

Keep in mind that there are a great many woodturners out there who think this method is nigh on sinful. They advocate a long and slow procedure of grinding, honing, and stropping, just as with other woodworking tools. If you have doubts as to the correct way forward, try both methods, and then use the one that works for you.

GRIND-HONING

Grind-honing woodturning tools is a pretty straightforward procedure, but you do have to have just the right equipment. You need a wet grindstone with a vertical medium-grit wheel about 7 to 8 inches in

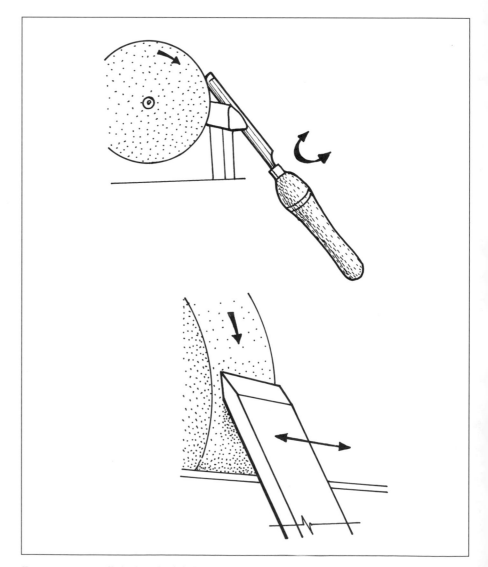

Fig. 6-8. Top, roll the bevel while keeping the point of contact at a constant same to the stone. Continue until the bevel is bright. Bottom, hold the tool at $12^1/_2$ to 15 degrees to the stone, and slide the tool from side-to-side along the rest. Make sure that your hold is firm but not heavy.

diameter that revolves toward you. And of course, you must also be outfitted with safety goggles.

Grind-honing a Roughing Gouge. Start by setting the grindstone's tool rest so that its top is level with the pivot point of the stone. This done, take the gouge, and set the back of the blade down on the rest so that the handle is low down, and the bevel is just clear of the stone. Now, with the tool held at an angle of about 40 to 45 degrees, lift the handle until the bevel is in contact, and then roll the handle first one way and then the other so that the whole bevel makes contact (see 6-8). The whole success of the operation depends on your holding the tool gently but firmly at a constant angle. Don't bear down too heavily on the tool, and don't keep lifting the tool up to see how the bevel is coming along; once or twice is enough. Finally, when you are happy with the bevel, jab the cutting edge into a block of softwood to remove the burr.

Grind-honing a Chisel. Some square-ended woodturning chisels are ground only on one side, and others are ground with a different bevel angle on each side, but most woodturners opt for identical angles between 12 1/2 and 15 degrees on both sides, adding up to a total sharpening angle between 25 and 30 degrees.

Set the chisel down on the tool rest at an angle between 12 1/2 and 15 degrees to the stone, and then advance the tool and run it from side to side across the face of the stone so that all of the bevel makes contact. When you have done one side of the blade, simply flip the chisel over and repeat the procedure on the other side (see 6-8 bottom).

Hold the tool firmly and yet lightly, that is, without too much downward pressure. On no account

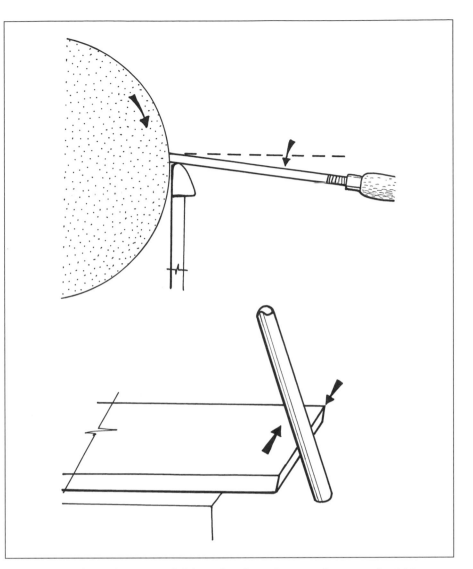

Fig. 6-9. Top, *lower the scraper slightly so that the end is ground to an angle of 80 degrees.* Bottom, *turn the burr over by rubbing the leading edge with the back of a hardened steel tool or with a piece of round section bar.*

must the handle be allowed to swing from side to side.

Finally, when you have achieved the bevel, remove the burr on the inside of the blade by jabbing the cutting edge down into a block of softwood.

Some woodturners favor having the chisel bevel ground at a total angle of 25 degrees. With the bevel being so hollow ground, what they have in effect is a micro-bevel. These woodturners even hone and strop to a polished finish. There is no doubting that micro-bevel geometry will outperform a ground-honed bevel at first cut, but the

micro-beveled edge will be so weak that it will fail in a few minutes. So it's up to you to choose: Do you want a supersharp tool for a few seconds? or Do you want a tool that's going to stay sharper longer?

Grind-honing a Straight Scraper. Scrapers are quite different from chisels and gouges in that they are ground to an edge of 80 degrees. They are first ground off at the end to a square angle of 90 degrees, and then the end is ground back slightly to 80 degrees.

Start by removing the old burr by rubbing the top face of the scraper across a bench stone. This

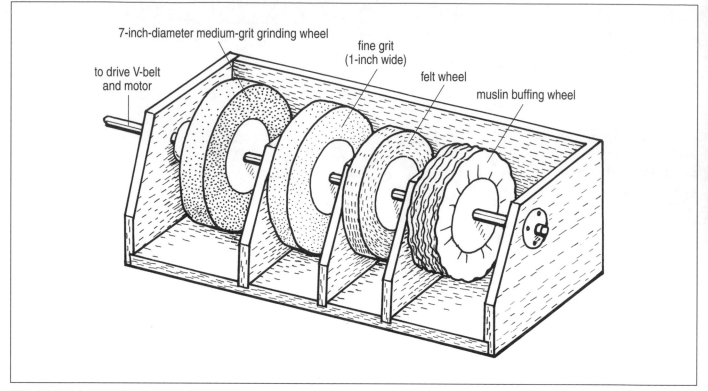

Fig. 6-10. A homemade all-in-one sharpening and tuning system. Be warned: You should always run at a low speed, and you should always wear safety glasses.

done, hold the scraper down flat on the grindstone's tool rest so that the heel is just clear of the wheel, advance so that the heel makes contact, and then drop the handle slightly until you achieve the 80-degree angle. Finally, take another round-section tool, like say the gouge, and rub the back of the shaft across the leading edge of the scraper to turn over the burr (see 6-9).

TUNING WOODTURNING CHISELS AND GOUGES

As with tuning joinery and woodcarving chisels and gouges, the procedure of tuning woodturning chisels and gouges is defined as maintaining your tools in good condition or, you might say, in a condition that best suits your way of working. On the face of it, this would seem to be a straightforward business of replacing a handle or regrinding a bevel. There appears, however, to be a unique and overwhelming desire, right across the board, for turners to completely change their tools to the extent that we wonder why they bothered buying them in the first place. For example, one well-known woodturner starts by knocking the handles off his tools and replacing them with turned handles of his own design.

Another turner that we know of first changes the bevel angles of his new gouges, and then he regrinds the

backs, turns new handles, and weights the ends of the handles with lead shot. Another guy, contrary to all current thinking, hollow-grinds the bevel of his skew chisels to a very slender angle. This tradition of turners spending time fine-tuning and customizing their tools is borne out by the amount of space in tool catalogs given over to grinding and sharpening systems that are specifically designed for swift-and-easy shaping and sharpening. It is also true that the process of turning is so hard on the tools that almost as much time is spent on fine tuning and sharpening as is spent on the actual turning. All this adds up to the fact that it is almost impossible to give you specific advice on tool tuning, other than to say that the cutting edges need to be sharp and the handles need to be well balanced and comfortable to hold. We can say for sure that you need a sharpening system. We know of a woodturner who has built his own tuning system that grinds, hones, strops, and polishes. All it is, in effect, is a shaft, motor driven by means of a V-belt. From left to right along the shaft are four wheels: a medium-grit grinding wheel, a fine wheel, a felt wheel, and a mop wheel (see 6-10). He uses this machine for all his tuning procedures, everything from grinding the bevel and honing to cleaning away all signs of rust and the final polishing.

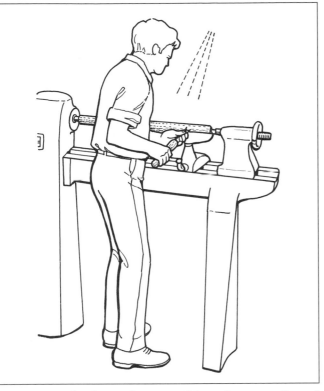

Fig. 6-11. Stand with your feet in a well-braced position. Control and maneuver the tool by locking your arms and moving the top part of your body. To start a cut, raise the handle until the bevel makes contact, and then lift the handle some more so that the tool arcs and cuts into the wood.

Fig. 6-12. With your elbow more or less in line with the lathe center, hold the tool at a sloping angle to the rest, support the handle against your thigh, and then advance the cut.

STANCE AND CONTROL WITH WOOD-TURNING TOOLS

While working at the lathe, you can stand at the front, with the workpiece being turned inboard between centers (see 6-11), or you can stand to the left of the headstock, with the workpiece on the outboard end of the drive shaft (see 6-12). Your choice of stance at the lathe is pretty limited. It's not like carving, where you can, say, sit cross-legged on the porch or stand up in the garage; the lathe is stationary, and you have to present yourself to it. So stand in a well-balanced position, with your legs astride and well braced so that you can get your weight behind the tool. Your height and build will govern the precise way that you hold the tool, but what you are aiming for is a tight compact stance, with the tool always held close to the body. You don't move your arms or your hands much when you want to change the direction of the cut, but rather, you move your hips and the top part of your body and slightly increase your height by flexing your feet. The lathe stays put, you stand more or less in the same position, and your arms stay close by your side; all the movement is in your hips, your shoulders, and your feet.

One of the big stance-and-control dilemmas facing beginners to woodturning—the difficulty that most holds them back—is how best to secure the wood while it is being turned. You can, to a great extent, learn about the tools by trial and error, but the question of how to hold the wood safe and secure must be decided right from start. The following tips on stance and control will get you on your way.

TURNING WITH A FOUR-JAW CHUCK

Nowadays there are all kinds of patent woodturning chuck systems, some with spigots, some with pins, some with rings, pins, and spigots, and some with a whole bunch of weird and wonderful additions besides. One of the best all-around systems is the traditional four-jaw chuck as used by metalworkers (see 6-13). In woodturning, this beautifully efficient, tried-and-true device is used to hold and secure the workpiece on the lathe while it is being turned. It's wonderfully easy to use. You just screw the chuck on the headstock mandrel and then get started. When the chuck key is turned, the four jaws are screwed in geared unison toward the center so that the workpiece is automatically held and centralized. In action, you mount the square-section wood in the open chuck, tighten up the jaws, and get started. You don't have to deal with first turning the wood to a round section or fiddle around with pins and rings. And just in case you are thinking that a three-jaw chuck is much the same thing—it isnt! Although three-jaw chucks are a good deal less expensive and much easier to find second-hand than the four-jaw, they can, of course, be used only to hold and centralize wood that has already been turned to a round section. The four-jaw chuck, on the other hand, is perfect for holding both round- and square-section workpieces.

TURNING BETWEEN CENTERS

Turning between centers is the procedure of turning spindles, cylinders, and the like with the workpiece held and pivoted between the headstock and the tailstock center. So, for example, you might fit the four-jaw chuck and have the wood held in the chuck and pivoted on the tailstock center, or you could hold the workpiece between a pronged drive center and a live tailstock center (see 6-14), and so on. No matter how the workpiece is held, turning between centers means that the workpiece is pivoted between the headstock and the tailstock. Keep in mind that the maximum size of the workpiece is governed by the horizontal distance between the headstock and the tailstock and the vertical distance or "swing" between the center of spin and the top of the lathe bed or tool rest.

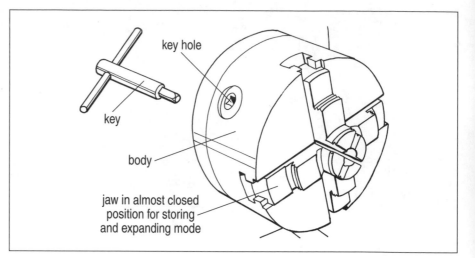

Fig. 6-13. *In the position as shown, the four jaws of the chuck are fully closed and ready to be opened and used as a large pin chuck. The four jaws can be removed and reversed so that they can be used in a gripping mode.*

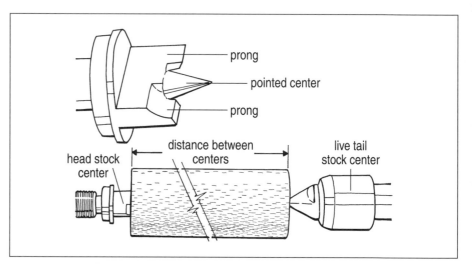

Fig. 6-14. Top, *the two-pronged center is best used for hardwoods.* Bottom, *the distance between centers determines the length of the work.*

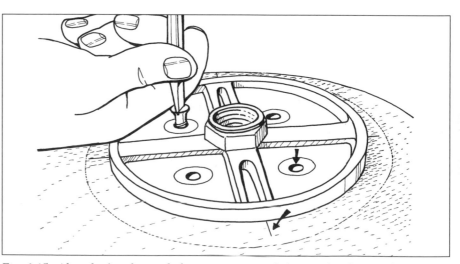

Fig. 6-15. *Align the faceplate with the center point guide lines and make sure that the screws fit the countersinks. Drive the screws in on opposite sides in the order N, S, E, and then W; remove them in reverse order.*

TURNING WITH A FACEPLATE

If you are looking to turn large bowls, without going to the expense of buying a four-jaw chuck or one of the other special chucks, then the best method is to use a traditional faceplate, a steel disc or blank with a threaded center that fits the screw size of your drive mandrel. In use, all you do is fix the faceplate to the workpiece with woodscrews (see 6-15), and then swiftly fit the faceplate onto the lathe drive either over the bed or over the outboard drive. Faceplates are safe and relatively easy to use; the only problem is that you finish up with screw holes in the base of the workpiece.

SCREW CHUCK

Screw chucks or wood screw chucks are diminutive attachments that are traditionally used for holding small turnings like eggcups, little bowls, and such (see 6-16 top). In use, the chuck is screwed directly into the center of the workpiece by means of a wood screw that is either loose or fixed, and then the whole works is mounted directly onto the lathe's headstock. Although the wood screw chuck is certainly inexpensive; once again, you do finish up with a screw hole in the base of the workpiece.

TURNING WITH A DRILL CHUCK

A drill chuck is usually no more than a Jacob's-type chuck that is mounted on an arbor that fits into a taper in the back of the chuck body. Chucks of this type can be directly mounted onto the headstock spindle or onto the tailstock barrel (see 6-16 bottom). They can be used for holding very small turnings like bobbins or drill bits and shell augers, and so on. You can use your drill chuck mounted on the tailstock in conjunction with Forstner drill bits, for boring holes through turned-between-center items like pepper mills, lampstands, toys, or anything that needs to be bored with an accurate hole.

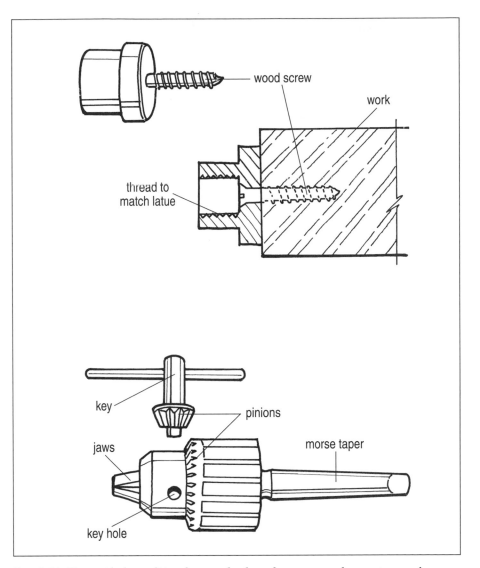

Fig. 6-16. Top, *with the traditional screw chuck as shown, a wood screw is passed through a hole in the back of the chuck and driven into the workpiece. The thread size of the chuck needs to match that on the drive spindle.* Bottom, *the traditional Jacob's-type screw chuck is opened and closed by means of a key. The Morse taper needs to fit your tailstock spindle size.*

WOODTURNING CHISEL, GOUGE, AND SCRAPER TECHNIQUES: STEP-BY-STEP METHODS

Most beginners to woodturning are eager to get started. There is no denying that enthusiasm is a good thing, but we would say that when it comes to woodturning, you do have to rein yourself in and temper your enthusiasm with caution. The problem, of course, is that a lathe is potentially very dangerous. It's not a toy!

Okay, your lathe is set up and in good working order, *you have read through the manufacturer's warnings,* and you are ready to go. Keep in mind that the following projects aren't intended to be complete in themselves; they are no more than exercises. The idea is that you can gain confidence by working through the basic techniques, and then go on to greater things.

USING A FOUR-JAW CHUCK TO ROUGH DOWN A CYLINDER

Take a length of square-section wood, say, about 12 inches long and 3 inches square, and establish the center point on one end by drawing crossed diagonals (see 6-17 top). (If you opt for using a pronged drive center as well as the tailstock center, then you would of course have to establish center points on both ends.)

1. Set the workpiece in the jaws of the chuck, bring the tailstock up and locate the center on the center point, and then tighten up the chuck. Bring the tool rest up to a comfortable height that is just below the center of spin. Make adjustments so that it is as near the workpiece as possible without actually touching.

2. Switch on the power and observe the way the corners of the wood show up as a blur.

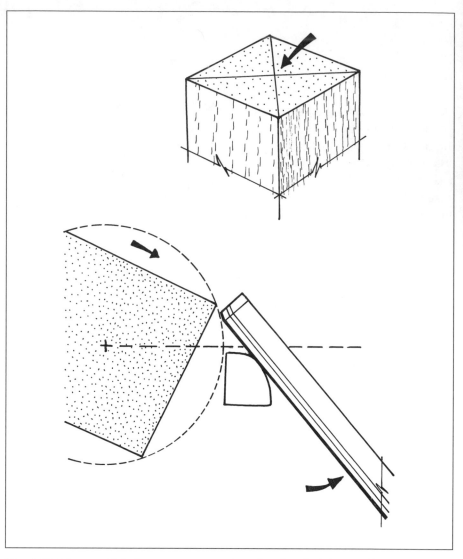

Fig. 6-17. Top, *establish the center point on the tailstock end of the wood by drawing two crossed diagonals.* Bottom, *set the tool rest just below the center of spin so that it's just clear of the workpiece.*

3. Set the 1-inch roughing gouge on the middle of the rest so that the flute is looking to the sky, and then advance and lift the handle so that the cutting edge of the gouge makes contact with the workpiece (see 6-17 bottom). You should feel a little tap as the cutting edge touches the "blurred" corners of the square-section wood.

4. Roll the gouge over so that the flute is looking to the right and then traverse to the left. When you are just short of the chuck, roll the gouge over so that the flute is looking to the left, and then traverse toward the tailstock end of the lathe (see 6-18). You will be able to watch and rate your progress by the every-decreasing width of the blur. Continue backward and forward along the workpiece until you achieve a smooth cylinder.

Although you could turn down the rough without rolling the gouge, the rolling action does, as it were, spread the load by putting all the bevel to work.

DRILLING A HORIZONTAL HOLE WITH A FOUR-JAW CHUCK AND A DRILL CHUCK

You are working with the wood held securely in a four-jaw chuck. You have just turned a cylinder about 3 inches in diameter and 8 inches long that needs to be bored horizontally. You have a drill chuck and a set of Forstner drill bits.

1. Turn off the power and wait for the workpiece to come to a standstill. Give a few extra turns with the chuck key just to make sure that the workpiece is going to stay put, and then wind back the tailstock and remove the center. be careful that you don't jolt the workpiece off center.

2. Fit the drill chuck in the tailstock end of the lathe, and set your chosen Forstner bit in the chuck and tighten up. Now, very carefully advance the tailstock so that the pointed center of the Forstner bit runs into the existing center hole (see 6-19) so that it becomes in effect the supporting center at the tailstock end.

3. When you are happy with the setup, switch on the power and gently advance the drill by winding up the tailstock spindle. Run the drill in to a depth of about $^1/_2$ inch, and then back out so as to clear the waste (see 6-20). Continue running the drill in and out until the proper depth is reached, all the while being sure to work slowly and with care and caution.

If you find that the drill starts to screech or gets hot, chances are that either you are trying to sink the hole too fast, or your drill bit needs resharpening, or the grain is tough.

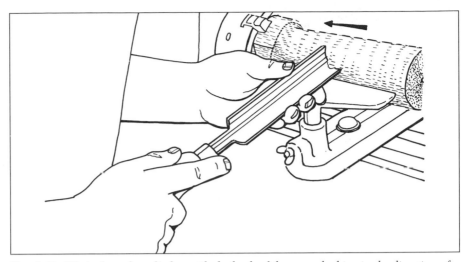

Fig. 6-18. Work along the cylinder, with the back of the gouge looking in the direction of the traverse.

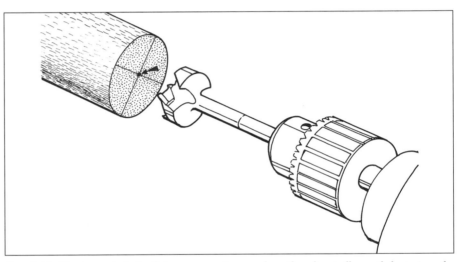

Fig. 6-19. Having switched off the power, advance the tailstock spindle until the point of the bit is on target in the existing center hole.

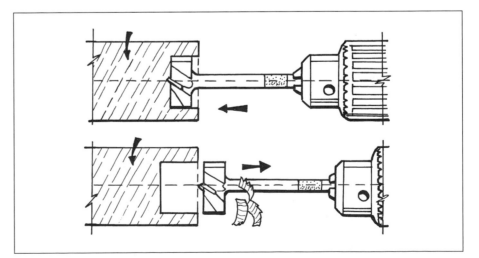

Fig. 6-20. Top, wind the tailstock up so that the bit runs into the wood to a depth of about $^1/_2$ inch. Don't force the pace; go at it very slowly. Bottom, back up enough to clear the waste, and then repeat the procedure until the proper depth is achieved. Note the piece of masking tape wrapped around the shank to act as a depth gauge.

MOUNTING A BLANK ON A FACEPLATE

You want to prepare a blank and mount it on the lathe—say, a disc or blank for a bowl about 6 inches in diameter and 3 inches thick.

1. Check your 7-by-7-inch-square slab of wood over for possible problems; avoid loose knots, cracks, stains, and anything else that may suggest that the wood might twist, split, or otherwise fail.

2. Having first established the center point by drawing crossed diagonals, set the dividers or compasses to a radius of 3 inches and scribe out a 6-inch-diameter circle (see 6-21).

3. With the circle in place, move to the band saw and cut out the disc. If you haven't got a band saw, then draw tangents at the four diagonal-circle intersections, and clear the corners of waste with a handsaw (see 6-22).

4. Finally, set the faceplate in place on the wood, align the faceplate's center hole with the crossed diagonals, and fix with four screws that run about 1/4 to 3/8 inch into the workpiece. Bear in mind that the success of a project of this nature has to do with three factors: the care taken in selecting the wood, the care taken when centering the blank on the faceplate, and your choice and placing of the screws. You have to think the project through right from the start and make some decisions as to how to proceed. You can mount the blank bowl base-to-faceplate, and then turn it with the single chucking so that you finish up with the screw holes in the base of the bowl (see 6-23 top). Or you can mount the blank rim-to-faceplate, and then use a screw chuck so that you finish up with a single hole in the base (see 6-23 bottom).

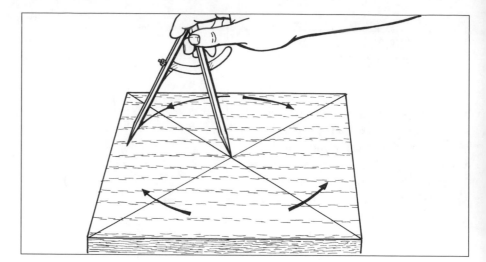

Fig. 6-21. *Spike the point of the dividers or compasses down on the diagonal crossover point and scribe out a circle. If you are using a set of dividers and the grain is rugged, then you might need to change the direction to suit the run of the grain.*

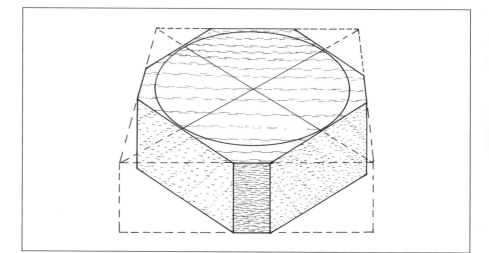

Fig. 6-22. *You can use a handsaw to clear away most of the waste wood.*

Some turners prefer to glue a piece of scrap wood to the bowl blank, with a layer of paper between the waste piece and the blank, and then mount the workpiece on the faceplate. The idea is that there is less chance of the tool edge coming into contact with the faceplate, there are no holes in the finished work, and the paper layer allows a natural dividing line when you want to remove the waste piece.

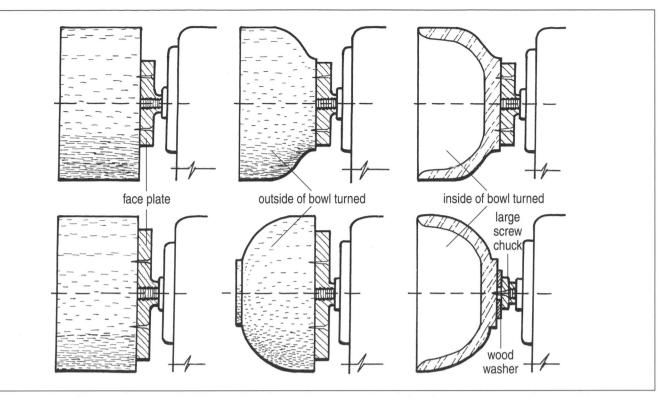

Fig. 6-23. Top, *from left to right, mount the blank so that the foot side is screwed to the faceplate; turn the outside shape of the bowl; finish by turning out the inside hollow. Bottom, from left to right, mount the blank so that the rim side is screwed to the face-plate; turn the outside shape of the bowl, complete with the foot; reverse the half-turned bowl, fix it to a screw chuck, and turn out the inside hollow.*

TURNING WHEELS FOR TOYS ON A SMALL LATHE

You want to turn a set of four small wheels about 3 inches in diameter, and you are working at a small underpowered lathe with no chuck, just a forked center.

Although we usually advocate turning the wood directly from a square section, some so-called beginners' lathes are so pathetically underpowered that it's essential that you clear some of the waste before you get started.

1. Take a $^1/_2$ inch length of $3^1/_2$-by-$3^1/_2$-inch square-section wood, and establish the end centers by drawing crossed diagonals. Adjust the dividers to a radius of $1^1/_2$ inches, and set each end of the wood out with a 3-inch-diameter circle. Draw tangents at the diagonal–circle intersections, link up the

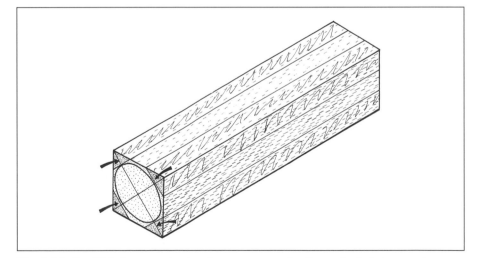

Fig. 6-24. *Establish the waste by drawing tangents at the diagonal–circle intersections, and then run linkup lines along the length of the wood. If it helps, shade in the areas of waste.*

resultant end of-wood octagons to establish the corner waste (see 6-24), and then use a plane to swiftly cut the wood down to an octagonal cross section.

2. Having cleared the bulk of the waste, set the workpiece between centers, tighten up the tailstock, ease it back slightly, and dribble a small drop of oil on the

Fig. 6-25. *Experienced turners would take a calipers' reading with the machine running. If you are a nervous beginner, then for safety's sake, switch off the lathe and drop the legs of the calipers over the workpiece before it comes to a standstill.*

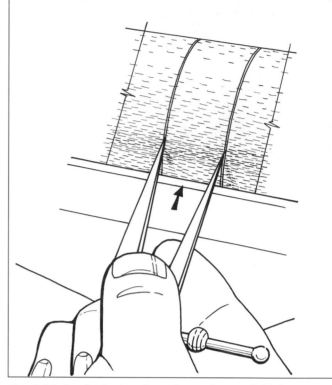

Fig. 6-26. *Set the dividers down flat on the rest, hold them firmly, and run the points into the workpiece.*

tailstock point of spin. Position the tool rest so that it is at a good height for your comfort and for the size of your gouge—usually just below the center height.

3. Having switched on the power, take the roughing gouge and swiftly turn down to a cylinder (see 6-18). Start by roughing the wood with the center of the gouge; when the wood has been roughed to a cylinder, set the gouge over on its side and traverse away from the flute. When you get to the tailstock end, roll the gouge over and traverse to the left. Always move the gouge along so that the corners can't dig in. Frequently along the way, use calipers to check the diameter (see 6-25).

4. When you have achieved a cylinder 3 inches in diameter, with ruler and dividers mark off alternate step-offs along the length of the wood: 1 inch for headstock waste,

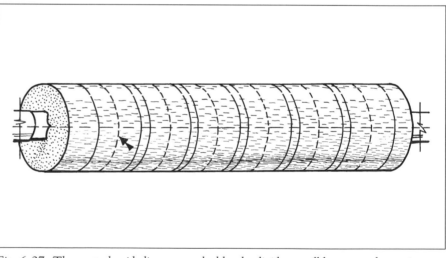

Fig. 6-27. *The central guide line, as marked by the dividers, will become a decorative feature.*

$1^1/2$ inches for the first wheel, $^1/4$ inch for parting waste, $1^1/2$ inches for the second wheel, $^1/4$ inch for parting waste, and so on along the length of the wood until you reach the tailstock end (see 6-26). This

done, reset the dividers to $^3/4$ inch and divide every $1^1/2$-inch wheel width in half (see 6-27).

5. You should finish up with six $1^1/2$ inch step-offs with parting waste in between. The idea is that

you do your very best to make six identical wheels, and then select the best four. With the 1½-inch-wide step-offs nicely scored with the points of the dividers, set the calipers to 1 inch, and then work along the cylinder with a parting tool sinking the between-wheel waste and the head and tail waste to a depth of 1 inch (see 6-28). If you have done it right, the central between-wheel core should finish up at 1 inch in diameter.

6. Having raised the tool rest so that you can work more to the top of the wood, use the skew chisel to turn each wheel down to a part-circle round-nosed profile. Working from left to right, the procedure is as follows: Set the bevel of the chisel down on the first wheel so that the short point is 1 inch to the right of the center line and, looking to the right, plane down and around to the right (see 6-29). Then do the same thing on the other side of the center line, only this time have the short point of the skew chisel looking to the left. Continue for all six wheels: Cut to the right and then to the left, and so on along the length of the wood.

The secret of using the skew chisel for this cut is to have the bevel of the skew rubbing so that the cutting edge shears through the wood. The other thing to watch out for is that the long point doesn't catch as you turn the blade over the curve and down into the parting waste.

7. Having first brought the surface to a smooth finish with the skew chisel, use the parting tool to reduce the between-wheel waste to a ¼-inch diameter. Finally, remove the whole works from the lathe, use a fine-toothed saw to cut the wheels apart, drill axle holes while the centers are still visible, and then run sandpaper down the faces of each wheel.

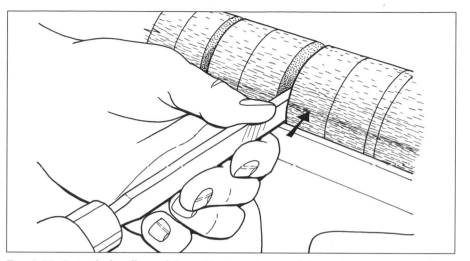

Fig. 6-28. *Raise the handle until the tool begins to bite, and then advance to remove the waste to a depth of 1 inch.*

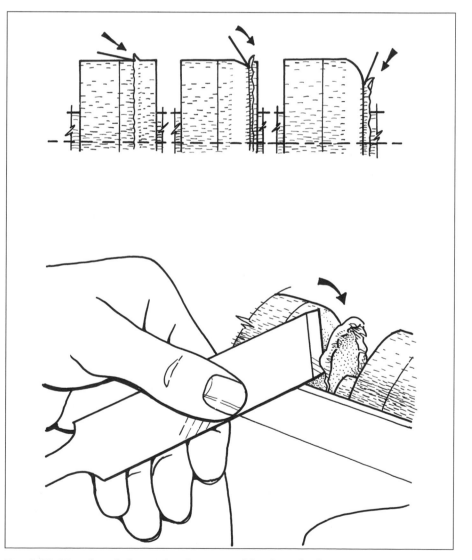

Fig. 6-29. Top, from left to right, *the action of the skew chisel as it rounds over the shoulder of the wheel*. Bottom, *with the tool rest set close and high, roll the skew chisel so as to cut and define the curve. Only a small part of the blade needs to be in contact.*

TURNING BALLS

You want to turn two identical balls about 4 inches in diameter, say, for a game of croquet. You are working on a large lathe with a four-jaw chuck.

1. Check over a 12-inch length of $4^1/2$-by-$4^1/2$-inch-square wood to make sure that it is free from loose knots, splits, and any other defects that look as if they might make things difficult. Find the end centers by drawing crossed diagonals, and mount it securely on the lathe.

2. Use the roughing gouge to turn the wood down to the largest possible diameter (see 6-18); set the callipers to 4 inches, and then slowly turn the wood down to 4 inches. The 4-inch-diameter size is critical, so spend time getting it right. This done, work from left to right along the length of the wood setting out the step-offs with the dividers: 2 inches for chuck waste, 4 inches for the first ball, 1 inch for the between-ball parting waste, 4 inches for the second ball, and 1 inch for the tailstock waste. When you are happy with the measurements, sink the waste in to a depth of $1^1/2$ inches so that you are left with a 1-inch-diameter core, and then set a center line into each 4-inch ball width (see 6-30).

3. With the lathe switched off, adjust the tool rest so that it is a little above spin height and so that the bevel of a smallish round-nosed gouge (one about $^1/2$ to $^3/8$ inch will be just fine) will rub toward the top of the wood.

4. Switch on the lathe. Set the gouge down on the rest with the bevel rubbing on the center line of the first wheel, raise the handle slightly so that the cutting edge just begins to bite, and then pivot the handle toward the right so that the cutting edge swings down and around toward the left. If you are

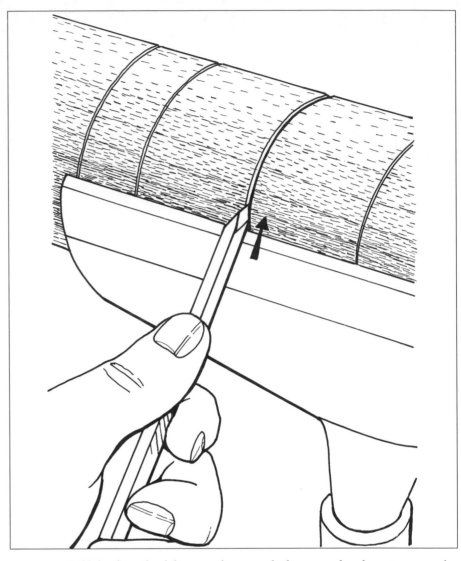

Fig. 6-30. *Hold the skew chisel down on the rest and advance so that the point sets-in the center line point with a decorative V-cut.*

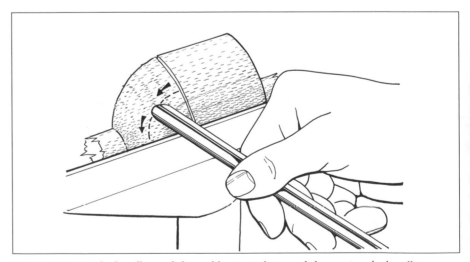

Fig. 6-31. *Raise the handle until the tool begins to bite, and then swing the handle in an arc while using the other hand to roll the gouge blade to plane over the surface.*

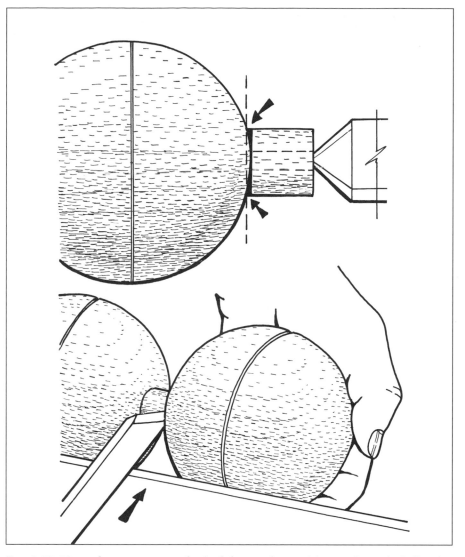

Fig. 6-32. Top, *when you come to the final shaping, be careful not to leave the ball with* "*flats*". Bottom, *support the ball in one hand and run the tool through for the final parting cut.*

doing it right, the swing-and-pivot movement will result in the gouge cutting with a paring action (see 6-31). Continue swinging the handle to the right to shape the left-hand side of the ball, swinging the handle to the left to shape the right-hand side of the ball, and so on, for both balls. Move backward and forward from ball to ball so that both balls are always more or less at the same stage. You may find that this little-by-little approach is much easier than turning one ball to completion before going on to the other one. There is no big secret to turning balls other than to take your time, and to try not to force the tool around the curve.

5. When you have achieved the two ball shapes, first use the parting tool to reduce the core to a ¼-inch diameter (see 6-32 top), and then use the point of the skew chisel to carefully part the right-hand ball from the tailstock waste. Wind the tailstock back out of the way. This done, swing the tool rest over the bed so that you can approach the ball end on to tidy up the parting scar.

6. Having cleaned up the end of the right-hand ball, part it off (see 6-32 bottom) and finish up the left-hand ball in the same manner as already described.

(*Note.* See chapter 7 for a project on turning chisel and gouge handles.)

Woodturning Project 1: Taper and Ring Chuck

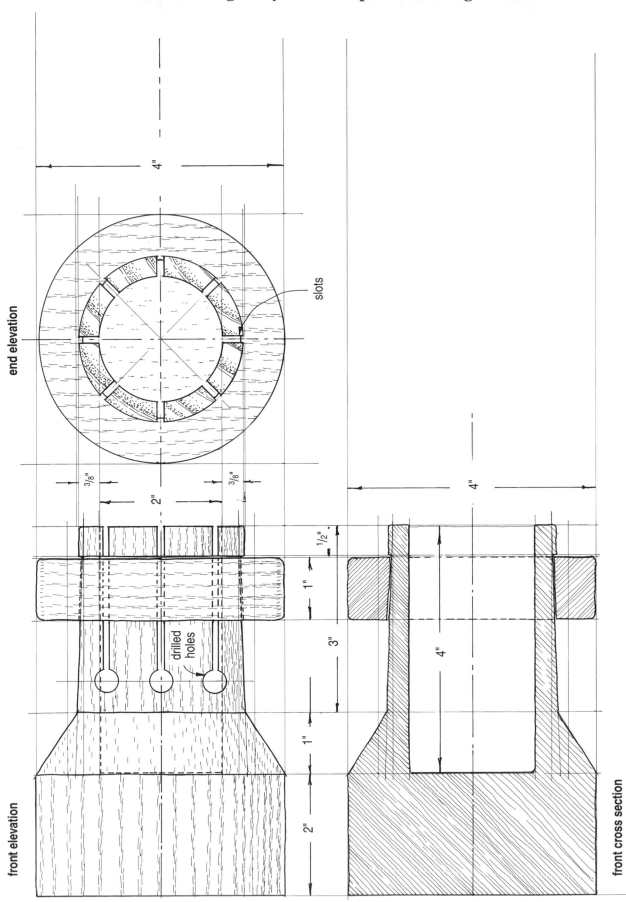

end elevation

slots

4"

3/8" 2" 3/8"

1/2"

1"

3"

1"

drilled holes

2"

4"

4"

front elevation

front cross section

Woodturning Project 2: Ring and Wedge–Peg Chuck

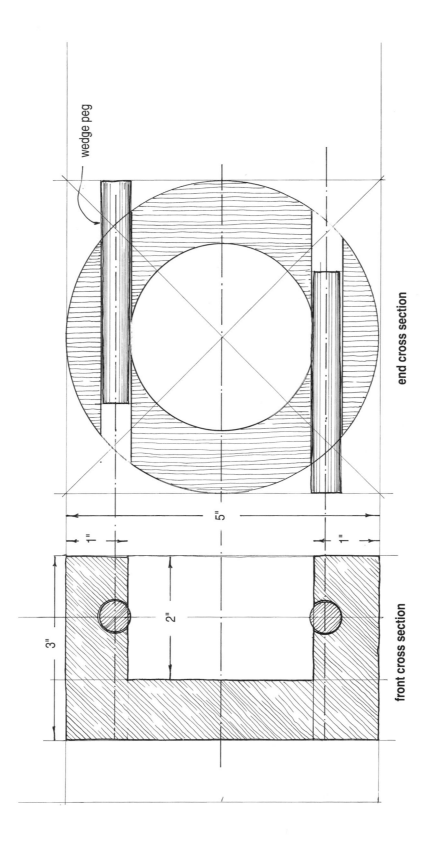

wedge peg

end cross section

5"

1"

1"

2"

3"

front cross section

CHAPTER SEVEN

Woodworking Machines

Though in the past, most home woodworkers used hand tools—either by choice or by economic necessity—there is now an ever-increasing push toward using machines. Although we are woodworkers who resist using machines—we don't like the noise, the dust, or the expense—we have got to admit that some small machines do most certainly cut the sweat and effort out of some of the more tedious backbreaking operations. Though we find very little hands-on satisfaction in using the machines, our pleasure comes from knowing that our stint with the planer, the band saw, or other power tool will leave us more time for the special quiet pleasures of using our hand tools.

The following listing describes the five machines that beginners to woodworking most commonly acquire.

THE LATHE
A lathe is like no other woodworking machine. If you want to make round sections like chair legs, tool handles, bowls, dishes, platters, balls, rods, dowels, beads, goblets, and all the rest, then there is no other way than to turn them on the lathe.

One of the biggest mistakes made by beginners to woodworking is that they nearly always opt for the cheapest, smallest lathe that they can afford, no doubt thinking that they can upgrade when the time is right. You can upgrade with a band saw or a drill press, but it is not so easy with a lathe. The average small inexpensive lathe so underperforms that it is either technically unable to do the task or so mechanically inefficient that it is dangerous. When things go wrong, the beginner doesn't know that his seeming inability to turn a spindle has nothing to do with his skill level or effort, but all to do with the lathe. What usually happens is that the average beginner to woodturning gets so demoralized, or just plain scared of getting hurt, that he or she gives up. The following listings and definitions will tell you what

to look for when choosing a lathe so that the above doesn't happen to you.

LATHE TYPE
First and foremost, you must get the highest-powered, heaviest lathe that you can afford. It's no use getting a tidy little lathe that clips onto your electric drill, or a lathe that is part of a universal machine, because it simply won't do the job. In woodturning—when buying a lathe at least—there is no such thing as "small is beautiful." Nor is there really any point in getting a lathe that is dedicated to turning small items, because even the smallest of small turnings is much better made on a big lathe. And, of course, whereas you can turn anything from a lace bobbin to a table leg on a huge lathe, your options are strictly limited with a small one.

As to weight of the lathe, you do need plenty of it to counteract the swing and the momentum that can occur when a piece of off-center wood is being worked. If the lathe body is lightweight or screwed to a table or bench, the chances are it will vibrate to the extent that it does damage both to the lathe and the workshop. It's vital that the lathe is going to stay put: no play in the bearings, no vibration, no off-center spin, and no creep. For this reason, we always recommend that beginners get a good traditional floor-standing lathe, one with a cast-iron or extruded beam body (see 7-1).

If you already have a good-sized table with a boxed sheet metal lathe, then it's a good idea to add triangulated braces and to sit bags of sand in the base. You will find that the braces will stop side-to-side and backward-and-forward rocking, and the sand will deaden vibration.

You have to decide if you want a lathe with a variable speed, meaning that you turn a knob to regulate the speed, or a lathe with a belt drive and various pulley speed options that require you to physically move the belt from one wheel to another.

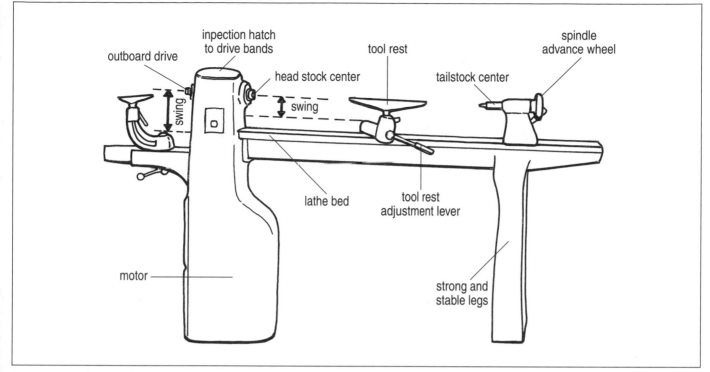

Fig. 7-1. Woodturning lathe.

Bed. The bed of the lathe is the horizontal bar that links the headstock end to the tailstock end. The length of the bed, sometimes described as the "distance between centers," defines the potential of the lathe, meaning the length of work that it is able to manage. So, if you want to turn legs for tables and such, don't get a bed length less than about 32 inches. The bed also supports and acts as a runner or track for the tool rest. Because turning produces mountains of shaving, plus turning requires that you are always moving the tool rest backward and forward along the bed, choose a lathe designed so that the shavings can't fall down into the track and prevent the tool rest from moving.

Swing. The "swing" is the vertical distance between the center of spin and the topmost surface of the tool rest (see 7-1). To put it another way, the swing and the radius capability of your lathe are one and the same. So, for example, if the swing of your lathe is 6 inches, then it follows that the fattest item that you can make is 12 inches in diameter. If your lathe is described as 36 inches between centers with a 5-inch swing, then the largest turning you can make is going to be a cylinder about 36 inches long and 10 inches in diameter.

Headstock. The business end of the lathe, the headstock, is driven either directly or by a pulley belt. The headstock drive spindle is threaded on the outside to take a chuck, and drilled on the inside to take a tapered bit (see 7-2). So when you are turning between centers you can either push a spurred drive in the spindle and

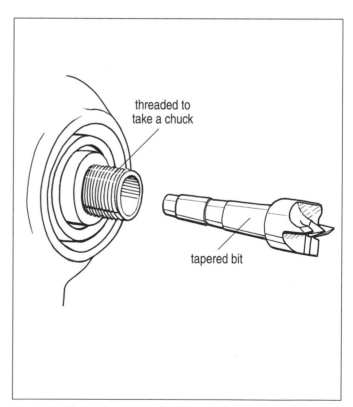

Fig. 7-2. The headstock spindle is threaded on the outside to take a chuck, and drilled on the inside to take a tapered bit.

have the workpiece gripped between the spurred drive and the tailstock center, or you can screw a chuck or faceplate on the spindle and have the workpiece gripped in the chuck or screwed on the faceplate and

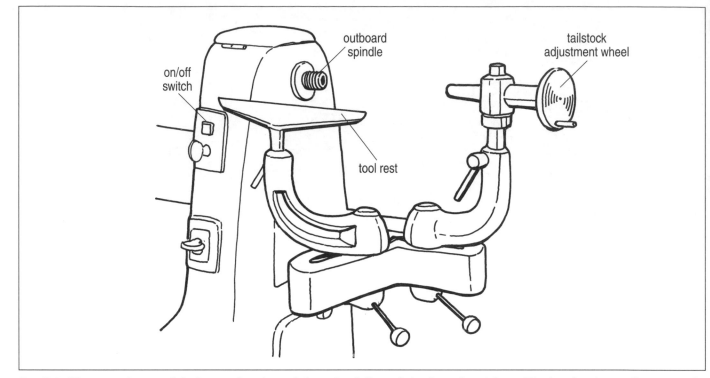

Fig. 7-3. This particular top-of-the-line machine has a dedicated on/off switch for the outboard drive. The fact that the spindle turns in the same direction as the inboard drive means that you can use the same faceplates and chucks—a very useful feature.

pivoted on the tailstock center. Our preferred setup for most jobs is to have a four-jaw chuck on the drive spindle, even when we're turning between centers. The size of the lathe and the consequent size of the drive spindle thread do to a great extent determine the potential of your lathe. A lathe with a 1-inch spindle thread is heavy enough to take a pretty large four-jaw chuck.

Outboard Drive. Sometimes known as back or rear drive, outboard drive is an option on some lathes that allows you to turn large dishes and bowls (see 7-3). Whereas on the front headstock drive end your radius capability is restricted by the bed, the only restriction to radius on the outboard drive is from the height of the tool rest fixing. On older lathes, the drive spindle runs straight through the headstock, turning counterclockwise to your approach over the bed and clockwise on the outboard end. On more modern lathes, the whole headstock swivels around to run in a counterclockwise direction to your approach for both inboard and outboard turnings.

Tool Rest. The tool rest or T-rest is a T-shaped piece of metal that slides along the bed track. Its function is to support the tool. The most efficient rests are curved on the front and straight faced at the back (see 7-4). Such a rest allows you to get very close to the workpiece while providing a smooth curve for various rocking-and-

rolling motions of the tool. Because T-rests are fixed on top of the bed, the size of the fixing does have to be taken into account when you are estimating the size of the swing. So, for example, if the T-rest fixing plate is a hefty 1½ inches thick, and the swing distance between the center of spin and the top of the bed is 6 inches, then the actual workable diameter for between-center turnings is reduced to 9 inches.

Tailstock. The tailstock unit sits on the right-hand end of the bed. It is made up of a spindle, a center, one or more locking levers, and a spindle advance wheel. In action, when you are turning between centers, you set the workpiece in, say, the four-jaw chuck, slide the whole tailstock unit up to the workpiece and lock it off, advance the spindle until the center is in contact with the wood, and then lock it off. Though there are a number of different tailstock designs, there are a couple of features that you must look out for. You must have a hollow spindle that allows you to fit a drill chuck (see 7-5). The other thing is to be sure the tailstock has a live center, meaning one that has bearings.

LATHE SAFETY
The lathe is potentially an extremely dangerous machine. Before you switch on the power, always run through the following checklist:

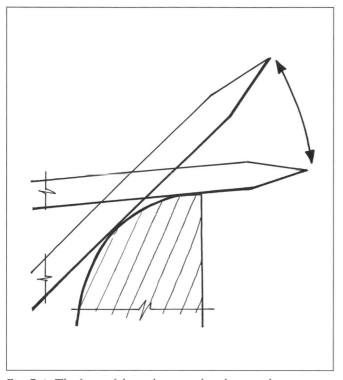

Fig. 7-4. *The front of the tool rest needs to be curved so as to allow for an even uninterrupted movement of the tool, and the back needs to be straight so that the rest can be positioned as close as possible to the workpiece.*

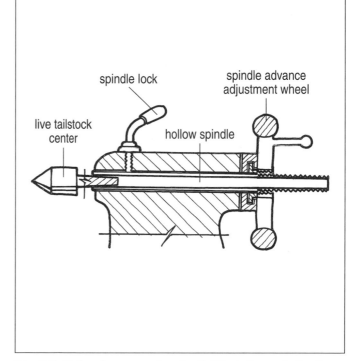

Fig. 7-5. *Tailstock cross-section detail. The hollow spindle allows you to fit all kinds of centers and chucks, plus you can run a long drill bit through the spindle for boring holes through lamps, handles, and such.*

- Make sure that the workpiece is well mounted.
- Turn the workpiece over by hand to make sure that it is well clear of the tool rest.
- Tie back your hair, roll up your selves, and generally make sure that you or your clothes aren't going to get dragged into the machine.
- Make sure that you are wearing goggles or, better still, a full-face mask.
- Make sure that the shop-vac is up and running.
- Make sure that interested parties—especially kids —have a clear view but are out of harm's way.

When you have switched on the power always follow these guidelines:

- Stop, or at least slow down, before testing with a template, dividers, or calipers.
- Move the rest out of the way when sanding.
- Make sure that your chosen wood is nontoxic.
- Never wrap the cloth around your fingers when burnishing with wax—it might get tangled up; but, rather, fold up the cloth so as to make a pad.

WOODTURNING TECHNIQUES STEP-BY-STEP: TURNING CHISEL AND GOUGE HANDLES
You have got yourself a nice set of tools, and you want to turn special custom handles. For each handle that you

want to make, you need a piece of 2-by-2-inch square-section wood at 16 inches long and a 1-inch-long, 1-inch-diameter brass ferrule.

Use boxwood, beech, ash, maple, or almost any close-grained wood that is strong along its length; it's best to avoid endangered exotic species.

1. Check over your length of wood for possible problems. Tight knots are okay, but don't use anything that looks as if it might be cracked. If there is a knot, make sure that it's placed well away from where the tang will be.

2. Pencil one end of the wood "pommel" and the other "ferrule." Draw crossed diagonals on the ferrule end of the wood, and mount it on the lathe in the four-jaw chuck so that the ferrule end is pivoted on the tail center (see 7-6 top).

3. Take the roughing gouge and swiftly turn the wood down to the largest possible diameter. Traverse from one end to the other until you achieve a crisp round section. Try to visualize the finished handle (see 7-6 bottom).

4. Use the inside calipers to take readings directly from the ferrule, and then transfer the reading to the outside calipers (see 7-7). Turn the tailstock end of the wood down with the parting tool so that it's a tight push-fit in the ferrule. The best procedure is to swiftly turn down to an oversize fit, and then repeatedly skim

and check with the calipers. It's got to be right, so don't rush; work little by little.

5. When you have achieved a nice clean spigot, slide the tailstock back, remove the center, set the brass ferrule in place between the workpiece and the tailstock spindle (see 7-8), and then wind the spindle out so that the ferrule is pushed into place on the spigot. It should be a close push-fit—not so tight that it crushes the wood, nor so loose that you can push it on with your hands.

6. Having pushed the ferrule into place on the spigot, refit the tailstock center, and use a smaller gouge to turn the cylinder down to what you consider is a comfortable good-to-hold shape. Don't attempt to part the pommel end off at this stage; leave a piece of waste about 3/4 inch in diameter. Use the skew chisel to plane the surface of the handle down to a supersmooth finish (see 7-9).

7. When you are happy with the shape and finish, slide back the tailstock, remove the center, and fit a drill chuck with a bit size to suit the tang. Determine this by measuring halfway up the tang from the end of the tapered point. Advance the tailstock so that the drill bit is located in the end of the workpiece, in the center hole in the middle of the ferrule (see 7-10). Switch on the power and very gently advance the tailstock spindle and run in a hole to a depth of about 2 inches. To avoid binding or overheating the drill bit, wind the drill in and out repeatedly, until the proper depth of the hole is achieved.

8. Finally, part off the handle, set the tang of the tool in the hole, and then gently bounce the handle on its end until the whole thing is a nice straight fit.

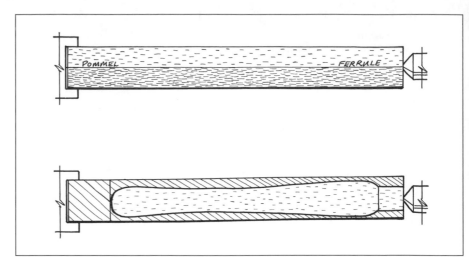

Fig. 7-6. Top, *the square-section blank mounted and ready to start the roughing out stage.* Bottom, *visualizing the finished handle; the shaded area marks the waste that needs to be removed.*

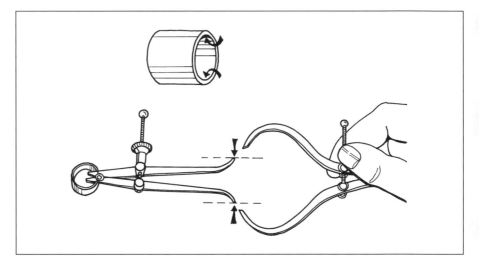

Fig. 7-7. *Having used the inside calipers to take a reading from the inside of the ferrule, transfer the measurement to the points of the outside calipers. The best way to do this is to set the inside calipers down on the work surface, and then repeatedly drag and adjust the outside calipers over and past the points until they catch.*

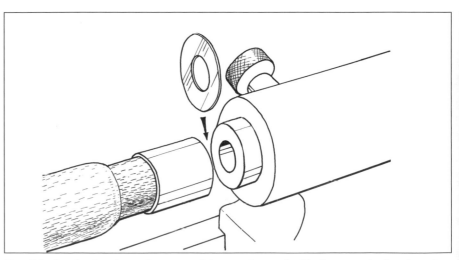

Fig. 7-8. *Set the ferrule on the spigot, slide a washer or the like between the ferrule and the spindle, and then wind up the spindle so that the ferrule is forced into place.*

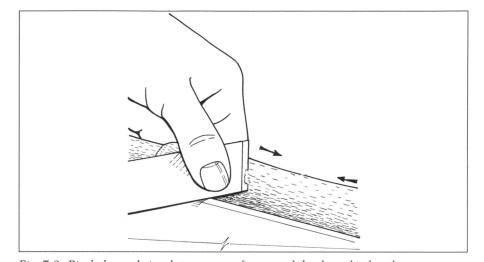

Fig. 7-9. *Pinch the workpiece between your fingers and the skew chisel so that your thumb is applying pressure.*

THE DRILL PRESS

The traditional drill press—sometimes also called the bench drill, the column drill, or even the pillar drill—is a large bench-standing drill that is fitted out with its own integral base, column, and worktable (see 7-11). In use, you select the speed by moving the drive belt; insert the drill bit into the chuck, which is tightened up with a key (see 7-12); clamp the workpiece to the worktable, which is raised or lowered and pivoted left or right so that the drill bit is near the workpiece and on target; and set the depth gauge. Then the feed lever is pulled forward (see 7-13), the chuck comes down, and the hole is drilled. When the hole has been bored, you ease back the lever so that the return spring lifts the bit clear.

On the face of it, you might think that a drill press is no big deal —a hole is a hole is a hole—but its action is so accurate and positive that it is possible to bore perfect holes every time. It is a vital piece of equipment. As to the choice of machine, we advise you to go for a straightforward full-size traditional drill press, one with solid cast-iron construction to minimize vibration,

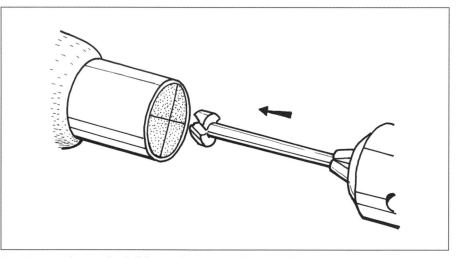

Fig. 7-10. *Advance the drill bit until it is perfectly centered.*

and one that is dedicated to the job. Don't be tempted to go for a small clip-on portable drill option, because it simply won't perform. Way back, when a good friend told us that we needed a drill press, our first reaction was, won't a brace do the job? But once we had the drill press set up, its advantages were obvious. We could use large-size Forstner bits to sink perfect smooth-based holes, we could lower the waste on relief carvings, we could use a mortising attachment, a small routing bit, a sanding attachment, and the list goes on. If we had to sum up the ad-

vantages of a drill press over a shaky handheld drill in two words, the words would be "confident control." If you do get a drill press, then you can't do better than set yourself up with a full set of Forstner drill bits (see 7-14). Not only do Forstner bits bore out perfect, smooth-sided, smooth-based holes, but better still, the design of the bit is such that you can even drill holes that overlap. If you have in mind to make exhibition standard items with large-size holes, or items with decorative plugs—such as furniture and toys— where it is important that the edges

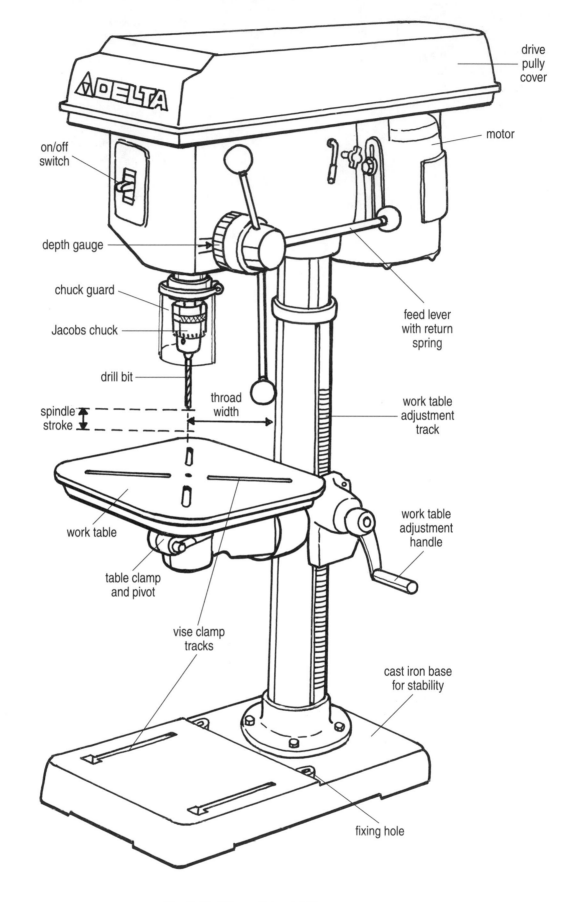

drive
pully
cover

on/off
switch

motor

depth gauge

chuck guard

Jacobs chuck

feed lever
with return
spring

drill bit

throad
width

spindle
stroke

work table
adjustment
track

work table

table clamp
and pivot

work table
adjustment
handle

vise clamp
tracks

cast iron base
for stability

fixing hole

Fig. 7-11. The traditional drill press.

of the holes be perfectly crisp and clean, then you need a set of Forstner bits.

As to the size and specifications of the machine, we recommend one with a large throat width of about $4^3/4$ inches and a spindle stroke of 2 inches.

DRILL PRESS SAFETY

As with all other machines, it's vital that you read the manufacturer's safety checklist before you switch on the power. But just in case you have a secondhand machine, the important dos and don'ts s are as follows:

- Always wear eye protection or, better still, a full-face visor.
- Always make sure that your hair is tied back and your sleeves are rolled up.
- Never wear swinging jewelry.
- Always clamp the workpiece if you are drilling a hole bigger than $1/2$ inch in diameter.
- Always remove the chuck key before switching on the machine.
- Never use the machine if you are tired or feeling woozy, or if your attention is being drawn to other things—kids, pets, the phone, etc.

DRILL PRESS TECHNIQUES STEP-BY-STEP: DRILLING OVERLAPPING HOLES

You want to use the drill press to clear the waste from the center of a solid wood box, say a pencil box. Let's say that the wood is cherry, the area to be cleared is 2 inches wide, 1 inch deep, and 7 inches long, with a 2-inch-diameter half circle at each end—a bit like the shape of a bathtub.

1. Fit the 2-inch-diameter Forstner bit in the chuck and tighten up with the chuck key.

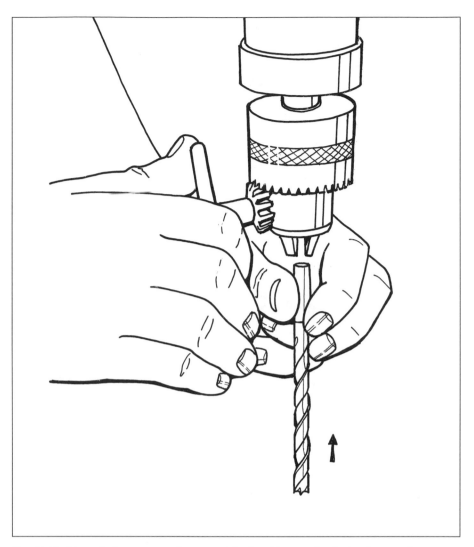

Fig. 7-12. Turn the key to open the jaws of the Jacob's-type chuck. Make sure that you remove the chuck key before starting the motor.

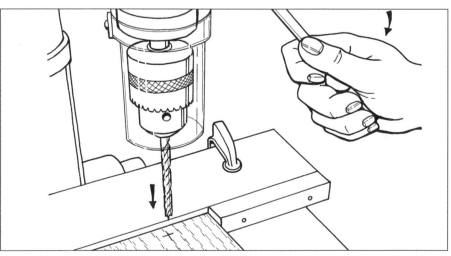

Fig. 7-13. Lower the drill bit by pulling down on the feed lever. When the hole has been bored to the desired depth, ease back on the lever so that the spring return lifts the chuck into the "rest" position. Note how the plastic guard is in the down position. Use a jig clamped to the worktable to speed up batch work.

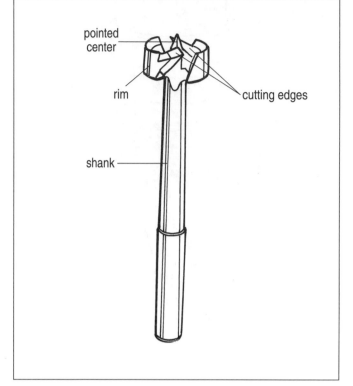

pointed center

rim

cutting edges

shank

Fig. 7-14. The Forstner drill bit is the perfect bit for boring smooth-sided clean-bottomed holes. Whereas most bits are guided by their center point, the Forstner bit is guided by its rim. It can be used at almost any angle and is capable of boring a hole that runs off the edge of a board.

2. Establish where you want the sunken area to be centered, and draw in a 7-inch center line accordingly. Working from left to right along the line, set out center points at 1 inch, $1^1/_4$ inch, $1^1/_4$ inch, $1^1/_4$ inch, and $1^1/_4$ inch. What you should have is a 7-inch-long line with five center points set $1^1/_4$ inches apart (see 7-15 top). As the 2-inch holes are bored, the next center point in line should be on the remaining high wood (see 7-15 bottom).

3. With all the guide lines in place, clamp the workpiece securely to the drill press table, wind up the table so that it is just clear of the drill bit, and then set the depth stop at 1 inch.

4. The drilling procedure is as follows:
   • Swing the table around so that the Forstner point is aligned with one of the center points, and tighten up the toggle.
   • Switch on the power and run the drill slowly in and out until the depth stop brings it to a halt.
   • Repeat the process for all five center points (see 7-16).

5. Finally, clear the little peaks of waste with a chisel (see 7-17) or even a hand router, and then use a small-width scraper to bring the whole works to a smooth finish.

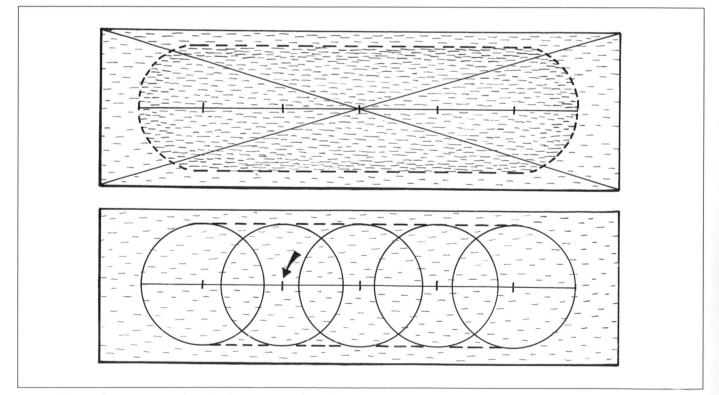

Fig. 7-15. Top, draw in a center line, fix the position of the drilling points, and shade in the area of waste. *Bottom,* with this design of overlapping holes, no matter the drilling sequence, the bit is always able to center on an area of raised wood.

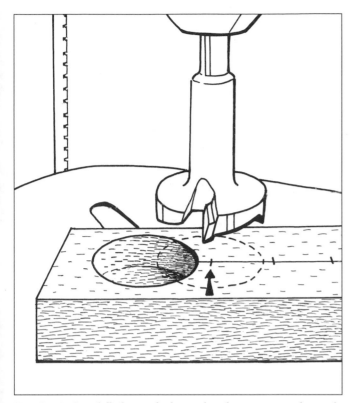

Fig. 7-16. *Carefully lower the bit so that the point is on the mark and check the alignment before switching on the motor. If you are boring holes bigger than* $^1/_2$ *inch in diameter, then you always need to have the workpiece clamped securely.*

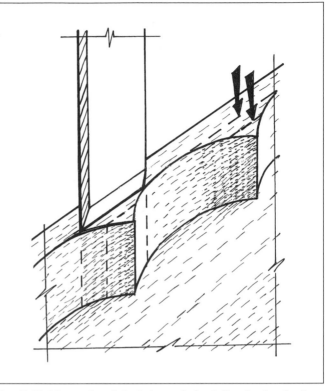

Fig. 7-17. *Having bored the holes with the drill, take the chisel and pare away the remaining little peaks of waste. Make successive cuts that back up to the line.*

THE SCROLL SAW

The scroll saw, sometimes also called a jigsaw or a fretsaw, is a power-driven fine-bladed bench saw designed specifically for cutting tight and intricate curves in wood up to 2 inches thick. That said, although it can indeed struggle through 2-inch-thick wood, it is ideally suited to cutting veneers and thin plywood. The blades come in various tooth sizes and grades and are cheap and easy to replace. The scroll saw is a wonderfully easy-to-use machine, perfect for the small workshop (see 7-18).

In use, the power is switched on, and the workpiece is pressed down hard on the table with both hands and fed into the reciprocating blade. The trick is to judge the speed of the advance so that the blade is always fed with the line of next cut.

Plain-end blades are better for intricate fretwork. The absence of the end pin seen on larger-width blades means that you can drill very small pilot holes, about $^3/_{32}$ inch in diameter. Go for blades described as "skip tooth"; they cut a much cooler and cleaner line.

The scroll saw is particularly useful for making interior or "window" cuts. The procedure is as follows:

- Drill a pilot hole.

- Release the blade tension, unhitch the top end of the blade, pass it up through the hole in the workpiece, and rehitch the blade (see 7-19 top).
- Tighten up the blade until it "pings" when plucked.
- Switch on the power and gently feed and maneuver in the workpiece toward the blade so that the line of cut is slightly to the waste side of the drawn line (see 7-19 bottom).
- When the cut is complete, switch off the power and remove the workpiece by unhitching the blade.

We purchased a machine specifically to make fretted chair backs and small plywood toys. It's a relatively fragile machine, and the blades do break frequently, but they are easy and inexpensive to fit, and the machine is safe, quiet, and reliable. If you are considering getting yourself a new scroll saw, then you must be aware that there is a wide range of machines out there—some brilliant, some good, and some just plain awful. And it doesn't follow that the most expensive machines are the best. You won't go far wrong if you make sure that your machine has the following features:

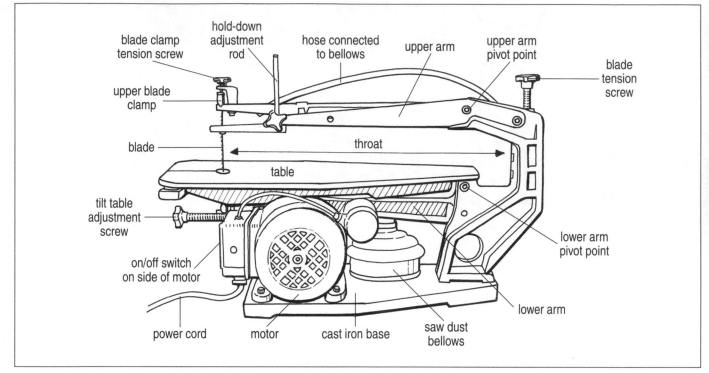

Fig. 7-18. *Top-of-the-line scroll saw.*

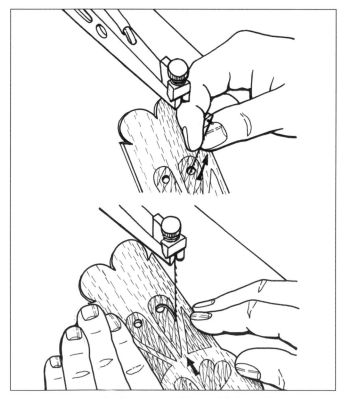

Fig. 7-19. Top, *unhitch the top end of the blade and pass it up through the pilot hole. Bottom, cut a little to the waste side of the drawn line. Make two cuts to achieve a sharp corner.*

- Large easy-to-turn thumbscrew fittings for clamping the blade in place. Make sure that the actual blade clamps are made from blue steel, rather than soft aluminum, and avoid allen screw clamps. (Some machines have a little blade-holding option that allows you to use pin-end blades without going to the bother of clamping; this is a very useful extra.)
- A dust blower operated from an integral bellows that blows the wood dust away from the point of cut—but not into your face!
- A large table with a tilt option that allows you to run angled cuts through the wood.
- A deep wide mouth that allows you to cut wood up to 2 inches thick.
- A deep throat that allows you to cut a good distance away from the edge of the workpiece.
- A good stroke length. The greater the distance that the blade moves, the cooler and more efficient the cut.
- A machine with a variable speed control so that you can adjust the speed to suit the wood.

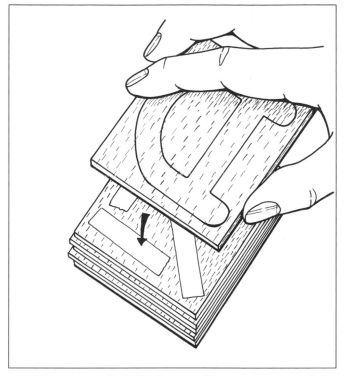

Fig. 7-20. Build little stacks of plywood and put double-sided tape between the layers; make sure that the penciled letter is on top of the stack.

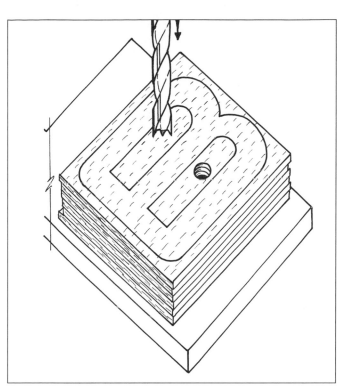

Fig. 7-21. Drill a good-sized hole through the enclosed window of waste that is big enough for the blade to pass through. If you are working with pin-end blades, then you will need to design the size of the letters accordingly.

SCROLL SAW SAFETY

Although the scroll saw is just about the safest machine around—even safe enough to be used by supervised children—you do have to follow the safety checklist. The important dos and don'ts are as follows:
- Always wear goggles or a full-face visor.
- Never work if you are tired.
- Always tie back your hair and roll up your sleeves.

SCROLL SAW TECHNIQUES STEP-BY-STEP: CUTTING SCROLL SAWN LETTERS

You have just got yourself a nice new scroll saw, and you want to practice your technique by cutting uppercase letters from $1/8$-inch-thick plywood offcuts. Perhaps you are going to give your workshop a name, or maybe you have in mind to put up signs like "EXIT," "FIRE," "WATER"; in any case, you have decided to fret out multiples of some of the letters. Let's say that you want eight cutouts for each letter.

1. Having drawn suitable letter forms to size and made tracings, spend time press-transferring the letter forms onto the plywood. Aim for simple letter forms that are about 2 to 3 inches high. Draw only one example of each letter.

2. When you have transferred the letters, set about building little eight-piece stacks of plywood with the transferred-letter piece on the top of the stack. Use double-sided sticky tape to sandwich the offcuts together (see 7-20). If you have done it right, you should finish up with stacks each at a little over 1-inch-thick.

3. Carefully pencil in each letter so that there is no doubting the line of cut, shade in the areas that need to be cut away, and then run pilot holes through all the enclosed windows at a size to suit your blade size (see 7-21).

4. Fretting out the open letters is simplicity itself. The procedure is as follows:
- Fit a new blade with the teeth pointing down, adjust the tension so that it "pings," and switch on the power.
- Take a stack, hold it firmly on the cutting table, and run it into the blade.
- Work at an easy pace, being ready to turn and maneuver the workpiece so that the blade is fed with the line of next cut. Run the cut a little to the waste side of the drawn line (see 7-22).
- When you come to a tight angle, ease back and mark time so that the cut broadens slightly at the point of turn to the waste side of the drawn line, and then change the direction of the cut. Be

warned: If you try to run rapidly in and out of a sharp angle, chances are you will spoil the line of cut or break the blade.

5. When you come to fretting the enclosed letters, the procedure is as follows:

- Switch off the power, release the tension, and unhitch the top end of the blade.
- Pass the blade up through the pilot hole, refit, and tighten up the tension until the blade "pings" when plucked.
- Switch on the power and run the line of cut a little to the waste side of the drawn line (see 7-23).
- Finally, when the cut is complete, unhitch the blade and go on to the next letter.

SPECIAL TIP: If you use top quality multicore plywood from Europe or the USA, and if you work with a new well-tensioned blade, and at a steady pace, it is easily possible to achieve a cut edge that is so smooth that it doesn't need sanding. On the other hand, if you use Malaysian "soft heart" plywood, or dark-faced coarse-centered plywoods, then you are going to be in trouble. Plywood of this character is half the price, and it's no wonder: Malaysian soft heart plywoods are so open grained that they always need filling, they are so coarse that the edges always need sanding, they are so badly glued that the laminations break down, they are difficult to paint, and they aren't always waterproof. Apart from that, they are a pretty good buy!

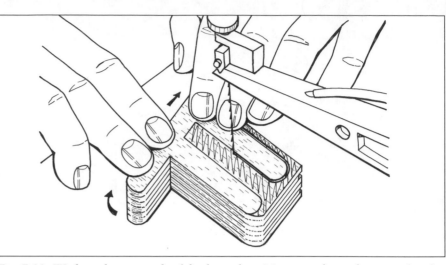

Fig. 7-22. Work on the waste side of the drawn line. Maneuver the workpiece so that the saw blade is always presented with the line of next cut. If you use a fine-toothed blade and work at an easy pace, then the cut edge will need only a minimum of sanding.

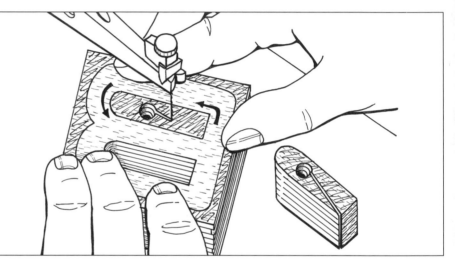

Fig. 7-23. Cut directly into the corner, and then follow around the drawn line until the window of waste falls free.

THE BAND SAW

A band saw is a power-operated bench machine consisting of a looped metal blade running over and driven by two or more wheels (see 7-24). This is the perfect tool for sizing lengths and for cutting curves in thick-section plank wood. It is possible to obtain blades in many sizes and grades. So, for example, you can use a very fine small-toothed blade for cutting thin sections in hardwood or a wide rip-toothed blade for ripping down the length of 4-inch-thick planks. A good general-purpose blade for small work is ¼ inch with six hook teeth to the inch.

If you are thinking of buying a band saw, start by appraising your needs. Are you in the main going to be cutting relatively thin stuff, say, up to about 3 inches thick? Or do you need to cut great balks? If you have a mind to do a fair amount of woodworking, then we would say that it's a good idea to get yourself a medium-size, two-wheeled bench-top machine. Our band saw is well able to cut through

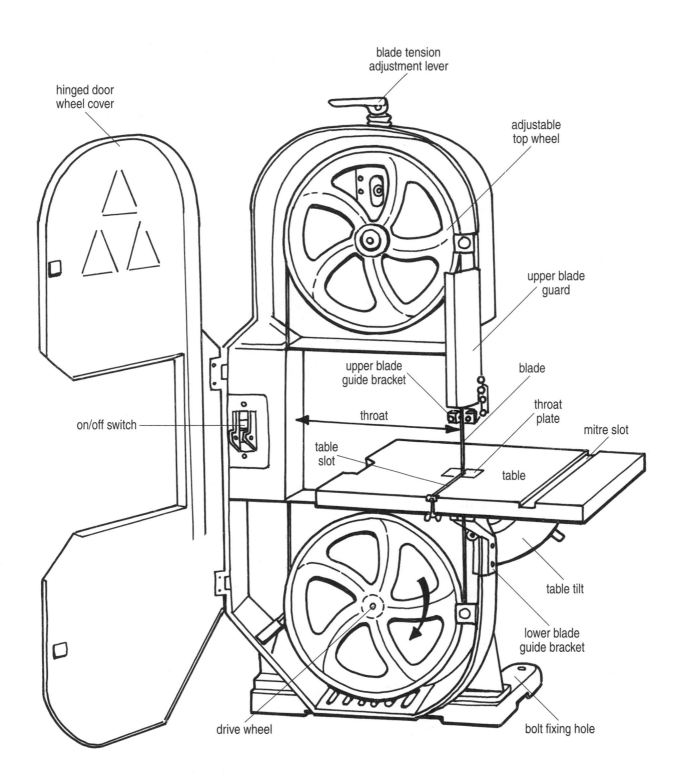

blade tension
adjustment lever

hinged door
wheel cover

adjustable
top wheel

upper blade
guard

upper blade
guide bracket

blade

throat
plate

mitre slot

on/off switch

throat

table
slot

table

table tilt

lower blade
guide bracket

drive wheel

bolt fixing hole

Fig. 7-24. Two-wheeled band saw. The workpiece is supported on the table, which can be tilted and has a slot for a miter attachment. There is a slot at the front of the table so that you can fit a new blade. The sacrificial throat can easily be removed and replaced.

4-inch-thick wood, and it is also very useful for thinner wood that is a little too thick for the scroll saw. You should be aware that the band saw is potentially a very dangerous piece of equipment, arguably one of the most dangerous machines that you are likely to use. It is most important that you read through the supplier's manual. Perhaps more than anything else, it is vital that you spend time setting the blade correctly.

Though, of course, your machine might have specific tuning requirements, the following general tips will set you on the right track:

- Having donned your gloves, mask, and safety glasses, carefully adjust the top wheel so that the blade runs centrally.
- Adjust the thrust bearings and the guide blocks so that the blade is correctly aligned.
- In use, lower the guidepost so that there is about $1/4$-inch clearance above the workpiece.
- If you want the blade to run squarely through the wood, then use a square to make sure that the table is at 90 degrees to the blade.
- The thrust bearings need to be set about $1/64$ inch behind the blade.
- The guide blocks need to be set with a gap of about $1/64$ inch at the point where the blade is welded.

When you have tuned the blade correctly, test for squareness as follows: Take a scrap of wood about 2 inches wide, and run a center line around both sides so that you have a right-angled cross marked at top and bottom. With the wood set with the cross uppermost, run a kerf up to within $1/16$ inch of the cross, but don't touch it. This done, turn the wood over and run another line in from the other

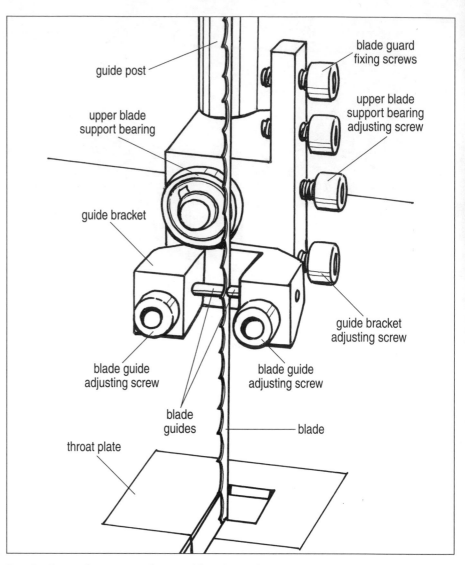

Fig. 7-25. Band saw top guide assembly. The guidepost holds both the guide assembly and the blade guard (the guard has been removed so that you can see what's going on). In use, the guard is raised and lowered to suit the different thicknesses of wood. The bearing support, sometimes called a thrust bearing, takes the strain when the blade is being pushed backward. The blade guides at each side of the blade prevent the blade from being twisted or pulled sideways. A good part of the tuning procedure has to do with getting the spacings between the blade, the guides, and the support bearing just right.

side. If all is square, the cuts will be perfectly aligned; if they are offset, you will need to readjust the table.

The band saw needs to be placed squarely on a stand or table in a place where the workpiece can be fed directly across the cutting surface and have plenty of room to exit, so it's no good having the machine set on a bench that is up against a wall. Set up the machine on a bench in the middle of the

room so that you can move freely around the working area.

In action, the wood is fed and maneuvered so that the blade is always presented with the line of next cut. Be aware that this machine is completely unforgiving, so keep your fingers away! The good news is that the one-direction movement of the blade makes it a very easy task to hold and move the wood. Unlike the scroll saw, where the machine is forever trying to jerk the wood out of your hands, the rapid "down" movement of the band saw means that the wood can be held with the lightest touch. That said, the simple rule of thumb is, don't allow your fingers to get to within 6 inches of the front of the blade. If the size or shape of the workpiece requires that you get closer than 6 inches, then control the workpiece with a couple of bird's-mouth push sticks (see 7-26).

Beginners often ask, "Do we need a band saw?" We can only say that it really depends on what you want to do with it. Certainly, there is no doubt that a band saw is a wonderfully speedy machine for cutting curves in slabwood, say, for chair seats, woodturning blanks, large toys, curvy pieces of furniture, and the like. But then again, we know woodworkers who claim they can get the job done more efficiently with a large bow saw. If you do get a band saw, you will also have to add on the expense of a dust extractor and mask.

BAND SAW TECHNIQUES STEP-BY-STEP: CUTTING A CABRIOLE LEG BLANK ON A BAND SAW

Many items in woodworking call for sawing on two surfaces; they are sawn out as they are seen in both front and side views so that you finish up with a three-dimensional form. One such item is the classic Queen Anne cabriole leg (see 7-27). While making cabriole legs is one of those procedures that completely mystifies the uninitiated—we suppose because the end result looks so stunning—the good news is that cutting the blank on the band saw is a very easy and straightforward technique. If you follow a set sequence of cuts, you finish up with a leg that requires a minimum of hand shaping. For this

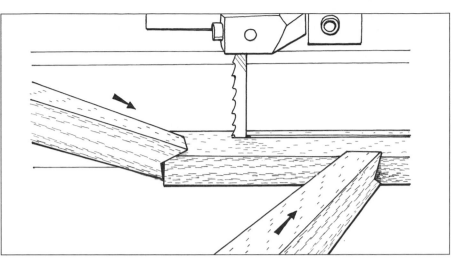

Fig. 7-26. Keep your fingers away from the blade. If you are working with a small piece of wood, then for safety's sake, the best procedure is to use a pair of bird's-mouth push sticks to guide the wood. The sticks can easily be made in a few minutes to suit the size and shape of the job at hand.

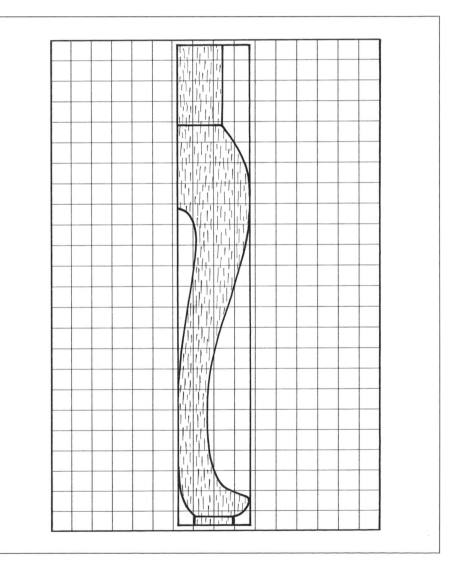

Fig. 7-27. When you need to cut out multiples of the same complicated shape, as with this leg, it's always a good idea to draw out a master design or template so that you always have a good reference.

project, you need the use of a band saw with a ¹/₄-inch blade and a nice piece of straight-grained 20-inch long and 3-by-3-inch-square wood for each leg. Use something like lime, cherry, or sycamore.

1. Check over your chosen piece of prepared wood for possible problems. Avoid knots, end splits, wild grain, and anything else that looks as if it might be a nuisance. Carefully press-transfer your full-size tracing or template of the leg to neighboring faces of the wood. Shade in the waste so that you know what needs to be cut away (see 7-28). If you have any doubts, then pencil label the various faces so that you can keep track of where you are.

2. Fit a ¹/₄-inch-wide blade to the band saw, adjust the various pins and guide wheels so that the blade is well tensioned, aligned, and supported, and switch on the power.

3. Set down the wood and cut out the profile as seen in one view, keeping in mind that you need to keep the pieces of waste. We find that the easiest procedure is to start at the top of the leg and work down (see 7-29 top). Cut from the top of the post down to the knee, then from the knee down to the ankle, then the underside of the footpad, and finally the curves at the back of the leg (see 7-29 bottom).

4. When you come to the pad of the foot, turn the leg around and make cuts up from the bottom (see 7-30 top). This done, turn the leg around and cut the curve at the bottom of the leg to meet the pad cut (see 7-30 bottom).

5. When you have sawn out the leg as seen in one view, tape the waste scraps back in place, and repeat the whole procedure on the other side of the wood (see 7-31). Finally, remove the various bits of

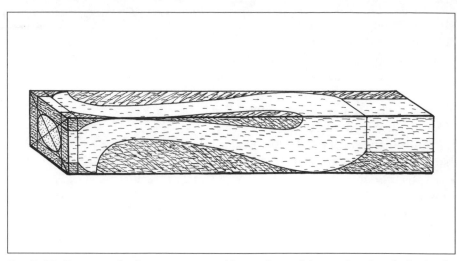

Fig. 7-28. *Draw out the design on two neighboring faces of the wood so that the heels of the legs are more or less touching each other.*

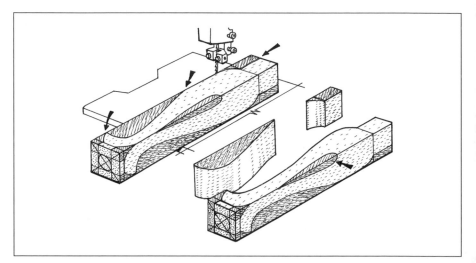

Fig. 7-29. Top, *start cutting at the top of the post. Make sure that you cut close up to the waste side of the drawn line.* Bottom, *arrange and keep the pieces of waste; you will need them for the second stage.*

tape and waste. The blank is now ready to carve and shape.

THE PORTABLE THICKNESSER PLANER

There are many machines that might well be categorized as planers, for example, the surface planer, the thicknesser, the planer thicknesser, the jointer, and one or two other machines besides. The machine that we think is best suited to the small home workshop is a beautifully designed machine known as

a portable thicknesser planer (see 7-32).

First, it's got to be said that this machine is not portable in the sense that you can hold it under your arm and run it up the stairs. At 60 pounds, you can lift it up in both arms and move it from one side of the workshop to the other—but that's about it. Second, although noisy and dusty, planing is finished in a very short time, leaving you extra time for the more pleasureable tasks.

In use, you wind the handle one way or the other to raise or lower the cutterhead—a bit like an old-fashioned mangle or wringer—and then you feed the wood through the resultant slot (see 7-33). The action of the cutterhead drags the wood across the rollers, in one side of the machine and out the other, to leave the wood smoothly surfaced on the top face. To thickness the wood, you simply push it through and plane, flip it over, lower the cutterhead slightly, and then repeat the procedure for the other side. Our particular machine is able to take boards up to 12 inches wide and 6 inches thick. If you have limited workshop space or you are looking for a machine that you can transport to the boatyard, or to another room in the house, or whatever, then this is the machine for you.

As with all machines, it's most important that you read through the manufacturer's manual and safety checklist before switching it on. The primary dos and don'ts are as follows:

- Always keep the guards in place while the power is switched on.
- Never allow children to be alone with the machine.
- Always wear safety glasses.
- Always use a shop-vac alongside the machine to remove most of the dust at the source.
- Always wear a dust mask—or better yet, a full-face respirator.
- Always wear ear protection, because it's a very noisy machine.
- Never try to make a cut deeper than $3/32$ inch.
- Never try to plane single boards that are thinner than $3/4$ inch.

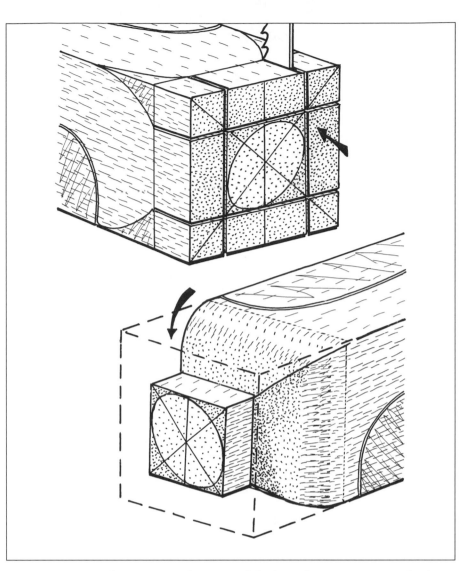

Fig. 7-30. Top, *cut the waste away from around the footpad; run a cut up into the sharp angle*. Bottom, *complete the cut and define the shape of the underside of the foot by running a second cut into the first.*

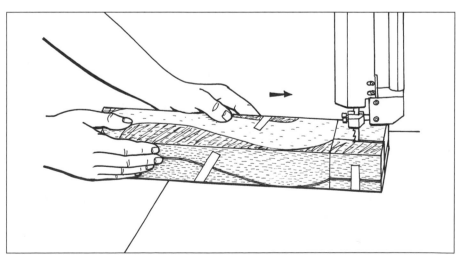

Fig. 7-31. *Tape the waste pieces back in place, and then cut the leg out as seen in the other view.*

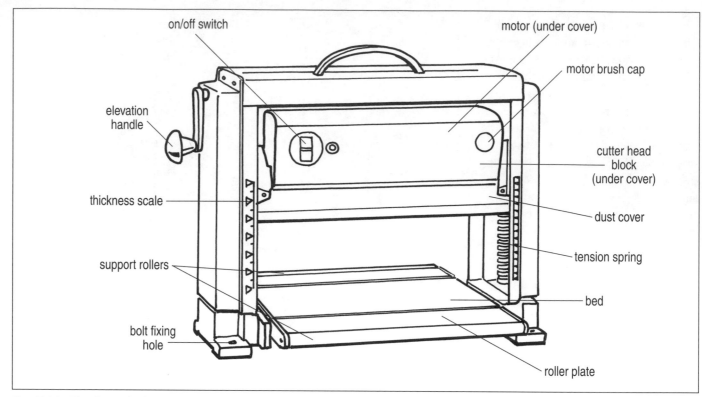

Fig. 7-32. The planer thicknesser.

- Never stand directly in line with the infeed or outfeed; always stand a little to one side.
- Never try to make any blade or guard adjustments while the power is switched on.

PLANER TECHNIQUES STEP-BY-STEP: THICKNESSING AND JOINTING A BATCH OF BOARDS ON A PORTABLE PLANER

Although the portable planer is designed as a thicknesser, it is possible to joint the edges of boards that have been clamped together in batches to make a stable block that will stand on edge.

Let's say you have ten or so sawn boards at $3/4$ inch thick and $5 1/4$ inches wide, and you want to plane them all to a finished size of $1/2$ inch thick and 5 inches wide.

Before starting the project, read through the manufacturer's safety checklist and make sure that the

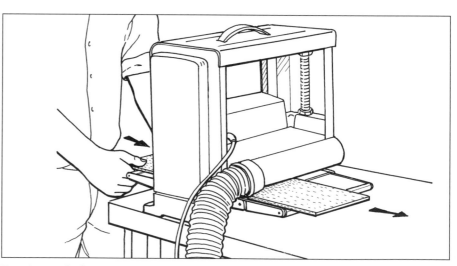

Fig. 7-33. The knives and moving parts of the planer are well enclosed for safety. The chip and dust deflector hood can easily be connected to a vacuum. In use, the action of the machine drags the workpiece across the rollers.

machine is in good working condition.

1. Set up the dust extractor and put on your filter mask and ear protection. Start by running the boards through one at a time to bring one face to a good finish (see 7-34). To do this, wind down the cutter a

whisker and pass all ten boards through one at a time, then wind down another whisker and pass them through again, and so on, until all boards have been smoothed on one side. Make sure that you always feed in the direction of the grain.

2. Having faced one side of every board, measure the thickness—just so you don't make a mistake—and then repeat the whole procedure on the flip sides. The only difference this time around is that you need to stop planing when you reach the finished thickness of $1/2$ inch. An easy way of working is to start out with the boards stacked on one side of the machine and to stack them on the other side after the pass. So, take a board from the right, put it through the machine, stack it on the left, and so on through the stack. When all the boards are in a single stack on your left, wind the cutterhead down a shade, and then reverse the procedure. Working in this way, you will find that you can keep track of the number of times each board has been planed.

3. When you have smoothed and thicknessed all ten boards so that they are down to $1/2$ inch thick, set them side by side and on edge in a block, and clamp them together. Have one clamp wrapped around each end so that the body and the thumbscrew part of the clamp are at the center of the 5-inch width and well away from the edges that are going to get jointed.

4. Having switched off the power and pulled out the plug, wind the cutterhead up, and set the stack of boards in place through the machine and across the rollers. This done, spend a good long time with an engineer's adjustable square making sure that the boards are stacked square both with each other and with the bed of the machine (see 7-35). The success of the whole operation hinges on the boards being clamped up squarely, so spend time getting it right.

5. When you are absolutely sure that the face side of the stack is perfectly square with the bed of the machine, then tighten up the

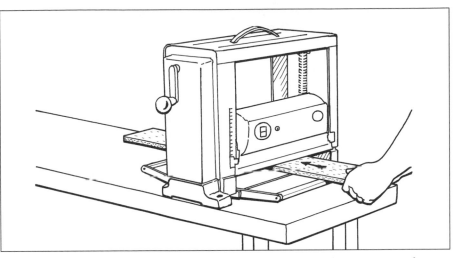

Fig. 7-34. *The pointer scale tells you how thick the wood is after planing. In use, the wood is fed in the direction of the grain.*

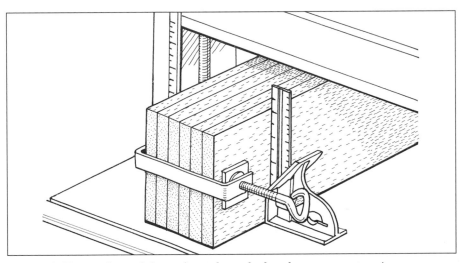

Fig. 7-35. *Having clamped the stack together at both ends, use an engineer's square to make sure that it is square with the bed, and send the stack through the machine.*

clamps, withdraw the stack, plug in the machine, and switch on the power. When you have double-checked that the clamps are well clear of the edges, wind down the cutterhead, and then have several trial runs until the blades begin to cut. At this point, wind down the cutters some more and make several passes until the edges are smooth. Repeat the procedure for the other side until you reach the 5-inch-wide board width.

CHAPTER EIGHT

Primary Marking and Testing Tools

When Alan was a kid doing woodworking with his granddad, his granddad would always begin a project with the same little ritual. He would set his old wooden ruler down on the bench, take out a little bone-handled penknife and his pencils, and spend a minute or two bringing the pencils to beautiful fine points. And while he was shaving the pencils, he would look from Alan to the knife, ruler, and pencils and say, "It all starts here." And, of course, he was absolutely right. The success of a project—the way the component parts fit together—hinges on good measuring and setting out. If the faces and edges of the wood are square and true, and the measurements are accurate, then the chances are that good sawing, planing, and jointing will follow. Put another way, it doesn't matter how wonderful your planing and jointing skills are if you have made a mistake in the initial measuring and setting out.

Accurate work is only possible if the tools are in good condition and the wood is set out correctly. While marking out can be done with a sharp pencil, precision joinery is best achieved using a sharp knife. The idea is, of course, that a knife-worked line more precisely positions the tools with the line of cut.

When you are working with exacting measurements where fractions are involved, it's the easiest thing in the world for small inaccuracies to creep in.

It's a good idea to use a stick to take a reading of the measurements. So, for example, you might have all the measurements that go to make up a fancy turned chair leg set out on the same stick. You can then use this "story" stick to set out the other legs without the need for further measurements.

WOODEN RULER

Though there are all sorts of rulers—one-piece bench rulers, steel rulers, plastic rulers, and all the rest—we think that the two most useful rulers for woodworking are the traditional fourfold wooden ruler and the wooden zigzag ruler. We currently use two fourfold rulers, one at 24 inches long for general work (see 8-1), setting out, sizing wood, and the like, and the other at 12 inches for setting out joints, measuring the widths of chisels, measuring the depth of holes, and all the other small tasks (see 8-2). Rulers of this type are very convenient to hold and small enough to slip into your pocket. They are set out variously in inches, $1/2$, $1/4$, $1/8$, $1/10$, $1/12$, and $1/16$ inches. That is, there might be $1/8$-inch step-offs at one end, $1/2$-inch step-offs at the other end, and so on. And, of course, there are metric rulers of the same type.

The wooden zigzag ruler (see 8-1) is much the same as the folding rulers just described, the main difference being that the sections are pivoted together rather than hinged. A 5-foot zigzag ruler gets used for the bigger tasks, like measuring doors and cupboards. It is particularly useful because it doesn't sag when in use. As to why it is 5-feet long rather than 6-feet—perhaps you can tell us!

ENGINEER'S STEEL RULER

The engineer's steel ruler is much the same as one made of wood, except that it is much more accurate. If you are working with both American and European plans and designs, then get a ruler that is set out with both English and metric measurements (see 8-3). The steel ruler doubles up very nicely as a straightedge, an edge to cut against, and a sighting edge.

METAL TAPE

The metal tape or flexible metal tape measure (see 8-1) is a ruler consisting of a strip of spring steel that is wound into a little hand-sized case. In use, the tape is pulled out, the measurement is taken, and then the tape is released so that it automatically rewinds back into its case.

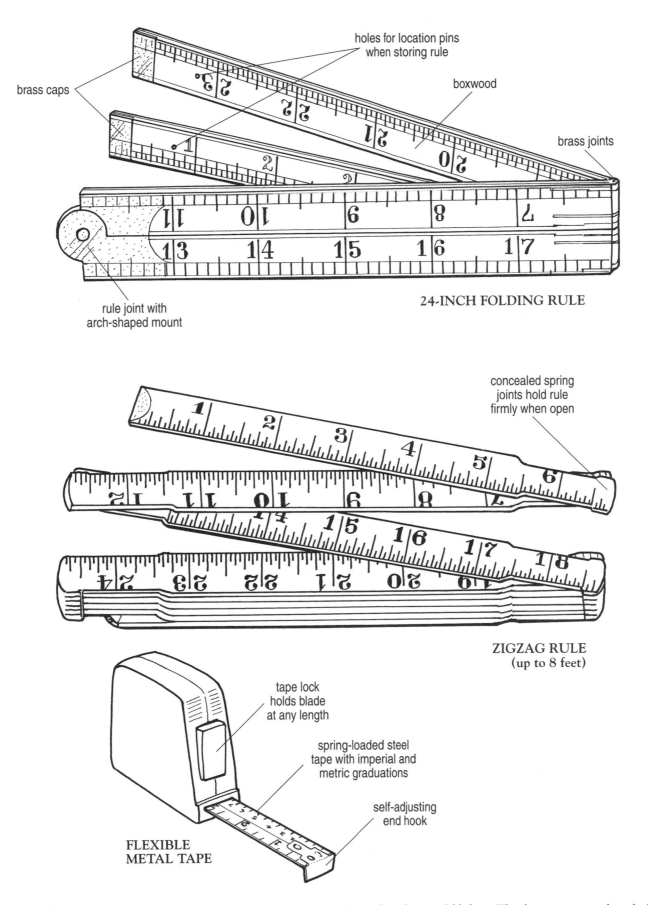

24-INCH FOLDING RULE

holes for location pins when storing rule

boxwood

brass caps

brass joints

rule joint with arch-shaped mount

concealed spring joints hold rule firmly when open

ZIGZAG RULE
(up to 8 feet)

tape lock holds blade at any length

spring-loaded steel tape with imperial and metric graduations

self-adjusting end hook

FLEXIBLE METAL TAPE

Fig. 8-1. *Well-made rulers have a catch or pins that hold the sections in place when they are folded up. This feature protects the rule from twisting and wrenching damage.*

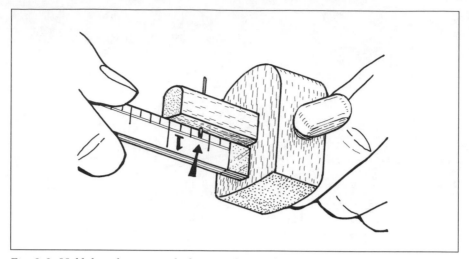

Fig. 8-2. *Hold the ruler against the beam with its end touching the face of the fence or stock. Move the fence along until the pin is set to the correct reading, and then lock in place with the thumbscrew. Be sure to add an extra $1/32$ inch to the required size for smoothing and finishing waste.*

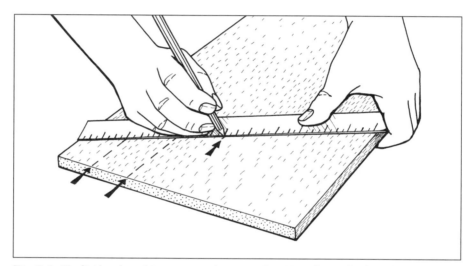

Fig. 8-3. *To divide a board into six equal parts with a 12-inch metal ruler, place the ruler diagonally across the board so that both 0 and 12 are touching the edges of the board. Draw a line along the ruler and make marks every 2 inches. Remove the rule and run parallel lines along the length of the board. This system is particularly useful when the board is an odd, difficult-to-divide width.*

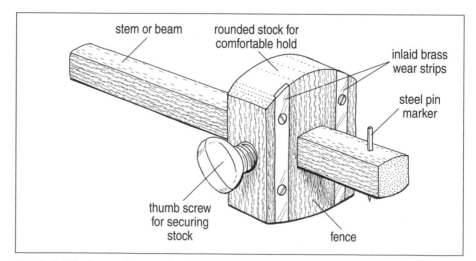

stem or beam

rounded stock for comfortable hold

inlaid brass wear strips

steel pin marker

thumb screw for securing stock

fence

Fig. 8-4. *The fence of the marking gauge is locked at the required distance from the pin, butted hard up against the edge of the workpiece, and then either pushed or pulled so that the pin makes its mark by being dragged across the workpiece. (Note: in England the wooden block is known as the "stock," and in the USA it is known as the "fence.")*

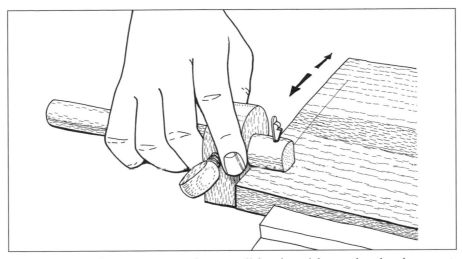

Fig. 8-5. In use, the cutting gauge is best run off the edges of the wood so that the cutter is dragged from the middle of the board and off the edges. Many woodworkers use the cutting gauge for marking across the grain, because unlike the marking gauge, it cuts the fibers of the wood rather than tearing them.

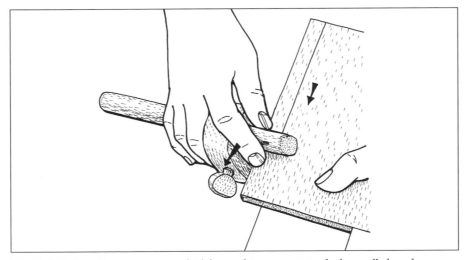

Fig. 8-6. It doesn't matter too much if the marking gauge is pushed or pulled, as long as the point is being dragged. The gauge needs to be held so that the thumb is pushing down on the pin while the rest of the hand is being used to ensure that the fence is held hard up against the workpiece.

Although the tape measure is gaining favor, we use it only for measurements greater that 6 feet and for measuring around curves. The metal tape is flawed on several counts; the numbers swiftly wear off, it doesn't like being kinked, it is relatively fragile, and it is heavy and cold in the pocket.

MARKING GAUGE

The simple wooden marking gauge consists of a fence that slides along a beam or stem. The stem has a scribing pin at one end, and the fence has a tightening screw or wedge (see 8-4). The gauge is used primarily for marking guide lines with the grain or on end grain. Some woodworkers also use a gauge with a modified flat knifelike pin to mark across the grain (see 8-5). In use, the fence is moved a measured distance away from the scribing pin and held in position with the screw or wedge. The fence is held hard up against the true side edge or side face of the workpiece, the stem is tilted so that the pin is at a dragging angle, and then the gauged line is struck (see 8-6). There are lots of opinions as to the best type of gauge. All you really need to know is that if the tool is held with the fence hard up against a true edge and then either pushed or pulled so that the point is dragged, the resultant gauged line will be parallel to the true edge.

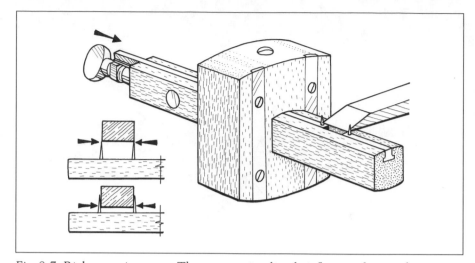

Fig. 8-7. Right, *mortise gauge. The gauge setting directly influences the way the tenon is cut. For example, if you set the chisel on top of the points* (top left), *then the saw cuts need to run to the waste side of the scribed line; if the chisel is set between the points* (bottom left), *then the saw cuts need to be run on the scribed line.*

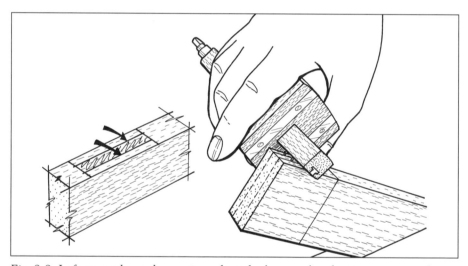

Fig. 8-8. Left, *to mark out the mortise, adjust the fence so that the pins are centered on the wood so that it doesn't matter on which side of the wood the fence is run.* Right, *to mark the tenon, use the same gauge setting and run the scribed lines along the sides and across the end.*

MORTISE GAUGE

The mortise gauge is identical in all respects to the marking gauge, apart from the fact that it has two spurs instead of one: one fixed, and the other attached to a slide that moves along the stem (see 8-7).

The mortise gauge is used, as its name suggests, for marking the double-track parallel lines that are needed when setting out mortise and tenon joints (see 8-8).

In use, the pins are set to correspond with the width of your chisel, the fence is fixed so that the pins are centrally aligned on the workpiece, and then the two lines are struck.

If you have in mind to make joints, then you need a good mortise gauge.

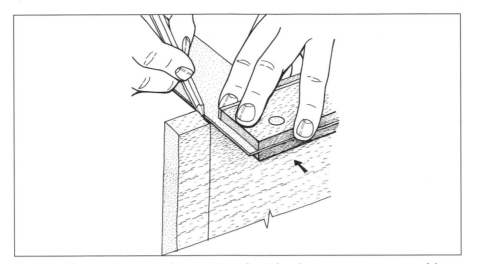

Fig. 8-9. *The try square is used for proving right angles, for testing squareness, and for generally setting out joints. The wooden part is generally termed the "stock" or the "handle." In use, the stock is held hard up against a true edge, and the line is run along the edge of the steel blade.*

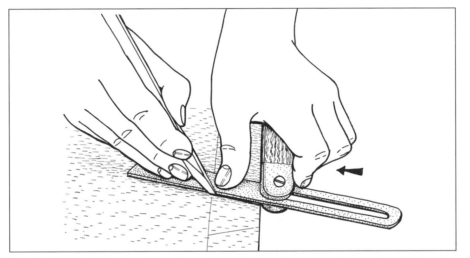

Fig. 8-10. *The sliding bevel has a loose blade that can be set at various angles. It is used for striking off lines that are not at right angles—as with dovetail joints. In use, the blade is set at the required angle, the fence is clenched hard up against the workpiece, and the knife is run along the side of the steel blade. For maximum accuracy, use a Japanese-type knife that has a bevel only on the outside face of the blade so that the flat face can be held up against the workpiece.*

SQUARES, MITER SQUARES, AND SLIDING BEVELS

Because the success of most woodworking projects hinges on successive cuts and faces being at right angle to each other, it follows that the square is one of the most important woodworking tools. Though, traditionally, most woodworkers used three squares—the classic wood and metal square for measuring right angles (see 8-9), a miter square for drawing 45-degree angles, and a sliding bevel for fixing all the other angles (see 8-10)—more and more woodworkers are now using one or other of combination all-metal squares (see 8-11). We currently use two all-metal squares: one with a square head that has a spirit level vial and its own integral sliding rule used for marking 90- and 45-degree angles, and one with a protractor head used for just about everything else (see 8-12).

Whereas there is no doubting that the traditional metal and wood square is an attractive tool to use and handle, to our way of thinking, the all-metal squares win out for their versatility and accuracy. In use, the sliding head is set in place and secured with the locking nut, the head or stock is pushed hard up against the true edge or face of the

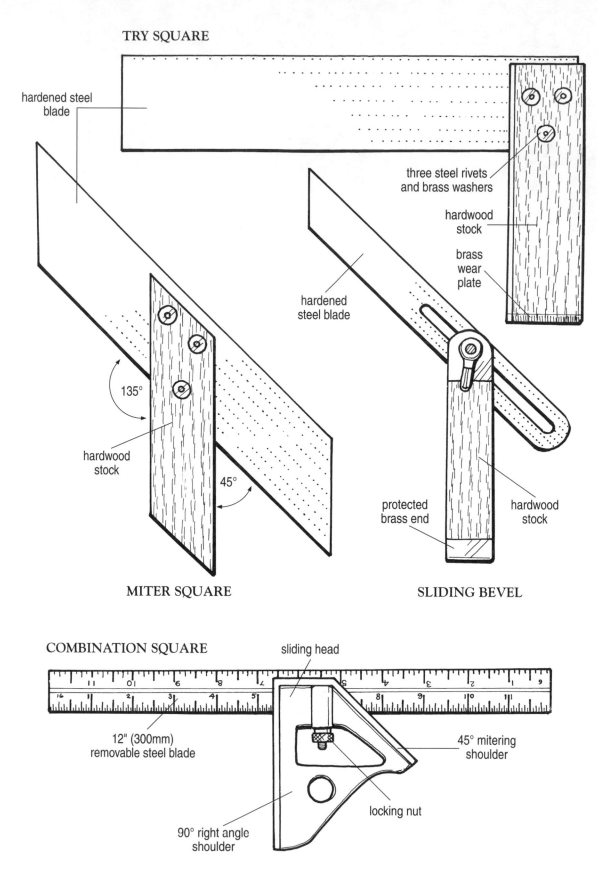

TRY SQUARE

hardened steel blade

three steel rivets and brass washers

hardwood stock

brass wear plate

hardened steel blade

135°

hardwood stock

45°

protected brass end

hardwood stock

MITER SQUARE

SLIDING BEVEL

COMBINATION SQUARE

sliding head

12" (300mm) removable steel blade

45° mitering shoulder

90° right angle shoulder

locking nut

Fig. 8-11. Top, *the try square is set at a right angle (90 degrees) and used to check and mark right angles to face sides and edges, and to check that frames and joints are true. Middle left, the miter square, set at 45 degrees, is used to set out miters. Middle right, the sliding bevel is used in conjunction with a protractor to set out angles from 0 to 180 degrees. Bottom, the combination or engineer's square is set at both 45 and 90 degrees. This square is especially useful since it can be used to draw out both inside and outside right angles.*

workpiece, and then the line is struck along the side of the blade (see 8-13). The other good thing about the all-metal combination-type or engineer-type squares is that, unlike the wood and metal squares, they are true on both inside and outside faces of the angle (see 8-14).

The accuracy of an all-metal combination square does of course depend on the trouble you take with the setting. If you set it a couple of degrees out, or the locking screw slips, then your work is going to be less than perfect.

As to the best buy for beginners, we see from the catalogs that it is possible to purchase the three traditional wood and metal squares —a try square, a sliding bevel, and a miter square—all for less than half the price of a good quality all-metal combination square. If you are short of cash, search around for a top quality secondhand combination square.

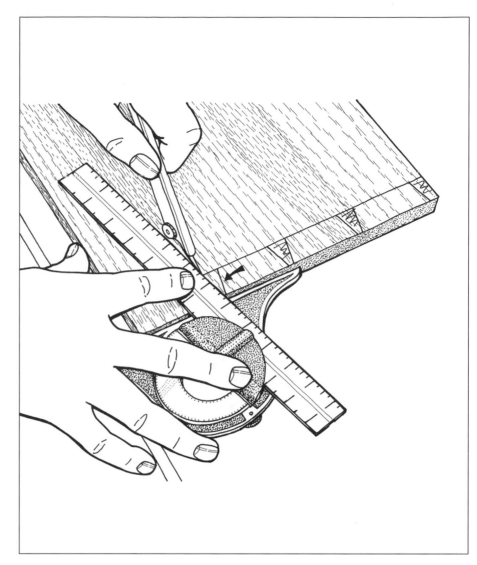

Fig. 8-12. The protractor head combination square is a precision tool that is particularly useful for setting out dovetails. In use, the thumbscrew is loosened, the ruler is rotated to the required protractor reading, and then the screw is retightened.

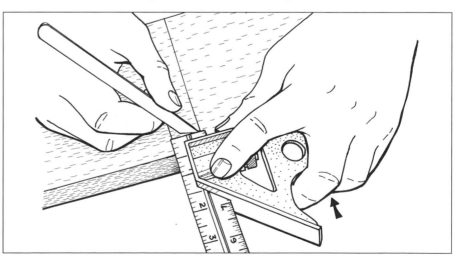

Fig. 8-13. In this instance, the engineer's square is being used to mark out a stopped housing joint. The shoulder lines are run across the width of the board, lines are extended across the edge, and then the marking gauge is used to set out the depth of the stop, as shown.

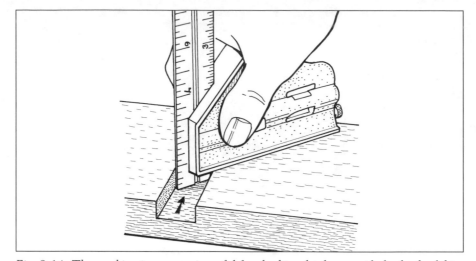

Fig. 8-14. *The combination square is useful for checking depths, as with the depth of this housing. The depth measurement is read off on the rule.*

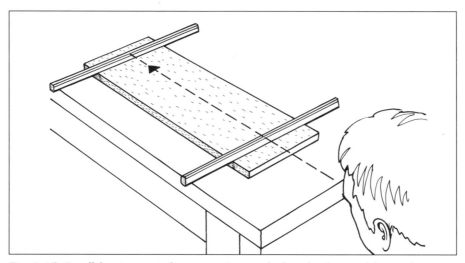

Fig. 8-15. *Parallel strips or winding strips. In use, the board to be tested for wind or twist is set on a known flat surface, and the strips are set apart and parallel to each other and at right angles to the edge of the board. You sight down the length of the board and across the strips. If you can line up the top edges of the strips, one with the other, then the board is true.*

PARALLEL STRIPS

Sometimes also called winding strips, these are no more than strips of wood at 12 to 18 inches long, $1^{1}/_{2}$ inches wide, and $^{1}/_{2}$ to 1 inch thick that are parallel along their lengths. They are used to test whether surfaces are free from dips, bumps, and winding. In use, the two strips are set one across at each end of the board, and then the woodworker sights from one strip to another (see 8-15). If the board is true, then it is possible to align the two strips one with another so that the top edges are parallel. The best strips are made in dark straight-grained hardwood and broad based in cross section, with pale wood inlay lines set slightly down from the top edge. The idea is that it's easier to sight from one strip to another if there is an easy-to-see sighting line. Traditionally, most woodworkers made their own strips; it was a matter of pride to make them as fancy as possible.

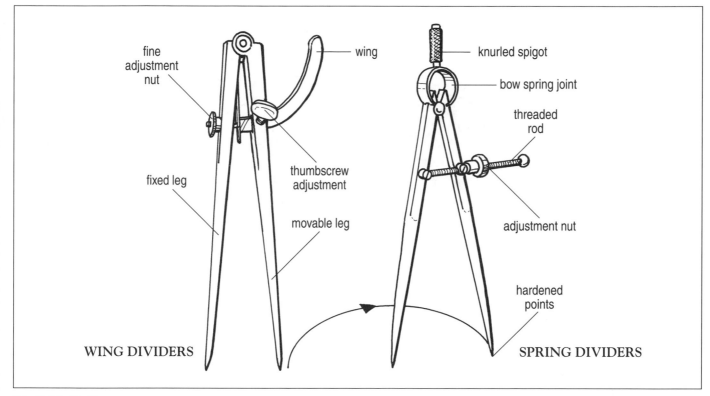

fine adjustment nut

wing

knurled spigot

bow spring joint

threaded rod

thumbscrew adjustment

fixed leg

movable leg

adjustment nut

hardened points

WING DIVIDERS

SPRING DIVIDERS

Fig. 8-16. Dividers.

DIVIDERS

Dividers, also known as compasses, (see 8-16) are instruments that are used variously for scribing out circles and arcs, for transferring measurements from the ruler to the workpiece, for drawing polygonal motifs—six-pointed stars, octagons, church window tracery, and the rest —and for trial-and-error dividing.

In use, you simply fix the legs a set distance apart, tighten up the screw or wing nut, spike one leg of the dividers down on the workpiece, and then scribe the arc or make the step-off.

We tend to use the dividers mostly for swiftly dividing a distance into a number of identical parts. Let's say, for example, that you want to divide a line into four equal parts. All you do is guess the measurement by eye and set the dividers accordingly. You then make four step-offs along the line. If the last step-off runs over the mark, you decrease the setting by one quarter the distance of the overrun; if the step-off doesn't reach the mark, then you increase the setting by one quarter the underrun. And so you continue, making step-offs and readjusting the dividers until the last step-off spikes exactly on the mark.

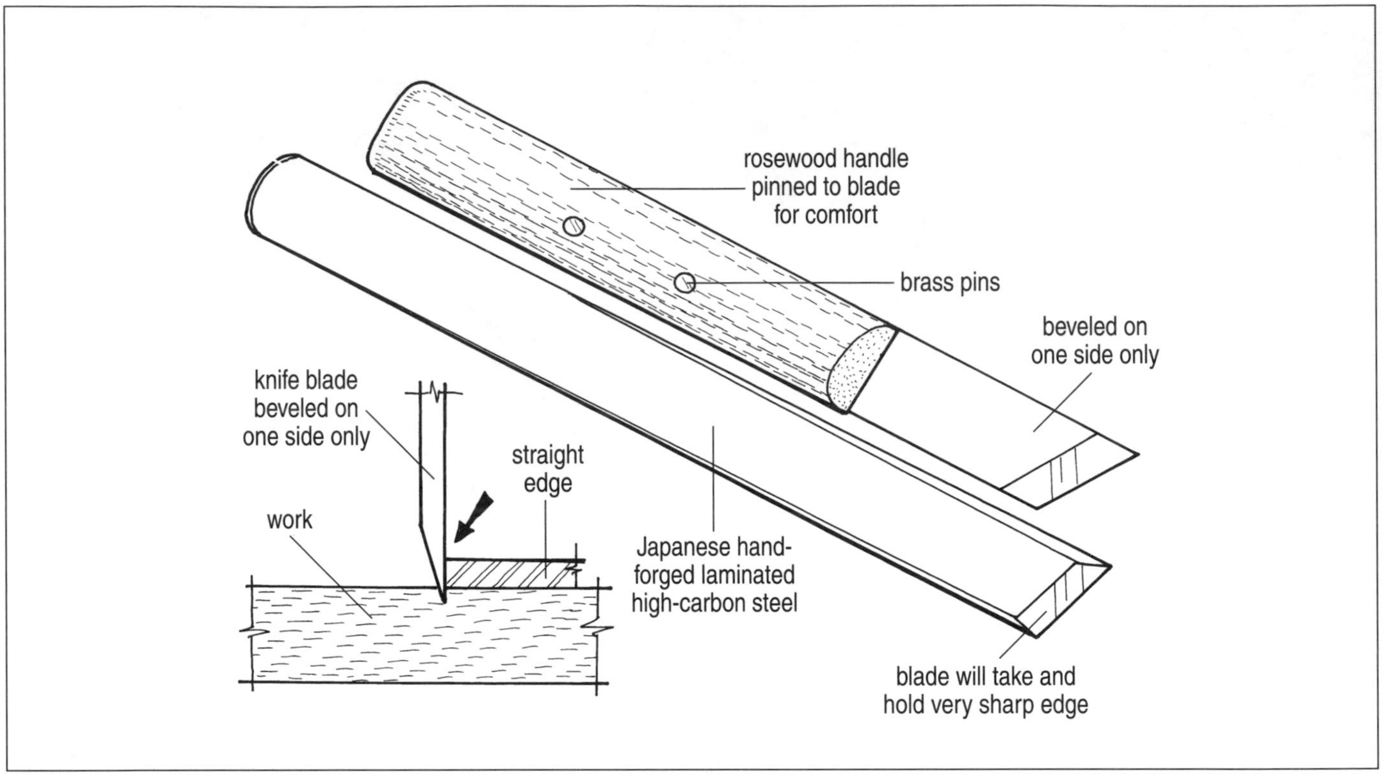
rosewood handle
pinned to blade
for comfort
brass pins
beveled on
one side only
knife blade
beveled on
one side only
straight
edge
work
Japanese hand-
forged laminated
high-carbon steel
blade will take and
hold very sharp edge

Fig. 8-17. Marking knives

MARKING KNIFE

The marking knife is a skew-bladed knife that is ground to a bevel only on one side of the blade (see 8-17 top).In use, the flat side of the blade is struck along the straightedge (see 8-17 bottom), making the cut very accurate because it is square on the finished side of the line and beveled on the waste side. In contrast, if you use an ordinary penknife to run a cut down the side of a straightedge, you will see that the cut is inaccurate because it is half the thickness of the blade away from the straightedge.

Of course, you can only really use a knife when the cut line is going to be removed by subsequent sawing or planing, but, that said, the knife generally leaves a line that is clearer to follow than a pencil mark.

CHAPTER NINE

Drilling Tools

The ability to drill just the right type of hole to just the right depth and width is important to good woodworking. Beginners often make the mistake of taking hole-making tools for granted. Having made the beautiful carved chair seat or cabinet, they then take up the nearest power drill and zap the holes. What often happens is that the ill-chosen drill bit exits in a mass of splinters or splits the workpiece. What beginners fail to appreciate is that there are all sorts of requirements when it comes to holes. Sometimes it doesn't matter too much if the hole is a bit ragged, whereas other times the hole needs to be perfectly smooth sided. All this adds up to the fact that you must use the right tools for the task. The following listing will help.

BRACE

While old wood and brass braces are most attractive and highly collectible, they are pretty useless when it comes to drilling good holes. They are hard work, and they are liable to break. The modern ratchet brace, on the other hand, is not only a beautiful tool to hold, but it is also a highly sophisticated and extremely efficient tool, perfect for almost every hole-making task (see 9-1).

The modern brace employs a turning power or force to the bit by means of a cranked frame. For horizontal or vertical drilling (see 9-2), the bit is fitted into the chuck, the ratchet is engaged so that the brace pushes on the clockwise stroke, the head of the brace is butted into your abdomen or against your chest, and then the handle is turned in a clockwise direction (see 9-3).

The diameter of the circle taken up by the handle in its turning or throw is referred to as the "sweep"; braces are sold by the half-sweep or radius of the circle. The ratchet can be used in tight situations to enable the brace to move with a forward-and-back part-circle stroke: forward a quarter turn, and then back

a quarter turn, and then forward a quarter turn, and so on.

Before you buy a brace, you have to decide whether you need a 5-inch brace with a large 10-inch sweep for slow work but high efficiency, or whether you want to sacrifice efficiency for speed by going for a smaller 4-inch brace with an 8-inch sweep. If you decide to go for a secondhand brace—and lots of woodworkers do— then it's always a good idea before you buy to dismantle the brace, just to make sure that it's in good condition. Start by unscrewing and removing the shell from the chuck so that you can check for wear on the alligator jaws (see 9-4). If the jaws are in reasonable condition, they should meet face-to-face when you push them together with the minimum of twisting and deformation. If there are any signs of cracks, if the metal looks mangled, or if the spring is twisted, broken, or missing, then look for another brace. Check the head of the brace; make sure that the bearings are in good working order. If the head is very wobbly or it won't turn, keep looking.

When you have selected and purchased what you consider is a good tool, then give it a thorough going-over. Remove the chuck case, the jaws, and the head, and clean away all the dirt and debris. Grease the moving parts and reassemble. Finally, squirt a small amount of light oil in the head oilhole, in the ends of the crank, under the handle and collars, and in the ratchet, and the brace is ready for action (see 9-5).

BRACE BITS

A brace and bit go together like bread and cheese and salt and pepper; the one is useless without the other. It follows, of course, that it's no good having the best brace in the world, if your bits are worthless. There are many types of bits, each and every one designed for a specific boring scenario. The best thing to do is to have a good

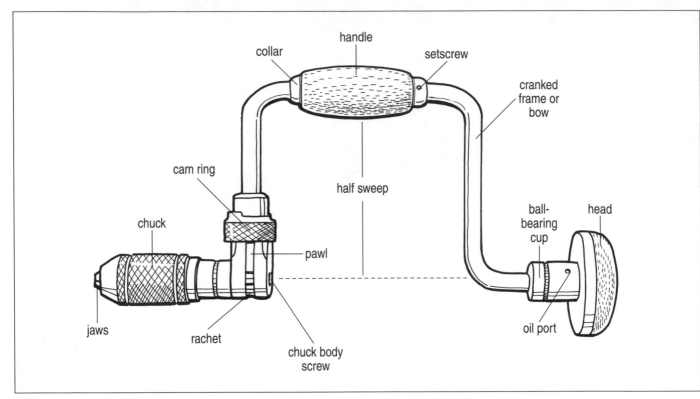

Fig. 9-1. The modern brace has a self-centering two-jaw chuck that takes bits of all sizes.

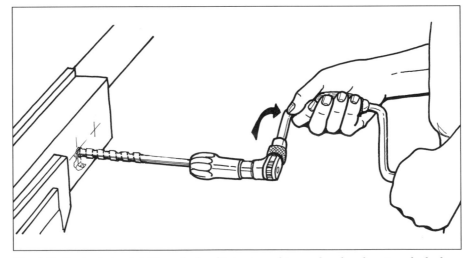

Fig. 9-2. For horizontal drilling, the head is supported in one hand and against the body, and the handle is cranked clockwise. The drill needs to be carefully aligned before beginning the cut.

selection of different bits so that you are always prepared for the next task. New bits are relatively expensive, but you can fill up an old 36-pocket bit roll with good secondhand bits at a fraction of the price of new ones.

Not only are secondhand bits inexpensive, but perhaps more to the point, some older out-of-production bits can only be obtained secondhand. If you like searching around yard sales and flea markets, and you are into collecting tools, then making an exhaustive collection of brace bits will be a pleasurable lifelong challenge.

The following listing will help you choose your bits.

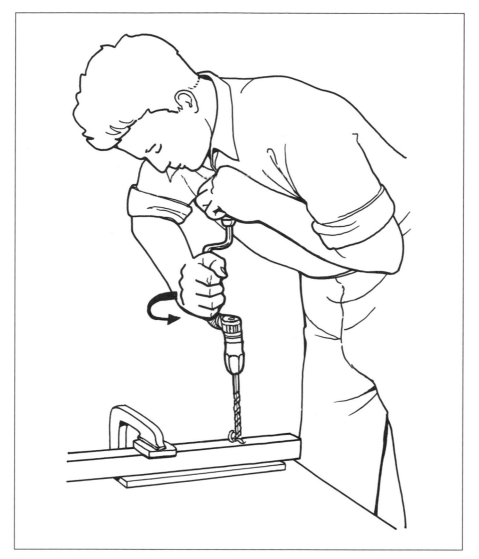

Fig. 9-3. *For vertical drilling, the head is cupped in one hand while force is applied by leaning over so that the chest rests on the hand. The handle is cranked clockwise. A piece of waste is used to prevent drill exit breakout.*

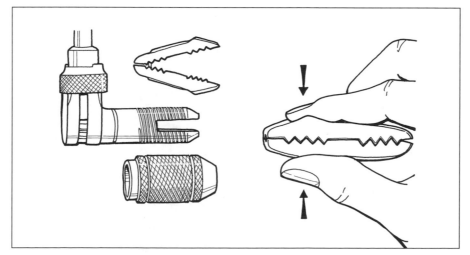

Fig. 9-4. Left, *the disassembled chuck showing the sintered alligator jaws, the chuck body, and the chuck shell.* Right, *testing the jaws for correct alignment.*

AUGER BIT

The auger or twist bit is designed specifically for cutting deep straight holes. Whereas modern catalogs show two patterns of auger bits—the Jennings and the solid center (see 9-6)—we see from an old catalog dated 1911 that there are at least six pattern types: the bright Scotch, the solid nose, the Gedges screw, the Jennings screw, the Gedges dowel, the Jennings dowel, and the wagon builder's fast. The chief advantage of the auger bit, and the reason that it has remained so popular, is that once started, the cutting action is such that the bit always stays on course. Though this is a big plus if you want to drill deep straight holes, you do have to spend extra time at the outset, with a square or by eye, making sure that the bit is correctly aligned and on course. It's no good running the drill in $^1/_2$ inch or so and then trying to change course!

To avoid bit-exit breakout, drill from one side until the tip of the screw appears, and then drill from the other side (see 9-7).

When you buy auger bits, either new or secondhand, it is important that you know your needs. Auger bits come in lengths ranging from 8 inches to 17 inches and diameters from $^3/_8$ inch to $2^1/_2$ inches. Some types of bit are made with a choice of "fine," "medium," or "coarse" lead screws, and other types are designed specifically to bore into end grain. You do need to know the type of auger bit that you require, its length and diameter, and also the type of lead screw.

The auger bit is a beautiful tool to watch in action. If you look closely, you will see that, sequentially, the lead screw pulls the bit into the wood, the flukes or spurs cut the circumference of the hole, the cutting lips skim off layers, and the twist or spiral sends the waste

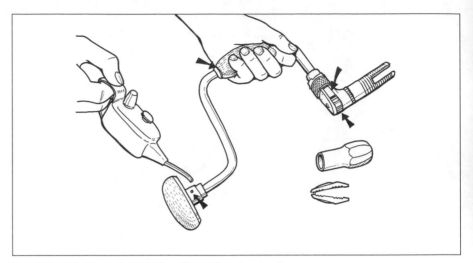

Fig. 9-5. Oil the ratchet, the handle, and the head holes.

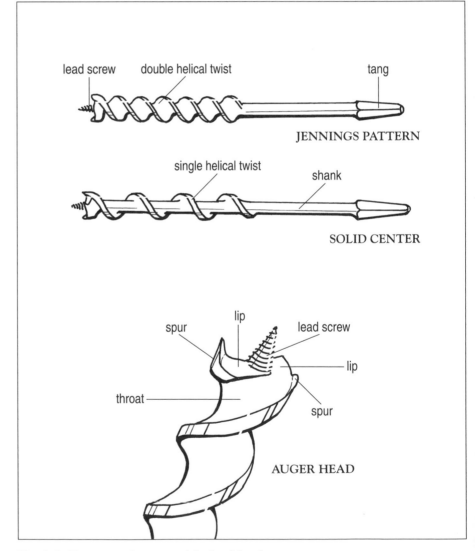

Fig. 9-6. Two types of augers and the head detail.

back up out of the hole (see 9-8). All the parts work in unison, with each part preparing the way for the next. Because one part prepares the way for another, or you might say one part depends on the other, so it is all the more important that each and every part of the bit be kept in good working order. Don't expect the lead screw to pull if it's clogged (see 9-9) or the spurs to cut if they are dull.

EXPANSIVE BITS

Whereas auger bits can drill deep holes up to about 2 1/2 inches in diameter, and center bits can drill shallow holes up to about 3 inches in diameter, the expansive bit, sometimes called the expansion or expanding bit, can drill deep holes up to 4 or 5 inches in diameter. Expansive bits are most interesting little gems of engineering. In design, they are essentially solid center bits or even auger bits, but without the twist, and with an extra spur cutter (see 9-10 top). The design of the spur cutter is such that it can be moved out from the center to increase the diameter of the swing. All you do is undo the screw, slide the spur out along its track to the correct radius, and then tighten up the screw and get on with the job (see 9-10 bottom left).

While expansive bits are attractive and relatively easy to set up, the off-center design of the outrigger cutter means that the cutting action is not so easy to control. To put it another way, don't think that you can set a used and abused expansive bit to, say, 3 inches, pop it in a small swing brace, and set to work swiftly drilling an easy hole in a piece of end-grain oak. It just won't happen! The trick with expansive bits is to make sure that they are in peak condition. The lead screw must be clean and unclogged, and the two spurs and the

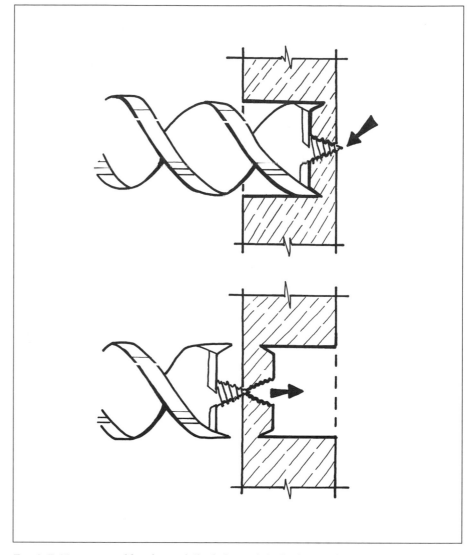

Fig. 9-7. Top, *to avoid breakout, drill a hole until the lead screw breaks through.* Bottom, *start over from the other side. Work at an easy pace until the lead screw finds its way.*

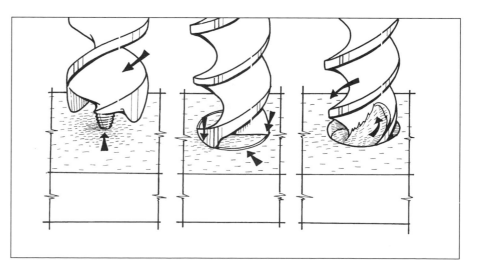

Fig. 9-8. Left, *the auger is pulled into the wood by the lead screw.* Middle, *the spurs cut the circumference of the hole.* Bottom, *the lips skim off the layers, and the waste exits up the spiral throat.*

cutting lip must be razor-sharp. Then you take the largest possible brace and go at it nice and slowly. If you study the working action closely, you will see that, in sequential order of cut, the lead screw pulls the bit into the wood, the primary spur makes contact and scribes out an inner circle, the primary lip clears the waste from the inner circle, and the outrigger spur then scribes the diameter of the hole while the outrigger cutting lip shaves off the layers of waste. What is happening, in effect, is that two holes are being drilled, one ahead of the other: an inner one that clears the bulk of the waste and an outer one that establishes the diameter of the hole (see 9-10 bottom right).

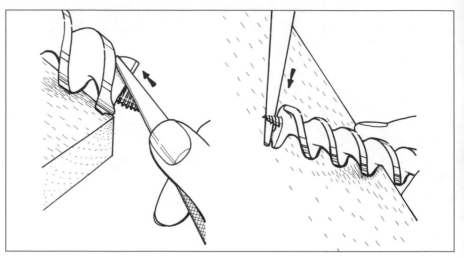

Fig. 9-9. Left, *to sharpen the auger, rest the head on a piece of waste wood and use a smooth-faced file to file the lips on the top leading surface.* Right, *only file on the inside of the spurs.*

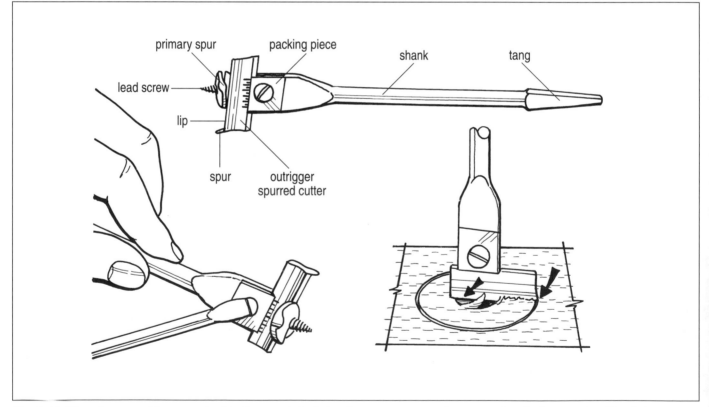

Fig. 9-10. Top, *the parts of the expansive bit.* Bottom left, *fitting the outrigger cutter.* Bottom right, *the bit in action. Two holes are bored: first the inner and then the outer.*

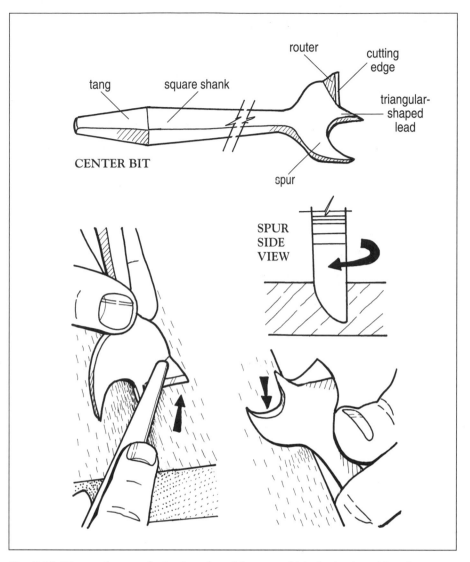

Fig. 9-11. Top, *make sure the cutting edge of the center bit isn't pitted or chipped on a secondhand tool.* Bottom left, *to sharpen, spike the lead spur into a block of wood and use a safe-edge file on the outer cutting edge.* Bottom right, *the tip of the spur should be sloping; sharpen the spur only on the inside edge.*

CENTER BITS

The old-fashioned flat-nosed center bit with its spike lead, spur cutter, and cutter lip is thought to be the archetypal bit. Not so long ago, before auger bits were introduced, the center bit was the one commonly used by most woodworkers (see 9-11 top). A flat center bit is just as useful now as it ever was. If you are looking to clear waste from a relief carving or to bore a large-diameter shallow hole, and you aren't too bothered about the sides being clean, then this is an easy bit to use and maintain (see 9-11 bottom).

FORSTNER BIT

If you are looking to drill a shallow accurate smooth-sided hole, then the Forstner bit takes a lot of beating (see 9-12). With its pointed center, cutting edge and rim, and absence of a lead screw, the Forstner bit is quite unlike an auger bit in that it requires a good deal of downward pressure before it starts to cut. To our way of thinking, the Forstner bit is the perfect bit for boring out clean-bottomed holes in

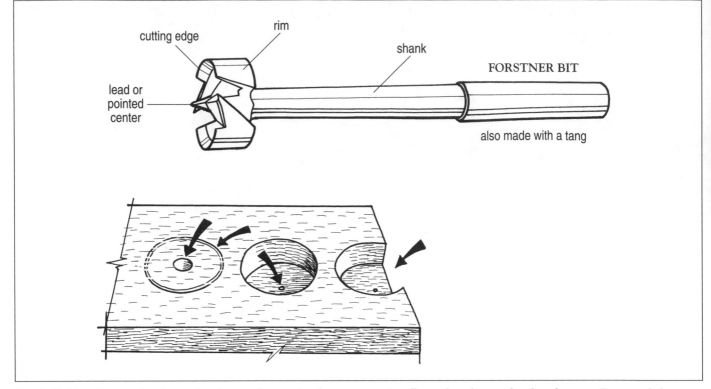

Fig. 9-12. Top, *Forstner bits have a bevel-ground outer rim that may occasionally need stroking with a fine slipstone.* Bottom, left to right, *the hole is scribed by the cutting edge. The Forstner produces flat-bottomed holes; it can even drill close to the edge.*

carving and in woodturning, when you want the hole to be on exhibit. (See chapter 7 section on the drill press for more about Forstner bits.)

BREAST DRILL AND HAND DRILL

Whereas the brace is designed for boring out wide and deep holes, the breast drill and the hand drill are the choice tools for swift small holes (see 9-13). As a general rule, the brace is used to bore out holes from, say, ¼ inch to 4 to 5 inches, and the breast and hand drills are most useful for making holes from ¼ inch down to ¹/₁₆ inch.

The characteristic hand drill has a cast-iron frame, a large gear wheel, one or two pinion gears that are meshed with the gear wheel, a three-jaw chuck, a top handle and a drive handle. The breast drill is

much the same, the only differences being that the whole thing is bigger, there are two speeds, there is a side handle, the top handle is replaced by a curved saddle-shaped breastplate, and on some models you need a chuck key to replace the bits. In use, the hand drill is held in one hand and operated with the other (see 9-14), and the breast drill is held in one hand and operated with the other while the user applies extra pressure by leaning against the breastplate (see 9-15). Both drills are designed to be used in conjunction with twist drills.

To fit the bits in the drill, hold the large gear wheel firmly against the frame while turning the chuck shell counterclockwise to open the chuck. Center the bit in the chuck, and then turn the chuck shell clockwise and give it a final clench-

ing. When the job is done, reverse the procedure to remove the bit.

TWIST DRILL BITS

Two types of twist drills are used with the hand drill and the breast drill: the common twist or Morse drill and the brad point twist or dowel drill (see 9-16). Much the same in design, they both have two helical flutes running along the length of the body. But the Morse drill has an angled chisel head with two cutting lips, whereas the brad point has a leading point or brad and cutting spurs. Common twist drills are suitable for boring all the everyday run-of-the-mill holes for nails, screws, pins, and the like, and the brad point drills are much preferred for drilling holes into hard end grain and for drilling precise holes for dowels.

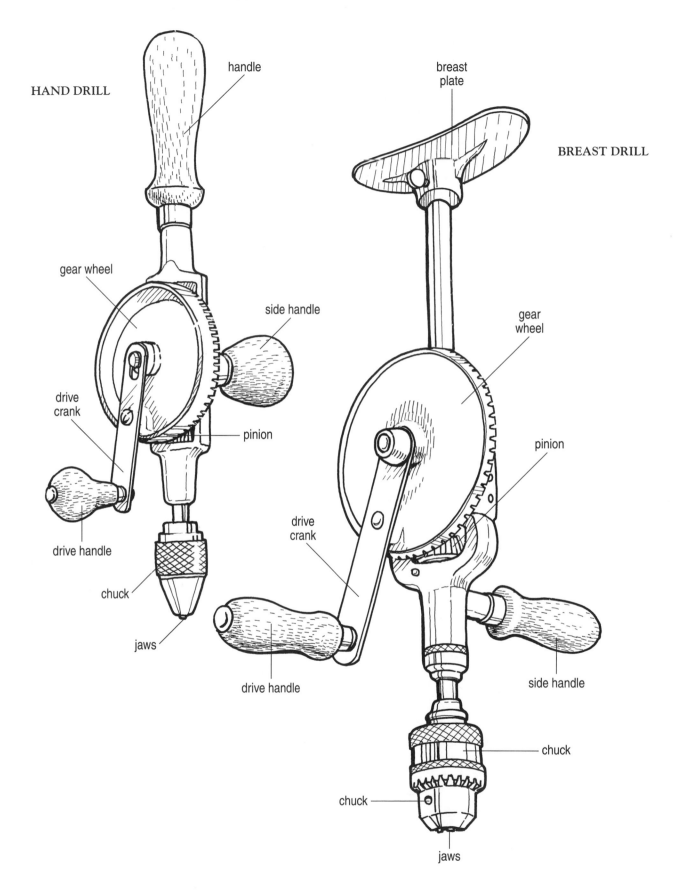

HAND DRILL

BREAST DRILL

handle

breast plate

gear wheel

side handle

drive crank

pinion

drive handle

chuck

jaws

gear wheel

pinion

drive crank

drive handle

side handle

chuck

chuck

jaws

Fig. 9-13. The hand drill and the breast drill.

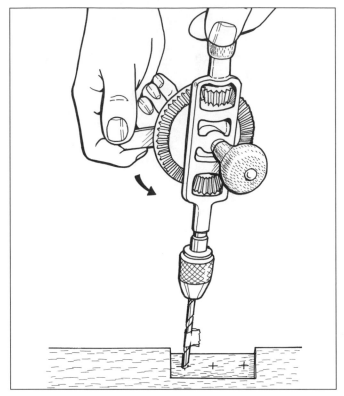

Fig. 9-14. *The hand drill is a good drill for working small holes. Note the tab of tape on the bit that is used to act as a depth guide.*

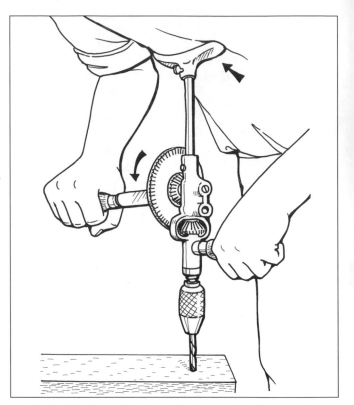

Fig. 9-15. *The breastplate is used to increase the downward pressure.*

In use, twist drills are best used with a light pressure and at high speed, but you do have to be careful not to overheat or bend the metal. The best procedure is to drill some and then retract the bit to clear the waste, and then drill some more, and so on; at the top end of the size range, when you are using the 1/4-inch drills or even some of the larger-stepped shank drills, the balance between speed and overheating becomes even more of a problem.

Some woodworkers are happy to use their twist drills to destruction. Although some of the cheaper twist drills are so low priced that they can be considered as throwaways, we think it is much better to buy higher-priced better-quality drills, and then treat them with care. Bear in mind when you are buying Morse twist drills that carbon steel drills are only suit-able for wood, whereas the HSS drill can also be used on metal.

GIMLETS

The gimlet is a handheld tool shaped a bit like a corkscrew that is used to bore shallow holes. If you want to make a quick hole for a nail or screw, then the gimlet is a good first-choice tool. The gimlet is much easier to use than, say, a bradawl simply because it has a lead screw at the tip that draws the tool into the wood. Though the gimlet is pretty easy to use (see 9-17), you do have to watch out that it doesn't split the wood.

There are three types of gimlet in common use: the auger gimlet for large holes, the shell gimlet that tends to be used for rough work, and the half-twist gimlet that is used for more delicate holes (see 9-18).

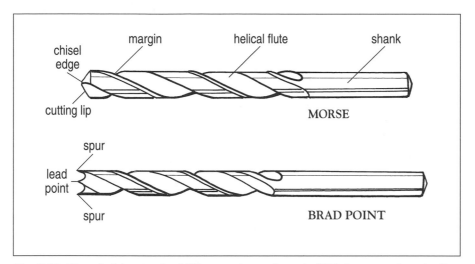

Fig. 9-16. Top, *the Morse twist drill has a point angle total of 118 degrees and cutting lips of equal length. Bottom,* the brad point twist drill is designed specifically for use on wood. *The two spurs are good for working hardwood.*

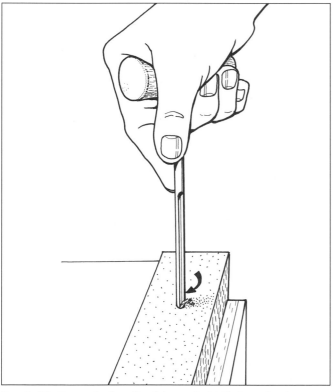

Fig. 9-17. *Grasp the handle of the gimlet with the index finger extended along the shank. Twist in a clockwise direction to bore the hole; reverse to remove.*

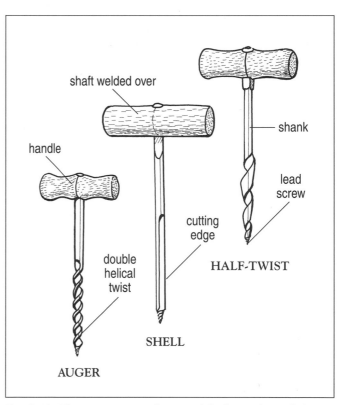

Fig. 9-18. *The auger-type gimlet is used for boring larger holes than the half-twist. The shell gimlet is less likely to split the wood —good on end grain.*

CHAPTER TEN

Knives and Scrapers

Though knives and scrapers have, for a long time, been mistakenly considered as rather folksy tools that are totally unsuited to sophisticated work, they are currently undergoing a revival. A whole new generation of woodworkers is gradually coming to realize that knives and scrapers are the archetypal tools from which all the fancy power machines have sprung, and as such, they deserve respect. But more than that, this new generation is coming to understand that knives and scrapers in all their various guises are supremely useful and versatile tools. Since the turn of the century right up until the 1980s, more and more woodworkers had been advocating a complete mechanization of woodworking—more power planers, power saws, power routers, power sanders, and all the rest. Now, at long last, many woodworkers appreciate that the humble knife and scraper not only get the job done, but also leave finishes that are uniquely beautiful. Okay, so a hand scraper and a knife might not be as swift as a power sander and a power planer, but more to the point, they are silent, they produce shavings rather than harmful dust, they cost pennies, and most important of all, they put the woodworker in contact with the wood.

So if you are looking to get back to basics, and you want to get as close as possible to the wood, and you want to cut down on the noise and the mess, then the following listing will show you how.

HAND KNIFE

The hand knife is, at one and the same time, one of the most versatile of all woodworking tools and one of the most underrated. To our way of thinking, this sorry state of affairs is encouraged by the tool catalogs, which usually feature one or two cheap general-purpose craft-type do-it-all throwaway knives, and not much else. When the beginner gets to use these horrible badly designed knives, with their nasty unbalanced handles and their can't-be-sharpened blades, they swiftly come to the false conclusion that all knives are inferior.

The knife is one of the most important of all the woodworking tools. It can be used for whittling, carving, trimming, scraping, cutting dowels, splitting pegs, rounding sticks, and a whole host of other tasks. The important thing here for you to realize is that just like planes, saws, and chisels, there are all types of knives, with each and every one being designed for a specific task. There are hooked and crooked knives for carving hollows (see 10-1), chip-carving knives for cutting pyramidal patterns (see 10-2), sheep's-foot whittling knives for fine shaving (see 10-3), sheath knives for general rough work (see 10-4), penknives for fine detailing (see 10-5), and so on. If you are a beginner, then one of the best ways into knife use is to start a collection of secondhand knives, and then tune them up and use them. We have a Northwest coast Indian crooked knife that we use for hollowing out the backs of masks and for carving the bowls of spoons (see 10-6), a little bone-handled penknife that we use for fine modeling, a Swedish sloyd knife that takes the most amazingly sharp edge (see 10-7) and that we use for skimming chair legs and rods to a smooth finish, and an old pruning knife (see 10-8) that is good for whittling round sections. They are all choice tools, and they all get used.

DRAWKNIFE

In shape, the drawknife is no more than a single-beveled blade, with a tang and a handle at each end. While modern catalogs show only a couple of drawknives, if any, old catalogs show drawknives or drawing knives of just about every conceivable type, shape, and size. Every woodworking trade had its own shape of knife. An old listing includes American drawing knives, English

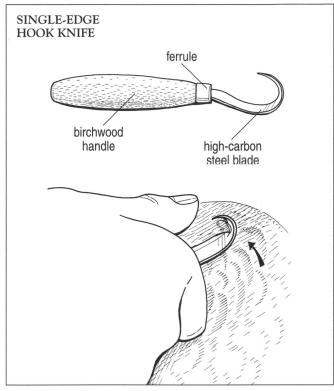

SINGLE-EDGE HOOK KNIFE

ferrule

birchwood handle

high-carbon steel blade

Fig. 10-1. *The single-edged hooked knife is used for working concave shapes—the hooked end doesn't dig in. A paring action is used, with the thumb acting as a lever.*

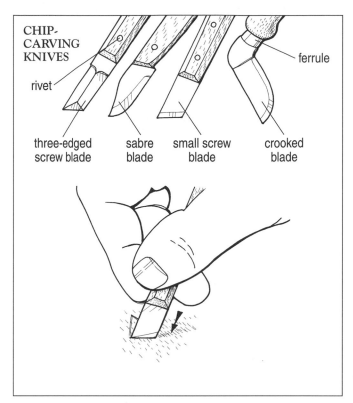

CHIP-CARVING KNIVES

rivet

ferrule

three-edged screw blade

sabre blade

small screw blade

crooked blade

Fig. 10-2. *Chip-carving knives are small knives designed to remove small chips of wood. The blades are pushed down at an angle into the wood and drawn toward the user's body. A sequence of cuts is used to remove a chip.*

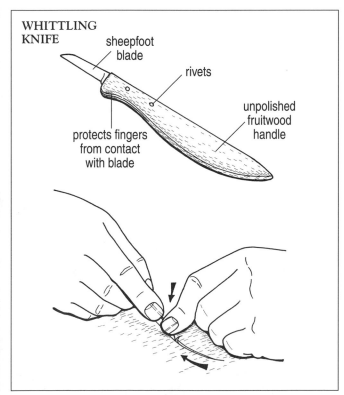

WHITTLING KNIFE

sheepfoot blade

rivets

unpolished fruitwood handle

protects fingers from contact with blade

Fig. 10-3. *Top, the whittling and carving knife is a sturdy little knife perfect for working small details. Bottom, the most common grip is the pencil hold, which can be reinforced by using the index finger of the other hand to lever down on the back of the blade.*

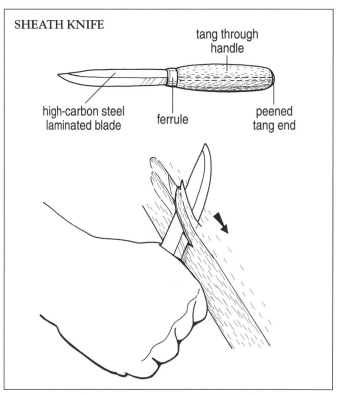

SHEATH KNIFE

tang through handle

high-carbon steel laminated blade

ferrule

peened tang end

Fig. 10-4. *Top, use the sheath knife to remove large amounts of waste. Bottom, grasp the handle and push the knife away from your body. This is safe if you always make sure that the supporting hand is behind the blade.*

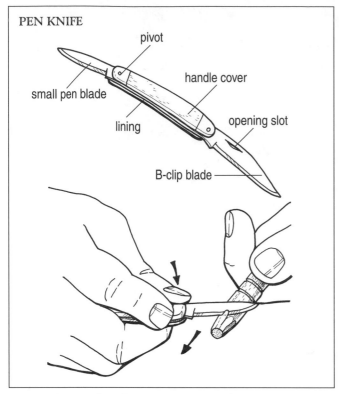

Fig. 10-5. A small penknife is great for small detailing, for cleaning out crevices on large sculptural works, and for intricate modeling.

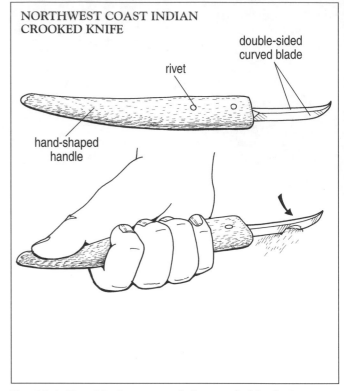

Fig. 10-6. Top, Northwest coast Indian crooked knife. Bottom, hold the handle daggerlike, with the thumb extended along the handle, and paddle the blade by pushing with your thumb.

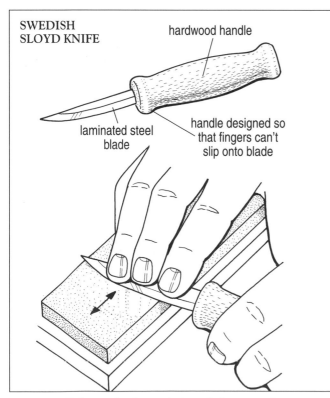

Fig. 10-7. To hone a knife, work through the stones from coarse to fine. Secure the stone flat on the bench, set the blade down and raise it up until only the bevel is resting on the stone, then rub backward and forward. Repeat this procedure on all the grades of stone.

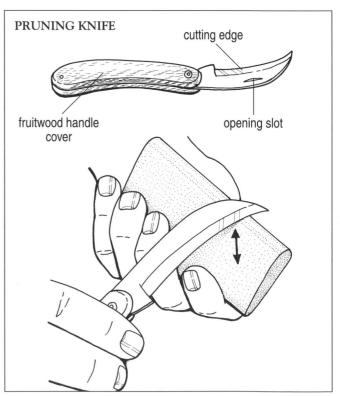

Fig. 10-8. To hone the shaped blade of a pruning knife, find a slipstone that fits the curve. Work the blade back and forth with a slight skewed action. Do both sides.

drawing knives, drawing knives used for debarking trees, carpenters' drawknives, chairmakers' knives, gentlemen's drawing knives, ladies' drawing knives, knives for gunsmiths, coopers, wheelwrights, shipbuilders, spar makers, and the list goes on. The pity of it is that a good many woodworkers now dismiss the drawknife as being a good tool for rough wasting, swift shaving, and maybe for preparing billets for the lathe, but not for much else. Of course, it is good for all of those activities, but for much more than that; it is a tool that is capable of very fine and sophisticated work. For example, the drawknife can be used for the total operation of shaping chair legs and stretchers; in fact, many chair leg makers use the drawknife instead of the lathe. It can be used for the final shaping of steambent chair backs, and it can be used for fine planing the edges of thin-section wood, and so on. We have at least three drawknives: one with a rather thick straight blade and egg-shaped handles that we use for splitting slender sections and for cutting stopped chamfers; one with a wide blade at about 12 inches long that we use for roughing out everything and anything; and a very nice one with a narrow blade at about 7 inches long that we use for fine skimming (see 10-9).

When you are looking to get yourself a drawknife, our best advice is to buy one secondhand. We say this because older knives usually have laminated steel blades that stay sharper longer. Search out a knife by one of the English toolmakers like Sorby, Ridge, or Hildick. Check the knife over and make sure that the tang runs right through the handle. Avoid handles that are in any way wobbly or split. To sharpen, all you do is hone the bevel with a slipstone in much the same way as for a knife (see 10-10).

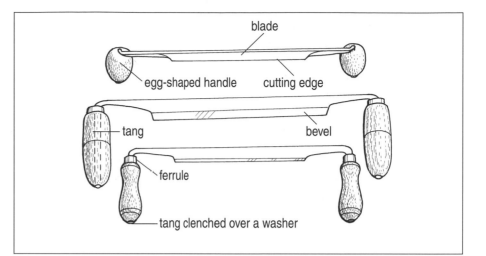

Fig. 10-9. Though there are many different designs of drawknives, they all have tapered tangs that angle off from the blade and pass through the handle to be clenched over against a washer.

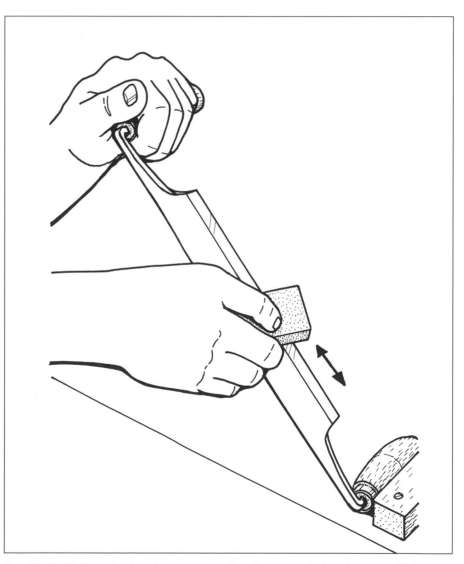

Fig. 10-10. To hone the drawknife, prop one handle against the bench stop, hold the other up at an angle, and rub the stone across and along the bevel. Use the stones from coarse to fine.

For shaving long planks and the like, a drawknife can be used with the workpiece held in a vise. But for many of the stick, leg, and dowel operations, the drawknife really needs to be used in conjunction with a shaving horse or donkey, a benchlike seat with a foot-operated clamp at one end. In action, you sit astride the horse, set the workpiece in the clamp, push the bottom end of the clamp with your foot, and then you set to work with the drawknife (see 10-11). The clever thing with this arrangement is that the very action of bracing your foot against the bottom end of the clamp, and then drawing with the knife toward your body, automatically results in the workpiece being held fast. The more effort that you put forth and the harder you push with your foot, the tighter the hold on the workpiece. The drawknife is held in both hands, with your elbows tucked into your waist. As to the oft-asked question of whether to have the bevel up or down, all you have to remember is that the knife tends to run away from the bevel. So if you hold it bevel downward, then it rises from the cut, and if you hold it bevel upward, then it wants to make a deeper cut. Assess each situation, and then use the knife accordingly. Another feature of the drawknife is that it can be held and used at an extremely skewed angle, making it particularly useful for delicate shaving and paring strokes.

For safety, always hold and handle the drawknife with both hands (see 10-12). Beginners are sometimes worried that they might pull the drawknife so hard that they will lose control of it and cut themselves. My answer to this fear is that if your elbows are tucked hard into your waist, then it's not possible to cut yourself. Try it and see!

Fig. 10-11. Sit astride the shaving horse, place the work on the surface and under the clamp, and hold the work securely by pushing against the pedal with your foot. Your hands are now free to use the drawknife.

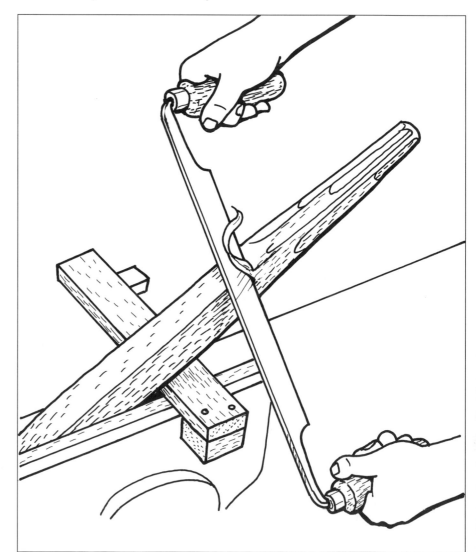

Fig. 10-12. Working at a slight angle, grasp the tool with both hands, and with the bevel side down, pull the blade toward your body. Progress in stages, turning the wood and retreating along the length.

The best procedure for making the cut is to start at the near end of the workpiece, and then work away from your body. So, for example, with a chair leg, first mark the ends of the wood to the correct diameter, and then work with a longer and longer reach, all the while trying to shave the rest of the waste down to the finished end. Periodically check with calipers.

INSHAVE

The inshave, sometimes called a round shave or a scorpe, is no more than a drawknife with a part-circle blade that is used for scooping out hollows (see 10-13). While this tool is a bit specific, it is a wonderful tool for certain tasks. For example, it is the best tool that we know of for finishing the hollows that go to make up a Windsor chairseat. In use, it is held in both hands, and then pulled with a tight elbows-in-the-side stroke. As to the bevel, some inshaves have the bevel on only the outside edge, but for the most part, they have a bevel on both sides of the blade. Our particular inshave was made in England by a firm called Marsden. It is particularly comfortable to hold because the beautifully turned handles cock outward. This feature results in a very tightly controlled cut.

SHAVE

A shave is basically a knife edge with a handle at each end. Although there are many types of shaves—a basket shave, a chairmaker's shave, a coach builder's shave, a bucket maker's shave, a handrail shave, a mast maker's shave, and so on—the shave that we all now most associate with general woodworking, is the wheelmaker's spokeshave. The traditional wooden spokeshave is sort of a cross between a plane and a drawknife. It consists of a wooden stock with a

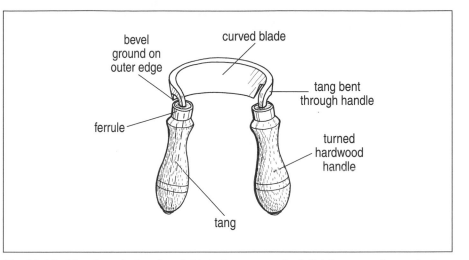

Fig. 10-13. Note how the handles of this inshave are cocked slightly outward to make it more comfortable to use.

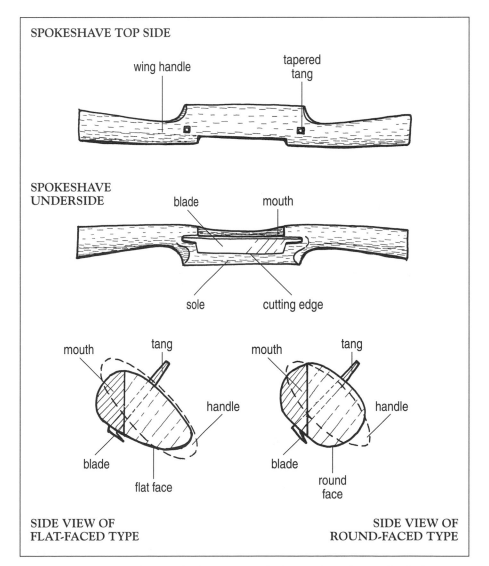

Fig. 10-14. The tapered tangs of a shave are a tight friction fit in the wooden body. Tap the ends of the tang with a hammer if you need a fuller or deeper cut. If the tangs become loose, secure them with a sliver of veneer. Use the flat-faced type for convex curves and the round-faced for working hollows.

handle at each side and a metal cutter. We have three wooden spokeshaves: a flat-faced type that we use for general work and for convex shapes, a large round-faced one that we use for big broad concave shapes, and a small round-faced tool that we use for little tight concave shapes (see 10-14).

In use, the shave is held in both hands, with the thumbs placed on the back edges to control the angle of approach, and then it is pushed in much the same way as you would push an old-fashioned router (see 10-15). The cutting action is similar to that of a plane: As the blade planes across the surface, the waste shavings run up between the sole of the shave and the blade. And just as with the plane, for best effect, it is necessary always to work in the direction of the grain. This means that for most multicurve forms—cyma curves, chairseats, and the like—it is necessary to change direction for the various sweeps (see 10-16). As with the drawknife, the design of the spokeshave is such that you can have one hand slightly forward of the other so that the shave is at a skewed angle. This way of working is especially good for shearing cuts on some corners and curves. While there are now spokeshaves made of metal, our preference is for wooden shaves. Certainly metal shaves are easier to sharpen and adjust (see 10-17), and they have a longer life, but wooden spokeshaves come in a wider range of sizes and designs, and better yet, they are altogether more responsive than metal ones. Another good quality of the wooden shave is its usefulness on the pull stroke. So, for example, if you're working a concave or convex curve, you don't have to move yourself or the workpiece to work in a different direction to the run of the grain; simply turn the shave

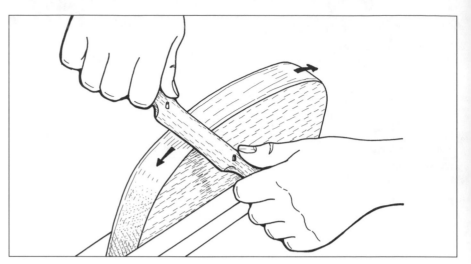

Fig. 10-15. Grasp the wing handles and arrange the shave so that you can see the back of the blade. For a well-controlled cut, place your thumbs behind the tangs. As you start the cut, rock the tool slightly to engage the blade. Keep the sole level with the surface being worked. Use a shearing skewed action on tough end grain.

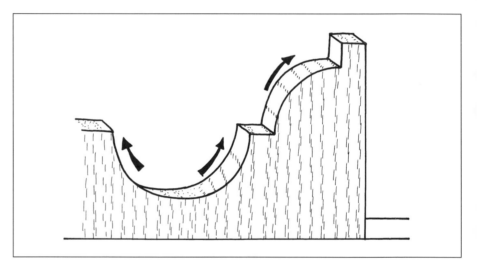

Fig. 10-16. Work in the direction of the arrows to follow the grain.

around and work on the "pull" stroke rather than on the "push."

HAND SCRAPER

Hand scrapers are no more than pieces of thin tool steel that are held and flexed in the hands and used to scrape surfaces to a smooth finish (see 10-18). We regularly use two scrapers, both about $3/64$ inch thick. One is a 3-by-6-inch rectangle that we use for cabinetwork, and the other one is kidney shaped; we use it for concave surfaces like the insides of bowls and the like.

The scraper has a wonderful quality that most beginners either never get to experience or simply fail to appreciate: It can produce a finished surface that is many times smoother than that produced by the finest of fine-grade sandpaper. Whereas a piece of sandpaper leaves a smooth fluffy characterless surface—like a flour-covered board—a scraper, on the other hand, leaves a surface that is glazed and burnished. And whereas a sanded surface looks mechanically perfect but dead, the scraped surface looks

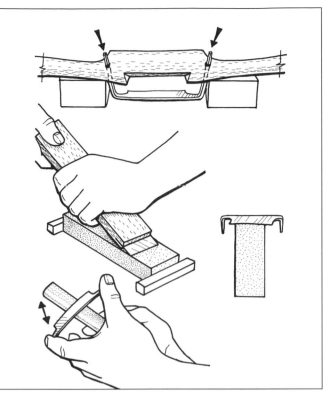

Fig. 10-17. Top, *to remove the blade, bridge the shave between two pieces of waste so that the wood on the handle side of the tang is supported, and then give the tang a gentle tap with a small hammer. Middle left, to sharpen the blade of a metal spokeshave, set it in a slot cut in a length of hardwood. Middle right, for flat blades, use the stone on edge with the blade held flat. Bottom, for curved blades, hold the cutter between thumb and finger and rub the blade over a curved-section slip.*

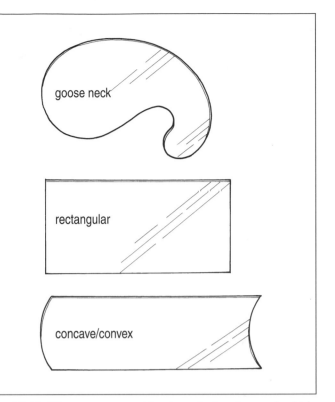

Fig. 10-18. *The scraper cuts with a burred edge. It must be thick enough to hold the burr but thin enough to flex—about $1/16$-inch thick is fine. Choose a scraper shape to match the surface being worked.*

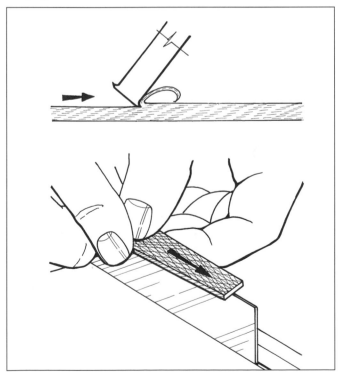

Fig. 10-19. Top, *the scraper blade is held at a leaning angle of about 70 degrees and pushed or pulled so that the burr is dragged. The burr bites into the wood and takes a shaving. Bottom, hold the file with the fingers on the underside to act as a guide. Press down keeping the file square to the edge of the scraper. Pass it along several times in a continuous stroke.*

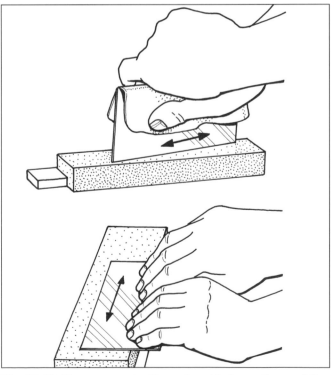

Fig. 10-20. Top, *remove the file marks with the medium and fine stones. Hold the scraper at a skewed angle to prevent wearing ridges in the surface of the stone. Use a cloth to protect your hands. Bottom, to clean the edges, wipe both faces flat down on the stone.*

altogether more vibrant and lively. If you have it in mind to make revival furniture or folk art pieces, then the best way of achieving an authentic surface is to use a scraper.

First, before you can even use a scraper, you have to learn how to sharpen it. A scraper cuts with a burr (see 10-19 top) rather than with a beveled cutting edge like that of a plane blade. To create the burr on a scraper, proceed as follows:

- First clean up the edge with a file, cut it so that it is at right angles to the face (see 10-19 bottom).
- Smooth the edge on a whetstone until it's perfectly true. If you are working on a rectangular scraper, true up the other long edge (see 10-20 top)
- Smooth both faces on the whetstone (see 10-20 bottom).
- To create the burr, draw the edge over with the back of a gouge. Draw the tool first one way and then the other, and then flip the scraper over and repeat the procedure on the other side (see 10-21). There should be a raised hooklike burr along the cutting edge on both sides.

In action, the hand scraper is always used with a dragging stroke. It doesn't matter whether it is pushed or pulled, as long as the burred edge is dragged. Hold the scraper with both hands, with the thumbs placed near the cutting edge. Press with the thumbs until the metal begins to bow, lean the top edge away from you, push the scraper at a slightly skewed dragging angle until the burred edge begins to bite, and then make the stroke (see 10-22). The success of the cut depends on four factors: the type of wood, the size of the burr on

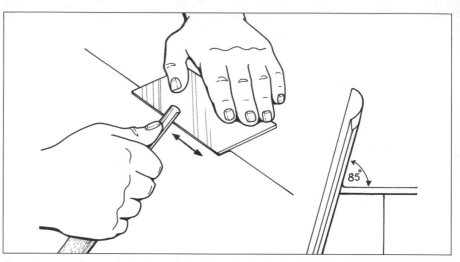

Fig. 10-21. Left, *use the back of the gouge as a burnisher. Make two or three fairly light passes with the gouge held at a slightly skewed angle.* Right, *the back of the gouge should meet the edge of the scraper at about 85 degrees.*

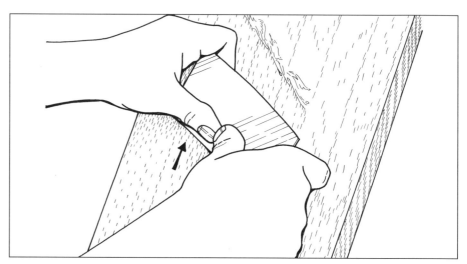

Fig. 10-22. *Hold the scraper at a skewed angle to the grain, tilted at about 70 degrees, press with your thumbs to bow the scraper, and push in the direction of the grain.*

the edge of the scraper, the dragging angle at which the scraper is held, and the amount of pressure applied with your thumbs.

When the scraper loses its initial keenness, swiftly burr over the edges with the back of the gouge, and then get on with the job. You can draw up the burr three or four times before you have to go back to the filing and honing stages.

SCRAPER PLANE
The double-handed scraper plane, or cabinet scraper, is the choice

tool for bringing a level surface to a good finish. It works in just the same way as the hand scraper, the only difference being that it is more comfortable to hold, with a good deal less strain on the thumbs, and the angle of drag is constant. We use an old Stanley 80 scraper plane; it's the perfect tool for scraping tabletops and the like (see 10-23).

As for sharpening, unlike the edge of the hand scraper blade, which is ground to 90 degrees prior to the burr being drawn, the edge of the cabinet scraper is first ground to a bevel of 45 degrees (see 10-24).

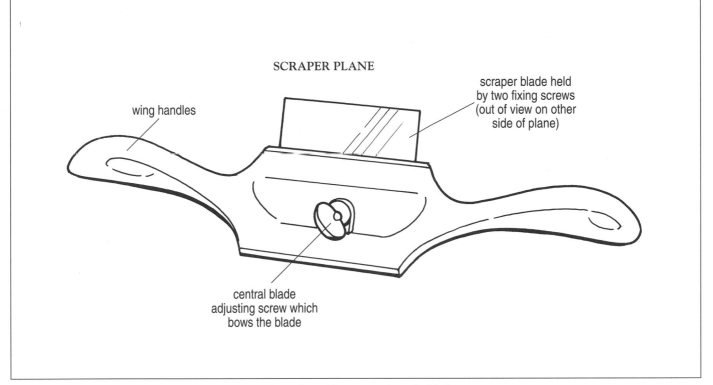

SCRAPER PLANE

wing handles

scraper blade held
by two fixing screws
(out of view on other
side of plane)

central blade
adjusting screw which
bows the blade

Fig. 10-23. The scraper plane has wing handles and an adjustable screw to bow the blade.

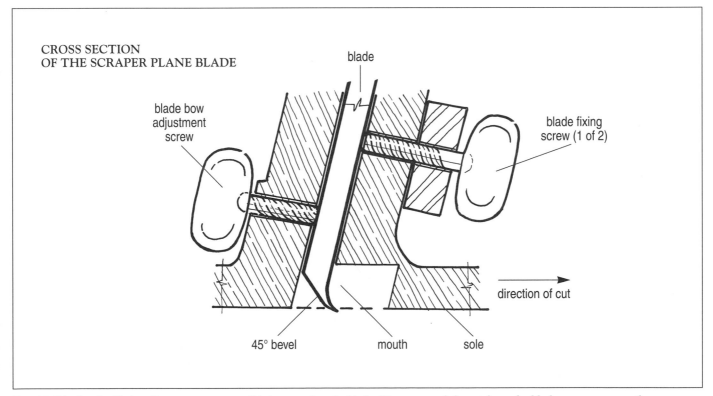

CROSS SECTION
OF THE SCRAPER PLANE BLADE

blade

blade bow
adjustment
screw

blade fixing
screw (1 of 2)

direction of cut

45° bevel   mouth   sole

*Fig. 10-24. Set the blade adjustment screw until it just touches the blade. Try a cut and then tighten the blade some more until you are
happy with the amount of bite.*

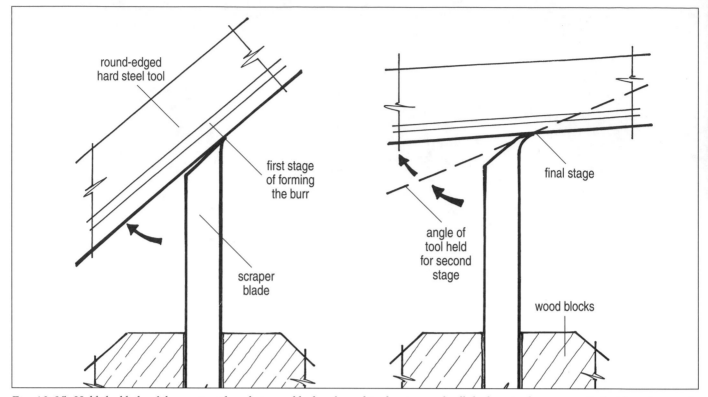

Fig. 10-25. *Hold the blade of the scraper plane between blocks of wood in the vise, and roll the burr in three stages.* Left, *place the round-edged tool on the blade, raise it slightly, and then draw it across the burr.* Right, *raise the tool and repeat the stroking action a couple more times. At the final stage, the burnisher should be about 15 degrees off the horizontal.*

The blade is then held between blocks in the vise to create the burr (see 10-25).

When honing the scraper blade, hold it in a grooved piece of hardwood, similar to that used for the metal spokeshave blade (see 10-17). The setting-up or tuning sequence is as follows:

- Set the plane sole down on the bench, slacken the two fixing screws that hold the bar in place, and loosen the thumbscrew.
- Drop the newly drawn blade into place so that the bevel is looking toward the thumbscrew, and

make sure that the cutting edge is in close contact with the bench (see 10-24).

- Tighten up the two fixing screws so that the blade is held securely. Then give the adjusting thumbscrew a tweak until the blade begins to bow.
- Try the plane on a piece of scrap hardwood, and then make adjustments accordingly.

In use, the stock is set sole down on the workpiece and managed in much the same way as for a spokeshave, that is, with the top of the blade leaning away from you and the bevel dragging.

CHAPTER ELEVEN

Hammers and Mallets

HAMMERS

Inasmuch as the poor old hammer is, all too often, the luckless tool that the woodworker takes for granted, all the more reason to choose one with extra care and consideration. A good hammer needs to fit your hand and do the job, without your giving it a moment's thought.

Though we do take hammers for granted, sometimes to the extent that we use them to death, the simple truth is that we can't do without them. Certainly, a hammer is in no way as glamorous as a chisel, nor is it as exciting to use as, say, a plane, but it is just as vital to the total quality of the finished woodwork. We think that part of the reason why most of us tend to take hammers for granted is that they are often the one and only woodworking tool that most families possess. Most kids just pick up the family hammer, usually a claw hammer and proceed to whack everything in sight from nails, rocks, posts, and bricks to bike parts and whatever else happens to be around. Once this cycle of misuse is set in motion, beginners to woodworking tend to follow it up by using just any old hammer—no matter that it is totally unsuited to the task. They whack in the nail and, surprise surprise, the hammer glances off and the work-piece is forever marked.

As a woodworker, you have to appreciate that a well-chosen hammer is a boon to good woodworking. If you carefully select two or three good quality hammers, they will be friends for life.

So if you don't want your projects to be tattooed with hammer marks, and if you do want to drive nails home without mashing your fingers, then the following listing will help you on your way.

CLAW HAMMER

Though the claw, ripping, or adz-eye hammer is, strictly speaking, a tool that is used more by carpenters than by, say, furniture makers, simply because carpenters are much more likely to use large-size nails that need extracting, we think that all woodworkers need at least one claw hammer (see 11-1). Our preference is for a straightforward wooden-handled hammer of 8 to 11 ounces of the adz-eye type. Hammers of this type are easy to recognize, because the hammerhead eye extends down the handle to act as a sleeve.

You could go for a one-piece solid steel hammer with a leather grip, or a tube steel handle pattern with a rubber or foam-cushioned grip, or even a hammer with a resin fiber handle, but we think these hammers are all somewhat flawed; either the shock of banging in large nails gets to be uncomfortable or the handles are simply out of balance and bothersome to hold, and rubber sleeve handles soon get greasy and slippery. To our way of thinking, there is nothing so unpleasant in the small world of hammers as a foam-cushioned handle that is slick with grime. A good quality hickory or ash handle, on the other hand, absorbs the shock, it is good to hold even if your hands are warm and moist, it is slightly flexible, it is relatively inexpensive, and best of all, it can be replaced.

As to the question of whether or not to replace a handle if it is broken, we would say that it's only worthwhile if the face of the head is in reasonable condition, meaning not chipped, cracked, or rounded. The procedure is as follows:

- Cut away as much of the broken handle as possible.
- Set the hammerhead upside down so that it is bridged over a couple of hardwood blocks, and use a drift to drive out the stub of broken handle (see 11-2 top).
- Measure down the handle shaft to where the bottom of the cheek should fit, and then use a knife

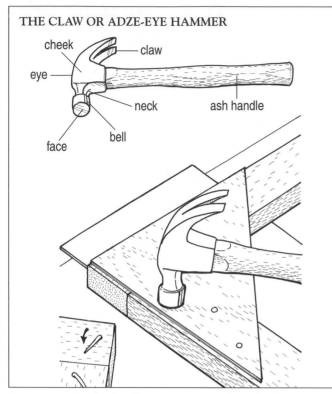

THE CLAW OR ADZE-EYE HAMMER

cheek — claw
eye
neck — ash handle
face — bell

Fig. 11-1. Top, *the claw hammer*. Bottom left, *clenching or clinching nails against a metal plate. The nails are driven through the joints, and the points strike the metal plate and roll over to become clenched.*

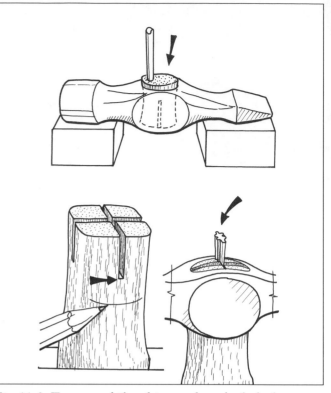

Fig. 11-2. Top, *use a drift to drive out the stub of a broken handle*. Bottom left, *make saw kerfs about two-thirds down the depth of the eye*. Bottom right, *the metal wedge is driven in after the wooden wedges have been trimmed to shape.*

to whittle the end of the handle to a snug push fit.

- Secure the handle upright in the vise and use a saw to cut two kerfs down across the end of the shaft about two-thirds down the depth of the eye (see 11-2 bottom left).
- Tap the head on the handle, and then drive one or two hardwood wedges down into the kerfs to expand the top of the shaft across its width.
- Saw off the ends of the wedges, and then drive in two metal wedges at right angles to the wooden wedges so as to expand the top of the shaft across its length as seen in cross section.

Holding and Using the Hammer. The claw hammer comes into its own when it is being used to drive in good-size nails. In use, it is held toward the end of the handle (see 11-3) so that it is nicely balanced, and then it is swung with confident well-measured strokes. The curious thing about using a hammer is that if you think too hard about what you are doing, the chances are you will miss your mark. The best approach is to keep your eye on the nail, use short strokes to get the hammer on target, and then to follow through with good smart strokes. If you watch a carpenter at work—someone like a roofer, who gets to bang in a lot of nails—you will see that the rhythm of his work goes something like tap-tap-bang, tap-tap-bang, and so on. The two taps are the little trial runs that help him to get his stroke on target.

As for the claw part of the hammer, it is used to draw out misplaced or bent nails. In action, the claw is slid under the head of the offending nail (see 11-4), a piece of waste wood is set between the hammerhead and the work surface, and then the handle is levered over to extract the nail. A clever little ruse to use with difficult long nails is to start with a thin piece of waste and gradually switch to thicker and thicker pieces of waste as the length of the extracted nail allows.

PIN HAMMER

The long-handled pin hammer is really no more than a lightweight Warrington-style hammer that is used to drive in small pins or tacks. There are two types in use by woodworkers, both at about 4 ounces in weight: the ball peen, which is favored by woodworkers who need to round over the odd pin or rivet, and the more common cross peen, which is used for most small nailing and pinning operations (see 11-5). If you have in mind to do lots of little fussy tasks, like fixing small applied moldings, making picture frames, and such, the pin hammer is a good choice.

CROSS PEEN HAMMER

Though not so long ago just about every county in England and the USA had its own unique style of cross peen joiner's hammer in a whole range of handle lengths and weights, now most woodworkers have no other choice but to use what is described as the standard Warrington pattern cross peen at 10 to 11 ounces. The cross peen (see 11-6) is used to start the nail that is held between your fingers, and then, once the nail is holding, the hammer is turned around in the hand, and the nail is driven home. When you are choosing a hammer, have a good close look at the forged head. Make sure that the face is flat, the peen is nicely rounded, and the cheeks, neck, and eye are free from rough edges. If there are any problems, then look for another hammer.

COACH TRIMMER'S OR CABRIOLET HAMMER

Although we wouldn't give most secondhand hammers a second look because the faces are usually well rounded and the handles cracked, we would buy a secondhand coach trimmer's or upholsterer's hammer for the plain and simple reason that they are almost impossible to buy new. We have such a hammer (see 11-7). It has a long pointed head, with a round face at one end and a claw at the other; the head is fixed to the handle by means of two side straps. The handle itself is particularly comfortable to hold; it swells out at the end, and it is unvarnished. A characteristic feature is the magnetic face that allows the user to select small tacks with minimum of effort. The smallness of the face means

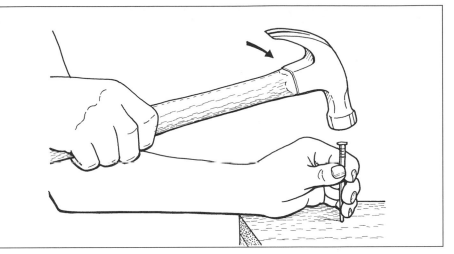

Fig. 11-3. Hold the hammer handle near its end; start with small taps and increase the stroke. Aim to hit the nail centrally.

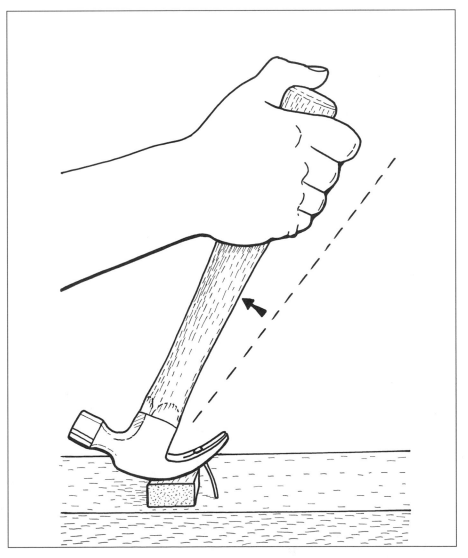

Fig. 11-4. To remove a nail, the claw hammer is held upside down with the head resting on a small block of waste. The claw is engaged with the nailhead and the handle is pulled and levered back.

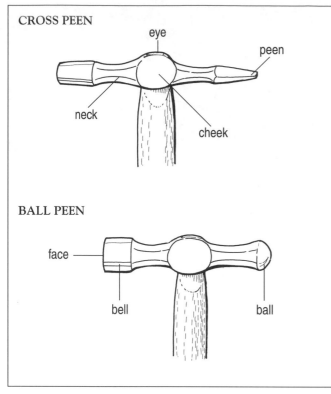

CROSS PEEN

eye

peen

neck

cheek

BALL PEEN

face

bell

ball

Fig. 11-5. Top, *the woodworker's cross peen hammer, with the horizontal peen.* Bottom, *the metalworker's ball peen, used for knocking over rivets and nails.*

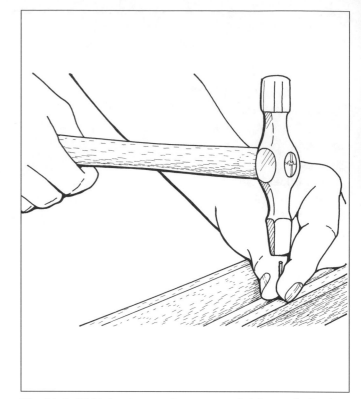

Fig. 11-6. *Hold the pin or tack in position, lightly tap the head with the peen, and then turn the hammer over and complete the task with the head. If you are working with profiled beading as shown, then it's a good idea to complete the task with the pen.*

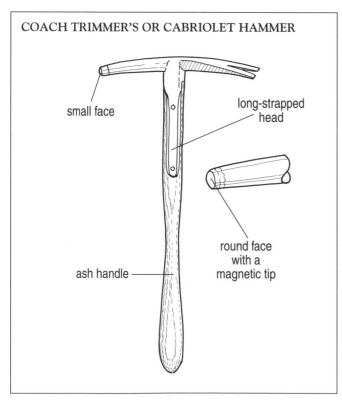

COACH TRIMMER'S OR CABRIOLET HAMMER

small face

long-strapped head

round face with a magnetic tip

ash handle

Fig. 11-7. *The coach trimmer's or cabriolet hammer has a magnetic tip to help with handling small pins on very fine work.*

that the hammer can be used to drive in small tacks without doing damage to the surrounding area. Though we use this hammer in much the same way as a pin hammer, an old coach builder once told us that the magnetic end is used for taking the tacks from the mouth. The idea is to fill your mouth with a hundred or so tacks, and then somehow or other maneuver the tacks around with your tongue so that the heads of the tacks are presented to the magnetic face of the hammer. We're not advocating this technique you understand, for a simple reason that this old guy went on to explain: He reckoned that most coach builders swallowed hundreds of tacks over the course of their working lives!

MALLETS

Traditional mallets are best considered as hammers made of wood. They are used to strike a piece of wood in situations where a metal hammer might do damage. A good memory aid is metal for metal, and wood for wood. So mallets are used for striking chisel handles, for knocking frames together, for woodcarving, for cutting joints, and for all the other tasks and procedures where the metal hammer might bruise the workpiece.

And, of course, whereas the face of a hammer is so small that you might well miss the end of a chisel handle, the face of a mallet, on the other hand, is so big that it would be difficult to miss your mark.

CARPENTER'S OR JOINER'S MALLET

The common mallet, as used by carpenters and joiners, is the choice tool for driving chisels and for tapping frames together and apart (see 11-8). Though it looks to be no more than a block of wood on the end of a handle, a good mallet is designed so that the head is part of a circle—like a piece cut from the rim of a wagon wheel. In fact, at one time, when wooden wheels were commonplace, old and broken wheel felloes were salvaged, sawn up into chunks, and turned into mallet heads. The idea is that because the faces of the part-circle head are tapered or canted toward the end of the handle, when the mallet is being swung in an arc the face will always strike the work fair square and at right angles. And if that isn't clever enough, both the eye and the handle are tapered toward the user so that when the mallet is being swung, centrifugal force tends to throw the head out so that it tightens up on the handle. There is no risk of the head flying off.

Traditionally, carpenter's and joiner's mallets were made from close-grained woods like beech and apple, or ash if they were cut from old wheel felloes. Modern mallets come in a whole range of sizes—4, 5, 6, or 7 inches, and bigger—but a 7 incher at 28 to 32 ounces is a good all-around mallet.

WOODCARVER'S MALLET

The head of the traditional woodcarver's mallet is round in cross section and a sort of cone or bun shape as seen in side view. Made on the lathe in such woods as beech, box, and lignum vitae, a mallet of this type is the first-choice tool if you have in mind to take up woodcarving (see 11-9). The all-around shape allows you to strike the chisel or gouge from any direction without the need to shift your grip, but more than that, you can deliver

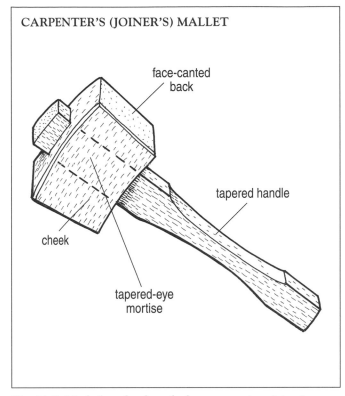

CARPENTER'S (JOINER'S) MALLET

face-canted back

tapered handle

cheek

tapered-eye mortise

Fig. 11-8. Made from hardwood, the carpenter's or joiner's mallet can take a heavy beating. Unlike hammers, they are best held close to the head.

lively glancing blows, where the head of the mallet bounces or ricochets off the tool.

PLASTIC AND RUBBER MALLETS

Although soft-faced rubber, plastic, and leather mallets are being used more and more for carpentry and joinery, as well as for woodcarving, we have got to say that we get pleasure from hearing wood strike wood. Compound heads last longer, and white-head mallets can be used without marking the wood, but we still prefer wooden mallets. One reason for this seeming illogicality might well be that we are of the opinion that a good part of the pleasure of woodworking has to do with making your own tools. What is the sense of buying a compound head mallet if you can make your own customized wooden mallet?

HOMEMADE MALLETS

There is a long-standing tradition among woodworkers to make as many of their own tools as possible. The mallet is one such tool. While carpenters and joiners made their mallets from sections cut from wagon wheel

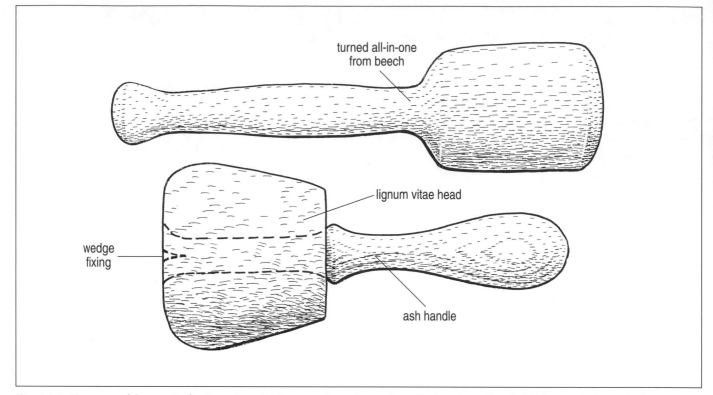

turned all-in-one
from beech

lignum vitae head

wedge
fixing

ash handle

Fig. 11-9. Top, *turned from a single piece of wood, this type of woodcarver's mallet is only really suitable for very light work. Bottom, designed to take a lot of punishment, this kind of mallet is used to deliver a lot of forceful blows. Used in conjunction with a gouge, it is perfect for the swift removal of waste.*

felloes, and boatbuilders made theirs from bits and pieces of rib offcuts, and woodturners turned theirs from a single piece, woodcarvers tended to carve and whittle theirs from whatever wood was at hand. Over the years, we've made mallets from cut-down baseball bats, wickedly knotty lumps of burl wood, old bowling balls, gnarly pieces of root, pieces of driftwood, and various other bits and pieces that have been lying around. We have a favorite mallet that we made from an old wooden ball that blacksmiths used to weight down some part of

the rope that they used to tie the horse to a rail. It was a pierced wooden ball about 6 inches in diameter—a bit like a huge bead. All we did was cut a handle to fit through the ball and then fix it with a wedge. It sounds a bit rough, we know, but since the ball is made from a piece of burl wood, it is very heavy and tough and so it works for us on many levels: There is the pleasure of knowing that we made it at no cost, it is an attractive artifact in its own right—it looks and feels good—and it does the job.

CHAPTER TWELVE

Clamps, Cramps, and Holdfasts

I t doesn't matter whether you call it a "clamp," a "cramp," a "cram," or a "glaun," as long as you understand that these are all names for a device used for holding and pressing wood together while it is being screwed, glued, or otherwise worked. Though it doesn't matter what name they go by in your neck of the woods, you do have to be aware that when you are searching through tool catalogs, they might be indexed as "clamps" or "cramps" or both. We've always used the term "clamp."

There is hardly a task in the workshop that doesn't require the wood to be held securely. We started out with a couple of old clamps that a friend gave us, and then gradually over the years we have gathered more and more. Every time we see a good-quality clamp at a garage sale or a flea market, we buy it. That said, although we've now got fifty or so different clamps, there are still times when we need more, or a different size, or an identical pair, or whatever. So the more you have, the greater your choice, and the easier it will be when you come to putting your projects together.

Though the following listing isn't in any way complete, it will give you a good idea of the various options.

C-CLAMP

The good old C-clamp, known as the G-clamp in Britain, is one of the most useful clamps in the workshop. With its C-shaped malleable frame, it is the perfect device for all manner of clamping operations. In action, the frame is set in position so that the anvil and the shoe are centered on the area to be clamped, small pieces of waste or blocking are slid between the workpiece and the clamp, and then the screw is tightened up by means of the sliding tommy bar or wing nut (see 12-1).

C-clamps come in many shapes and sizes, from long-reach bar clamps, edge strip clamps, and special giant-size clamps used by boatbuilders to small clamps used by musical instrument makers and patternmakers, clamps that can be closed with one hand, and very light duty clamps that can be used for model making (see 12.2).

The main thing that you have to remember when buying C-clamps is that the cheap stamped steel type are dangerous as well as worthless. Whereas good quality malleable iron clamps might well buckle and twist if they are put under too much pressure, the stamped steel variety are likely to fail catastrophically. When this happens, not only does the metal crack and shatter, sending lots of jagged-edged fragments flying all over the shop, but there is also a likelihood that a sprung board might fly up and hit you or knock something off a surface. In any case, the glued works are likely to be ruined.

Good clamps are quite expensive, so if you are short of money, the best thing to do is to buy your clamps secondhand. Look for English and American clamps, especially ones with labels that read "dropped forged." Inspect the clamp closely; make sure that the screw is straight, the swivel shoe is in place, and the shoe meets the anvil at the center.

WOODEN HAND SCREW

The traditional wooden hand screw is made from two hardwood blocks or jaws about 12 to 18 inches long and 2 inches square in section. Clamps of this kind have two wooden screws: one set toward the center that passes freely through one block to be screwed into the other block, and the other set nearer the end of the jaws, where it is screwed through one block to run into a blind hole in the other block (see 12-3 right). Although this arrangement might seem a little unusual, we think that the design has something to do with lessening the risk of stripping the threads of the wooden screws and optimizing the pressure at the ends of the jaws. We

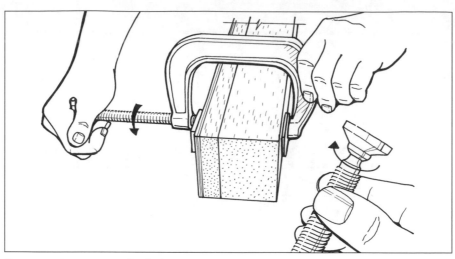

Fig. 12-1. Top, *respect the C-clamp's capacity; it is one of the most powerful clamps. Protect your work with blocks and hand tighten.* Bottom, *adjust the C-clamp by rolling the screw between fingers and thumb.*

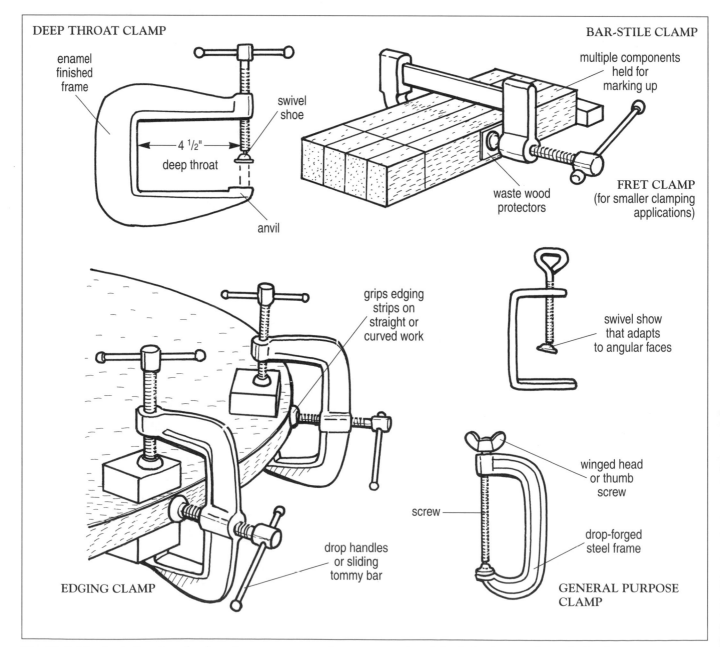

DEEP THROAT CLAMP

enamel finished frame

swivel shoe

4 1/2"
deep throat

anvil

BAR-STILE CLAMP

multiple components held for marking up

waste wood protectors

FRET CLAMP
(for smaller clamping applications)

grips edging strips on straight or curved work

swivel show that adapts to angular faces

winged head or thumb screw

screw

drop-forged steel frame

drop handles or sliding tommy bar

EDGING CLAMP

GENERAL PURPOSE CLAMP

Fig. 12-2. *The simple function of a clamp is to exert pressure between two points. Match the clamp to the work. It is better to use many clamps moderately tightened than one or two giants clamps overtightened.*

know for sure that clamps of this type are capable of exerting a great deal of pressure. Wooden clamps are also kinder than metal clamps to the surfaces being clamped; the wood-to-wood contact is less likely to leave pressure marks.

In use, the jaws are adjusted by holding the handles and pedaling one around the other (see 12-3 left), the workpiece is set between the jaws, the jaws are brought up to the face of the work by means of both screws, and then the outer screw is given a couple of extra turns. If you look closely, you will see that at the last couple of turns, the ends of the jaws tilt in to grip the workpiece with a pincerlike action. You can even clamp work that is slightly angled.

There is a modern version of the traditional hand screw with metal screws instead of wooden ones (see 12-4 left). Its working action is slightly different from the traditional hand screw in that both screws are threaded through both blocks (see 12-4 right). Although this arrangement is certainly stronger, we feel that it is slightly flawed, because not only does the introduction of metal increase the risk of rust and staining, but more than that, having both screws threaded through both blocks results in a cutback of pressure at the ends of the jaws. That said, they are pretty good clamps that might well suit your needs.

FAST-ACTION CLAMP

Although modern fast-action clamps are used in much the same way as C-clamps, they are generally used in circumstances where the need is for speed rather than pressure. In use, the jaws are swiftly pushed together so that they are in contact with the workpiece, and then the final clenching adjustment is made variously by means of

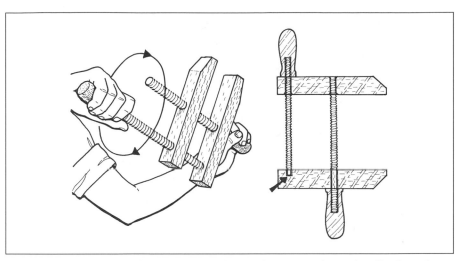

Fig. 12-3. Left, *to adjust the jaws of a wooden hand screw, cycle one handle about the other.* Right, *the tip of the back screw fits a hole that is cut into the stock.*

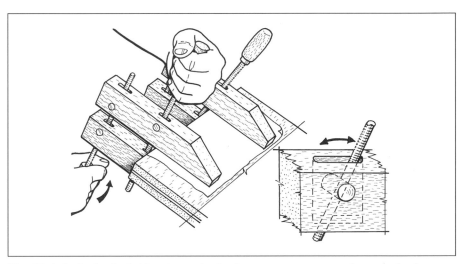

Fig. 12-4. Left, *the final tightening and releasing movements are made on the back screw. Use waxed paper to protect the jaws from glue.* Right, *both screws pass through a mortise and a captive nut, resulting in a pivotal movement.*

a screw, trigger ratchet, or cam, depending on the design of your specific clamp (see 12-5). There is a place in the workshop for clamps of this type, especially when speed is important, but we haven't as yet come across a situation where they do the job as efficiently as traditional C-clamps. That said, there is a little European-made, all-wood, cam-operated, fast-action clamp on the market that is really useful in extradelicate situations where the prime need is for light pressure without marking (see 12-6).

BAR CLAMP

Known variously as bar clamps, sash clamps, T-section bar clamps, door clamps, and one or two other names besides, clamps of this type are used in situations where the need is for strength and long reach. These are the clamps for clamping up doors, frames, windows boards, and the like.

As to the various designs, each and every type of clamp has been developed to cope with specific needs. For example, the bar clamp proper (see 12-7 top), which is usu-

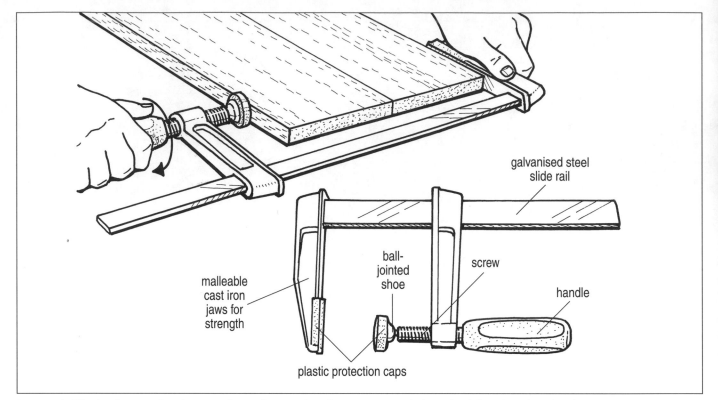

Fig. 12-5. The fixed jaw is placed against the workpiece, the other jaw is moved along the slide rail, and the handle is turned to automatically lock the clamp.

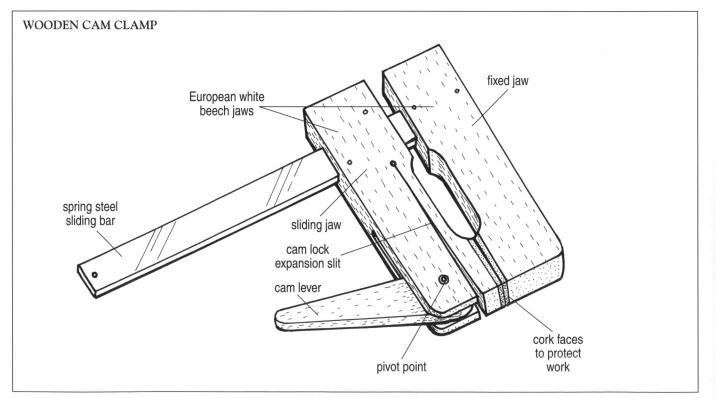

WOODEN CAM CLAMP

Fig. 12-6. The wooden cam–operated clamp is best used for light clamping tasks like veneering. It exerts about 330 pounds pressure when fully cocked.

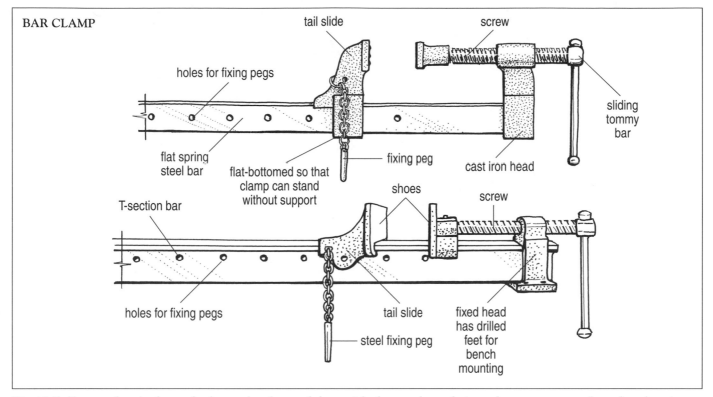

BAR CLAMP

tail slide

screw

holes for fixing pegs

sliding tommy bar

flat spring steel bar

fixing peg

cast iron head

flat-bottomed so that clamp can stand without support

shoes

screw

T-section bar

holes for fixing pegs

tail slide

fixed head has drilled feet for bench mounting

steel fixing peg

Fig. 12-7. Because there is always the danger that the metal shoes might damage the workpiece, always use scraps of wood as clamping blocks.

ally made from $1^1/_4$-by-$^1/_4$-inch bar with malleable ends and clamping heads, and obtainable in lengths from 18 to 66 inches, is the perfect clamp for medium-light long-reach tasks like pulling frames together. Although the T-bar clamp looks, at first glance, to be more or less the same item, the T-section bar is so strong (see 12-7) that it can be used for just about any heavy long-reach situation that you can throw at it. The T section resists bending in all directions. These extra–heavy-duty clamps are available in lengths right up to 78 inches and are designed with drilled feet that allow them to be bolted to a bench. If you have it in mind to make something like large windows or a massive slab tabletop, then these are the clamps to use.

In use, the bar clamps are arranged on the floor or the bench, the workpiece is set dry in the clamps—just so that you know what goes where and how—pieces of waste are cut to fit between the shoes and the workpieces, and the glue is prepared. When all is ready, you smear glue on all mating faces of the wood, position the wood in the clamps, slide the waste pieces in place, check the alignment, and then tighten up just enough

to hold. This done, you check once again for alignment and squareness, and then you tighten up some more (see 12-8). The important dos and don'ts are as follows:

- Work on a clean level surface large enough to support the whole piece.
- Make sure at the trial clamping stage that the whole works is going to clamp up squarely.
- Don't think that you can pull a bad joint together by putting extra pressure on the clamps.
- Make sure that the clamps are clean and in good order.
- Plan out the whole operation before you start spreading the glue around.
- Don't put so much glue on that it oozes all over the shop.
- Don't wipe dribbles of glue away with a damp cloth; it's much better to wait until the glue is semidry and then to remove it with a chisel.
- Don't have the clamp so tight that the wood is scrunched up.
- Make sure that the clamping blocks are the right size and in the right place.

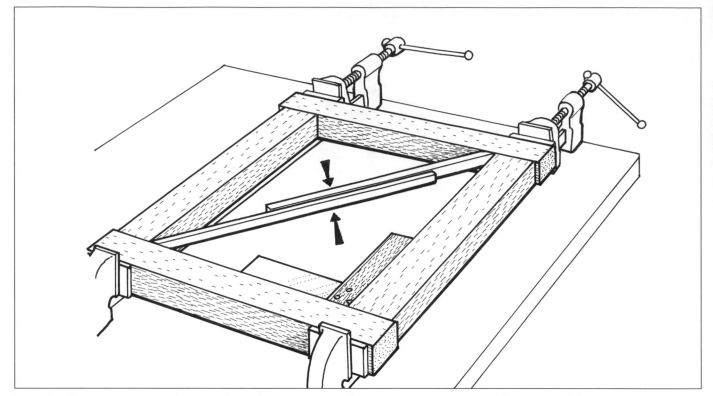

Fig. 12-8. To test alignment, sight across the work; use a straight-edge as a reference. Reposition the blocks and clamps accordingly. Use a try square to check for squareness or use two rods set across the diagonals. The diagonal measurements should be equal.

PIPE CLAMP

The pipe clamp is much the same as the bar clamp; the only real difference is that the clamp heads are mounted on a round section bar (see 12-9). The main advantage of having round section bars is their relatively low cost and versatility. All manner of fixing and holding options can be achieved simply by boring holes in the bench or in blocks of wood. For example, by boring a hole down through the bench top, and then sliding the bar down through the hole, you can make a really useful hold-down or holdfast (see 12-9 right). Keep in mind that pipe clamps are only suitable for relatively light work. They are good for frames and the like, but if you try to use them for anything too hefty, the pipes are going to bend.

CLAMP HEADS

Clamp heads are a good inexpensive option to sash, bar, and pipe clamps because you only need to buy a clamping head set. They are designed to fit wooden battens that are 1-inch wide by a minimum of $1^1/2$ inches deep. All you do is drill holes at 1-inch intervals all the way along the batten and fit the heads with the pins provided (see 12-10). There is no denying that such clamps aren't as strong as bar clamps proper; clamping head sets are only as strong as your chosen battens.

There is no reason why you can't fit the heads on larger-section battens at, say, 1 inch wide and 3 inches deep. The same set of loose clamp heads can alo be used on a selection of different-length battens.

MITER CLAMPS

Miter or corner clamps are used when joining two 45-degree mitered members to create a 90-degree corner—as with picture frame moldings. There are all manner of designs, some made of plastic with straps, some made of metal with screws or ratchet mechanisms, some made of wood, some with fancy additions, and so on (see 12-11). One pattern has two screws—one for each piece of molding. All you do is smear glue on the mating faces, set the members in the clamp so that the glued faces are pushed together, and then tighten up. Although this design is most certainly the strongest and the simplest, it doesn't force the joint together. The best miter clamp is one that automatically draws the joint together as the clamp head screw is tightened up. Better yet is a type of clamp with a design feature that allows T- and L-joints to be clamped.

ROPE AND WEB CLAMPS

One of the best clamping arrangements that we know of for clamping up irregular structures, such as woodcarv-

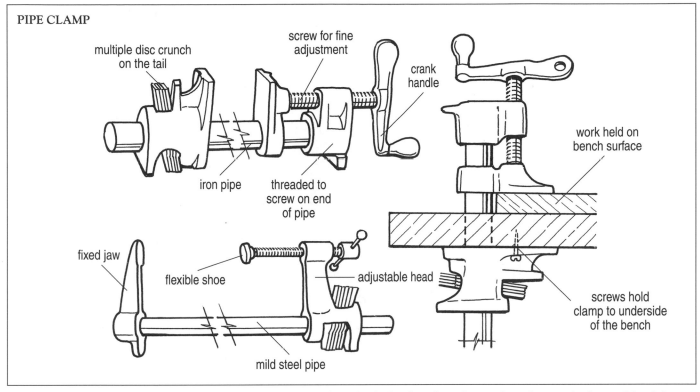

PIPE CLAMP

multiple disc crunch on the tail

screw for fine adjustment

crank handle

iron pipe

threaded to screw on end of pipe

fixed jaw

flexible shoe

adjustable head

mild steel pipe

work held on bench surface

screws hold clamp to underside of the bench

Fig. 12-9. Left, the iron or mild steel pipe is threaded on one end to take the head- or the tailpiece, depending on the design. The sliding jaw is locked into place by a simple clutch mechanism. Right, the pipe clamp is beautifully versatile; it can even be used as a bench holdfast.

ing blanks, consists of a length of natural hemp rope, a selection of wooden wedges, and a good-sized ash or hickory hammer handle. In use, the rope is first dampened so that it stretches, then it is wound several times around the workpiece and the ends are knotted together. This done, the handle is pushed through the binding and repeatedly twisted around until the rope is as tight as possible, and then one end of the handle is tied to the binding (see 12-12 left). If the rope is still a bit slack and the irregular shape will allow it, wedges are banged in place between the bindings and the workpiece. If this still isn't tight enough, when the rope begins to dry out it shrinks, and everything is clenched absolutely drum-head tight. A variation on this rope, wedge, and stick theme is the web clamp. It works for all sorts of irregular structures and situations: for building blanks for large sculptural woodcarvings, for clamping up chairs (see 12-12 right), for making repairs to odd-shaped pieces of cottage furniture, for steambending boards, for building large chests, for clamping up large garden items like gates, and so on.

HOLDFAST

The traditional holdfast has been around since Roman times. The modern holdfast has the shape of a forged bar, with a screw-operated lever pivoted at the top end.

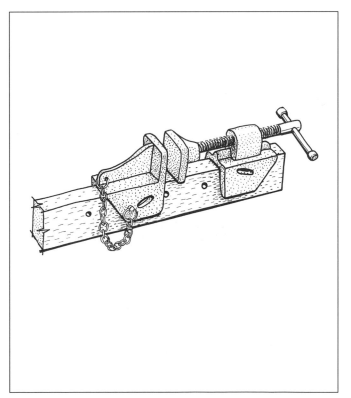

Fig. 12-10. Clamp heads are relatively inexpensive. They can be swiftly fitted onto a length of 1-inch-thick wood that has been drilled at regular intervals. They are a good answer for the small workshop.

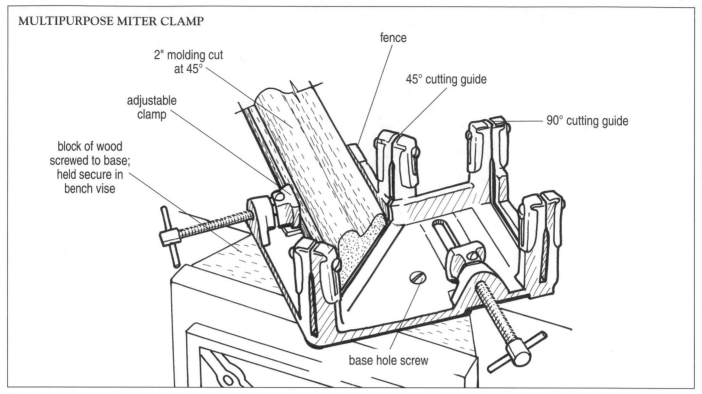

MULTIPURPOSE MITER CLAMP

fence

45° cutting guide

90° cutting guide

2" molding cut at 45°

adjustable clamp

block of wood screwed to base; held secure in bench vise

base hole screw

Fig. 12-11. *A set of multipurpose miter clamps with both 90- and 45-degree cutting guides are good for both cutting and clamping.*

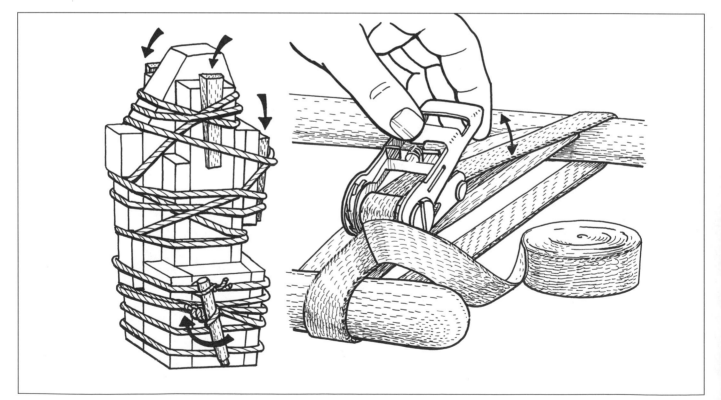

Fig. 12-12. Left, *rope and wedge clamps are great for large irregular shapes. Right, the 1-inch-wide nylon web clamp exerts a steady 1,500 pounds of pressure—a good clamp for certain tasks.*

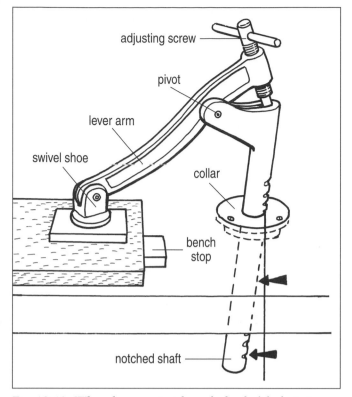

Fig. 12-13. When the screw is tightened, the shaft locks in its hole, and the shoe exerts downward pressure.

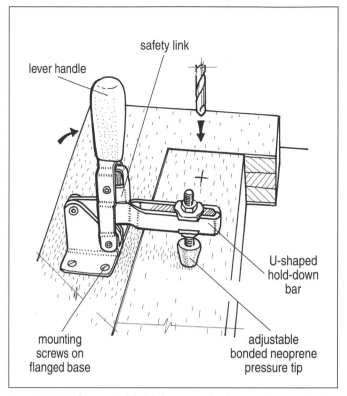

Fig. 12-14. The vertical hold-down toggle clamp is just perfect for setting up small jigs.

In use, the notched main pillar or shaft is dropped down through a hole in the bench, the shoe is positioned on the item to be secured, and the screw is given a couple of turns, clamping the workpiece down hard on the bench (see 12-13). When you want to release the workpiece, all you do is give a few counterclockwise turns to the screw and it's done.

The wonderful qualities of the holdfast are its strength, its swiftness, and its no-nonsense reliability. We've had ours for about twenty years, and it's seen a lot of hard use and is still going strong. As for the primary function of the holdfast, meaning the tasks for which it is best suited, it is just about the best clamp that we know of for holding down flat items like panels, boards, and dishes while they are being carved. If you rig your bench with a pattern of holes, a bunch of wooden stops, and two holdfasts, then all you do is set the workpiece down on the bench, butt it up against one or more stops that you have banged in the holes, and then clamp it down with one or both of the holdfasts. This arrangement is a winner on several counts: It is inexpensive and easy to set up, it is totally flexible, and it is swift to operate.

As to the various designs of holdfasts, there is one with a beautiful plastic swivel shoe that negates the need for having a waste block set between the shoe and the workpiece. We would say, though, that its design is

flawed because the pillar is rectilinear in section. The problem is that whereas round holes can be swiftly bored all over your bench, it's not so easy to chop rectangular mortise-type holes.

TOGGLE CLAMPS

Toggle clamps are a relatively new idea that have been developed primarily for making jigs, meaning when you want to repeatedly rerun the same working sequence. So, for example, let's say that you have got a couple dozen component parts all cut to the same size, and you want to bore them through with the same-sized hole in the same position. All you need to do is work out a board with a set of toggle clamps. In action, you fix the board to the drill press, drop the component piece in place on the jig, lever over the clamps so that the workpiece is held fast, bore the hole, and then go on to the next component (see 12-14).

There are all sorts of toggle clamp designs—some that push straight down, some that push in from the side, some with long handles, some that have rubber bung shoes that squash down on the workpiece, and so on. While they might be used in hundreds of different situations, they are really aimed at the woodworker who is doing repeat functions, say, on the router, or gluing up

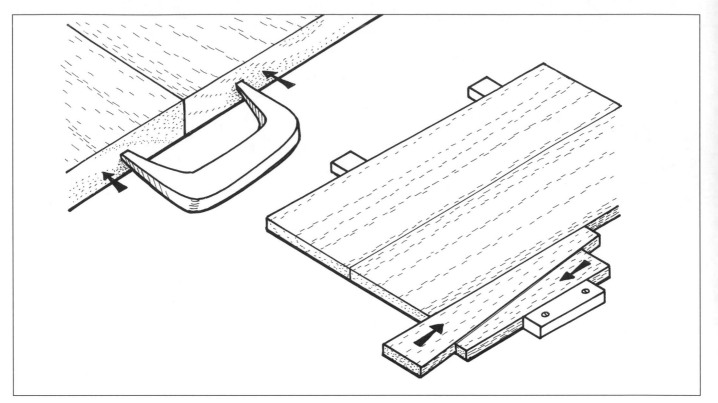

Fig. 12-15. Left, *dog clamps draw the boards together when they are driven into the end grain.* Right, *the nose-to-nose wedges lock the workpiece in place.*

a sequence of small parts, or on the drill, that is, when it pays to spend time and money making a jig.

DOG CLAMPS

Known variously as joint dogs, joiners, pinch dogs, joint clamps, and one or two other names besides, these are little U-shaped pieces of iron—like bridge-shaped staples—that are used when making rubbed joints to link the ends of boards (see 12-15 left). Although there are several ways that they can be used, we find that the best procedure is to glue and butt-joint the boards, set a couple of clamps across to hold them in place, and then knock the dogs in at each end and remove the clamps. Using the dogs frees the clamps for other tasks. That said, the dogs are, in fact, designed to be used without clamps. The idea is that the tapered shape of the dogs automatically draws the boards together. When using the dogs in this manner, the edges of the boards are brushed with glue, the boards are then butted together and rubbed, and then the dogs are driven in. This is a perfectly good technique, but you do have to make sure

that the boards are planed so that they are free from hollows and carefully aligned.

HOMEMADE CLAMPS

Even if a woodworker has a good selection of clamps, there always comes a time when he or she will need to improvise and come up with some sort of homemade design. Depending on the project, we are very fond of using wedges. It's the easiest thing in the world to set some boards down on the bench so that they are butted up against a couple of stops, screw a batten down about 2 inches or so to the other side of the boards, and then drive a pair of folding wedges between the boards and the batten (see 12-15 right). It's also possible to make a couple of bar clamps that use wedges. All you do is make up a length of wood or bar with a fixed block at one end and a movable block or shoe that can be screwed in any position along the bar. In use, you set the workpiece on the bar, move the shoe close up to the workpiece, and then knock the folding wedges in between the shoe and the workpiece.

Metric Conversions

INCHES TO MILLIMETERS

IN.	MM	IN.	MM
1	25.4	51	1295.4
2	50.8	52	1320.8
3	76.2	53	1346.2
4	101.6	54	1371.6
5	127.0	55	1397.0
6	152.4	56	1422.4
7	177.8	57	1447.8
8	203.2	58	1473.2
9	228.6	59	1498.6
10	254.0	60	1524.0
11	279.4	61	1549.4
12	304.8	62	1574.8
13	330.2	63	1600.2
14	355.6	64	1625.6
15	381.0	65	1651.0
16	406.4	66	1676.4
17	431.8	67	1701.8
18	457.2	68	1727.2
19	482.6	69	1752.6
20	508.0	70	1778.0
21	533.4	71	1803.4
22	558.8	72	1828.8
23	584.2	73	1854.2
24	609.6	74	1879.6
25	635.0	75	1905.0
26	660.4	76	1930.4
27	685.8	77	1955.8
28	711.2	78	1981.2
29	736.6	79	2006.6
30	762.0	80	2032.0
31	787.4	81	2057.4
32	812.8	82	2082.8
33	838.2	83	2108.2
34	863.6	84	2133.6
35	889.0	85	2159.0
36	914.4	86	2184.4
37	939.8	87	2209.8
38	965.2	88	2235.2
39	990.6	89	2260.6
40	1016.0	90	2286.0
41	1041.4	91	2311.4
42	1066.8	92	2336.8
43	1092.2	93	2362.2
44	1117.6	94	2387.6
45	1143.0	95	2413.0
46	1168.4	96	2438.4
47	1193.8	97	2463.8
48	1219.2	98	2489.2
49	1244.6	99	2514.6
50	1270.0	100	2540.0

U.S. TO METRIC

1 inch	=	2.540 centimeters
1 foot	=	.305 meter
1 yard	=	.914 meter
1 mile	=	1.609 kilometers

METRIC TO U.S.

1 millimeter	=	.039 inch
1 centimeter	=	.394 inch
1 meter	=	3.281 feet or 1.094 yards
1 kilometer	=	.621 mile

INCH-METRIC EQUIVALENTS

Fraction	Customary (IN.)	Metric (MM)	Fraction	Customary (IN.)	Metric (MM)
$1/64$	.015	0.3969	$33/64$	.515	13.0969
$1/32$	.031	0.7938	$17/32$	.531	13.4938
$3/64$	.046	1.1906	$35/64$	.546	13.8906
$1/16$	.062	1.5875	$9/16$	.562	14.2875
$5/64$	.078	1.9844	$37/64$	.578	14.6844
$3/32$	.093	2.3813	$19/32$	.593	15.0813
$7/64$	.109	2.7781	$39/64$	.609	15.4781
$1/8$	.125	3.1750	$5/8$	.625	15.8750
$9/64$	.140	3.5719	$41/64$	.640	16.2719
$5/32$	.156	3.9688	$21/32$	.656	16.6688
$11/64$	.171	4.3656	$43/64$	.671	17.0656
$3/16$	.187	4.7625	$11/16$	.687	17.4625
$13/64$	.203	5.1594	$45/64$	.703	17.8594
$7/32$	.218	5.5563	$23/32$	.718	18.2563
$15/64$	.234	5.9531	$47/64$	.734	18.6531
$1/4$	.250	6.3500	$3/4$	.750	19.0500
$17/64$	.265	6.7469	$49/64$	.765	19.4469
$9/32$	.281	7.1438	$25/32$	.781	19.8438
$19/64$	.296	7.5406	$51/64$	.796	20.2406
$5/16$	.312	7.9375	$13/16$	.812	20.6375
$21/64$	.328	8.3384	$53/64$	.828	21.0344
$11/32$	.343	8.7313	$27/32$	.843	21.4313
$23/64$	.359	9.1281	$55/64$	.859	21.8281
$3/8$	.375	9.5250	$7/8$	.875	22.2250
$25/64$	.390	9.9219	$57/64$	.890	22.6219
$13/32$	.406	10.3188	$29/32$	.906	23.0188
$27/64$	.421	10.7156	$59/64$	.921	23.4156
$7/16$	.437	11.1125	$15/16$	.937	23.8125
$29/64$	.453	11.5094	$61/64$	.953	24.2094
$15/32$	.468	11.9063	$31/32$	.968	24.6063
$31/64$	.484	12.3031	$63/64$	.984	25.0031
$1/2$	.500	12.7000	1	1.000	25.4000

The above table is exact on the basis: 1 in. = 25.4 mm

Index

allonge tools, *106*, 107

backsaws, 7–8, *10*
    bead, 10, *10*
    dovetail, 8, *9*
    gent's, *10*
    handle, plans for, *42*
    stance and control with, *21–22, 22*
    tenon, 8, *9*
Bailey, Leonard, 54
Bailey patent, 54
band saws, 168–171, *170, 171*
    cutting a cabriole leg blank with, 171–72, *171–173*
    two-wheeled, 169
bead saws, 10, *10*
beading scrapers, *134*, 135
beeswax polish, *161*
bench hook plans, *35*
bench planes, metallic, 45–47, 54
    body and sole, 56
    cap iron and cutter, 54, *56*
    cutting action of, *56*, 56–57
    disassembled, *55*
    frog assembly, 56
    lateral lever, 56
    lever cap, 54
    sharpening, 59–62, *60–61*
    sharpening shaped blades of, *62*
    stance and control with, 65–66, *66*
    tuning, 62–65, *63–65*
bench planes, wooden, 45–47, 57
    adjustable toe, 57
    adjusting screw, 57
    body and sole, 57–59
    cap iron and cutter, 57
    cutting action of, 59, *59*
    disassembled, *58*
    regulator, 57
    sharpening, 59–62, *60–61*
    sharpening shaped blades of, *62*
    stance and control with, 65–66, *66*

tension screw, rod, spring, and knob, 57
    tuning, 62–65, *63–65*
bent gouges
    back, *106*, 107
    carving a bowl with, 128–129, *129*
    front, *106*, 107
    modeling a relief carving with, 126–127, *127*
    wasting and grounding a relief carving with, 124–126, *125–126*
bevel-edged chisels, 84, 85
    cutting a lap or drawer dovetail with, 99–102, *100–102*
    making a through dovetail with, 98–99, *99–100*
    paring a half-lap with, 97, *97*
bird's mouth cutting board plans, *36*
block planes, 47–49, *51*
    adjustable, 48
    adjustable mouth, 46
    shearing end grain with wooden, *74*, 74–75
    stance and control with, 66–67, *67–68*
bow saws, 8, *10*, 10–11
    cutting a lathe blank with, 31–32, *31–32*
    stance and control with, *22*
bowl scrapers, heavy–duty, *134*, 135
bowl-turning gouges, *134*, 136
brace bits, 187–188
    auger, 190–191, *190–192*
    center, 193, *193*
    expansive, 191–192, *192*
    Forstner, *164*, 193–194, *194*
braces, 187, *188–190*
    bits for, 187–194, *190–194*
breast drills, 194, *195, 196*
    twist drill bits for, 194–196, *197*
bruzz chisels, English, 83, 84
bullnose rabbet planes, 46, *51*
    stance and control with, 70, *70*

chiseling projects
    gallows shelf bracket, *104*
    oilstone box, *103*
chiseling techniques, 96
    chopping a deep through mortise, 97–98, *98*
    chopping out a blind mortise, 96, *96*
    cutting a lap or drawer dovetail, 99–102, *100–102*
    making a through dovetail, 98–99, *99–100*
    paring a half-lap, 97, *97*
chisels, joinery and cabinet, 83, 84
    American framing, 83, 84
    anatomy of, 85–87
    bevel-edged/pattern makers paring, *84*, 85
    blade, 87
    bolster, *86*, 87
    cranked handled, *84*
    cutting action of, 87–88, *88*
    cutting bevel, *86*, 87
    cutting edge, *86*, 87
    English bruzz, 83, 84
    ferrule, *86*, 86
    firmer, 83
    handle, 85–86, *86*
    heavy-duty registered, *84*, 85
    horizontal paring with, 93–94, *94*
    joiner's mortise, *84*, 85
    leather shock absorber, *86*, 86–87
    primer, *84*
    registered mortise, *84*, 85
    sash mortise, *84*, 85
    sharpening, 88–92, *89–92*
    ships slicker/socket slick, *84*, 85
    shoulder and neck, 87
    side bevel, 87
    socket, *86*, 87
    stance and control with, 93–95
    swan-neck/lock mortise, *84*, 85
    tang, *86*, 87

tuning, 92, 93
  vertical mortising with a mallet
    and, 94–95, 95
  vertical paring with, 94, 95
  what to use and when, 83–85
  see also individual names
chisels, woodcarving, 105, 106
  allonge, 106, 107
  anatomy of, 108–112
  bent or curved, 105–107
  blade, 111, 111
  bolster, 110, 111
  corner spoon bit, 106
  cutting action of, 112–114,
    112–114
  cutting bevel, 111, 112
  cutting edge, 112
  ferrule, 110, 110
  fishtail, 106, 108
  fluteroni, 106
  handle, 110, 110
  leather shock absorber, 110,
    110–11
  long pod, 106, 107
  macaroni, 106
  mallet work with, 122, 122
  modeling with, 122, 122
  parting, 106, 107, 107
  relief carving with, 120–122,
    120–122
  sharpening, 114–119, 117–118
  spoon scooping with, 123, 123
  stance and control with, 119–123,
    120–123
  straight skew, 105, 106
  straight square, 105, 106
  straight strong cuts with, 122–123,
    123
  tang, 110, 111
  techniques, 123–129, 124–129
  tuning, 119, 119
  veining, 106
  what to use and when, 105–108
  wing parting, 108, 108
  see also individual names
chisels, woodturning, 133
  anatomy of, 136–138
  cutting action of, 139, 139
  cutting bevel, 138, 138
  ferrule, 137, 138
  handle, 137, 138
  high-speed steel, 136
  long-and-strong flat-bladed skew,
    134, 135
  long-and-strong square, 133, 134
  oval-bladed skew, 134, 135
  sharpening, 140, 141
  tang, 137, 138
  techniques, 146–153
  tuning, 142, 142
  turning handles for, 159–160,
    160–161
  see also individual names

clamps, 215
  bar, 217–219, 219, 220
  bar-stile, 216
  C, 215, 216
  deep throat, 216
  dog, 224, 224
  edging, 216
  fast-action, 217, 218
  fret, 216
  general purpose, 216
  head, 220, 221
  holdfast, 221–23, 223
  homemade, 224, 224
  miter, 220, 222
  pipe, 220, 221
  rope and web, 220–221, 222
  toggle, 223, 223–224
  wooden hand screw, 215–217, 217
combination planes, 53–54
  cutting a deep dado or housing
    with, 77, 77–78
  cutting a double-bead return with
    Stanley 45, 78–80, 79–80
  Stanley 45, 46, 53
compass planes, 46, 52
compass saw handle plans, 43
coping saws, 8, 11, 11
  cutting a coping with, 33–34,
    33–34
  cutting through dovetails with,
    28–29, 29–31
  stance and control with, 23
corner spoon bit chisels, 106
cow planes. See scrub planes
cranked handled chisels, 84
crosscut saws, 7, 8, 12–13
  handles, plans for, 40, 41
  sizing plank on bench with, 25–26,
    26
  stance and control with, 21, 21–22
  teeth, 9, 12
curve-cutting saws, stance and control
    with, 23

dado planes, metallic, 49
dados, 52
Delta Universal wet and dry grinder,
  115
diamond scrapers, 134
diamond-section parting tools, 134,
  136
dividers, 185, 185
dovetail saws, 8, 9
  cutting through dovetails with,
    28–29, 29–31
drawknives, 198–203, 201–202
drill presses, 161–163, 163
  drilling overlapping holes with,
    163–164, 164–165
  Forstner drill bit for, 164
  safety, 163
  traditional, 162

drilling tools, 187
  braces, 187, 188–190
  breast drills, 194–196, 195, 196
  gimlets, 196, 197
  hand drills, 194–196, 195, 196
  see also drill presses

E. C. Emmerich (E.C.E.), 57

fillister rabbet planes, 46, 49
  cutting a cross-grain rabbet with,
    75–77, 76
firmer chisels, 83
fishtail tools, 106, 108
fluted parting tools, 134, 136
fluteroni gouges, 106, 108, 108
framing chisels, American, 83, 84
fretsaws, 8, 11
  cutting a profile in thin wood with,
    34, 34
  stance and control with, 23

gallows shelf bracket plans, 104
gent's saws, 10
gimlets, 196, 197
gouges, woodcarving, 105, 106
  allonge, 106, 107
  anatomy of, 108–112
  back bent, 106, 107
  bent or curved, 105–107
  blade, 111, 111
  bolster, 110, 111
  cutting action of, 112–114,
    112–114
  cutting bevel, 111, 112
  cutting edge, 112
  ferrule, 110, 110
  fishtail, 106, 108
  fluteroni, 106, 108, 108
  front bent, 106, 107
  handle, 110, 110
  leather shock absorber, 110,
    110–111
  long pod, 106, 107
  macaroni, 106, 108, 108
  mallet work with, 122, 122
  modeling with, 122, 122
  parting, 106
  relief carving with, 120–122,
    120–122
  sharpening, 114–119, 117–118
  spoon bent, 106, 107
  spoon scooping with, 123, 123
  stance and control with, 119–123,
    120–123
  straight square, 105, 106, 107
  straight strong cuts with, 122–123,
    123
  sweep, 107, 109
  tang, 110, 111
  techniques, 123–129, 124–129
  tuning, 119, 119
  veining, 106, 108, 108

what to use and when, 105–108
wing parting, 108, *108*
see also individual names
gouges, woodturning, 133
  anatomy of, 136–138
  bowl-turning, *134*, 136
  cutting action of, *139*, *139*
  cutting bevel, 138, *138*
  ferrule, 137, *138*
  flutes, 137, *137*
  handle, 137, *138*
  high-speed steel, 136
  long-and-strong, 137
  round-nosed (finger–nail), *134*, 136
  sharpening, *140*, 141
  square-nosed roughing-out, *134*, 136
  tang, 137, *138*
  techniques, 146–153
  tuning, 142, *142*
  turning handles for, 159–160, *160–161*
  see also individual names
grinders
  Delta Universal wet and dry, *115*
  traditional floor-standing wet, *115*
grooving planes, 51–52
  stance and control with, 67–68, 69

half-round left scrapers, *134*
half--round right scrapers, *134*
half-round side-cut scrapers, *134*
hammers, 209
  claw, 209–210, *210*
  coach trimmer's or cabriolet, 211–212, *212*
  cross peen, 211, *212*
  holding and using, 210, *211*
  pin, 210–211, *212*
hand drills, *195*, 196
  twist drill bits for, 194–196, 197
handsaws. *See* crosscut saws; ripsaws

jack planes, 47, *48*, 49
jigsaws, stance and control with, *23*
jointer planes. *See* trying planes

keyhole saws. *See* pad saws
knives, 198
  chip-carving, *199*
  drawknives, 198–203, *201–202*
  hand, 198
  inshave, 203, *203*
  marking, 186, *186*
  Northwest coast Indian crooked, *200*
  pen, *200*
  pruning, *200*
  shave, 203–204, *203–205*
  sheath, *199*
  single-edge hook, *199*

Swedish sloyd, *200*
whittling, *199*

lathes, 133, 156
  bed, 157
  headstock, *157*, 157–158
  outboard drive, 158, *158*
  safety, 158–159
  swing, *157*, *157*
  tailstock, 158, *159*
  tool rest, 158, *159*
  turning wheels for toys on small, *149–151*, 149–151
long pod tools, *106*, 107

macaroni gouges, *106*, 108, *108*
mallets, 213
  carpenter's or joiner's, 213, *213*
  homemade, 213–214
  plastic and rubber, 213
  woodcarver's, 213, *214*
marking and testing tools, 176
  combination squares, *182–184*
  dividers, 185, *185*
  engineer's steel rulers, 176, *178*
  folding rulers, *177*
  marking gauges, *178–179*, 179
  marking knives, 186, *186*
  metal tape measures, 176–178, *177*
  miter squares, 181–183, *182*
  mortise gauges, 180, *180*
  parallel strips, 184, *184*
  sliding bevels, *181*, 181–183, *182*
  squares, *181*, 181–183
  try squares, *182*
  wooden rulers, 176, *178*
  zigzag rulers, *177*
measuring tools. *See* marking and testing tools
miter shooting board plans, 82
miter squares, 181–183, *182*
molding planes, 48, 54, *54*
  working with classic "sprung," 77–78, *78–79*
mortise chisels
  chipping out blind mortise with sash, 96, *96*
  joiner's, 84, *85*
  registered, 84, *85*
  sash, 84, *85*
  swan-neck/lock, 84, *85*
multiplanes. *See* combination planes

narrow-bladed saws, 10, *32*, 32–33
  bow, *10*, 10–11
  coping, 11, *11*
  fretsaws, 11
  pad, 8, 11

oilstone box plans, *103*
oval-bladed skew chisels, *134*, 135
  chopping a deep through mortise with classic, 97–98, *98*

pad saws, 8, 11
  cutting a cat door with, *32*, 32–33
parallel strips, 184, *184*
paring chisels, pattern makers, *84*
parting tools, *106*, 107, *107*, *134*, 136
  diamond-section, *134*, 136
  fluted, *134*, 136
  wing, 108, *108*
planes, 45
  adjustable block, 48
  adjustable mouth block, 46
  anatomy and cutting action of special, 62
  anatomy of metallic bench, 54–57
  anatomy of wooden bench, 57–59
  bench, 45–47, 54–59
  bench rabbet, 46, 49
  block, 47–49, 51
  bullnose rabbet, 46, 51
  combination, 53–54
  compass, 46, 52
  dado, 49
  fillister rabbet, 46, 49
  grooving, 51–52
  jack, 47, 48, 49
  metallic, 46
  molding, 48, 54, *54*
  plough, 46
  rabbet, 48, *51*
  router, 46
  scrub, 45, 47, 48
  sharpening, 59–62
  shoulder, 49–51
  side rabbet, 53, *53*
  smoothing, 46, 47, 48, *50*
  special-purpose, 47–54
  stance and control with, 65–71
  Stanley 45 combination, 46, 53
  tongue-and-groove, 52
  trying, 47, 48, *50*
  tuning, 62–65, *63–65*
  wooden, 45, 48
  see also individual names
planing projects
  miter shooting board, 82
  ramp shooting board, 81
planing techniques, 71
  cutting a cross-grain rabbet, 75–77, *76*
  cutting a deep dado or housing, 77, *77–78*
  cutting a double-bead return, 78–80, *79–80*
  edging, *73*, 73–74
  facing a board, 71–72, *71–72*
  shearing end grain, *74*, 74–75
  shooting end grain, 75, *75*

thicknessing, 72–73, *72–73*
working with classic wooden "sprung" molding plane, 77–78, *78–79*
plough planes, *46*
plywoods, tip concerning, *168*
primer chisels, *84*
projects
  backsaw handle, *42*
  bench hook, *35*
  bird's mouth cutting board, *36*
  compass saw handle, *43*
  crosscut saw handles, *40, 41*
  gallows shelf bracket, *104*
  miter shooting board, *82*
  oilstone box, *103*
  ramp shooting board, *81*
  ring and wedge-peg chuck, *155*
  ripsaw handle, *39*
  saw vise, *37*
  sawhorse, *44*
  taper and ring chucks, *154*
  toolbox saw clip, *38*
  woodcarver's bridge hold-down, *132*
  woodcarver's cleat, *131*
  woodcarving bench, *130*

rabbet planes, *48, 51*
  bench, *46, 49*
  bullnose, *46, 51*
  fillister, *46, 49*
  side, *53, 53*
  stance and control with, 67–68, *69*
ramp shooting board plans, *81*
registered chisels, heavy-duty, *84, 85*
ring and wedge-peg chuck plans, *155*
ring-cutting scrapers, *134,* 135–136
ripsaws, 7, 8, *12–13*
  converting large plank with, 24–25, *24–25*
  handle, plans for, *39*
  stance and control with, *20,* 20–21
  teeth, *9, 12*
roughing planes. *See* scrub planes
round-nosed (finger–nail) gouges, *134,* 136
  long-and-strong, *136*
round-nosed scrapers, *134*
router planes, *46*
  stance and control with, *70,* 70–71

saw vise plans, *37*
sawhorse plans, *44*
sawing projects
  backsaw handle, *42*
  bench hook, *35*
  bird's mouth cutting board, *36*
  compass saw handle, *43*
  crosscut saw handles, *40, 41*
  ripsaw handle, *39*
  saw vise, *37*

sawhorse, *44*
toolbox saw clip, *38*
sawing techniques, 24
  converting large plank, 24–25, *24–25*
  cutting a cat door, *32,* 32–33
  cutting a coping, *33–34, 33–34*
  cutting a lathe blank, 31–32, *31–32*
  cutting a profile in thin wood, *34, 34*
  cutting a tenon, 26–28, *27–28*
  cutting through dovetails, 28–29, *29–31*
  sizing plank on bench, 25–26, *26*
saws, 7, 8
  anatomy of, 12–13
  backsaws, 7–10
  band, 168–172
  bow, 8, 10–11
  cleaning and waxing, 19
  coping, 8, 11, *11*
  crosscut, 8, 9, *12–13*
  cutting action of, 12–13
  cutting man-made board with, 12
  fitting, 14–15, *16*
  fitting crosscut, 15, *17*
  fitting ripsaws, 14–15, *17*
  fretsaws, 8, 11
  handles, plans for, 39–43
  jigsaws, 23
  jointing, 14, *15, 16*
  narrow-bladed, 8, 10–11
  overhauling handle of, *18, 18*
  pad, 8, 11
  ripsaws, 8, 9, *12–13*
  selecting tips, 11
  setting teeth on, *16, 17*
  sharpening, 14–16, *15*
  sharpening and tuning equipment for, 14
  stance and control with, 19–23
  starting cut with, *19,* 19–20
  storing, *18,* 19
  straightening buckled, *18, 18*
  teeth, *13, 13*
  tuning, 16–19
  see also individual names
scrapers, 198
  hand, 204–206, *205–206*
  plane, 206–208, *207–208*
scrapers, woodturning, 133, *135*
  anatomy of, 136–138
  beading, *134,* 135
  cutting action of, 139–140, *140*
  cutting bevel, 138, *138*
  diamond, *134*
  ferrule, 137, *138*
  half-round left, *134*
  half-round right, *134*
  half-round side-cut, *134*
  handle, 137, *138*

heavy-duty bowl, *134,* 135
high-speed steel, 136
ring-cutting, *134,* 135–136
round-nosed, *134*
sharpening, *141,* 141–142
tang, 137, *138*
techniques, 146–153
scribes, *52*
scroll saws, 165–168, *166*
  cutting letters with, 167–168, *167–168*
  safety, 167
scrub planes, 45, *47, 48*
scud planes. *See* scrub planes
ships chisel slicer/socket slick, *84, 85*
shooting boards
  miter, *82*
  ramp, *81*
shoulder planes, 49–51
  stance and control with, *69,* 69–70
skew chisels
  long-and-strong flat-bladed, *134,* 135
  oval-bladed, *134,* 135
  straight, 105, *106*
sliding bevels, *181,* 181–183, *182*
smoothing planes, 46, *47, 48, 50*
  shooting end grain with metallic, *75, 75*
  thicknessing with wooden, 72–73, *72–73*
spoon bent gouges, *106, 107*
  modeling a relief carving with, 126–27, *127*
  wasting and grounding a relief carving with, 124–126, *125–126*
square chisels, long-and-strong, 133, *134*
square-nosed roughing-out gouges, *134,* 136
squares, 181–183
  combination, *182–184*
  try, *181, 182*
Stanley 45 combination planes, *46*
  cutting a double-bead return with, 78–80, *79–80*
  disassembled, *53*
  setting-up, 79
straight chisels, 105, *106*
  wasting and grounding a relief carving with, 124–126, *125–126*
straight gouges, 105, *106, 107*
  carving a bowl with, 128–129, *129*
  carving incised letter forms with, 127–128, *128*
  modeling a relief carving with, 126–127, *127*
  outlining and setting-in a relief carving with, 124, *124–125*
  wasting and grounding a relief carving with, 124–126, *125–126*
straight skew chisels, 105, *106*

carving incised letter forms with, 127–128, *128*

modeling a relief carving with, 126–127, *127*

taper and ring chuck plans, *154*

tenon saws, 8, 9

cutting tenon with, 26–28, *27–28*

testing tools. *See* marking and testing tools

thicknesser planers

portable, 172–173, *175*

safety, 173–174

thicknessing and jointing a batch of boards on, 174–175, *175*

tongue-and-groove cuts, *52*

tongue-and-groove planes, metallic, 52

toolbox saw clip plans, *38*

traditional tools, x

trying planes, 47, *48*, *50*

edging with, *73*, *73–74*

facing a board with, 71–72, *71–72*

twist drill bits, 194–196, *197*

universal planes. *See* combination planes

veining gouges, *106*, 108, *108*

vises, 4, 5

V-tools, outlining and setting-in a relief carving with, 124, *124–125*

winding strips. *See* parallel strips

wing parting tools, 108, *108*

woodcarver's bridge hold-down plans, *132*

woodcarver's cleat plans, *131*

woodcarving bench plans, *130*

woodcarving projects

woodcarver's bridge hold-down, *132*

woodcarver's cleat, *131*

woodcarving bench, *130*

woodcarving techniques, 123–124

carving a bowl, 128–129, *129*

carving incised letter forms, 127–128, *128*

modeling a relief carving, 126–127, *127*

outlining and setting-in a relief carving, 124, *124–125*

wasting and grounding a relief carving, 124–126, *125–126*

woodturning, 133

between centers, 144, *144*

with a drill chuck, 145, *145*

with a faceplate, *144*, 145

with a four-jaw chuck, 143–144, *144*

screw chuck, 145, *145*

woodturning projects

ring and wedge-peg chuck, *155*

taper and ring chuck, *154*

woodturning techniques, *146*

drilling horizontal hole with chucks, 147, *147*

mounting a blank on faceplate, 148, *148–149*

polishing handles, *161*

turning balls, 152–53, *152–53*

turning chisel and gouge handles, 159–160, *160–161*

turning wheels for toys on small lathe, 149–151, *149–151*

using a four-jaw chuck to rough down cylinder, 146, *146–147*

woodturning tools, 133, *134*

cutting action of, 138–140

sharpening, *140–141*, *140–142*

stance and control with, 143–145, *143–145*

tuning, 142, *142*

what to use and when, 133–138

workbenches, 2–4, *3*

bench dogs, 4

vises, 4, 5

workshops, 1–2

electrical outlets, 6

garage layout, *2*

garden shed layout, *3*

heating, 5–6

lighting, 5

tool storage, 4–5

ventilation, 5

wood storage, 4, 6

workbenches, 2–4, *3*, 4